prepare a personal data sheet
write it out

W9-CZB-386

test Thur. Mar. 10

✓ Spelling

✓ Unit 6 — study # on Synonyms & antonyms.

✓ Review list of text books — Give name
   of one encyclopedia, etc.

✓ P.110 - 5 rules on how to use reference books.

P.129 — 8 characteristics of business letter.

P.138 — 5 different letters Sec. writes.

        58
        52
    ——————
   2) 19 10
    ——————
      9 5

128-145

Applied Secretarial Practice

APPLIED

Secretarial

Drawings by Jane Oliver

GREGG PUBLISHING DIVISION

Practice

THIRD EDITION

JOHN ROBERT GREGG

ALBERT C. FRIES
Professor and Chairman
Department of Secretarial Administration
and Business Education
University of Southern California, Los Angeles

MARGARET ROWE
Head, Department of Business Education
Thomas C. Howe High School, Indianapolis, Indiana

McGraw-Hill Book Company, Inc.
New York   Chicago   San Francisco
Dallas   Toronto   London

APPLIED SECRETARIAL PRACTICE, Third Edition

Copyright, 1952, 1941, 1934, by Gregg Publishing Division of the McGraw-Hill Book Company, Inc. All rights reserved. This book, or parts thereof, may not be reproduced in any form without permission of the publishers. July, 1954 KP

Library of Congress Catalog Card Number: 52–5348

Code No. 24391

PUBLISHED BY GREGG PUBLISHING DIVISION
McGraw-Hill Book Company, Inc.

Printed in the United States of America

Preface

Applied Secretarial Practice, Third Edition, continues a series of secretarial practice texts that have been leaders in the field for many years. It retains the popular features of preceding editions and offers a number of new ones that represent timely trends in the training of secretaries and other personnel for employment in today's offices.

Applied Secretarial Practice, Third Edition, opens with an overview of the office and the duties and qualifications of secretaries. Many of these same duties and qualifications apply to office workers other than secretaries, and a special effort is made throughout the text to direct its contents and instructions to the varied job objectives of business students who may be enrolled in the course.

Following the helpful orientation of the student through the overview, *Applied Secretarial Practice*, Third Edition, launches into a practical, realistic treatment of personal qualities and work habits—factors that are largely responsible for the job success of office employees. The importance of these qualities is substantiated by personnel studies, which show emphatically that employee dismissals and failures are usually caused by unsatisfactory personal qualities or work habits.

This text does not confine its treatment of personal qualities and work habits to a unit or two. It features a program of self-evaluation and self-improvement that runs throughout the text. The program includes a series of eighteen Personality Pointers—one preceding each unit—and a set of personality questions, problems, and projects based on each Personality Pointer. Each Pointer is written in an engaging, informal, conversational style and is accompanied by a clever, original drawing designed to convey the theme of the Pointer.

Applied Secretarial Practice, Third Edition, contains more than two hundred illustrations, many of which are based on original photographs made expressly for this text. All business data and reproduc-

tions of business forms and charts are, of course, right up to date.

A happy combination of important business knowledge and sound skill training has always been a distinction of this series of texts. The initial text in the series—*Office Training for Stenographers* by Rupert P. SoRelle—was the very first text to provide a program of business information and applied skills needed to train secretaries and other office workers efficiently and adequately. That program has been refined and improved in each succeeding text and reaches a new high of development in *Applied Secretarial Practice*, Third Edition. Each unit of the text is concluded with a systematic pattern of review, discussion, and problem exercises.

Applied Secretarial Practice, Third Edition, is based on the early work of Rupert P. SoRelle and of John Robert Gregg, inventor of Gregg Shorthand, who joined the authorship of the series in 1927. The new coauthors, Dr. Albert C. Fries and Mrs. Margaret F. Rowe, have made significant contributions to the Third Edition. Like the authors of preceding editions, the present authors have made a painstaking effort to assure the accuracy and practical, businesslike quality of the contents of the book. In this connection, they acknowledge gratefully the co-operation and assistance of the following in checking sections of the manuscript and in furnishing illustrations: Miss N. Mae Sawyer, Director, American Institute of Records Administration, Remington Rand Inc.; Mr. George P. Oslin, Publicity Director, The Western Union Telegraph Company; Mr. A. S. Smith, Copywriter, New York Telephone Company; Mr. Robert F. Keiling, Monroe Calculating Machine Company, Inc.; New York Central System; American Railway Express Agency; American Airlines; Addressograph-Multigraph Corporation. Special acknowledgment is made of the contribution of Clyde I. Blanchard, University of Tulsa, Tulsa, Oklahoma, to the preceding edition of *Applied Secretarial Practice*, in his capacity as general editor with the publishers at the time of the publication of that edition.

The authors also express their special appreciation to Mr. Wilson Chatfield, Assistant to the Vice President, Shaw-Walker Company, for the use of the Shaw-Walker showrooms in posing several original photographs for the text as well as in furnishing a number of illustrations, and to Esther E. Brooke, Carl H. Cummings, Ola Day Rush, Hazel Craig Thompson, and Elizabeth F. Trumper for their helpful assistance in preparation of the manuscript.

THE PUBLISHERS

Contents

Unit 18   Job Finding and Job Success **509**

Section 1. Preparation for Job Finding
Section 2. Applying and Interviewing for the Job
Section 3. Your Job Success

PERSONALITY POINTERS

Text-Films correlated with
APPLIED SECRETARIAL PRACTICE

Getting a Job. Correct techniques in applying for a job; the job interview; the test; refusal of one job, acceptance of another. (53 frames)

The First Job. The initial job; indoctrination of new employees; reporting to the department; meeting co-workers; first assignment. (50 frames)

Secretarial Attitudes. Working under pressure and meeting deadlines; shows correct technique for telephoning, greeting callers, and for following instructions. (57 frames)

Adjusting to the Job. The first job promotion; dictation by several distinct types of individuals; decisions regarding office mail. (51 frames)

Secretarial Co-operation. Importance of teamwork between stenographers and secretaries; "breaking in" one's replacement; filing. Further illustration of correct telephoning, greeting of callers, taking of dictation. (52 frames)

Job Growth. Presents the model secretary's difficulties and successes during her first two years of work. (49 frames)

These films also include six records (12″, 2 sides, 78rpm, 10 minutes), and Teacher's Guide in convenient album.

Personality Pointer

DO YOU LIKE PEOPLE?

"My secretary is not only expert, she is liked by everyone in the organization."

"We like to have people in our office working together in harmony. We like a friendly atmosphere—the 'one big family' idea."

If you were to make a study of the successful secretary's personality, you would find that you were analyzing her ability to get along well with people and to make favorable impressions on them. You would discover that the secret of adjusting oneself to others is included in the simple formula: "Treat others as you would like to be treated by them."

Always keep in mind that it takes all kinds of people to make a world. You can't expect everyone to have the same particular likes and dislikes that you have. Each person is of a different temperament and disposition. It is not unusual to find someone in an office who is a little difficult to get along with, but this person has some quality that is agreeable to you. Accept him as he is; think of his good qualities; don't try to make him over. Be tolerant. When you can make allowances for differences in individuals, you have taken the first step toward increasing your interest in other people.

The next step is to expand your friendships to include personalities different from those of your usual acquaintances. Make a deliberate and determined effort to meet and know such people. By cultivating the friendship of contrasting personalities, you grow in tolerance and understanding, broaden your points of view, and in turn become more interesting to others.

1

The Secretary on the Job

People in the United States make their living in many different ways. It has been said that there are over 21,500 different kinds of occupations. Many of these jobs, of course, are somewhat similar in that they require the same basic skills, training, and personality traits. Fortunately, therefore, although you are preparing yourself thoroughly for one kind of job, you may also succeed in many different jobs.

You may have decided to prepare yourself thoroughly for a position as secretary. If so, you have chosen one of the most important positions in a business organization. It is natural that you will want to learn as much as possible about secretarial work while you are yet in school. But remember, if you are fully qualified for a secretarial career, you are also prepared to handle many of the numerous different jobs that come up in a modern office.

This unit discusses four fundamental questions that you should ask yourself as a prospective secretary and office worker and that you should understand clearly before you are ready to take your first job.

Where does the secretary work?
What are the duties of a secretary?
What are the qualifications needed by the secretary?
Are there good opportunities in secretarial work?

The discussion in the four sections of this unit will give answers to these questions. It will point out the kinds of situations you may expect to find in the office in which you may work, as well as the requirements you may quite logically expect to meet as a secretary.

Section 1. WHERE THE SECRETARY WORKS

The young person who plans a career in office work is on the right road for entering the business world. Office positions have been the entering wedge into business careers for countless numbers of young people, many of whom have later become successful business executives.

You, as a student looking forward to your career in business and to your first position as an office worker, want to know where the secretary works. You should know much more than a particular system of shorthand, how to use the typewriter, how to operate office machines, or the basic filing rules.

Whenever you are able, you should visit the place where the secretary works—the office—and observe what goes on. True, you may see some workers who do not follow all the principles stressed in this book. Do not, however, use these workers as your example. You can learn much by observation of all kinds of secretaries in the business offices you may visit.

What Is an Office? Stated very simply, an office is the *place* in which the numerous and varied activities requiring the "paper work" of an organization are carried on. The efficiency of the office worker is directly influenced by the equipment provided to make work performance as easy as possible. You will be working in an office and with people.

The office may be large, with people working at desks, tables, machines, or filing cabinets. Some workers may be writing, taking dictation, transcribing, telephoning, recording, interviewing, filing, or operating different office machines. Or, the office may be a private one in which work of a confidential nature is done. In other words, you may be employed in a large or a small office.

Kinds of Office Work. Office work deals generally with four main activities:

1. *Recording.* Records may be made, they may be used, or they may be filed for future reference. For example, there are records of financial data, accounts receivable, production schedules, contracts, orders, inventories, or correspondence. Often the person who deals with records is called a clerk, and the work may be called clerical work. Stenographers and secretaries may, however, be asked to take over some of the recording duties.

Courtesy Burroughs Adding Machine Company

Every secretary should have a working knowledge of the operation of an adding machine.

2. *Computing.* Office work involves figures and computations. In most business firms, prices, costs, discounts, and production figures must be determined, computed, and analyzed. Business management requires these computations in order to make comparisons among the data, to find out the current trends, and to compile the statistical results in an understandable form. Again, the secretary may be asked to help in these activities in the office.

3. *Classifying and Filing.* A considerable portion of the office work in any particular enterprise consists of the classifying and filing of various office papers concerned with past and future transactions. These papers are frequently necessary at some future date.

4. *Communicating.* Both inside and outside communications are important activities in office work. Interoffice memorandums and telephone calls, employee bulletins and instructions, and committee

Courtesy Shaw-Walker Company

The filing department is an important storehouse of information for any firm. No matter what your other duties may be, you need to know how to find valuable papers in the files.

minutes and reports are examples of communications within the business. Outside communications include letters, credit memorandums, telegrams, purchase orders, and the like.

What Is the Connection Between the Office and the Business? Office work forms an important part in the operation of a modern business; almost all the activities of the executives and managers, in fact, are influenced to some extent by office work. During the normal course of business, many operations are started or stopped as the result of written forms, orders, letters, memorandums, telegrams, and telephone calls. In addition, the facts needed for managerial analysis, discussion, planning, action, direction, and control are supplied by the office. Most managers consider reports, data on operations, calculations on cost, and information on possible future activities as necessary tools in the carrying out of managerial assignments.

It is important, therefore, that the secretary, as one office worker, understand her connection with the office work to be done.

The office worker should understand fully that the work done in the office is actually the *connecting link* between the production, distribution, and service phases of the business. Every activity of a business enterprise is in some degree dependent on the work done by the office force. Likewise, the activities of the office are dependent on the goods produced, the selling of these goods, and the performing of services.

Office Work Is Productive Work. The office worker should consider her work as productive. While her work is quite different from that of the factory worker whose product is sold to a consumer, her office work is none the less important in the total operation of the business. To illustrate, the clerk who makes entries on a card or who files a card is performing an activity valuable to the conduct of the business.

It is true that in a sense office work produces no direct profit. It is, rather, a kind of service work done to assist the various departments of the business. For example, office work is a service to the production department, the sales department, the finance department. They could not function without this vital service. In certain service-type businesses, such as banks, insurance companies, and governmental agencies, office work is the main part of the total work picture. The secretary, as an office worker, is a productive worker in every sense of the word!

Section 2. DUTIES OF THE SECRETARY

The preceding discussion suggests the kinds of responsibilities and duties likely to be assigned to the secretary. The size of the firm and the attitude of your employer will determine the duties you will be assigned.

What Will Be Your Responsibilities? As you start your applied secretarial practice course, you naturally will wish to know what is required of the secretary.

Three things are required of an efficient secretary: (1) superior stenographic skill, which is a combination of shorthand, typing, and transcribing skills; (2) a clear understanding of business customs and procedures, including a familiarity with the commonly used business records and business machines; and (3) certain character and personality traits, such as dependability, courtesy, initiative, judgment, loyalty, resourcefulness, and, above all, adaptability and common sense.

You already have a certain amount of stenographic skill. You will need more. Do not neglect this phase of your training. Take at least one letter a day and transcribe it—more if you have time. You know something about business, and you possess many of the traits necessary for success as a private secretary to a business executive. Up to this point in your training, however, seldom, if at all, have you been called upon to merge these three qualifications while working on a practical assignment.

The major purpose of this course, therefore, is to build on the foundation you have already laid: to increase your stenographic skill until it has reached an acceptable business standard, to enrich your business knowledge so that you will be familiar with the customs and procedures that you must deal with on the job, and to strengthen those desirable traits you already possess and develop those other desirable traits that may be lacking so that you will have an employable personality.

The major purpose of the secretarial assignments in this course is to give you the opportunity of applying your knowledge, your skills, and your personality traits as if you were actually engaged as a private secretary in a business office.

You are to assume throughout the course that you are an employee of the United Products Corporation, producers and distributors of merchandise of all kinds. The main office of this corporation is located at 500 Madison Avenue, New York 22, New York, and it has branches in the principal cities of the United States.

You will start to work for the office manager of the main office of this corporation. From time to time you will be transferred to other departments and branches of the corporation, so that by the end of the course you will have a fairly general understanding of the secretarial duties of all major departments of the corporation.

Just as there is only one standard in business for a business letter that has been transcribed from dictation, so there is only one standard of proficiency for every assignment that is given the secretary. For business letters, the standard is mailability. If a letter, when transcribed, can be signed and mailed without any changes being made in it, the letter meets the standard set by business. If the secretary is asked for information about a subject with which she should be familiar, the only satisfactory answer is a complete and accurate one given at the earliest possible moment. In other words, business has no

place for a grade system consisting of excellent, good, fair, poor, and failure. Only two grades will be given by the businessman—satisfactory and unsatisfactory. If the work is not satisfactory, the secretary is likely to go off the payroll and on the unemployed list.

This standard does not mean that business asks the impossible of a beginner. On the contrary, the businessman is usually very lenient with a beginner. He is, as a rule, willing to overlook minor and even major mistakes the first time they are made but rarely the second time and never the third time.

Beginners who may not have had the opportunity of completing a secretarial-training course prior to their employment often go through a most trying breaking-in period. You are more fortunate than they. When you have completed this course, you will be "broken in" and may apply for your first position with confidence in your ability to do well the tasks assigned you.

Even though your abilities measure up to the acceptable business standards, there will be many things to learn in your new job. Most firms have some sort of orientation period, so that beginners will have a knowledge of the organization and the varied activities of the company. Try to learn as much as you can about your firm and the importance of your job.

Specific Performance Standards for Secretaries. At this point you may want to know what are the performance standards for secretaries. The standards listed below have been adapted from a recent study by Dr. Herbert A. Tonne, of New York University. If you can meet these, you are well on the road to being a successful secretary. Keep them in mind throughout your study of this text and the completion of the assignments.

DICTATION AND TRANSCRIPTION

1. Can make changes and insertions, in taking dictation, and take down special instructions properly and without confusion.
2. Calls attention to, and attempts to clear up, obvious errors before typing, such as incomplete sentences and omission of significant information. Corrects misspelled words.
3. Can transcribe with little or no loss of time because of clear notes.
4. Transcribes correctly what has been taken down.
5. Turns in letters and memos in proper form, complying with current office instructions so far as they have been given.

H. Armstrong Roberts

You may begin your career by working in a stenographic department like this one.

6. Turns in correspondence with the necessary filing references, enclosures, enclosure tags, cc notations on carbons, routing tags. Assembles file correctly. Types correct number of copies. Gets correct signature.
7. Can sort much "wheat from chaff" in conference discussion and take down all significant developments.
8. Recognizes and takes down decisions and assignments.
9. Can effectively summarize trends of discussion and digest notes taken.
10. Prepares concise, smooth-reading, and grammatically correct drafts that accurately reflect trends of discussion and that contain all decisions and assignments.
11. Prepares copy to go outside of office in good form, well balanced, with even margins, attractively spaced on page.
12. Produces copy that is free of uncorrected omissions and typographical errors, provided there has been opportunity to review it before turning it in.

TYPEWRITING

1. Keeps typewriter in good condition by cleaning and oiling it when necessary and reporting need for repairs immediately.

2. Makes clear-cut impressions; neat erasures; material is free from finger-prints, smudges, creases, and uncorrected strike-overs.
3. Prepares materials for temporary use with sufficient neatness and clearness, so that they may be read without distraction caused by poor typing or editing.
4. Observes and follows correctly instructions in regard to spacing, margins, etc.
5. Reads typed work and corrects typographical errors before turning it in, unless pressure of time prevents or unless she and the person for whom she is doing the work have a definite understanding.

Telephone

1. Can reach persons by telephone with little difficulty.
2. Obtains name and telephone number (exchange and extension) of callers.
3. Transmits all significant parts of messages both incoming and outgoing.
4. Notices obvious errors and omissions and attempts to clear them up on incoming calls.
5. Avoids errors in names and telephone numbers.

Communications

1. Sends notices in proper way (that is, by phone, post card, or letter-sized notice) at proper time.
2. In sending out notices, gives all essential information (that is, time, place, topic of discussion, and other special, important information).
3. If follow-up is indicated, makes it at proper time without being reminded.
4. Reads procedure letters carefully; notices and always makes all changes directed by letters.

Standards for General Activities

1. Keeps job moving.
2. Resumes work immediately after interruptions.
3. Works steadily, losing little time chatting about personal affairs, etc.
4. Does not dilly-dally or engage in "busywork."
5. Never does "extracurricular" reading unrelated to job.
6. Obtains enclosures and attachments required for work without unnecessary delay.
7. Meets all reasonable deadlines established for specific jobs unless delayed by superior or by conditions beyond control.

8. Establishes good will with, and is accepted and liked by, co-workers and by those outside with whom there is official contact.

9. Is usually able to get the co-operation of others, except under difficult circumstances.

10. Dresses neatly and appropriately so that there is no adverse comment.

11. Has well-modulated and pleasant voice; pleasant manner, never "bossy" or patronizing. Says and sounds as if she meant "please," "thank you," and "you're welcome."

12. Informs superior immediately if out of work.

13. Willingly and pleasantly helps with work of others when her own work is in fairly good shape, and when other work should have priority over what she is doing at the time.

14. Is willing to stay overtime, except in unusual circumstances; to adjust personal plans about lunch, leave, etc., to meet emergency situations.

15. Follows instructions readily and takes corrections with good grace.

16. Does not permit personal feeling to affect work.

17. Does not indulge in moodiness, sulkiness, "temperament."

18. Fulfills promises except when conditions beyond control prevent, in which case the persons affected are notified, well in advance if possible.

19. Can be relied upon to be ready and available for work when and where expected except under unusual circumstances, in which case the supervisor is notified, in advance if possible.

20. Produces consistent amounts and quality of work under similar conditions from day to day.

21. Does not request special privileges.

22. Discusses and attempts to adjust any work difficulties with superior rather than complaining to others.

Section 3. QUALIFICATIONS OF THE SECRETARY

The demands of modern business are increasing the need for secretaries with training beyond that of excellence of performance in the technical skills of shorthand, typewriting, and machine operation. This means that the secretary in today's business world must build a career based on a broad general education and a sound training in business fundamentals and understandings.

A Secretary Is More Than a Stenographer. A secretarial position and a stenographic position may differ in five respects. The secretary—

1. Has a closer personal contact with the employer and a knowledge of business secrets.
2. Spends less time on typewriting or performing stenographic duties.
3. Places increased reliance on personal initiative, judgment, and knowledge of business.
4. Has the ability to direct and supervise clerical workers.
5. Tries to assume responsibility for carrying out the most important details and performs minor administrative duties.

A stenographic position is largely "routine" in nature, while the secretarial position may be characterized as a "think-up" position. The secretary is often actually an assistant "boss" and as such must be qualified to carry on in the executive's absence. Keep in mind these distinctive features of the secretarial position toward which you are working. It is the goal toward which you will strive in this course.

Improve Your Character and Personality Traits. The vital importance of your ability to work well with others is stressed throughout this text. Your character and personality traits are likely to have a great deal to do with your success. Every study of employee failure shows, in most cases, that the secretary loses her position because of shortcomings in desirable personal qualities. You will find the section "Personality Pointer" and the personality assignments throughout the text helpful to you in improving yourself in these qualities.

Remember that you do not improve character and personality traits by wishful thinking. It takes action on your part. If you can develop those traits necessary for success, such as a friendly attitude, an unobtrusive initiative, and the willingness to do more than is required, you will go far in the business world.

Build a Well-Rounded Educational Background. Secretaries need a broad educational background. The education and training you have been receiving in your school program to date are preparing you for your initial position. You will continue your general education by reading, travel, recreation, hobbies, conversation, and possibly by continuing school, such as an evening school.

Develop Superior Stenographic Skills. Of course your technical skills must be very fine in order to obtain your first job. A sound knowledge of filing, dictation and transcription skills, correct speech, good telephone manners, the ability to compose letters are examples of these basic requirements. These skills are your most salable asset in obtaining your first position. For the secretary, however, the technical skills

should be considered primarily as immediate goals and as the *entering wedge* into a business career of increasing responsibility.

Understand Business Practices and Procedures. In addition to the qualifications of the secretary briefly described in the preceding paragraphs, you need to understand and appreciate modern business practices and procedures. Remember, you must use your technical skills in business situations; therefore, you need sound training in business fundamentals and understandings. If, for example, you wish to become a secretary in the marketing research or accounting department of a business firm, you should by all means familiarize yourself in the basic aspects of marketing or accounting. This will insure an understanding and an interest in the firm's business, essential requirements so necessary for advancement to positions of increased responsibility.

Section 4. OPPORTUNITIES IN SECRETARIAL WORK

Your First Position, a Starter. It is not so important, in the long run, if you begin your business career as a clerk, typist, or stenographer. If you have good basic skills, if you have had training that developed your understanding of business, and if you possess those desirable personal traits and individual merit, you can be confident of building a successful secretarial career.

Promotional Opportunities. In office work, thorough preparation for one job means that you may be successful in many. In your first position you will not receive a high salary because you are a beginner. Remember, however, that each job is preparation for a higher one, and good workers receive recognition.

First positions as stenographers may lead to executive, private, medical, or legal secretarial positions. Your first position may also lead to some related kind of work with the firm, such as an office supervisor or manager, a buyer, or a credit manager. Jobs for efficient employees are secure for business today tries hard to select and train employees carefully with the intention of promoting from within wherever possible.

Be Ready for Advancement. What does it take to be promoted? There is no formula! Increasingly, however, the person who works hard with the next job ahead in mind is the one rewarded with the promotion. Advancement to the next position is always a possibility for

Courtesy The First National Bank of Chicago

Jobs in banks offer many opportunities for young people with good office training and good personality.

every worker. It means an increase in responsibility as well as additional salary and authority. Study the job you want and prepare yourself for it. Think of your first job as a steppingstone to advancement.

Applied Secretarial Practice—a "Plus" Course. The purpose of this course is to give you, while still a student in school, an opportunity to acquire some of the "plus" factors that make for success in secretarial work.

You have often heard of the secretary who is able to correct the boss's mistakes in a subtle way that convinces him he was right all along; who provides him with valuable ideas and makes him think that the ideas were his to begin with; who directs his taste, restrains his rash judgments, and improves his disposition without his having

the slightest inkling of what she is doing. You have heard that her office has been thrown into utter confusion by her three-day illness, but scarcely affected when the boss went on a month-long fishing trip. That secretary had all the plus factors.

Yes, *Applied Secretarial Practice* is designed to help you perfect your technical skills still further as you use them in the infinite variety of secretarial duties included in this text. At the same time, it is designed to help you add to them those plus factors so necessary for advancement to positions of increased responsibility.

Some Highlights of This Unit

1. To learn more about your prospective career as a secretary, visit business offices.

2. An office may be large or small and is the *place* where the numerous and varied activities are carried on that require the "paper work" of an organization.

3. Office work deals generally with four main activities: recording, computing, classifying and filing, and communicating.

4. The work done in the office is actually the *connecting link* between the production, distribution, and service phases of the business.

5. Office work is productive, although it produces no direct profit but is done to assist the various departments of the business.

6. An efficient secretary should have (*a*) superior stenographic skill, (*b*) a broad educational background, (*c*) a clear understanding of business practices and procedures, and (*d*) desirable character and personality traits.

7. It is possible to distinguish between a secretarial position and a stenographic position through a delineation of the duties and responsibilities of the positions.

8. There is no formula for advancement (promotion), but it is wise to be ready for the opportunity should it present itself.

Questions and Items for Discussion

1. Discuss the statement, "Even though you prepare yourself thoroughly for a certain kind of job, you may also succeed in many different jobs."

2. What can you learn by the observation of all kinds of secretaries in the business offices you visit?

3. How does office work contribute to the operation of a business?

4. Discuss the statement, "Office work is the means to a desired end; it is not the end itself."

5. Enumerate and discuss some of the specific performance standards for secretaries.

6. In what specific respects does a secretarial position differ from a steno-graphic position?

7. How can you prepare yourself for advancement to another position should the opportunity arise?

Personality Questions and Projects

(Based on Personality Pointer, page 1)

1. One section of the Jones Rating Scale in your Workbook names the per-sonality characteristics that contribute to a person's ability to get along with others. Give yourself a careful rating on this scale, using the form on Sheet 43.

2. Set out deliberately to make the acquaintance of at least one person dif-ferent from those with whom you ordinarily are associated. If you are known as the athletic type, then choose a person for your study from the so-called studious type. Or, if you realize that you have had an unconscious prejudice against certain persons, choose one of them to help you with your project.

You may find your study subject sitting right next to you in your class, or riding on the same school bus, or among your neighbors and friends of your family. You won't have to go far to find stimulating persons to cultivate.

One girl who was working on a project of this nature was having a hard time to overcome her timidity and didn't seem to be able to "break the ice" with those she did not know. One morning while running for the streetcar, she turned a corner suddenly and bumped into one of the girls from her school. They both fell down. When they got to their feet, they laughed and laughed. Talking to each other from then on was easy, and the timid girl decided to use this new acquaintance for her project study subject. They eventually became close friends.

When you have selected the person you want to know better, learn as much as you can about his attitudes, interests, and background of experience. Tell him about your project, if you like.

Say to him, for example, "I know you're very much interested in journal-ism. When did you discover your interest, and what do you plan to do with it after you finish school? I know very little about the subject myself, and if you will tell me a little about it, you will be giving me some mighty interest-ing information and helping me with my personality project at the same time."

After talking with this person two or three times, you will be ready to complete this assignment. Your new acquaintance may be a boy or a girl, a man or a woman. If you have difficulty in making friends with members of the opposite sex, this will be a good time to conquer your timidity.

Our guess is that you will find this exercise so fascinating that you will

continue your search for interesting personalities, perhaps to the extent of making it your hobby.

When you have studied your new acquaintance, record in writing in your notebook a discussion of each of the following topics, using not more than fifty words for each:

1. Describe the person, or persons, you met.

2. Why did you choose this person, and how did you make his acquaintance?

3. Name five or more characteristics you admired about this person.

4. What characteristics, if any, would you like to imitate and make a part of your own personality?

5. Would you like to form a lasting and intimate friendship with this person?

Secretarial Assignments

As you undertake this course, it will be interesting and worth while for you to rate your qualifications for secretarial and other office duties and then to rate yourself at the end of the course and note your improvement. The following secretarial assignments are intended for this purpose.

1. Detach the Jones Personality Rating Scale in your Workbook, Sheet 1, and carry out the following procedure:

Rate yourself; *keep* the Scale; try to improve yourself during the school term; use the second Jones Personality Rating Scale, Sheet 116, at the end of the term; compare the ratings.

An interesting variation of the rating procedure that may be used, if preferred, would be to place your name on the sheet; pass the sheet to three or four students in your class; have each student check the Rating Scale, using a distinguishing mark or color (no name).

2. Detach the Job-Proficiency Rating Scale from your Workbook, Sheet 2. Rate yourself and *save* the rating. At the end of the term or of each school grading period, rate yourself again and note the improvement.

Spelling Demons

list

accelerate	accommodation	acquaintance
accessory	accumulate	adjournment
accidentally	achievement	affiliated

Job Tips

1. Do important things first.

2. Think for yourself—outgrow your dependence on others.

3. Be orderly in mind and habit.

4. Know the "why" of things; your work will be pleasurable, accurate, and more meaningful.

Personality Pointer

DO YOUR HABITS WORK FOR YOU?

Whatever you would make habitual, practice it; and if you would not make a thing habitual, do not practice it, but habituate yourself to something else.
— *Epictetus*

Living would be more tedious if habits did not relieve you of the monotony and the tensions of repetition. Good habits are necessary to pleasant living and efficient work.

Much of your success in an office is dependent on the work habits you establish. Office jobs are made up of many little tasks that are small but necessary parts of the general routine. Make the performance of these tasks habitual. When you have systematized your routine, you do not worry about the possibility of forgetting or omitting some detail.

Filing should be done daily if you would make light work of it.

Lois Thompson was an efficient private secretary who possessed all the qualifications of an expert secretary except one—she never kept her files up to date. A drawer in her desk was a catchall. Lois would rather search among the accumulated papers for some particular item than take time each day for routine filing. When asked why she left her filing to the last minute, Lois replied, "I hate it so." Lois would not have felt this way if she had learned to "do today's work today."

Note, also, that habits must admit of adjustment—your attitude toward habits must be flexible. At times a change in office policy affects the routine you have set up. That means you have to break down one set of work habits and build up a new set. Your value to

19

your employer is determined by the ease with which you adjust your-self to the new routine. There is no place in business for the person who gets set in his ways and cannot change.

As in all phases of personality, it is comparatively easy to point out the good habits we possess; but it is difficult to name and isolate the bad ones. We are not good critics of ourselves; we cannot see ourselves as others see us.

What are some of the good habits that a successful secretary can and should acquire?

Arrive promptly at the office each morning. Write down messages and instructions. Be neat in your work—neat erasures, for example, are just as easy to make as poor ones, though they take a little more care. Keep files orderly—replace each file folder properly; allow no papers to appear carelessly inserted. Be courteous. Say "Thank you," "Please," "Good morning," "Good night," and be sure to say them pleasantly.

The following annoying habits should have no place in the routine of an efficient secretary. You can probably add others to this list. Examine yourself carefully to see if you have any of these habits now. If you have, they should be broken as soon as possible and replaced by good habits.

Undesirable Work Habits

1. Borrowing erasers, pencils, fountain pens, or other equipment con-tinually
2. Not returning borrowed equipment in the condition in which it was received
3. Asking that instructions be repeated
4. Being inaccurate and satisfied with less than perfect work
5. Making excuses when confronted with an error instead of acknowledg-ing the error
6. Interrupting others when they are doing detailed, exacting work
7. Interrupting another employee to ask questions regarding English usage, punctuation, or spelling instead of looking up the answers
8. Delaying for "just a minute" when asked to carry a message or perform a task.

Undesirable Personal Habits

1. Filing nails, refreshing make-up, and putting on other finishing touches at the desk
2. Being careless about personal appearance

Undesirable Social Habits

1. Repeating over and over again certain words and phrases in conversation
2. Talking about "me," "my job," "my family"
3. Talking in a high, squeaky voice
4. Mumbling and speaking indistinctly
5. Interrupting others when talking
6. Being inquisitive about other people's business
7. Limiting associations, not making an effort to increase the number of acquaintances and to get broadening experiences

UNIT **2**

Your Personal Effectiveness

Your own experience in life thus far has made you well aware of the fact that your success is a very personal affair. It has been said that success is the sum total of you, your job, and your effort.

Your personal qualities and your work habits all add up to your personal effectiveness. They are extremely important in the success that you achieve in your work. As a matter of fact, studies of employee failures show that the worker (and this includes secretaries, too!) loses his position in most cases because of unsatisfactory *personal effectiveness*—weaknesses and shortcomings in personal qualities and work habits.

A study of 4,000 workers who lost their jobs, after being employed in the offices of 76 different companies, was made by H. C. Hunt. He found that in 90 per cent of cases—nine cases out of every ten—the workers lost their jobs because of some personality weakness or defect. In only 10 per cent of the cases were the workers discharged because of inadequate or otherwise unsatisfactory skills.

Personality is also a vital factor in getting ahead on a job. Mr. Hunt, in studying employees who were denied promotions, discovered that 76 per cent were not promoted because of unsatisfactory personal characteristics, while but 24 per cent were not promoted because of unsatisfactory skills.

It is evident that personality is of basic importance to secretaries and all office workers in achieving success on the job. One of the major purposes of *Applied Secretarial Practice*, therefore, is to help you improve your personality.

22

Section 1. YOUR PERSONAL QUALITIES

Personality is a difficult thing to define. It is intangible; something that you cannot see or hold. But it is definitely something that you can feel inwardly and that can be felt outwardly by others.

To some people, personality is the sum total of an individual's personal qualities or traits. To others, personality is what you are, an expression of yourself; and to still others, personality is something *in action*—an effect produced on others in a given situation.

It is necessary to think of personality in terms of your individual personal qualities, in order to study yourself and improve your personality. The study and improvement must be undertaken quality by quality. At the same time, it is highly desirable to think of your personal qualities as being in action and having an effect on others.

You are constantly making impressions on people, and these impressions are an essential part of the opinion that people form of you. They may say that your personality is interesting or dull, charming or unpleasant, stimulating or depressing. Your aim, therefore, is to improve your personal qualities, so that together—in action—they produce a favorable effect on those with whom you associate.

In order to improve your personality, it is necessary to build up the desirable elements or parts that make it up—the qualities or characteristics of a good personality. You must first realize and appreciate the importance of improving your personality, and then you must recognize and understand the desirable personal qualities that you should constantly try to develop. Many statements and lists of them have been compiled. The Personality Pointers in this text, one of which precedes each unit, present and develop in an informal, conversational manner several major personal qualities. Each Personality Pointer should be read and studied carefully, along with the corresponding personality questions and assignments that appear at the conclusion of the unit following the Personality Pointer.

The following personal qualities are of particular importance and value to you as a future secretary or office worker and even now as a student:

1. *Character*. Character underlies all personality and personality development. Character is based on moral principles and on a proper sense of values. It leads to self-confidence, self-reliance, personal

honesty, forthrightness, and courage in all your contacts and dealings with other people.

2. *Respect for Others.* Probably no human quality is so important in getting along with others as the quality of respecting others. This quality recognizes that everyone is different—different in make-up, in background, in experience. Respect for others leads to a genuine interest in others and a tolerance of the other person's point of view. It means being friendly and helpful.

3. *Sincerity.* Genuine sincerity is a quality that always impresses others. Be honest and sincere in everything you say and do.

4. *Courtesy and Tact.* Courtesy, tact, and good manners are based on consideration of the other person's needs, comfort, and convenience. They are among the first and most distinguishing characteristics of a good personality. They are the essence of a person's desire to please others.

5. *Enthusiasm.* Be cheerful in your outlook and in your associations with others. Enthusiasm is a big help in getting work done and in getting it done well and pleasantly. It's contagious, too, and helps others to be happier and more productive.

6. *Poise.* Poise comes from emotional stability. It reflects your confidence in yourself to do a job or to handle a situation. Poise creates the impression of efficiency and self-reliance. Emotional outbursts and and displays of moods or temper are avoided by a poised person.

7. *Gratitude and Co-operation.* The appreciative person is always appreciated by others. He doesn't take others for granted—neither them nor their kindnesses and assistance. He is quick to praise others when the praise is deserved and to express his appreciation for kindnesses and co-operation. He is always ready to return helpfulness for helpfulness.

8. *Sense of Humor.* A sense of humor is based on the ability to see the bright and the light side of things. It enables you to make the best of a situation and to take things in your stride. It helps you to maintain your mental balance and perspective. It helps you to stave off worry and anxiety and to take an occasional personal offense or disappointment.

9. *Loyalty.* Loyalty is a quality to be prized—loyalty to your friends, your company, your boss. Misplaced confidence or trust is soon found out and leads to serious consequences. Support others in prob-

lems and controversies honestly and constructively. Refrain from griping about conditions and people. It wastes time and nerves—your own and those of others!

10. *Receptivity to Ideas, Criticisms, and Suggestions.* Openmindedness is an essential quality of a good personality. You should have confidence in group thinking and seek the ideas, opinions, and advice of others. Respect the views of others and be willing to learn and to be shown.

Avoid being argumentative or antagonistic. Do not be offended by criticisms and suggestions of others. Welcome them and make the most of them. They will help you increase your efficiency and advancement.

Courtesy Betty Place

11. *Speech.* Speech is our most commonly used means of communication. Your telephone manners should also reflect a pleasing personality.

used means of communication. It is a means of conversing with others, giving and receiving instructions, presenting ideas to others, and so on. Your voice, your choice of words, your grammar—all are a part of your personality. Your voice should be pleasant in tone and balanced in volume. Words should be selected appropriately and combined in easy-to-follow sentences. Speak clearly, distinctly, and accurately. In conversation, be a good listener as well as a contributor.

12. *Health.* Good health is a basic essential of good personality. It is basic to numerous important personal qualities—enthusiasm, poise, emotional balance, sense of humor, and so on. It is the basis of vitality and energy—both essentials of a good personality. Eat the proper food, get sufficient sleep, and do those things in your free time that will give you relaxation and recreation.

13. *Appearance.* Appearance is a composite of several factors—dress,

grooming, posture, and so on. It is one of the most significant elements of personality—so significant and comprehensive a subject that it is treated separately and in detail in Unit 3 of *Applied Secretarial Practice*.

14. *Ambition*. Ambition is an essential characteristic of a good personality. Having an objective—looking ahead to something bigger and better—tends to pull together and concentrate your thought and effort on an objective. It helps you to make the most of your talents, training, and experiences. It stimulates thinking and ideas. It helps you over the rough spots and helps you to keep your perspective. It generates enthusiasm and effort.

Section 2. YOUR WORK HABITS

Your work habits are an essential part of your personal effectiveness. They are the means by which you get the most out of your talents, personal qualities, training, and experience. They work for you in getting more out of your job!

Work habits consist of attitudes toward work and ways of doing work. Right now, as a student, you have a set of work habits—attitudes toward your schoolwork and ways of doing it, such as studying, preparing lessons, participating in class discussions, and so on. You realize, of course, that in order to do your schoolwork well and to use your time and energy to the best possible advantage it is necessary for you to have good work habits. So it is on the job; in order to achieve maximum success for yourself and maximum returns from your efforts for your employer, it is necessary for you to use good work habits.

What are some work habits that are known from experience to produce good results in secretarial and other office jobs? Here's a selected list of them—not all the items that could be mentioned by any means, but they're all highly important work habits for you to develop and follow:

1. *Be production-minded*. The "pay-off" with the employer is production. That's what he pays wages to obtain. He is concerned, of course, with the steps taken and the materials used to get production; but your production is the measure of your success and of your value to

your employer. Consequently, strive for production—fast production that is at the same time satisfactory in quality, accuracy, and economy of materials. The things you do, the way you do them, the decisions you make should all lead directly and efficiently to the goal of *production*.

2. *Do the job in the "one best way."* There is a "one best way" of doing any job—the way that yields the best results (best production) with the least expenditure of time, effort, and materials. It may not be the "one best way" for all time. We learn from experience. But it is the "one best way" for the present. In undertaking a particular piece of work—perhaps transcribing some dictation, duplicating a memorandum, addressing a mailing, and so on—here is a suggested procedure for finding the "one best way" of doing it:

a. Study the job, breaking it down into parts or steps.
b. Arrange the steps in the best order or sequence.
c. Arrange the materials, tools, and equipment in the most satisfactory order, probably in accordance with the sequence of steps.
d. Do the job according to the plan, at the most satisfactory time, and preferably without interruption.

3. *Put first things first.* This work habit may sound a little trite. Naturally, a person thinks he "puts first things first"; but actually he does not more often than he does.

To "put first things first" requires thinking, judging, planning, and acting. Usually, it means doing the most urgent things first. Sometimes, it means planning ahead for days and keeping parts of a job moving concurrently with other work, so that at a designated time the entire job will be completed. Sometimes to "put first things first" means to do the *most difficult* things first. Often, we are inclined to delay doing the more difficult task; we put it aside until "another day." But the job stays with us mentally. We think about it; worry about it. It upsets our mental balance, cuts down on our efficiency, and consumes energy. Then when the day of reckoning comes and the job must be done, it is even more difficult to do than would have been the case had it been done promptly at first. The mental disturbance has been costly, and probably complications have been caused by the delay. To "put first things first" often means, therefore, to do the most difficult thing first. This procedure, however, usually has

a *positive* effect, for after the most difficult thing is done, the other tasks are "a breeze."

4. *Meet your deadlines.* In business, many things have to be done by a designated time—perhaps the four o'clock mail, the fifteenth of the month, and dozens of other possibilities. These designated times are known as "deadlines." Whenever you are given a deadline for a job, or know that a deadline exists, be sure to meet it. Plan your work in such a manner as to meet the deadline, and plan it early! Then, follow through on your plan. Deadlines are common in business. They're a part of the momentum of office work. They can be exciting. In all events, they must be met. When they're not, the employer knows it!

5. *Finish the job; don't flit!* Often it's a temptation, for one reason or another, to flit from one job to another, spending only a few minutes on each job; sort of a "blue-plate-special" performance—a little of each. Such a procedure is wasteful of time and energy, and disorganizes your thought and effort. It is far more desirable to see a job through and then to proceed to the next one. Of course, there are times when you may be forced to drop a job and turn to another because the latter is more urgent, or for some other understandable reason; but as a matter of policy, see one job through to the finish before starting the next.

6. *Keep your working tools handy and in good condition.* As in any job, the tools you work with in a secretarial or any other type of office job are very important. They are important to the quantity and the quality of your production—the dictation you take, the letters you transcribe, the reports you type, the memorandum you duplicate, and so on. Your working tools—pencils, pens, notebooks, erasers—should be adequate in variety and quantity. They should be properly cared for and kept in good condition. They should be put and kept in places where they may be reached for use easily and quickly.

7. *Take good care of your equipment.* In order to achieve neat, accurate, quantity production, good care must be given to equipment such as typewriters, staplers, and many other items that are discussed in *Applied Secretarial Practice.*

8. *Keep your materials and supplies up and in good order.* In secretarial and other office work, a large variety and quantity of materials and supplies are used—stationery, second sheets, carbon paper, onion-skin paper, ink, and so on. Judgment and foresight must be used in order to have on hand an adequate quantity of office supplies. They must be

kept and arranged in such a manner as to protect them from soil and waste and to make them quickly and easily available for use. Watch *Applied Secretarial Practice* for specific and practical suggestions on this important work habit.

9. *Be neat and accurate with your work.* Speed is important but not for its own sake. It must be speed that is consistent with neatness and accuracy. The employer can sign the quick transcript only when it is neat and accurate; only, when it is mailable. By all means, work fast; but your work must primarily be neat and accurate. Speed is in vain if the product cannot be used.

10. *Follow through; let the boss forget it.* Many words have been written and said about reliability and dependability. It is a real compliment for an employer to say that an employee is reliable and dependable; it is usually "money in the bank" for the employee. The employer means that, when the employee is given a job to do, he *knows* that it will be done—done on time and done well. He can forget it. When given instructions on a job, listen carefully, be sure you understand what is to be done, and then follow through—do it on time, and do it well. Soon you will develop that coveted reputation—reliable and dependable.

11. *Use your judgment.* Not every step, every move, or the answer to every question can be spelled out for you in detail. There are numerous opportunities for the secretary and other office workers to use judgment. Seek the help and advice of others, especially when you are new and inexperienced on a job, but don't develop the habit of depending on others to do your thinking for you. Develop your own ability to think things through and come to decisions. But while you are reaching that point, ask when in doubt. That's the way to learn.

12. *Use your initiative and resourcefulness.* Every business has a need—a vital need— of ideas; as a matter of fact, outside of people, ideas are the greatest factors in business. You—everyone—has suggestions and ideas to contribute or new and better ways of doing things. Don't hesitate to talk over your suggestions and ideas with your employer. They may mean savings and benefits for him, the employees, and the business. Take the initiative in starting and doing work on your own. Draw on your own resources for procedures and solutions to problems when you can do so with the confidence of satisfactory results.

13. *Be considerate with your time.* Always be on time—on time for work, for appointments, for completion of jobs. But in addition, consider your time during the course of the working day; don't

waste it in idle gossip, in clock-watching, and the like. Consider your time in meeting emergencies—the emergency letter that must be written or the report that must be finished, even though this may require working after closing hours. Of course, you have a right to expect your employer not to abuse your willingness to use your own time for emergencies; but in all cases, be sensibly considerate of your time.

14. *Get along with people*. Perhaps this is the most important of all work habits. In an office you will have co-workers—many of them in a large office. To be an effective worker yourself, you must be able to get along well with your co-workers.

Co-operation, friendliness, and enthusiasm are appreciated by co-workers as much as they are appreciated by employers. You should always remember that you are a member of a team in an office, working towards the same goal—the success of your employer's business.

Friendliness among co-workers need not be a close friendship

You may be very busy and it may be near closing time, but you should always be co-operative and help out, even if this sometimes means a little extra work.

Courtesy Shaw-Walker Company

outside of the office. In fact, it is sometimes better to have separate groups of friends in and outside an office in order to bring into your experience a variety of interests. In any case, show a friendly, but not too inquisitive, interest in the welfare and activities of your co-workers.

Enthusiasm is contagious. If you are enthusiastic about your work, your co-workers will be influenced by your example and will probably also become enthusiastic. Work in an office is more productive and flows more easily when employees are enthusiastic and cheerful.

Section 3. SELF-IMPROVEMENT

The improvement of your personal qualities and your work habits depends on what you, yourself, do about them. No one can improve them for you; the improvement must come from within you and be made by you. If is a self-improvement process.

Four steps are necessary to improve your personal qualities and work habits:

1) Recognize the importance of your personal qualities and work habits in achieving success.
2) Appraise or evaluate your personal qualities and work habits.
3) Formulate a plan of self-improvement.
4) Carry out the plan.

In the beginning of this Unit, preceding Section 1, Your Personal Qualities, the importance of personal qualities and work habits is emphasized. You have undoubtedly noticed how important they are by observing your friends and others in school and in your community. Their importance is supported by research studies of employee failures. This importance is demonstrated even more clearly in actual experience on the job. Consequently, it should not be difficult for you to recognize and appreciate the need for improving your personal qualities and work habits; and no matter how good your personal qualities and work habits are, they can be improved.

Probably the most satisfactory means of appraising or evaluating your personal qualities and work habits is by means of rating devices or scales. Several rating scales have been prepared. For example, you will find in the Workbook for *Applied Secretarial Practice*, Sheets 3 and 4, two personality rating charts. Analyze and rate yourself on the various qualities in these charts. In addition to using already prepared

charts and rating scales, it is quite possible to construct your own chart of personal qualities and to use it in analyzing and rating yourself.

The usual procedure in self-improvement, following the self-appraisal, is to formulate a plan of action. Such a plan should provide for:

1. The analysis and study of the personal qualities and work habits of other people, particularly the personal qualities and work habits of those people who, in your opinion, and on the basis of their actual success in school or in the community, have demonstrated that they have superior personal qualities and work habits.

2. Reading books on career planning and biographical sketches and biographies of people who have achieved success through their superior personal qualities and work habits, such as *Successful Women and How They Attained Success*, by Isabella Taves, published in New York by E. P. Dutton.

3. Practicing, through your own experience and association with others, to improve your personal qualities and work habits. Improve yourself by doing, by actually and conscientiously practicing superior personal qualities and work habits.

4. Rating yourself again and again periodically, noting the improvement, or lack of it, that has occurred.

5. Continuing with a systematic and conscientious study and practice program in between the rating periods.

The final step, of course, is actually to carry out your plan of self-improvement. This might seem to be automatic, but it is not. Carrying out the plan requires determination, patience, and self-discipline. You must stick to it. Fortunately, if you really and sincerely desire to improve your personal effectiveness, your effort to do so will become a habit after a period of conscientious, systematic effort. That habit is highly desirable, because the need of improving your personal effectiveness has such unlimited possibilities that a lifetime can and should be devoted to it.

Some Highlights of This Unit

1. Be specific in analyzing yourself in order to achieve an employable personality.

2. Some of the factors that make up a good personality for an office worker are: a sense of humor, dependability, good grooming, co-operativeness, loyalty, openmindedness, courtesy, and enthusiasm.

3. A genuine liking for people contributes to the ease with which a secretary gets along with others.

4. Experts agree we can change, at least slightly, all the factors that make up our personality.

5. After self-analysis, do something constructive in regard to those items in which you rate below average.

6. Personality plays a large part in job success and job failure.

7. Developing desirable traits will help you to develop a better personality.

8. Your work habits determine your efficiency—now as a student and later as a secretary.

Questions and Items for Discussion

1. Discuss the statement that success in your work experience "is the sum total of you, your job, and your effort."

2. How do you define "personality"? What is Webster's definition?

3. What are the desirable personality factors that an employer looks for in an employee?

4. It is said that "a genuine liking for people means you will get along well with others." Why is this statement said to be true? Might it be untrue?

5. Why is a fine personality more important to a secretary than, perhaps, to a stenographer?

6. How is a pleasing personality related to the amount of work that a secretary can turn out?

7. What qualities and traits do you most admire in other people? How can you improve these things in yourself?

8. What are desirable work habits for a student? for an office worker and secretary? What are *your* work habits?

Personality Questions and Projects
(Based on Personality Pointer, page 19)

1. On the form in your Workbook, Sheet 43, rate yourself on the Jones scales that measure the two important personality traits of thoroughness and industriousness. If your rating is not up to accepted business standards, inaugurate a program for improvement.

2. Since habits are results of repetitive practice, are you doing over and over again in your daily work those things that will become good job habits? What study habits are you forming? Do you write down instructions and assignments carefully? Do you carry through an assignment to completion? Do you budget your time, so that you can do your work thoroughly in the minimum time required? Are you acquiring habits of neatness in the care of your books and other equipment?

In your notebook make a list of the habits you are determined to acquire before the time of your employment. Beside each habit on your list note the

plan you intend to follow in order to acquire this habit. You may have to break an old habit before acquiring the new one. Be sure your notations include this factor.

Secretarial Assignments

1. Answer the questions in the Personality Mirror [1] in your Workbook, Sheet 3. Add the number of checks in the "yes" column *only*, and multiply that number by 4. For example, if you have checked 15 answers in the "yes" column, you would have a personality rating of 60 per cent.

If your score is between 35 and 65 per cent, you may certainly enter an occupation where you come in contact with people. This would include stenographic and secretarial work.

Of course, if your score is below 35 per cent, it might be wiser for you to choose a job in which your success does not depend on your ability to get along with people. Also, if your score is above 65 per cent, your personality has a definite cash value. You ought to do well in occupations in which success depends to a large extent on your ability to deal with, influence, and impress people.

2. Check your personality traits on the Charm Chart [2] on Sheet 4 in your Workbook. Use the key given to find your score. If your score is *above 240*, you have a personality that naturally attracts people to you. If your score is *above 180*, you have a pleasing personality. If your score is *under 120*, you should strive for a better rating.

Optional

3. Prepare a selected bibliography of books in your school library pertaining to the topic of "personality." Type up the bibliography in good form, classifying the books if possible.

4. What books in your school library have chapters in them on "personality"?

5. What magazine articles can you find that have been written on the subject of "personality"?

6. Construct your own chart of personal qualities and use it in rating some one you admire, some one you dislike, and yourself.

Spelling Demons

affirmative	allotment	apparatus
aggregate	aluminum	appropriate
allege	apostrophe	arrangement

[1] Esther E. Brooke. "Personality Mirror," *Guide to Career Success.* New York, Harper and Brothers, 1947.

[2] Hazel T. Craig and Ola D. Rush. "Charm Chart," *Clothes with Character.* Boston, D. C. Heath and Company, 1946.

Job Tips

1. There is always time to be courteous.
2. Be wise—keep your personal affairs to yourself.
3. Don't be supersensitive—be understanding and businesslike.
4. A well-modulated voice, a light tread, and the capacity to work quietly are among the finest characteristics for a secretary.
5. Speech affectations are highly undesirable.

Review 1st 2 units for test

Personality Pointer

ARE YOU GOING UP?

Even though your first job may be only a clerical one, you should keep yourself well dressed, like the secretary you hope to be, for some day a department head may say to the personnel manager: "I need a secretary. Is Miss X from the Filing Department available? They tell me she does fine work, and she always looks so well groomed."

Virginia, a newly employed secretarial graduate, called her secretarial training teacher one Saturday and said, "Everything is wrong on my new job. Won't you come down and have luncheon with me, so I can tell you all about it?"

When they met, the teacher learned that Virginia was employed in the Mailing Department of a large concern that occupied a ten-story building. Virginia's department was on the fifth floor. Her work was stapling papers. These were Virginia's complaints.

"You told me I had to wear a suit at the office. I'm the only one who wears a suit.

"You told me I shouldn't wear thin blouses to the office. Many of the other girls wear thin blouses.

"You told me I shouldn't use brilliant nail polish, that I had to dress my hair conservatively. You said I had to speak in a soft voice and not use slang.

"I don't look or act like the other girls in my department because I am following your instructions. What's wrong?"

The teacher laughed and replied: "You may feel uncomfortable now, Virginia; but those rules are still good. Remember that some day an executive is going to need a secretary; and if you want your immediate superior to recommend you, you'll have to show him that you can behave and look like a secretary.

"Monday, take a late luncheon hour if you can. Use part of it to walk down the corridor of each floor, from the fifth, where you are now, to the tenth, where the office of the executives and board of directors are. Then call me up and tell me what you discovered."

A few days later Virginia telephoned her teacher. "I get your point," she said. "The nearer I got to the tenth floor, the better dressed and more conservative in manner secretaries were. They seemed to be enjoying their work, too; but there was no loud talking or laughter to disturb the atmosphere of efficiency. I'm going to try to get that tenth-floor look."

Your Appearance

Many surveys have been made to determine what personal characteristics employers consider when hiring office workers. In one of these
surveys, employers were asked how important they considered the
satisfactory appearance of the secretary. The employers answered,
"Very important." When asked what they believed to be the most
serious faults in the appearance of a secretary, the most-often-checked
offenses were: uncleanliness, untidiness, inappropriateness in style of
clothes, too much make-up, and monotony of dress.

Your future employer will take your appearance into account as
one of your qualifications before hiring you. And later he will inevitably consider your daily appearance in deciding whether you
warrant a promotion. Remember that only *you* can change your
attitudes, your personality, or your appearance. Remember, too, that
it is what you say and what you do—and the way you say and do it—
that reveal your personality to others.

In Unit 2, the development of an employable personality was
emphasized. Now you will give particular attention to those appearance factors that are a part of your personality. This unit, through
suggestion and illustration, will help you become that top-notch
secretary every executive wants—an attractive, pleasant, efficient
worker. Three basic elements of your appearance are discussed:
(1) dress and grooming, (2) health and cleanliness, and (3) poise and
posture. They are closely related elements of appearance. As you
study this unit and complete the secretarial assignments, keep upper-
most in your mind that you can do a great deal to develop an employable personality and that appearance is an important part of it.

Section 1. DRESS AND GROOMING

The office worker's personality is expressed, to a considerable extent, by the attention given to appearance. You can make your appearance an asset. Although the business executive wants his secretary to be "easy to look at," he does not expect a Miss America or Mr. America. What he really wants is a business worker who always creates a favorable impression.

The well-dressed business worker creates a favorable impression. Because the secretary meets many different people daily, she must do so with ease and cordiality. Your appearance has much to do with the poise you will possess. For example, what you wear and how you wear it is very likely to help or hinder your frame of mind. With the right clothes and right grooming, you present an attractive, businesslike appearance and build your self-confidence and the confidence of others in you. Give serious thought and effort to the suggestions in this section and you can make your appearance an asset.

Dress Appropriately. The efficient secretary is appropriately dressed. She knows she must dress the part and she knows how to do it. Let us see how you, the successful secretary, will do it.

Suits. First of all, you will select a trim, well-made tailored suit in your favorite color. It gives you a businesslike appearance. A suit is an excellent investment. It may be worn most of the year. A suit that is well styled and of quality material is the best buy. Though its initial cost may be higher, it will hold its shape and appearance through many dry cleanings. A suit made of gabardine, worsted, or tweed will last you many seasons, especially if made on conservative lines that are not outdated by style changes.

Skirts. You can vary your wardrobe easily by adding a skirt to it to contrast with your suit jacket.

Blouses. The blouses worn with the suit or extra skirt can dress it up or down. They may be classic tailored shirts made of rayon, silk, cotton, or nylon. If the suit is a dark solid color, a gay print blouse will add interest. If the material of the skirt is a plaid or check, the blouses should be a solid color. But remember, whatever your blouse may be, it must always look fresh and crisp. That is why many office workers prefer nylon blouses, as these wash and dry quickly and require little ironing.

Dresses. Dresses are appropriate for office wear. They should be smart and tailored—never frilly or fluffy. Basic dresses are practical, too. They may be changed in appearance by varying the jewelry, belt, or scarf. Tailored clothes need not be drab or monotonous.

Shoes. The shoes you wear to the office every day should be tailored. They should be made of a leather that can be polished and kept clean easily. Nothing can spoil an otherwise well-groomed appearance as easily as scuffed-up shoes and run-down heels. Ballet slippers and flats are definitely out of place in an office. Your office shoe should have a medium heel, it should fit well, it should be comfortable.

Accessories. The secretary knows the importance of having the right accessories. Her bracelets do not jangle with every movement she makes or get caught in her typewriter or other objects. Neither are her earrings oversized and dangling, so that they interfere with telephoning. She uses a light, fragrant toilet water, not a heavy perfume. Her accessories—scarves, belts, jewelry—point up her dress but do not clamor for attention for their own sake. Always remember —go easy on accessories. It is better to have too little than a little too much.

Your handbag should harmonize with your costume and be large enough to carry the various beauty aids necessary for good grooming. Do not accumulate pencils, personal letters, and the like to spoil the shape of your bag.

Employers Do Care How You Look. Your boss is sure to notice how you look. He wants his secretary to look smart but conservative. He knows that the secretary who takes personal pride in her appearance will inevitably take the same amount of pride in her work.

Let's look at Flossy and see why the boss is going to replace her at the end of the week. Of course you may wonder why an employer would hire her in the first place! She attracts attention all right! What a hairdo! It requires constant care and attention! Her brilliant orange taffeta dress with a low neckline (strictly a party dress) has no place in the office. Flossy is slow in answering the telephone because of the fancy earrings she wears. She wears too much lipstick. One day she comes to work in shoes with high heels and the next day in dusty sports shoes with run-down heels. Her hair is dyed and much too long. Her tapering fingernails are too long for filing. Yes, and her desk is ready to "walk away." Papers that should have been filed are everywhere. Pencils are dull. The typewriter ribbon is faint. Desk drawers

are in complete confusion. The boss, of course, replaces Flossy at the end of the first week.

A Basic Wardrobe. As you look forward to your first secretarial position, you will be wise to plan a basic wardrobe similar to the following. It is suggested as the absolute minimum requirements for a well-dressed career girl:

A good suit, which may be changed in appearance with the addition of different accessories.

A smart basic dress, which may be toned up or down with accessories to fit dress or business occasions.

An extra skirt.

A date dress for after-five social events.

Two tailored blouses and a dressy blouse.

Two pairs of shoes—one pair for daily wear and one with higher heels for dress occasions.

Several pairs of nylon hose, all the same shade; thus if one stocking is snagged, the remaining one will match the next one that loses its mate.

One or two nonfussy hats.

A coat suitable for the season, cut to go over everything, in a neutral color that will blend with all your clothes. This means at least two—a heavy winter coat and a light spring or fall coat. In some climates a third coat—a "shortie," perhaps, or other casual type—is a smart idea.

A tailored bag for daily use and another bag for dress occasions.

Gloves for daily wear, plus washable "whites," for dress wear.

Ewing Galloway

Spic and span from head to toe, she's off to a good start on a successful career.

A practical suggestion to help you select clothes that will harmonize is called the color-chart system. In such a chart you would list the basic neutral colors across the top—black, gray, brown, blue. Under each color, the complementary colors would be listed. For example, under brown you would have yellow, rust, brick, beige, hunter green, and coffee. Under these complementary colors, you would list the contrasting colors. For brown they would be turquoise, royal blue, emerald green, white, and dusty pink. Let your teacher help you deter-

mine the complementary and contrasting colors for the other neutral shades.

After you are sure of the colors that will look well together, you can plan your purchase of a wardrobe to fit both your colors and your budget.

How Do You Select Your Clothes? In the preceding paragraphs you have read about the selection of becoming, attractive clothes. But

A man's appearance is a big factor in his job future.

how do you know they're going to look attractive on *you?* Remember, what's attractive on long, lanky Jane may look unattractive on short, stocky Barbara. Here are a few hints on selecting styles becoming to your type of face and figure.

If you are tall and slim with a narrow face, cut your height by wearing blouses with full sleeves, boxy jackets, peplums, dirndls, voluminous coats, and clothes made of stiff, standout fabrics. You can wear hats with wide brims, profile hats, and off-the-face rollers.

Are you the short and round type, with a wide face? Then you should try to stretch your appearance with long vertical lines that you will find in a classic dress buttoned down the front, or one with narrow center panels and a V-neckline. Don't wear short chubby jackets or clothes that are too tight. You will look well in turbans draped high, in berets, in tall hats. Remember to keep your hair smooth at the sides.

You may be a bit too heavy. Don't call attention to the fact by wearing a print blouse or overpadding your shoulders. Instead, wear an interesting skirt to draw attention. If, on the other hand, your hips are heavy, balance them by building up your shoulders. Wear skirts that are neither too wide nor too narrow. Don't wear full skirts with contrasting belts, and stay away from wide pleats and widely spaced stripes.

If you are a large girl, remember that darkish colors make you appear smaller. Well-tailored suits with long jackets will slim you, as

well as hats with wide brims. Don't wear a tiny hat; by contrast, it will make you appear larger.

If your neck is short, create the impression of length by wearing a dress with a deep V or a low square. If your neck is long, avoid low necklines. Wear stand-up collars and high, round necklines with choker necklaces.

A Word to the Boys. It is equally important that men in business offices dress the part. A well-fitting suit of conservative style and color is always "right" for the male secretary. Suits made of mixtures are practical; they do not show spots or mends readily. Your suit will get plenty of hard daily wear; so medium or dark colors are good. It is better to have fewer suits of good quality for long-lasting good looks than many suits of poor quality that will show wear quickly.

Be sure your coat and trousers fit easily and comfortably. Both single- and double-breasted coats are appropriate. Keep your shoes shined and the heels straight. A white shirt is always in good taste; but, whatever you wear, beware of frayed collars. There's something about wearing a good-looking hat that gives you an air of self-assurance. Keep it clean and well blocked. In selecting your hat, consider the shape of your face, your physique, your complexion, and your wardrobe.

Section 2. HEALTH AND CLEANLINESS

The quality of your work must be excellent. But you will first be noticed by your daily appearance. Fortunately, there are many ways in which you can make the most of your appearance. Some of them depend on your health and cleanliness.

Personal Cleanliness. Keep yourself clean. Bathe or take a shower daily. Use a reliable deodorant. Change your underwear and stockings or socks daily. The foregoing rules apply to boys and girls.

And now a word to the girls. After you have cleansed your skin thoroughly, either with soap and water or with a good cleansing cream, apply your make-up. Let a cosmetician advise you on the correct blending of your powder to harmonize with the tone of your skin. Use a conservative make-up for the office.

Cleanliness of Clothes. Have your clothes dry-cleaned and pressed frequently. Brush and polish your shoes and watch for worn-down

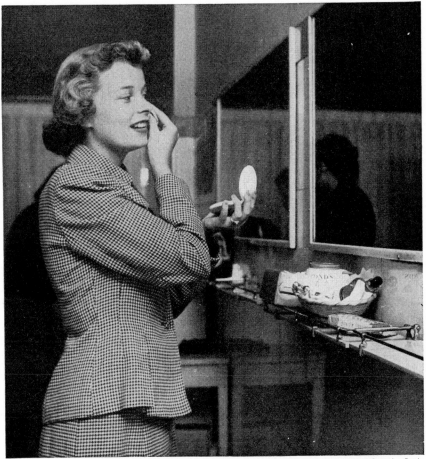

Courtesy Pond's Good Grooming Service

Take a few minutes during the day to freshen your make-up and check your grooming —but do this in the washroom, never at your desk.

heels. Baggy trousers, a shine on your suit, or dandruff on your coat collar do make a difference.

Care of the Eyes. The proper care of your eyes is essential on several counts. If you do much filing or keep a set of books, your eyes may easily become strained. Don't neglect getting glasses because you think you are not the type to wear them. Little wrinkles around your eyes and deep lines in your forehead will be definitely less flattering than a pair of smart specs! Select the right color and shape of frames to suit both your looks and your personality.

Care of the Hands. The secretary's hands are prominent in the performance of her duties. Keep them clean and well groomed. The fingernails should be well shaped and carefully trimmed. Long, glamorous nails may have their place in the social whirl—but not in the secretarial world. They must not take time from your duties. If you use fingernail polish, be sure it is never chipped.

Care of the Hair. Gleaming hair that is brushed faithfully between shampoos is definitely an asset. Keep your hair in a becoming style—one that will look trim and neat with a minimum of attention. Elaborate hairdos may look well one day but become very untidy before the next shampoo.

Care of the Teeth and Mouth. Well-brushed teeth are important. Visit your dentist twice a year. Clean your teeth at least twice a day. Use a mouth wash to avoid unpleasant breath.

Sleep. Get enough sleep—at least eight hours every day—so that your eyes sparkle and your mind is alert. You cannot look pleasant when sleepy. You cannot be efficient when tired.

Section 3. POISE AND POSTURE

Your Poise. Poise is that hard-to-define term that describes a dignity of spirit as well as a dignity in bearing or manner. It is that trait that enables you to look cool and calm and composed when you are inwardly seething at some difficult situation, at your boss, a fellow worker, or some tiresome client or visitor to your office. It is the trait, the self-discipline, that makes you pleasant and polite on a hot, muggy day, when you long to be down at the beach or relaxing at home with a cool, tall glass of lemonade. It is the ability to appear serenely and calmly dignified when your head aches or you are feeling frustrated or not up to par physically.

Poise, too, is that ability to be friendly yet businesslike. It is the way you control your movements to suggest efficiency without hurried or frantic efforts. There is the appearance of easy effort but an assurance that makes you appear "at home" in any situation that arises. It is the ability to be cordial and friendly without descending to familiarity, "apple-polishing," or backslapping.

Poise may be achieved by anyone who has the desire or willingness to cultivate it. You can never feel at ease if you are self-conscious about your appearance; hence poise requires the knowledge that you are

clean and neat and appropriately dressed. Graceful carriage of body is also essential—a poised person does not slump in his chair nor walk noisily or clumsily about. Neither does he go so far to the other extreme as to carry his "nose in the air" or give an attitude of haughtiness.

The secretary who can carry herself with a bearing of self-assurance but not smugness, who can be patient and pleasant to all whom she meets, and who can smile and radiate good cheer among her associates is a valuable employee.

Your Posture. Closely related to poise is posture. The way you walk, stand, or sit is an important attribute of your efficiency on the job. If

Keep a graceful, relaxed posture by sitting correctly at your desk.

AT SMALL OF BACK

RIGHT ANGLE

NO BIND

FEET FLAT ON FLOOR

Courtesy Shaw-Walker Company

you amble into the office shuffling your feet and drooping your shoulders, and flop awkwardly on your chair, you are definitely not promotional material. Show your interest in your job by walking into the office with a brisk step. Throw back those shoulders and lift your head high. Gracefulness in walking and sitting is easy to acquire and will bring a changed mental attitude about your work and your job.

Some Highlights of This Unit

1. Three basic elements in your appearance are dress and grooming, health and cleanliness, and poise and posture.

2. What you wear and how you wear it is very likely to help or hinder your frame of mind.

3. A secretary should look smart but conservative.

4. The right accessories are important.

5. The efficient secretary dresses appropriately.

6. It is equally important that men in business offices dress appropriately.

7. Keep your hair in a becoming style—one that will look trim and neat with a minimum of attention.

8. Get enough sleep so that your eyes sparkle and your mind is alert.

9. Cleanliness of person and clothes is of vital importance for your personal and job efficiency.

10. The way you walk, stand, or sit is an important factor in your appearance and efficiency.

Questions and Items for Discussion

1. What is meant by appropriate dress?

2. Discuss the use of color in accessories.

3. What is meant by a basic wardrobe?

4. What does good grooming mean to you?

5. What is meant by poise?

6. Mention five offenses that occur most frequently in a secretary's appearance.

Personality Questions and Projects

(Based on Personality Pointer, page 37)

1. Study the rating scale on personal grooming and personal appearance in your Workbook, Sheet 43. Place a check mark in the section that most nearly describes your appearance now. Are you going to be satisfied to remain at your present rating?

2. For young women: Consult some reliable books on the subject of appropriate and becoming clothes. Find out what is required to accentuate your most attractive features and to make your less attractive features inconspicuous. Study cosmetic charts and decide on the extent to which you will use cosmetics. If you have difficulty in deciding on the right colors and lines for you, ask the style consultant of your local department store to help you. Your secretarial instructor will also be able to help you.

3. For young men: Observe the clothes of the men in your community who hold executive positions and whom you consider to be well dressed. Write down a description of four different outfits that you conclude are appropriate for the office, and therefore appropriate for you to consider for yourself when you are employed. If you are in doubt as to styles and colors that would be becoming to you, consult with the buyer of a men's furnishings store in your community.

Secretarial Assignments

1. Fill out the Good Grooming Rating Chart [1] in your Workbook, Sheet 5. Score yourself according to the key given there. If your score is above 90, you rank superior. If your score is above 75, you are well groomed. If your score is under 50, you can do much to improve your grooming.

2. Check the contents of your wardrobe against the suggested basic wardrobe.

Optional

3. Select a book on personality, personal appearance, grooming, or posture. Read the book and make a report to the class.

4. Select one of the other neutral colors mentioned in the text and list the complementary and contrasting shades for it. After that, make a list of a basic wardrobe in that color scheme.

Spelling Demons

asphalt	assistance	attendance
assessment	asterisk	attorney
assignment	athletic	aviator

Job Tips

1. Immaculateness must be an unbreakable habit.

2. *Get up early enough* to dress completely *at home.* Arrive at your desk sure of your appearance in every detail.

3. Watch your appearance during the working day—your person, your desk, your workplace—but don't waste time at it!

[1] Elizabeth F. Trumper, "Good Grooming Rating Chart," *Today's Secretary* (April, 1951), p. 364.

*write a paper on a personality.
The most Unforgettable Character I'd
Ever met. Pose.*

Personality Pointer

WHAT TIME DO YOU HAVE?

You can answer this question glibly by giving the time of day! But, really, now, what time *do* you have to do all the things that need to be done and all the things that you want to do?

You have twenty-four hours a day! Sixty minutes each! Of course, you know this! But what do you do with the time that is given to you?

If you are like most people, you usually do one of three things.

One, you live each moment as it flits by letting things come and go in an aimless manner, waiting for something to happen—vegetating.

Two, you do some general planning, remembering certain things that should be completed within a period of time. Insofar as your plans go, this use of your time is an improvement over the first use.

Three, you plan each day's activities, making a plan that is flexible yet is a plan of action. Each day you have an average of eight hours sleep. Approximately eight hours you spend at school or at work. You need about two hours for leisurely eating. At least an hour a day you need for good grooming. Such planning, of course, reflects more thought in your use of time.

But what about those three, four, or five hours that you have not accounted for? These hours do not come in continuous minutes but are apportioned throughout the day in ten-, fifteen-, thirty-, and perhaps sixty-minute periods. Those are the minutes that count *for you* or are forever lost to you.

What time do you have? How do you spend it? Your answer is of vital importance *to you*.

Taking Dictation and Transcribing

When you think of working as a secretary, you probably picture yourself taking dictation. You have, therefore, been putting every effort into perfecting your ability to take dictation accurately and to read your notes readily. Certain techniques are described in this unit that will make your taking of dictation easier and more efficient.

You have also pictured yourself in the office transcribing the dictation into mailable copy. This unit will help you acquire transcribing techniques that will promote your success in this important part of the secretary's work.

In addition to the basic skills needed in taking dictation and in transcribing, you must develop the ability to *think* about the sense of the material dictated to you. As your skills in shorthand, in typing, and in English become automatic, you will have more time to concentrate on the meaning of the material.

Section 1. TAKING DICTATION

You will find that taking dictation in an office is different from taking dictation in a classroom. For example, the material dictated in class is carefully planned as to content, length, and speed of dictation. The material is read in an even tone of voice, each word being enunciated clearly. The desks are comfortable, and the room is comparatively quiet.

In a business office, the dictator is seldom so good a dictator as your teacher and seldom so considerate of your limitations in endurance and speed. Shorthand skill to him does not mean so many words a

52

minute. It merely means the ability to take down in readable notes what he dictates, regardless of the speed or the length of his dictation. Few executives dictate rapidly for any appreciable length of time. Each day you will become increasingly familiar with the vocabulary of the business of the firm, with the names and business transactions of its customers, and with the vocabulary and idiosyncrasies of the dictator. In time, much of the routine correspondence will be turned over to you to answer. Then you will have the responsibility for the message to be conveyed as well as the typing of the letter.

During this course, you have the invaluable opportunity of benefiting from the experience of others, as described in this text. Here are some helps and hints for taking and transcribing dictation on the job.

Your Dictation Equipment

The Notebook. The standard two-column shorthand notebook is 6 by 9 inches in size and contains 70 leaves (140 pages). The paper must be suitable for ink. The Spiral-bound notebooks lie flat when open.

Wherever practicable, use a copyholder for your notebook while transcribing. A copyholder will enable you to read your notes at the right angle and from the right distance, thus eliminating eyestrain. An inexpensive yet entirely satisfactory copyholder is illustrated on page 89.

When a notebook is filled, it is filed for possible future reference. This is one of the reasons why you will be careful of your notebook, keeping each day's notes clearly dated and writing names, addresses, instructions, and dictation material plainly so that all your notes can be read at any time after the notebook has been filed.

A rubber band placed around the used leaves of your notebook will make it easy for you to open the book at once to the first unused page.

When the notebook is filled, indicate on the cover the beginning and ending dates of the material included. An index of the contents pasted on the cover is helpful.

You may have to take dictation from several persons. If so, it is advisable to use a separate notebook for each person. If, for example, you are in the midst of transcribing the dictation of one person and you receive a call from another, you will not have to disturb the notebook from which you are transcribing if you use separate notebooks.

You will find that having separate notebooks for different dictators will also aid you in using the letter style that suits each dictator, because the different notebooks will remind you of the different styles. You may find it helpful, also, to have a special notebook close to your telephone in which to record telephone messages and any especially urgent dictation, such as a telegram or a cablegram.

A Tip to Left-Handed Writers. Left-handed writers may find it more convenient to write in the second column of the notebook first instead

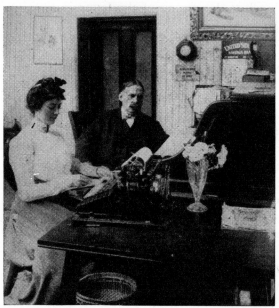

The latest style in offices at the beginning of the century—from the wicker wastebasket to the roll-top desk. Then, just as today in the picture on the opposite page, every executive placed great value on a well-trained secretary.

Culver Service

of the first column. "Upside-down" left-handed writers start at the extreme top of the opened book instead of at the top of the page below the binding.

Pen and Pencils. Write shorthand with a pen instead of a pencil whenever possible. The advantages of the pen over the pencil are so many that the pen has become the standard writing tool of the efficient secretary. A famous reporter, David Wolfe Brown, gave the following seven reasons for using a pen:

1. Less muscular exertion is required in using the pen. Hence the pen writer works for long periods with less fatigue than the pencil writer.

2. The pen permits and promotes a lightness of touch that is out of the question with the pencil. This lightness of touch contributes largely to speed.

Courtesy Shaw-Walker Company

Note the correct position of this secretary while taking dictation: she is ready to turn the page of her notebook with her left hand; the top of her fountain pen has been removed and is lying at her left; the dictated correspondence is also placed neatly at her left.

3. Pen notes are better adapted for preservation than pencil notes, which tend to blur with even ordinary handling. Notes that are to be filed away as a record should not be written with a pencil.

4. Pen notes are more legible than pencil notes, especially when they must be read at night. The young stenographer, looking forward to coming years, should preserve his sight carefully as a part of his business equipment and should realize that he cannot afford to abuse the only pair of eyes he will ever have.

5. Neater notes can be made with the pen than with the pencil, as the latter tends to encourage a habit of scrawling. The scrawling writer is nearly always a pencil writer. Some of the neatest writers in our profession use the pen constantly.

6. Pencil notes can seldom be transcribed (as pen notes constantly are)

by other persons than the writer. Such transcription by assistants is an immense advantage to many a hard-working executive and secretary.

7. The pencil point is liable to break at a most critical moment.

In purchasing a pen, see that you get one with a free flow. Try several points until you find one that suits your style of writing.

Many secretaries use either jet-black or purple ink to reduce the strain on the eyes while transcribing. Special permanent inks are advisable for important records.

When you arrive at the office each morning, check immediately to see that your pen is filled and in good working order. Have several pencils sharpened, including a red and a blue pencil, ready to be used for temporary memorandums on letters or papers, or in an emergency, should your pen fail to write properly.

Answer the Dictator's Call Immediately. A buzzer system is generally used in offices to signal different members of the staff. When your buzzer sounds, quickly pick up your notebook, pen, and pencils and go immediately to the dictator's desk. Answer the buzzer promptly even though you are in the midst of urgent duties. Even a slight delay on the stenographer's part is not only annoying to the dictator but may also interfere with important proceedings.

If you anticipate being away from your desk for some time, let the telephone operator or the person sitting near your desk know where you are and ask him to take your telephone calls for you. If you are expecting a business caller, leave instructions with the receptionist. In other words, you are supposed to be at your desk or have your whereabouts known. Don't permit personal calls when taking dictation.

Your notebook and pen must be ready for instant use, as there may be times when the dictator will be so engrossed in his business that he will not wait for you to get comfortably seated but will start dictating as soon as you approach his desk.

You will not always be comfortably seated. You should be prepared, therefore, to take dictation while standing; while seated, with your notebook on the edge of the desk or on your knee; while talking over the telephone; or while walking to the dictator's desk. No matter what the writing position, your notes must be legible.

Develop Your Personal Attitude. You should be at ease in your relations with your employer; yet when taking dictation, you cease to be a personality to your employer and are regarded by him as an effi-

Courtesy Shaw-Walker Company

Taking dictation while walking into your executive's office is not the ideal position. But be prepared to do it in a rush situation.

cient cog in the office machinery. Sit quietly and do not call attention to yourself by unnecessary motions or by fidgeting. Keep your mind focused on the matter being dictated so that, if you must ask questions, they will be intelligent ones.

Ask Questions. The situation determines *when* to ask questions. Each

dictator has his own likes and dislikes in this respect, and you must learn what they are. Remember not to interrupt when the dictator is speaking. Ask your question tactfully during a pause in the dictation or wait until the dictation is ended. If you keep your mind alert, you may find that a certain word that you did not quite understand will be repeated farther on in the dictation. Sometimes a proper name will puzzle you, but previous correspondence often will contain the answer to that question.

Be Alert During Dictation. A wise precaution for beginners is to take down instructions verbatim as they are given. As you become more experienced, a notation—merely a word or two of the instructions—will be sufficient. Special instructions, as "Send a copy to Mr. Brown of the Chicago office," should be clearly indicated in your notes; thus, "Copy to Brown, Chicago." Make the notation at the beginning of the dictated letter rather than at the end so that you will be saved the necessity of recopying the letter for Mr. Brown because you failed to make an extra carbon when typing the original.

You may be instructed to send a letter by air mail, to put certain letters in the mail immediately, or to send a telegram. Such notations should stand out prominently in your notebook. Some stenographers use a colored pencil for such special instructions.

Changes and Insertions. Sometimes the dictator wishes certain paragraphs crossed out. Or he may wish to have a paragraph that he dictated toward the beginning of the letter placed near the end of the letter. In either instance, make the notation in your notes immediately. If it is difficult to find the exact place for the changes without delaying the dictator, take down the instructions verbatim, marking them in such a way that you cannot overlook them when transcribing. Use a colored pencil or encircle the instructions. An X or an arrow placed at the beginning of the letter will act as a signal that it contains corrections and that special care will be necessary in transcribing the letter.

Your dictator may also wish to add paragraphs and make insertions. If he does this often, establish a system of numbering the insertions and indicating by a caret ($\wedge$) in your notes each place where an insertion is to be made. The paragraphs to be inserted should be written as near the insertion point as possible. The illustration on page 59 will show you how insertions and instructions should be indicated in your shorthand notes.

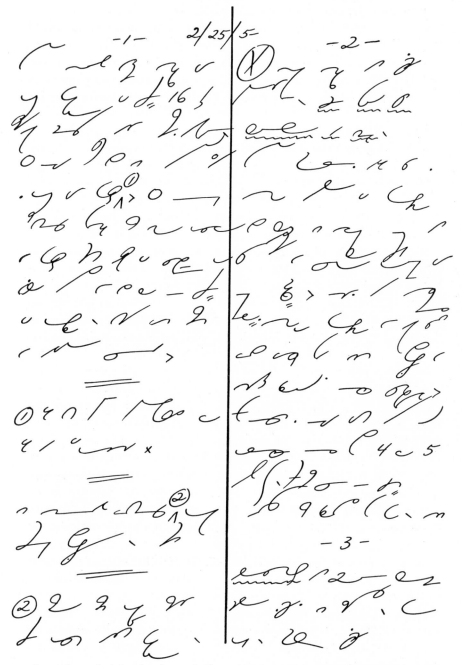

Correctly marked shorthand notes for inserts, carbon copies, rush letters, and telegrams.

Be sure you have some clear way of indicating the end of each letter in your notebook—for example, by a heavy single or double line drawn across the column at the end of the letter or, better still, by leaving two or three lines blank. These indications help you to estimate the length of the letter you are transcribing; and the blank spaces may be used for insertions, instructions, transcription date, and other data.

Pauses in Dictation. Do not allow your mind to wander when there are pauses in the dictation. Take this opportunity to read your notes and to make notations of punctuation, capitalization, and paragraphs. In this way you will speed up your transcription. Remember, you are to reproduce the dictated message in a mailable letter.

Endurance. Be prepared to take dictation for long periods at a time and school yourself to maintain an alert attitude at all times.

Names and Addresses. Most executives, when dictating an answer to a letter, do not dictate the name and address of the recipient of the letter. Often you will be given the letter to be answered. You can obtain the name and address from the letter itself and copy this information in your notebook in a space left for that purpose at the beginning of the answer. Another method is to place a number on the letter and the same number at the beginning of the shorthand notes of the answer.

Form the habit of writing names and addresses in shorthand, indicating peculiar spellings whenever necessary. These spellings will soon become familiar to you if the names represent regular customers of the firm. An efficient secretary memorizes as soon as possible the complete name, address, and business title of each person with whom her superior corresponds regularly. A card index of "Who's Who" is a great help in this respect.

Understand the Dictated Matter. It is essential that you understand the content of the message your employer is dictating. You may be called upon to read your notes back at any time, and you will wish to do so quickly and intelligently. This understanding comes from constant study of the firm's business. Learn as much as you can—as soon as you can—about how the firm does its business.

Leave the Dictator's Desk Promptly. When you leave the dictator's desk, take all your belongings with you, together with any correspondence or files that you will need when transcribing the dictation. Be sure

you understand all the instructions before you leave, while the correspondence is still fresh in the dictator's mind.

Improve Your Shorthand Skill. While you are studying this course in secretarial practice, take advantage of every opportunity outside of class to get at least five minutes of dictation a day, and either read your notes back or transcribe them on the typewriter. One five-minute take a day, dictated at your maximum speed, will maintain the speed you have and in many cases will increase it.

Some member of your family at home, some secretarial friend who also wants dictation, news commentators on the radio—all are possible sources of dictation. During this practice, keep clearly in mind that a shorthand writer is paid not only according to the speed with which he can write shorthand, but also according to the speed with which he can transcribe. Anything written in shorthand that cannot be read quickly is of little value in the business world.

You will be able to take dictation on the job with very little difficulty if you have mastered your shorthand theory and can write new matter for at least five minutes at from 100 to 120 words a minute. As soon as you are employed, learn the vocabulary of your business by reading its trade magazines and publications, by familiarizing yourself with its price lists and advertising materials, and by examining letters and documents that are available to you in the files. Make your own alphabetic list of words and phrases peculiar to your business; and if a special shorthand vocabulary for your business is not available, make up some special short outlines for the long and difficult terms that occur with great frequency.

Very little of this study should be done at the office. Get permission to take some of the printed material home—but return it promptly.

Remember that shorthand is a basic secretarial asset. Master it so that you may give your undivided attention to the many other duties that will be placed on your shoulders.

Section 2. TECHNIQUES OF TRANSCRIBING

One of the chief pleasures of a stenographer is to place on the dictator's desk a folder filled with beautifully typed, errorless letters ready for his signature. Never allow yourself to be satisfied with anything short of perfect transcripts.

Transcribing skill depends on four factors:

1. The ability to read shorthand notes quickly and accurately. This requires interpretive ability of a high order. There are times when shorthand forms should not be read too literally; they must be interpreted for *sense*. You may have misheard. Your chief may have dictated an involved sentence and lost the meaning. A literal transcript does not always make sense.

2. A thorough training in typing technique and artistic arrangement.

3. A working knowledge of English—spelling, punctuation, hyphenation, capitalization, paragraphing, rules of grammar and sentence structure—and a clear understanding of the meaning of business idioms.

4. The ability to visualize the completed transcript before you start to transcribe, so that the material need not be recopied because of poor setup or incorrect placement on the page.

Develop Efficient Transcribing Techniques. Your desk is your workshop. Arrange all your equipment so that you waste no motions. Place your notebook so that sufficient light falls on its pages; keep paper and carbon within easy reach; and have the correspondence to which you must refer close to your notebook, so that your eyes can travel from one to the other quickly.

After you have been working in the same office for some time, you will find that your transcription rate is much higher than it was on the day you entered that office. When you begin, you may have to read your notes completely before starting transcription. It is better for you to be cautious and sure of yourself when the materials dictated and circumstances encountered are strange. When you have become accustomed to the vocabulary and the mannerisms of your employer, you can save this prereading time and start transcription immediately.

Be sure to check all dates, numbers, and proper names with any records you may have. Do not forget to consult the dictionary when the spelling, divisions, or use of words puzzle you. When letter styles or report forms arouse the least doubt in your mind, consult a reliable authority, such as your secretary's handbook or an approved style manual. See pages 119-122 for a list of secretarial reference books.

Transcribe Intelligently. One of the major faults of the transcriber is to transcribe something that does not make sense to the dictator. Sometimes the resulting humor partially compensates for the mistake,

but you must not count on that. While you are learning, it is best to follow the rule that the dictator is always right. It is very easy to substitute imagination for interpretive ability and transcribe something that you imagined the dictator said, which may be farther from the true statement than what you actually had in your notes.

Each sentence should be tested on the basis of common sense before you start to type it. If you find passages in your notes that do not seem to make sense, ask the dictator about them after the other letters have been typed, unless the letter in question requires immediate transcription. If it does, go to him and get the matter cleared up at once. This procedure is much better than to transcribe the letter incorrectly and have to retype it. If you are alert when taking dictation, you will generally discover any lack of clearness and get the correct interpretation then instead of later.

Obvious errors of any kind made by the dictator should be corrected when transcribing. You will learn from experience and further acquaintance with your superior how much liberty you can take with his dictation.

Transcribing is not just a mechanical skill; it requires careful thinking and planning. You must learn not to let outside noises and activity disturb you. You should never become so engrossed in transcribing, however, that you are not aware of the activities that are going on around you, for your superior will expect you to keep your eye on many other things while attending to one thing.

Learn early in your stenographic career to "put first things first." If you have been careful when taking dictation, you will have your notebook clearly marked as to correspondence, telegrams, or special messages that should be transcribed first. Your notes will also indicate special instructions; for example, to register a particular letter or to send a letter by special delivery.

Display Your Letters Effectively. Every office requires its letters to be typed according to certain standard letter forms. The forms most commonly used are known as: (1) indented form, (2) blocked form, and (3) semiblocked form. In addition to these forms for outgoing letters, a standard interoffice form is also used.

These forms are illustrated on pages 65, 68-70. Note that the content of each letter describes that letter form in detail. An illustration of a two-page letter appears on page 76.

Your employer will tell you the letter form to use. Later your in-

Courtesy Dictaphone Corporation

In addition to knowing shorthand, a fully trained secretary should know how to operate transcribing machines.

creased responsibilities may include choosing an appropriate form for the letters you compose.

Remember, however, that a uniform style increases efficiency in the office. If there are few variations, the mechanics of letter writing become automatic.

Visualize Layout and Arrangement. As you visualize the letter to be written you consider the main parts of the business letter. They are: the heading, giving the writer's full mailing address (usually a printed letterhead in business), the date, inside address, salutation, body, complimentary closing, signature (including firm and/or writer), reference symbols (including enclosures and other notations). In addition, two other lines may appear: an "Attention" line (between the inside address and salutation) and a "Subject" line (between the salutation and the body of the letter). It is the responsibility of the secretary to see that typed letters are attractively placed on the page.

United Co-operative Association A

1243 *Canal Street* • *New Orleans 2* • *Louisiana*

February 15, 19-- B

Dr. James R. Kendall
Bureau of Labor Statistics   C
U. S. Department of Labor
Washington 4, D. C.

Dear Doctor Kendall: D

I was a member of the audience that heard you speak
yesterday at the Chamber of Commerce luncheon, here
in our city. I was particularly interested in the
portion of your address that dealt with the methods
you and your associates are using in creating your
new type of Consumer Price Index. I am very anxious
to have you speak at length on this subject before   E
our own executives and employees.

It is my understanding that you are going to be in
New Orleans again on March 15. Could you find time
to speak to our group of about 200 persons at 6:30
on that date and then to be my guest for dinner at
some quiet place afterwards? We shall all be very
much indebted to you if you can visit us.

Sincerely yours,   F

President   G

EHN:URS   H

(A) Printed letterhead. (B) Date line. (C) Inside address. (D) Salutation. (E) Body.
(F) Complimentary closing. (G) Signer's title. (H) Reference symbols—dictator's
initials, colon, and typist's initials. F G and H are together known as the "closing."

A modified block letter with the parts of a letter identified.

Should the letter contain unusual features, such as tabulated material, indented quotations, more than three paragraphs (each paragraph requires an extra blank line space), special attention or subject
lines, or extra lines in the reference-symbols section, the formula
must be adapted accurately. The added spaces required for such

typewritten material must be computed as accurately as possible, bearing in mind that the five-inch line will contain about ten short, pica-spaced words or twelve short, elite-spaced words.

A Simple Letter-Placement Table. Though the experienced secretary, striving for maximum artistry in placement, will vary the placement of letters depending on the number of words they contain (as illustrated on Model Form 1 in your Workbook), the beginner can get good results by using a standard 5-inch line width for all letters, as described in the following simple formula. This formula applies to single-spaced letters only. Do not double space a business letter unless it contains 50 words or less.

1. Type all letters 5 inches wide. On a pica-spacing typewriter this would be 50 characters wide; on an elite-spacing typewriter, 60 characters wide.

2. On all letters up to 100 words in length, type the first line of the inside address 24 spaces from the top edge of the paper. Reduce *one* space for each additional 25 words.

For example, in setting up a 175-word letter, you would type the first line of the inside address on the twenty-first line (24 minus 3) from the top edge of the paper.

$$\text{Solution: } 175 - 100 = 75 \text{ words}$$
$$75 \div 25 = 3 \text{ lines}$$
$$24 - 3 = 21 \text{st line}$$

The date may be typed so that it divides equally the space between the letterhead and the inside address *or* typed in relation to the letterhead.

To be able to make quick estimates of the number of words in letters to be transcribed from shorthand, it is suggested that you take a careful count of the number of words you write in a page of shorthand notes and thereafter use that figure in determining the length of letters to be transcribed. For example, if you write an average of 250 words to a page of shorthand notes and you are to transcribe a letter that takes one-half page in your notebook, you will adapt the above formula to a 125-word letter, typing the date on the fifteenth line and start the inside address on the twenty-third line from the top edge of the paper.

Margins. All typed material, whether it is a letter, a manuscript, or a report, should be artistically placed on the page. This is achieved by

maintaining artistic side, top, and bottom margins. The widest margin should *always* be at the bottom of the page; the margin at the top of the page should be slightly narrower, and the two side margins should be the narrowest and of equal width, exclusive of allowance for binding edge, if any. On letterheads, the top margin, of course, is fixed and is often narrower than the side margins.

To facilitate the setting of side margins, the paper should be placed in the typewriter so that its horizontal center always comes at 50 on elite and at 40 on pica typewriters. Then, if you wish to use a 40-space line, set a margin stop 20 spaces on either side of the line center. A 5-space leeway on the right margin is permissible for lines of irregular length.

Once the paper is inserted properly, the paper-edge guide should be moved so that it touches the left edge of the paper. Thereafter, all sheets will be inserted uniformly if the left edge of the paper is placed against the paper guide.

Carbon Copies. One or more carbon copies of all letters are usually required. Corrections should be made on both original and carbon copies before the work is taken from the machine. If errors are discovered after a letter has been removed from the machine, be sure that the corrections are made also on the carbon copy.

Remember that the carbon copy is the firm's permanent record of your work. Be proud of the carbon copies that bear your initials as typist.

Use the right kind of carbon paper for the specific job, as described in Unit 5, and change carbons often enough to insure readability.

When you must insert a pack of four or more sheets and carbons into your machine, you can keep the squared-off pack perfectly aligned by releasing the paper-feed rolls, pushing the tightly held pack around the cylinder, and straightening it before you return the paper release to normal (gripping) position. Operate the paper release occasionally as you type each page to release the accumulating tension that causes carbon paper to crease in fantastic "treeing" fashion, thus spoiling both the carbon paper and the copies. Check the top edges of the pack frequently to see that the sheets remain in alignment.

An even better way to keep the sheets in a pack evenly aligned while inserting them into the machine is to drop an envelope behind the cylinder with the flap down and facing you. Release the paper-feed rolls and shove the tightly held pack, using both hands, between

Circle 2-2441

Mutual Service Bureau
EVERYWHERE

1740 Broadway, New York 19, N.Y.

February
Twenty-ninth
19--.

My dear Senator:

 The date may be centered below the letterhead in the style shown. In very formal letters, the day of the month may be spelled out; in business letters, figures are always used.

 As this letter is in the form known as the "personal" arrangement, the inside address is typed below the body of the letter. In the indented style, each line of the inside address, after the first one, is indented five spaces.

 In close punctuation, the date line, each line of the inside address, the salutation, and the complimentary closing end with punctuation.

 The first line of each paragraph is indented five or ten spaces.

 The complimentary closing starts at the center. The firm name, typed title, or typed signature is indented five spaces.

     Yours truly,

     Production Manager

The Honorable John S. Randolph,
 United States Senate,
  Washington 25, D. C.

Indented style letter with close punctuation.

the flap and envelope, continuing until it appears in front of the cylinder. Hold the top edge of the pack firmly and pull the pack forward until you can remove the envelope. Straighten the pack against the paper-edge guide, press the pack firmly against the cylinder, and return the paper release to gripping position.

HORNER
BROTHERS

1618 FORD AVENUE · DALLAS 3 · TEXAS

THIRD AND WRIGHT STREETS · FORT WORTH · TEXAS

February 15, 19--

Miss Doris Black
241 First Avenue
San Francisco 6, California

Dear Miss Black

In the full block letter, every line begins at the
left margin. Typing time is thus saved, but the
results are not too artistic. A full block letter
is <u>never</u> <u>double</u> <u>spaced</u>.

In extreme open punctuation, no punctuation is used
at the end of any line outside the body of the
letter, except a line ending with an abbreviation.

If you use a company name, type it in all caps two
spaces below the complimentary closing. The dictator's name or title is typed four spaces below the
company name.

Very sincerely yours

HORNER BROTHERS

Secretary

CRM:HB

An extreme block letter with extreme open punctuation.

MONTGOMERY & METCALF  STEPHENS BUILDING
68 SOUTH STREET
ATLANTA 1, GEORGIA

November 18, 19--

Griffin & Hartley, Inc.
1853 Third Avenue, S. W.
Denver 8, Colorado

Attention of Mr. Graham

Gentlemen:

The modified block is the most generally used letter form in business.

Type the date so that it ends even with the right-hand margin. Use the backspacer to determine the point to start typing. Never abbreviate the date.

In standard open punctuation, no punctuation is used after the date or any line in the inside address except a line ending with an abbreviation; for example, "Inc." A colon is placed after the salutation and a comma after the complimentary closing.

Center the Attention line two lines below the inside address. A letter having an Attention line is addressed to a firm; therefore, the salutation must be "Gentlemen."

Note the different form used in the identification data. Where there is an enclosure, the abbreviation "Enc." is typed directly below the identifying initials.

On letters being sent by other than regular mail, you may indicate directions by typing in small letters below the identification data or enclosure how the letter is being dispatched, such as air mail, registered, etc.

Very truly yours,

MONTGOMERY & METCALF

R. C. Davis, Vice-President

rcd/ran
Enc.
Registered Mail

A modified, or semiblock, letter with standard open punctuation.

Erasing. Even the "perfect" typist makes mistakes and has to use her eraser. She does not make many mistakes, however; and what is more important, she erases those few mistakes neatly.

A neat erasure in many cases will save retyping an entire page; on

the other hand, a poor erasure might just as well not have been made at all, for any employer with average business standards will refuse to accept a typed paper containing a poor erasure.

If you erase so that the typographical error is still visible after the corrected letter has been struck over it, the erasure is unacceptable.

If you erase part of the surrounding letters and do not restore them to their original strength, you are not making an acceptable erasure.

An acceptable erasure is one that cannot be easily detected after it has been made. The first requirement is an eraser suitable for the grade of paper on which you are typing and for the kind of mark to be removed. If you are erasing ribbon impressions on a hard-finish bond paper, you should use a fairly gritty typewriter eraser. On the other hand, if you are erasing ribbon impressions on an inexpensive sulphite paper that gets "fuzzy" easily, you will do better with a softer eraser. All erasers should have an edge, so that they will erase single letters safely.

Old razor blades, steel erasers, and glass-fiber erasers are useful tools to have available for special erasing problems.

Always move the typewriter carriage to one side when erasing in order to avoid dropping erasure particles in the type-bar basket and the mechanisms at the printing point. It helps to blow the particles away as they gather.

If you are making carbon copies, place a small card between the original copy and the first carbon sheet. Using short up-and-down strokes, without too much pressure, erase the *entire* mistake on the original copy. Then erase the error on the first carbon copy by placing the card between the first carbon copy and the second carbon sheet. Repeat this operation until all carbon copies have been corrected. A card should *never* be placed against the inked side of a carbon sheet because one erasing operation rubs almost all the carbon on to the card, thus severely reducing the useful life of the carbon sheet.

If you damage part of a nearby character while erasing, you should touch up the entire character lightly until it is uniform in color. Then, retype the extra character and corrected matter with a slightly lighter touch than you ordinarily use, carefully retyping it lightly, if necessary several times, until your correction matches the rest of the page perfectly.

If an error is discovered after the paper has been taken out of the machine, place the sheet on a clean sheet resting on a smooth, hard,

and flat surface and erase. Then replace the paper in the machine, straightening it with the aid of the variable line spacer and the writing line scale. The line of writing should rest on the line scale.

Sometimes it is necessary to replace a word with another having more letters—a five-letter word with a six-letter word, for example. This can be done by crowding the letters slightly with the aid of the back spacer or by using the space bar on machines that move their carriages a half space on the downstroke and a half space on the up-stroke. After erasing the five-letter word neatly, type the first letter of the new word; then back space slightly and strike the second letter, back space a little more than you did for the second letter and type

```
opinion          savings
opinions         saving
```

the third letter, and so on. The sixth letter should come where the fifth ordinarily would come. Spacing can also be controlled by holding the carriage in the proper position with one hand. Keep your eye fixed on the paper at the printing point for skillful control.

Transcribe Mailable Letters. A mailable letter is one that is neat and attractive in appearance, well placed on the page, well typed with an even touch, and with few or no erasures. The right-hand margin must not be very ragged. The date must be correct. The initials of the dictator and stenographer (teacher and pupil) and all other identification data must appear in the proper place. There should be no serious deviations in the wording of the dictation, no incorrect spelling, no uncorrected typographical errors.

Select Extreme Open, Standard Open, or Close Punctuation. You will be told by your superior whether or not to use punctuation at the end of lines of the parts of the business letter (except the body). The various types of punctuation are commonly referred to as extreme open, standard open, or close punctuation. There may be a company policy on this matter, or the choice may be left to your discretion as a secretary.

If the *extreme* open punctuation style is followed, no punctuation is used at the end of any lines. If the *standard* open punctuation style is followed, no punctuation is used at the end of lines except after the salutation which is followed by a colon and after the complimentary closing, which is followed by a comma. If the *close* punctuation style is followed, appropriate punctuation is used at the end of all lines.

Strong, Moran & Duncan

May 22, 19--

Businessmen's Association
2881 Lincoln-Liberty Building
Philadelphia 7, Pennsylvania

THE SIMPLIFIED LETTER   1642 Stout Street, Denver 1, Colorado

This is something new in letter forms. It is recommended by
the National Office Management Association as an important
step toward improving business correspondence.

Each line begins at the left margin. The formal salutation
is omitted.

The subject is typed in capitals at least three spaces below
the address. Start the body of the letter three spaces below
the subject line.

Questions, listings, or like items in the body of the letter
may be indented five spaces from the left margin, except when
preceded by a number or letter.

Notice the following points:

1 Date location
2 The address
3 The subject
4 Periods omitted after numbers or letters in outline form
5 Name of the writer

The complimentary closing is omitted, and the signer's name
is typed in capitals five spaces below the end of the letter.

The initials of the typist are placed at the left margin, two
spaces below the signature. Enclosures are indicated below
these initials. The names or the initials of the individuals
receiving carbon copies are typed at the left margin, below
the typist's initials, enclosures, or the signature.

PAUL L. ROWE

LBA

The simplified letter form recommended by the National Office Management Association.

Note the illustrations on pages 68-70. The modern trend toward simplicity favors the standard open punctuation style.

The National Office Management Association is encouraging the Simplified Letter illustrated above. Note the elimination of the

salutation and the complimentary closing and the extreme blocked style.

Neatness. Your transcripts must not only be word perfect, but they must also be neat and attractive in appearance. Erase the slightest thumbprint or smudge with an Artgum eraser.

Keep your typewriter in good working order. Change the ribbon frequently, and clean the type often. Do not allow yourself to become careless in your typewriting. Never permit a strike-over. You may be tempted to make corrections with pen or pencil. Don't do it.

Submitting Transcripts for Signature. After transcribing the dictation, remove the carbon sheet and place it in the folder containing your supply of carbon paper or lay it away carefully in a suitable place in your desk. Attach the carbon copy to the correspondence and place the original copy of the letter on top of all the correspondence to which it pertains. Address the envelope and slip it over the top of the original letter. Place the letter, together with the carbon copy and the previous correspondence, on your employer's desk for his signature. If the letters are to be signed immediately, they should be placed right side up; otherwise, face down so that curious persons cannot read them. When the letters have been signed, take them to your desk for folding, insertion, and stamping, unless these duties are performed by a central mailing department. In that case, place the signed letters in the out-going-mail tray.

Enclosures. You must see that the right enclosures accompany the transcribed correspondence. Address the envelope first, and place the enclosures in it before starting to transcribe. In all cases, verify the enclosures with the letter itself before releasing the letter to the mailing department or mailing it yourself.

Fold the Business Letter Properly. Be careful to fold your letters properly for insertion in the envelope. Recommendations for folding letters are given in Unit 8 for your guidance. (See page 192.)

Transcribing Another's Notes. Increase your transcription ability, as you may be called upon to transcribe the shorthand notes of your employer or another employee. These may be memorandums to you or a complete letter in rough draft, or they may be the notes of another stenographer passed on to you to transcribe. To be able to read one another's shorthand notes is a great timesaver. The higher your own transcription ability, the better able you will be to read another's shorthand. Many offices require their stenographers to be able to transcribe one another's notes.

THE COLUMBIA MINING CORPORATION

INTEROFFICE CORRESPONDENCE

To   All Members of the Office Staff

From   Mr. Strong

Subject Letter Style for Interoffice Correspondence

Date   October 13, 19--

The following setup is used for all interoffice communications.

Note that the four lines in the heading are typed in blocked form and that only last names are used, unless there is another employee in the organization with the same name.

We begin paragraphs with an indention of five spaces, and we leave a double space between paragraphs.

Occasionally a letter will contain data that would be more legible and better emphasized if tabulated. It is usually advisable to tabulate:

Names and addresses
Any list of items

Interoffice communications are not signed in full but are signed with initials. The initials of the dictator and of the typist are typed two spaces below the signer's initials and at the extreme left margin.

Directly below these identification initials are placed special notations such as the one that appears on this letter. "Cc Mr. Jones, Mr. Smith" indicates that extra carbon copies of this letter were made and sent to both Mr. Jones and Mr. Smith.

F. S.

FS:vj
cc Mr. Jones
    Mr. Smith

An interoffice memorandum, semiblock style.

Canceling Your Shorthand Notes. As soon as you have completed transcribing a letter, draw a vertical line through your notes to show that they have been transcribed, and place the transcription date at the end of the notes for each letter. Carelessness in these seemingly small details may cause you some embarrassment later on.

Mr. W. McLean, Jr.   -2-   January 15, 19--

Never carry only one or two lines to the following page
or end a page with a hyphenated word.

A postscript appended to a letter is typed at least two
spaces below the identification data. Indent the first line
of the postscript five or ten spaces (depending on the indention of the paragraphs); type the dictator's initials below
the postscript. The postscript is used a great deal in sales
correspondence because of its "eye-catching appeal."

Yours truly,

Charles B. Collingsworth
CBC:DD   Secretary

P.S. The postscript may be used to add essential information that has been received after the letter was dictated.

C. B. C.

THE PROVIDENCE-ACME CORPORATION

Boise, Idaho   *2600 FIFTEENTH AVENUE WEST, SEATTLE 2, WASHINGTON*

Butte, Montana

Portland, Oregon

Spokane, Washington

January 15, 19--

Mr. W. McLean, Jr.
Director of Personnel
Dublin Bank & Trust Company
Market and Sansome Streets
San Francisco 12, California

My dear Mr. McLean:

Subject: Two-Page Letter

The modified block form with standard open punctuation
is the style most generally used in business. The date line
ends even with the right-hand margin. Use the backspacer to
determine the point to start typing. Never abbreviate the
date in any business letter.

The subject line may be centered two spaces below the
salutation. It is not uncommon to see the subject line
starting at the left margin; centering, however, is preferred.

Indent the paragraphs five or ten spaces. It is, however, usual to use five spaces in business letters. A good
rule to remember is that there should never be fewer than
five spaces.

Letters over 300 words in length generally require two
pages, particularly when typed on a pica-type machine. The
right, left, and bottom margins on the first page should be
balanced. The heading of the second page starts six line
spaces (1 inch) from the top and consists of the name of the
addressee, page "2," and the date. If possible, begin the
second page with a new paragraph. If this is impossible,
leave at least two lines of a new paragraph at the foot of
the first page; likewise, see that the first paragraph carried
to the second page has at least two lines at the top of the
second page.

Start the complimentary closing, the firm name, and the
signature near the center of the paper.

The two-page letter in semiblock form with standard open punctuation.

76

Courtesy Shaw-Walker Company

You should proofread your transcript by checking it against your shorthand notes before removing it from the typewriter.

Take, for example, the case of the stenographer whose employer asked her to get a copy of a telegram that was supposed to have been sent several days before. The stenographer remembered the telegram but could not find a copy in the files. She then checked in her notebook and found that the notes had been very definitely struck out, which would ordinarily indicate that the telegram had been transcribed. The telegraph company, however, had no record of having sent the wire. The stenographer examined her notes more carefully and discovered that in crossing off the notes of a letter dictated before the telegram, she had inadvertently drawn the canceling line through the telegram also. The stenographer did not lose her job because of this carelessness, but she learned the lesson regarding the importance of attention to small details.

Proofreading. Another one of the routines of transcribing is that of proofreading the letter before removing it from the machine.

Production Work. In order to get the maximum benefit from this secretarial practice course, you will approximate actual office conditions as you complete the secretarial assignments. You will really "produce" as you would on the job, including carbon copies, envelopes, and enclosures.

Reference Books. The secretary may often need to use reference books of various types when transcribing. Unit 6 contains many helpful reference sources for the secretary. You will probably use these reference sources many times as you study and complete the assignments in this book.

No "Clock Watchers" Wanted. Almost every day throughout this course you will be given the opportunity of actually taking dictation and of transcribing under conditions that approach real business conditions as nearly as is possible within the walls of a school building. If you find that your secretarial-training instructor is more exacting than your other teachers have been and insists on your increasing the amount of work you do without lowering its quality, be glad and give him your wholehearted support. He is bending every effort toward teaching you to attain a standard of production that will keep you on a payroll after you once get there. He is "breaking you in." He is giving you office experience. Don't watch the clock. Think only in terms of getting the job done and done right. The secretarial-training workroom is an interesting place after school hours!

Some Highlights of This Unit

1. When taking dictation, write instructions concisely and clearly at the beginning of the dictation to which they apply; use a colored pencil to indicate "rush" items.

2. If the dictator is likely to make changes, corrections, or insertions in his dictation, allow space for this by leaving an ample number of blank lines between letters.

3. Utilize the pauses in the dictation to read your notes, punctuate, capitalize, and make paragraph notations.

4. When proper names and addresses are dictated to you (unless the spelling is unusual), write the information in shorthand.

5. Familiarize yourself, as quickly as you can, with your firm's business, so that you will understand the dictated matter.

6. The basis of transcribing skill is fourfold:

    a. The ability to read shorthand notes quickly and accurately

    b. A thorough training in typing technique and artistic arrangement

c. A working knowledge of English

d. The ability to visualize the completed manuscript

7. To transcribe intelligently: (*a*) be sure the material you transcribe makes sense; and (*b*) correct obvious errors of the dictator (but be sure they are errors).

8. Correct *all* errors neatly.

9. Proofread the letter before removing it from the machine.

10. Carefully verify the inclusion of all enclosures.

11. Your transcripts must be word perfect and neatly prepared.

Questions and Items for Discussion

1. In what situations would it be wise for a stenographer to have two notebooks ready for instant use? Can you see some dangers in having more than one notebook in use at one time? What procedures would you suggest as desirable to follow in order to avoid possible mistakes when using more than one notebook?

2. Do you think you would be justified in presenting your side of the case when an error has been discovered that appears to be the result of your having made a mistake in carrying out instructions?

3. If you have difficulty in understanding your employer's dictation, what might be the possible causes? Suggest ways in which you can help overcome these difficulties.

4. Why is it better for a stenographer to take notes with pen rather than with pencil? Is the use of a pencil ever justified? In what situations?

5. When are you, as a stenographer, entitled to deviate from a verbatim transcript of dictated material? Under what circumstances will you need to ask permission to do so?

6. What are some of the ways by which you can avoid lost motion in the mechanics of transcribing?

7. Why will you, as an employed stenographer, wish to improve your transcribing skill to the standard of having every letter mailable without recopying?

8. What are some of the ways by which you can improve your transcribing skill while on the job?

9. Explain the difference between open, standard open, or close punctuation.

10. What are the distinguishing characteristics of the NOMA simplified letter?

Personality Questions and Projects

(Based on Personality Pointer, page 51)

Discuss the following questions:

1. Is there ever a time when a young person is justified in "sitting still"?

2. Why is a minimum of eight hours' sleep essential for most workers?

3. Why is it desirable to take time for eating leisurely?

4. To what extent should a person's time schedule be subject to change?

5. What do you do regularly each day that is a profitable activity?

6. What do you do regularly each day that is wasteful of time?

7. Are there any ways in which you could manage your time to better advantage?

Secretarial Assignments

1. Many organizations adopt a set of letter styles, so that all letters coming from that organization will present a uniform and attractive appearance. The United Products Corporation has adopted the three styles for letters shown on pages 68, 69, and 70 (see page 76 for two-page semiblock form), and the interoffice style on page 75.

Mr. Martin asks that you type copies of these four styles. This assignment will serve to acquaint you with the letter styles of this organization.

Type one mailable copy of each letter, making the necessary carbon copies; address envelopes. No envelope is needed for interoffice memos except for those that are confidential.

Use an interoffice memo sheet and three letterheads from your Workbook (Sheets 6, 7, 8, 9) for the original copies and the typing paper regularly used in class for the carbon copies and the second page of the two-page letter. Business firms usually prefer cheap Manila or other colored paper for carbon copies. If available, use onionskin for the extra carbon copies.

Assemble and clip together the four originals, the four first carbons, and the two second carbons. Submit the three sets to the office manager.

Instructions Regarding Carbon Copies and Envelopes

In order to get the maximum benefit from this course, you should prepare every assignment as if you were working in an actual office. When transcribing letters, therefore, you will make carbon copies and address envelopes just as you would on the job. You cannot hope to gain the required skill in making carbon copies and directing envelopes in two or three performances. No further mention regarding this matter will be made in the secretarial assignment instructions.

2. Your office manager will dictate the semiblocked letter on page 70 to you. Transcribe from your notes, without looking at the model. After you have completed your transcript, compare it critically with the model. Retype if necessary, but retype from your *notes*, not from the typed copy. Only mailable letters are accepted in this course. Use the letterhead from your Workbook, Sheet 10.

3. Your office manager will dictate to you the section in this chapter headed "Transcribe Mailable Letters." Transcribe this dictation in letter form, addressing the letter to your teacher and signing it yourself. Use the semiblocked form. Use Sheet 11 in your Workbook.

Transcription English

Transcribed letters should contain no errors in English. In Unit 7, you will find a summary of the rules of grammar most often violated. Review those rules often in which you are weak.

Information on the correct forms of address, salutations, and complimentary closings will also be found in that unit.

Optional

4. Ask your father or some business friend to lend you three actual business letters he has received. For each of these letters, make a pencil layout of the letterhead on a sheet of plain paper. Your pencil copy of the layout does not have to be artistic; you need it only to show what space remains for the typed letter. Use a ruler, however, in making it, so that your lines will be straight. Correct any errors in spelling, punctuation, capitalization, and word division that you find. Retype the letter on the layout you have made, improving the arrangement as much as possible.

Clip the retyped letters to the ones you have copied; show them to your teacher.

5. Your instructor will dictate an interoffice memorandum from the office manager to the head of the Billing Department, Mr. Sykes. Arrange the memorandum according to the instructions contained in it. If you wish, you may transcribe it roughly before typing the final draft, because this is a problem in arrangement. Use Sheet 12 in your Workbook.

6. This morning when you came to work, the cover was missing from your typewriter and the adjustments on your machine were changed; you, therefore, know someone used it. You cannot find the cover anywhere near your desk, and you wish to have it or another one. Prepare rough notes, for your own use, from which you will write a memorandum to the office manager, Charles F. Martin.

Like other executives, Mr. Martin gets beneath the surface by asking questions. You had better anticipate them and answer them before he asks them. You may foresee these questions and answer them in your note to him:

a. Why does your typewriter need a cover?
b. What happened to the old one?
c. Is there any good reason why your typewriter should not be used by other people when you are not using it?

Write a simple office memorandum to Mr. Martin, stating your case, accusing nobody, and expressing no emotional reaction. A typewriter cover is nothing to get excited about. Use Sheet 13 in your Workbook.

7. Your instructor will give you dictation for this assignment or will assign you to some other person who will dictate to you.

Spelling Demons

bachelor	beginning	business
ballot	benefit	cafeteria
battalion	bureaus	calendar

Job Tips

1. If it is necessary for you to consult with your employer, enter his office quietly; wait until he is aware of your presence before you speak to him.

2. Your employer gives you instructions for one purpose—for you, his secretary, to carry out. He expects to tell you only once!

3. If unusual or technical terms should appear in the dictation, ask for their meaning at the *end* of the dictation. If necessary, read the material back for checking.

4. If the dictator does not usually dictate addresses, write down those addresses that he *does* dictate. In such instances, he probably has no correspondence or memorandum for you to use as a reference.

5. Keep a spare notebook in your employer's office for emergency note taking—you should always have a pencil in your hand when you answer the buzzer.

TO THE STUDENT

Provide yourself with a file folder. All letters, carbon copies, envelopes, enclosures, and other papers that you prepare in working the assignments in Units 4-8 will be returned to you and held by you in this file folder. These items will be used in Unit 8, Assignments 2 and 3, and possibly in Units 13 and 14.

Personality Pointer

DO YOU CONTROL YOUR EMOTIONS?

How do you meet your daily problems? Do you show indifference, inattention, a "take-it-or-leave-it" disposition? Do you display a pitying smile, an overbearing "know-it-all" attitude? Or, are you patient, sincere, willing, and courteous? Do you show respect for the other person's feelings and efforts and, subordinating your personal reactions, meet the person halfway in a genuine effort to be helpful, agreeable, and appreciative? Do you put yourself in the other fellow's place?

A secretary must be able to handle all situations, under any and all circumstances, with common sense, confidence, and tact. She must give attention to the job at hand and consider her personal feelings and reactions of less importance. She must accept difficult situations and keep an even disposition. She is a representative of the firm for which she works; she owes loyalty to the organization; she ceases to be an individual, as such, during office hours.

Not only do your actions speak for you; but your words speak, also. Is your tongue sharpened with sarcasm, criticisms, or contradictions? "A soft answer turneth away wrath; but grievous words stir up anger. The tongue of the wise useth knowledge aright. . . ." A wise secretary avoids excess flattery, keeps out of arguments and disputes, refrains from gossiping, avoids boring others, and keeps confidences.

The ability to adapt oneself to any and all circumstances cannot be achieved in a moment or even a day. Self-control is a matter of *atti-*

tude, attitude acquired through conscientious self-discipline and the desire to be helpful to others.

The words of a prominent psychiatrist are pertinent here. He says, "Emotional maturity is ability to stick to a job and to struggle through until it is finished . . . to endure unpleasantness, discomfort and frustration . . . to give more than is asked for or required . . . to size things up and make independent decisions . . . to work under authority and to cooperate with others . . . to defer to time, other persons, and to circumstance."

Using Equipment and Supplies

In your first position, you must use the equipment and supplies given you and do the best you can with them, without making any complaints if they are not up to standard. Although many business offices are well equipped with the most modern and convenient secretarial desks, typewriters, files, lighting fixtures, office appliances, and supplies, some employers have not given sufficient thought to this matter.

You should be informed regarding the right kind of secretarial equipment and supplies and their efficient arrangement and use. You will then be in a position to assist in the selection of suitable equipment, should the occasion arise. You will also be able to help your employer reduce office costs.

This unit will tell you:

1. How to organize your work area
2. How to know office stationery
3. How to use office supplies economically

Section 1. SECRETARIAL EQUIPMENT

Today's office worker seldom works alone; she usually works in a rather close relationship with others. As a secretary, however, you will do much of your work and carry out most of your duties in your own work area. You may expect to have your own "workshop." This unit will help you to organize your work area, so that you can make your contribution to the reduction of office costs and at the same time enjoy the thrills that come from being efficient on the job.

The Secretarial Desk. Only one type of desk really deserves to be called a secretarial desk. In this style of desk (see below), the typewriter disappears into one of the pedestals, either the right or left, leaving the top of the desk free for other purposes. It is important, when ordering, to consider the direction of the light and other con-

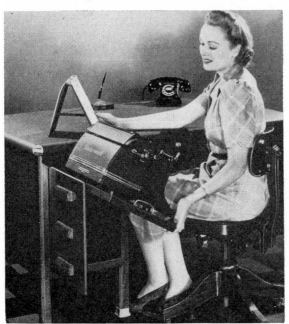

Courtesy Shaw-Walker Company

In this secretarial desk, the typewriter tilts down and disappears into the left pedestal.

trolling factors, so that you will specify the correct pedestal for the typewriter. Light should fall on your work over your left shoulder.

Secretarial desks may be obtained either in wood or metal. Various color combinations, such as a green body with a light-brown top or two-tone gray, are popular. The height of the desk has much to do with desk efficiency. The standard height, until recent years, was 30½ inches. Recently, however, efficiency engineers have found that lowering the height to 29 inches greatly increases working comfort. The height of the typewriter may be adjusted to individual needs by placing a pad or wooden block under it.

Another commonly used style of typewriter desk is shown on page 87 so that you will be familiar with it and be prepared to work efficiently with almost any type of office equipment supplied you.

Eyestrain. Scientists have found that eyestrain is one of the chief causes of fatigue among office workers. Every time the eye passes from the white color of the paper to the dark color of the desk top, the retina must adjust itself to the varying amount of light reflected. Scientists advise, therefore, that the desk top be kept as near the color

of the letters and papers on it as possible. Light gray, green, or brown have been found to be the most practicable for desk tops.

The Secretarial Chair. Doctors tell us that correct posture is of utmost importance. Correct working posture is almost impossible when the person is seated in certain old-fashioned, but all too common, types of chairs. The posture chair illustrated here has been designed especially to aid the secretary in maintaining correct posture. The seat and the back rest can be adjusted to meet the individual needs of the worker. The price of this type of chair is higher

Courtesy Shaw-Walker Company

A center-well typewriter desk.

than that of the customary office chair, but the additional cost is more than offset by the increased output of the worker and by the reduction in loss of time due to ailments resulting from faulty posture.

Writing Tools and Notebook. You have already learned that the pen is the standard writing tool of the efficient secretary and that the Spiral-bound notebook is recommended (refer to pages 53-56).

Courtesy Shaw-Walker Company

A secretarial posture chair.

The Typewriter. You are familiar with at least one make of typewriter. You should familiarize yourself with all the widely used makes so that your skill will not be handicapped by a change from one make to another. Five widely used makes of typewriters (arranged in alphabetic order) are the I.B.M., the Remington, the Royal, the L. C. Smith, and the Underwood.

The new electric typewriters should also be included in this list as their use is increasing rapidly. You will be able to adapt your typing skill rather quickly to the touch

of an electric typewriter. The Vari-Typer, with its many changes of type (see illustration on page 344), is useful in the office that wishes to send out bulletins and other material in a typewritten form that closely resembles a printed form. Its operation requires special training.

Files. A convenient secretarial file is shown on page 555. No further treatment of filing equipment is given in this unit because filing and filing equipment are discussed in Units 13 and 14.

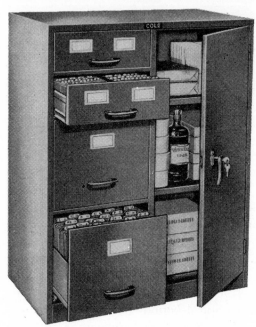

Courtesy Cole Steel Equipment Company, Inc.

A combination file and office-supply cabinet that a secretary will find convenient for her needs.

Miscellaneous Equipment. In addition to a desk, a chair, and a typewriter, you will possibly need an "In" tray and an "Out" tray on your desk. A wastebasket, preferably of fireproof material, is also essential. Where there is room, a separate telephone table with a shelf for directories is a great convenience. The telephone company has various models of telephone instruments and convenient installations for the secretarial desk.

A locker for wraps and for a small amount of supplies is highly desirable. If a locker is not available for wraps, you will need a costumer, set in some inconspicuous place.

The various office appliances with which the secretary should be familiar are treated in detail in succeeding units. Among these appliances are a stencil duplicator, hectograph or fluid duplicator, adding machine, calculating machine, check protector, dater, time stamp, stapler, paper punch, letter opener, paper cutter, staple remover, numbering machine, and postal scale.

Arrangement of Desk Space. When an executive walks through an office, he can generally tell who are the efficient workers and who are the inefficient ones by a glance at the desk top of each worker. If it is

cluttered with an assortment of papers, folders, paper clips, trays, and odds and ends, he classes the worker as "clutter-minded." If the desk top is clear except for the papers and materials actually needed for the job in hand, he sees an efficient worker. He knows that the working top of a desk is intended for one purpose only—a place to work

An "In" and "Out" tray for mail, a notebook holder with a Spiral notebook. The clamp on the notebook marks the place for the transcriber.

at one job at a time. There will always be an exception or two in every firm, but do not take "exceptions" as your models.

In the well-organized secretarial desk, there is a logical place to keep all things that are needed—each drawer doing its part to help organize the day's work and avoid confusion. The illustrations on page 90 show a well-organized secretarial desk in detail.

Now that you have obtained some familiarity with the equipment and supplies commonly used by secretaries, you are ready to study how to use such equipment and supplies efficiently when performing your secretarial duties.

Section 2. OFFICE STATIONERY AND SUPPLIES

The really competent secretary is characterized to a large extent by the way in which she uses the necessary materials. The secretary must be efficient and economical in the use of paper, letterheads, envelopes, carbon paper, and the many other office supplies. The secretary should know when to use and how to buy these supplies economically.

Paper. Paper has a multitude of uses in the business office. Probably the most frequent use is for correspondence. Most business letterheads are printed or engraved on bond paper, although parchment, ledger, and many book papers have been found suitable. Bond paper has tough, strong fibers that withstand rough handling. A bond paper may usually be distinguished from other papers by the watermark

Courtesy Shaw-Walker Company

The shallow center top drawer is convenient for pencils, erasers, paper clips, rubber bands, dater, ruler, scissors, and the rest of the indispensable little things you need all day long.

Letterheads and envelopes are easily accessible in the top side drawer.

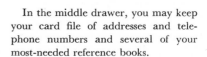

In the middle drawer, you may keep your card file of addresses and telephone numbers and several of your most-needed reference books.

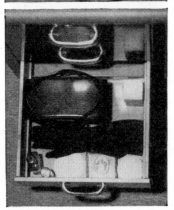

The lower drawer you reserve for your personal supplies—purse, gloves, make-up, tissues, an extra pair of hose.

90

that appears on each sheet. A *watermark* is a faint figure impressed in the paper. It is easily seen when the sheet is held to the light. Many concerns have their trade-marks watermarked into their stationery.

For carbon copies, a manifold paper is used. This kind of paper has most of the characteristics of bond paper, but it is lighter in weight. It may or may not be a bond paper. A very lightweight coated paper, known as onionskin, is often used for carbon copies. Many offices use a manifold paper on which the word "Copy" is printed in large outline letters. A cheap grade of manifold paper, often called a "second sheet" and obtainable in many colors, is also used for carbon copies.

Ledger paper is of exceptional strength and has a fine writing surface. As its name implies, it is used mainly for accounting records.

For mimeographing, a paper sometimes called "impression paper" is available. This paper has a soft surface, so that the mimeograph ink penetrates and dries quickly.

The most common size of paper used for letters, second sheets, and mimeograph work is $8\frac{1}{2}$ by 11 inches. The baronial size, $5\frac{1}{2}$ by $8\frac{1}{2}$ inches, and the monarch size, $7\frac{1}{4}$ by $10\frac{1}{2}$ inches, are sometimes used by executives for semisocial correspondence.

Paper for letterheads comes in various substance weights, such as $13\#$, $16\#$, $20\#$, and $24\#$. (In the paper trade, "pound" is represented by the symbol $\#$ following the figure.) These weights are based on the weight of 500 sheets of paper, 17 by 22 inches in size. A sheet this size will cut into four $8\frac{1}{2}$- by 11-inch sheets. Five hundred sheets of $20\#$ paper, therefore, would weigh only 5 pounds in $8\frac{1}{2}$- by 11-inch size. The commonly used weights for most bond letterheads are $16\#$, $20\#$, and $24\#$. Ledger papers weigh more, $24\#$ to $32\#$.

Letterheads. A letterhead reflects the character of the concern it represents. A letterhead that employs old-fashioned type or over-ornamented decorations that were in vogue a generation ago creates the impression of antiquated business methods. A poorly designed, indifferently printed job suggests careless or indifferent business methods. Crowding, cheap art work, poor-quality paper, and lack of or too much information result in letterheads having little or no prestige value.

A letterhead should contain only essential information—the firm name, the type of its business or products, and its complete address. Sometimes the telephone number and the names and titles of the officers of the firm are given.

Envelopes. Envelopes should match in quality, color, and weight of

paper the letterheads they accompany. The style of printing in the "card" (the return address in the upper left corner or on the flap) should harmonize with that of the letterhead.

Two sizes of envelopes are made for the usual $8\frac{1}{2}$- by 11-inch letterhead: (1) the more common is the No. $6\frac{3}{4}$ size. It measures $6\frac{1}{2}$ by $3\frac{5}{8}$ inches. (2) The No. 10 size, $9\frac{1}{2}$ by $4\frac{1}{8}$ inches, is used when a letter consists of several sheets or when several enclosures are to be inserted.

Suitable envelopes are also provided for baronial, monarch, and other styles and sizes of letterheads.

The window envelope is used a great deal in sending out bills and statements. It is not ordinarily used for general correspondence, however. This style of envelope contains a transparent address section, so that the inside address on the statement may also serve as the envelope address. The object of this arrangement is to save time and avoid an opportunity for error. Window envelopes come in all standard sizes.

Return envelopes, or self-addressed envelopes, are often enclosed with requests for information, to make it easy for a person to reply or mail an order, and for many other occasions. Return envelopes are slightly smaller than the standard-sized envelopes and are known as No. 6 and No. 9 respectively.

Carbon Paper. Black carbon paper is made by coating tissue paper with ink, wax, oil, and lampblack. Dyes are used to secure a variety of colored carbon papers. The weights (thickness) of basic tissue paper range from 4 pounds to 14 pounds per 500 sheets (20″ x 30″).

The thinness of the tissue, the thickness of the carbon on the tissue, and its hardness and finish determine in part the brightness and sharpness of the carbon copies made, the number of clear, readable copies that can be made, and how clean and resistant to smudging the copies will be. The thinner the tissue and the coating, and the harder the finish of the carbon, the sharper the impressions made by the carbon paper will be.

Other factors that determine the number of carbons, their cleanliness, and sharpness are:

The kind of typewriter used—Standard, Noiseless, Electric
The touch of the typist or the setting of the Noiseless and Electric controls
The size of the type (pica, elite, etc.), its sharpness or bluntness
The condition and hardness of the paper cylinder—the harder the cylinder, the more and sharper copies
The condition and cleanliness of the type

The thickness and quality of the typewriter ribbon

The thickness and quality of the paper used for receiving the original and carbon copies

In general, the heavier standard weights of carbon tissue are easier to handle than the medium and lighter weights. They also wear better than lightweight carbon paper. They are widely preferred for making one to three carbon copies, but produce somewhat thickened characters.

Except when making carbon masters for duplicating purposes, *record* carbon paper should always be used. *Copying* carbon smudges easily, erases messily, and fades rapidly. Black record carbon copies are relatively permanent.

The supplies representatives of the typewriter companies and specialty stationers selling carbon paper are always glad to study the carbon needs of any business office and recommend the kinds of carbon paper that should be used for particular manifolding jobs.

Carbon paper should be handled carefully, for it is easily damaged. When not in use, the sheets should be laid flat and preferably with the carbon (shiny) side down. The usability of a carbon sheet may be prolonged by turning it from top to bottom each time the sheet is used. When you are making several carbon copies in one operation, it is advisable to change the order of the sheets after each typing. This plan will help to distribute the pressure and make the sheets wear more uniformly. A minimum of twelve consecutive, single-spaced, legible copies may be expected from a standard sheet of carbon.

Typewriter Ribbons. Typewriter ribbons, like carbon paper, should be matched to the needs of the typist. Some of the factors affecting intelligent selection of typewriter ribbons are: (1) kind of typewriter; (2) size and style of type; (3) desired intensity of inked impression or "write"; (4) the typist's touch—light or powerful; and (5) the purpose for which the typing is to be produced.

Standard typewriters strike sharp, hammer blows; Noiseless machines literally press their type against the paper; while electric machines have devices that control the power behind each hammer stroke on the paper. The pressure controls on Noiseless and electric machines should be set carefully to insure the desired impressions.

Small type, such as elite, bites more into the paper than larger type, such as pica and billing sizes; hence a slightly less intensely inked ribbon should be used on small-type machines. Billing machines usually are equipped with heavily inked ribbons.

While some offices prefer a gray write, the trend is distinctly toward an intensely black write for greater readability and permanence.

A light touch may require the use of a ribbon inked with a higher degree of color than normal. A powerful touch should be tested to see whether better work can be done with a more lightly inked ribbon.

Most office typewriters are used for record purposes. Only "record" ribbons should be provided for such machines. If work is to be duplicated by a hectographic process (gelatin or fluid), a "copying" ribbon or copying carbon paper must be used. Combination "record-copying" ribbons are available where frequency of both kinds of work justify.

The better cotton ribbons are made from special cotton fiber. They resist fraying and battering of the type, require less frequent type cleaning, and produce sharper impressions than cheap cotton ribbons. Thin silk ribbons have long been used for extra sharp impressions, especially for producing copy for engraving and offset printing processes. Recently, nylon ribbons have been developed. For less than twice the price of good cotton ribbons, a nylon ribbon lasts three times as long, breaks down under battering much less quickly, holds ink longer, and requires less frequent type cleaning than a cotton ribbon. Several typewriter companies now supply carbon-paper ribbons that require a special spool mechanism for use in producing the sharpest possible, intensely black typewritten work needed for making satisfactory engravers' and offset copy.

The following chart will be helpful in selecting typewriter ribbons:

TYPEWRITER-RIBBON SELECTION CHART[*]

Kind of Typewriter	Style of Type	For Intense Black Impressions
Standard and Noiseless	Elite	Medium
	Pica	Medium Heavy
	Billing	Heavy
Electric	Elite	Light to Medium
	Pica	Medium Light to Medium Heavy
	Billing	Medium Heavy to Heavy

* These recommendations are made for top-grade *cotton* ribbons using a 16- to 20-lb. nonglazed original sheet or letterhead. *Nylon* ribbons of the same degree of inking wiil be satisfactory except in the case of Noiseless machines for which only cotton and silk ribbons are recommended. The next lighter degree of inking to that recommended here should be selected for *silk* ribbons.

There are several economies you may use to prolong the usefulness of typewriter ribbons. You can turn the ribbon for more even wear. You can cut off worn ends that have been damaged because of the improper working of the ribbon reversing mechanism. Some typewriters, moreover, permit you to type in three positions on the ribbon.

Handling Office Supplies. Orderliness in caring for office supplies is a great virtue. So many small items are involved and so many people use these items in such varied quantities that, unless a systematic method of storing, issuing, and ordering is installed and conscientiously followed, the resulting waste and confusion will be costly.

The Supplies Cabinet. A sufficient quantity of all office supplies for a determined period should be kept in a supplies cabinet or in a specially equipped stockroom. The reams of paper, boxes of envelopes, and other items should be stacked in orderly fashion on the shelves of the cabinet and labeled so they can be located easily. Many offices keep the supplies cabinet or room locked and require that all supplies be obtained from one person, who has the key. This plan is an excellent check on the careless use of supplies. With very little effort, a perpetual inventory record can be kept for each item. The use of this inventory will soon pay for itself in the saving effected.

Miscellaneous Supplies. The accompanying illustration shows a miscellaneous assortment of office supplies and appliances with which you should be familiar. Most of these items are found in the average office. Be constantly on the alert to find improved ways of handling

Miscellaneous supplies used by a secretary.

office details by means of timesaving and moneysaving devices such as these.

Keep a Clear Desk. A desk that looks like a junk heap hinders clear thinking and rapid performance of work. This condition generally means that you are behind in your work or are not an orderly "housekeeper" or both. If you will but take the following three steps, they will insure for you a clear desk:

1. Decide what to do
2. Decide who is to do it (probably you!)
3. See that it gets done

THINGS TO DO

on_____19__

*Mr.*_____

A. M.
A. M.
A. M.
A. M.
LUNCH
P. M.
P. M.
P. M.
P. M.
P. M.

One of the many desk-clearing forms that is helpful in forming efficient work habits.

These are three steps recommended by top executives to insure that unfinished business is handled as quickly and as satisfactorily as possible. Efficiency methods that are good for the executive are in the main good for his secretary.

To carry out each step successfully, the executive in most instances follows this simple but invaluable formula: "Put it in writing." Jobs put on paper leave no question of what is to be done and who is to do it. Carbon copies should be given to each person concerned (including the file clerk) for that essential follow-up to see that it gets done.

Too much "paper work," however, is a costly luxury in business; and judgment must be used at all times to avoid overdoing the advice to "put it in writing."

The desk-clearing form shown here has been used by many successful secretaries and executives. Familiarize yourself with these timesavers; and remember to put them to use to help you save time and keep your own desk clear. This or similar printed forms can usually be obtained from your local printers or stationers.

Some Highlights of This Unit

1. In a secretarial desk, the typewriter disappears into one of the pedestals, leaving the top of the desk free for other purposes.

2. Posture chairs with adjustable seats and back rests have been designed to aid the secretary in maintaining correct posture.

3. Try to familiarize yourself with all the widely used makes of typewriters, so that you can change from one to another without loss of speed and accuracy.

4. In your selection of carbon paper, consider the weight, style, and finish for the job you are doing.

5. When selecting typewriter ribbons, bear in mind (*a*) the kind of typewriter, (*b*) the style of type, (*c*) the desired intensity of inking, (*d*) the wearing quality of material, and (*e*) the cost.

6. A perpetual supplies-inventory record kept in a visible file will soon pay for itself in the saving effected.

7. Three steps recommended for the quick and satisfactory handling of unfinished business are: (*a*) decide what to do, (*b*) decide who is to do it, (*c*) see that it gets done.

Questions and Items for Discussion

1. Why is it desirable for you to know something about the various types of secretarial equipment and supplies?

2. Name the colors most desirable to avoid eyestrain in an office.

3. Outline the proper arrangement of the material in the drawers of a secretary's desk.

4. What information is always found in a letterhead?

5. Discuss briefly the different types of paper manufactured and the uses of each.

6. What is meant by "desk-clearing" form? Name and describe some of these forms.

Personality Questions and Projects
(Based on Personality Pointer, page 83)

1. List ten items that indicate a lack of self-control or emotional maturity.

2. List ten items that indicate a maturity of emotional control.

3. Refer to a book of synonyms. What is listed under "self-control," "emotion"?

4. Many books on personnel relations include rating charts and other material bearing on the subject of "emotional control." Report on one or more of these.

Secretarial Assignments

In order to familiarize yourself with the office equipment, stationery, and supplies discussed in this unit, do the following:

1. Assemble miscellaneous small office gadgets for a class demonstration of their use. For suggestions, see paragraph entitled "Miscellaneous Supplies" in this unit.

2. Collect paper and letterhead samples from business offices and from other sources.

3. Obtain carbon paper samples. Do this by contacting local distributors or by writing to the manufacturers.

4. Make a collection of desk-clearing forms used by businesses in your community.

Optional

5. Cut out the outlines representing office furniture that are drawn to scale in your Workbook, Sheet 14, and arrange each piece on the floor plan shown on Sheet 15 in order to obtain the most efficient use of the available space, without crowding.

6. From a list of supplies and prices given to you by your school purchasing agent, fill in and complete an estimate of the total yearly cost of twenty items used by your local school system. This is an exercise in practical mathematics, tabulating, and accurate typing of figures. Also, you should know something about the cost of these supplies.

The headings across the top of your table will be as follows: Estimated Yearly Quantity; Unit; Description of Item; Current Unit Cost; Yearly Cost. You may abbreviate some of these, but the abbreviations must be easily understood.

7. Visit an office-equipment company and have a salesman show you the features of their secretarial desks and posture chairs. Make a report to your class.

8. Visit the typewriter salesroom of a company selling typewriters unlike those with which your classroom is equipped. Make a report to your class.

9. Make a collection of office forms used in your community. Arrange them neatly in a loose-leaf scrapbook. Type a brief explanation of the purpose of each form to accompany the form.

10. Your teacher, or someone assigned by him, will dictate several letters and will give you instructions regarding them.

Spelling Demons

camera	career	census
campaign	carriage	chauffeur
carburetor	catastrophe	circular

Job Tips

1. Don't get into a rut! Keep an open mind about change and improvement in supplies, equipment, and printed forms.

2. Once or twice a year browse through a stationery or office-supply store to see the latest gadgets in small office supplies.

3. Office-supply and office-equipment salesmen can furnish valuable information concerning their products. Occasionally set aside a specified amount of time to listen to their sales talks—then use your good judgment.

p. 14 arrange an office.

Personality Pointer

HOW DO YOU DO?

There is a French word, now a part of our language, which exactly describes the popular definition or interpretation of poise. It is "savoir-faire," literally meaning "knowing how to do." As a part of childhood training, you were told always "to do the kindest thing in the kindest way." Since you are now more mature, you know that this means doing the right thing in the right way, the proper way, the graceful way.

A word of warning—poise is never finally achieved. It demands a sincere purpose of mind and the constant endeavor to improve. After you reach a state of improvement, you must be constantly on the alert to maintain what has been accomplished and to improve on the accomplishment.

Savoir-faire involves serenity and self-confidence. It involves knowing your abilities as well as your limitations. To achieve poise, you first must make a self-examination.

Do you get sufficient sleep and are you eating properly?

Are you certain that your body and your clothing are immaculate?

Have you applied make-up discreetly, so that it looks natural?

Does your hair show care, and is it attractively arranged for your type?

Have you selected a wardrobe that "goes together," that is appropriate for the occasion, and that is suitable for your type?

Can you sit, stand, and walk gracefully?

Is your voice pleasing to the ear and animated?

Do the words you select indicate attention to an average education?

101

Do you know and put to use the amenities of social etiquette? Do you have an earnest desire to be considerate of others?

An honest self-appraisal on these points will set you on the road toward being thought charming and poised.

read for Tuesday
list the book

UNIT **6**

Using Sources of Information

No executive expects his secretary to be a walking encyclopedia, but it is not unreasonable for him to expect his secretary to be able to locate needed information on a variety of topics. In order to do this quickly and accurately, with a minimum of lost motion, the secretary must be acquainted with the sources of business data. Some of these sources apply to all types of business. Each type of business also has its own reference sources. An important asset of the secretary is the ability to obtain information also from nonreference sources that may be helpful to her executive in carrying out his business.

Section 1. REFERENCE BOOKS ON ENGLISH

As transcription constitutes much of the secretary's work, reference books for verifying spelling, definitions, points of grammar, style, and quotations will be referred to most often. The first book on the list is, of course, the dictionary.

The Dictionary. An abridged (condensed) dictionary should be part of the desk equipment of every secretary. The illustration on page 105 is a reproduction of part of a page of *Webster's New Collegiate Dictionary*. You will see that some of the terms have been explained in the margin. In addition, every office should contain an unabridged dictionary to which the entire staff may refer. The two leading unabridged dictionaries are *Webster's New International Dictionary* and *Funk & Wagnalls New Standard Dictionary of the English Language*.

103

The dictionary contains a great deal of information in addition to spellings, pronunciations, and definitions; for example:

1. Grammatical information. The part of speech (noun, verb—whether transitive or intransitive—adjective, etc.), irregular plurals, principal parts of verbs, irregular comparatives and superlatives of adjectives and adverbs, and cases of pronouns.
2. Synonyms and antonyms.
3. Capitalization of proper nouns and adjectives.
4. The origin of all words listed (etymology).
5. Commonly used foreign words and phrases.
6. Prefixes and suffixes.

In addition supplementary information is given, sometimes in the body of the dictionary and sometimes in an appendix. This includes:

1. Abbreviations used in writing and printing
2. A pronouncing gazetteer (names of places and how to pronounce them)
3. Names of famous persons (biographical dictionary)
4. Tables of weights and measures
5. Common given names of men and women
6. Arbitrary signs and symbols
7. Atlas
8. Chronological tables
9. Preparation of copy for the printer, and proofreaders' marks

How to Use the Dictionary. The modern dictionary is the most comprehensive reference book ever published. Like any machine or tool, however, the technique of using it correctly must be mastered if the greatest benefits are to be obtained.

First, know your alphabet. If you lack a knowledge of the correct sequence of the letters of the alphabet, you will be handicapped:

1. In using the thumb index for opening the dictionary at the initial letter of the word you seek.
2. In finding the guide words at the top of the page containing the word you seek.
3. In quickly locating the word on the page.

Remember—words are arranged, first, according to the alphabetic order of their initial letters; then according to the alphabetic order of their second, third, and remaining letters.

Reprinted by permission, from an Outline for Dictionary Study, designed for use with Webster's New Collegiate Dictionary, copyright 1949, by G. & C. Merriam Company.

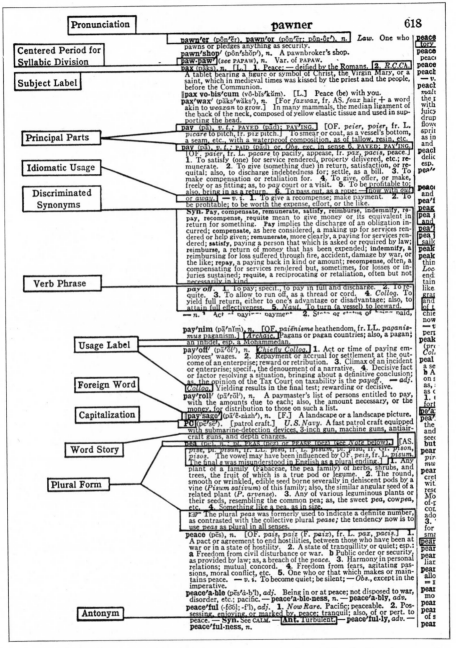

pawn′er (pôn′ẽr), **pawn′or** (pôn′ẽr; pôn-ôr′), *n.* *Law.* One who pawns or pledges anything as security.

pawn′shop′ (pôn′shŏp′), *n.* A pawnbroker's shop.

paw-paw (*see* PAPAW), *n.* Var. of PAPAW.

pax (păks), *n.* [L.] **1.** Peace: — deified by the Romans. **2.** *R.C.Ch.* A tablet bearing a figure or symbol of Christ, the Virgin Mary, or a saint, which in medieval times was kissed by the priest and the people, before the Communion.

‖**pax vo·bis′cum** (vō-bĭs′kŭm). [L.] Peace (be) with you.

pax′wax′ (păks′wăks′), *n.* [For *faxwax*, fr. AS. *feax* hair + a word akin to *weaxan* to grow.] In many mammals, the median ligament of the back of the neck, composed of yellow elastic tissue and used in supporting the head.

pay (pā), *v. t.;* PAYED (pād); PAY′ING. [OF. *peier, poier,* fr. L. *picare* to pitch, fr. *pix* pitch.] To smear or coat, as a vessel's bottom, a seam, etc., with a waterproof composition, as of tallow, resin, etc.

pay (pā), *v. t.;* PAID (pād) or, *Obs. exc. in sense 6,* PAYED; PAY′ING. [OF. *paier,* fr. L. *pacare* to pacify, appease, fr. *pax, pacis,* peace.] **1.** To satisfy (one) for service rendered, property delivered, etc.; remunerate. **2.** To give (something due) in return, satisfaction, or requital; also, to discharge indebtedness for; settle, as a bill. **3.** To make compensation or retaliation for. **4.** To give, offer, or make, freely or as fitting; as, to *pay* court or a visit. **5.** To be profitable to; also, bring in as a return. **6.** To pass out, as a rope: — now with *out* or *away.* — *v. i.* **1.** To give a recompense; make payment. **2.** To be profitable; to be worth the expense, effort, or the like.

Syn. Pay, compensate, remunerate, satisfy, reimburse, indemnify, repay, recompense, requite mean to give money or its equivalent in return for something. Pay implies the discharge of an obligation incurred; **compensate,** as here considered, a making up for services rendered or help given; **remunerate,** more clearly, a paying for services rendered; **satisfy,** paying a person that which is asked or required by law; **reimburse,** a return of money that has been expended; **indemnify,** a reimbursing for loss suffered through fire, accident, damage by war, or the like; **repay,** a paying back in kind or amount; **recompense,** often, a compensating for services rendered but, sometimes, for losses or injuries sustained; **requite,** a reciprocating or retaliation, often but not necessarily in kind.

pay off. **1.** To pay; specif., to pay in full and discharge. **2.** To requite. **3.** To allow to run off, as a thread or cord. **4.** *Colloq.* To yield full return, either to one's advantage or disadvantage; also, to attain full effectiveness. **5.** *Naut.* To turn (a vessel) to leeward. — *n.* Act of paying; payment. **2.** State or status of being paid,

pay′nim (pā′nĭm), *n.* [OF. *paiēnisme* heathendom, fr. LL. *paganismus* paganism.] [*Archaic.*] Pagans or pagan countries; also, a pagan; an infidel, esp. a Mohammedan.

pay′off′ (pā′ôf′), *n.* *Chiefly Colloq.* **1.** Act or time of paying employees' wages. **2.** Repayment or accrual for settlement at the outcome of an enterprise; reward or retribution. **3.** Climax of an incident or enterprise; specif., the denouement of a narrative. **4.** Decisive fact or factor resolving a situation, bringing about a definitive conclusion; as, the opinion of the Tax Court on taxability is the *payoff.* — *adj.* *Colloq.* Yielding results in the final test; rewarding or decisive.

pay′roll′ (pā′rōl′), *n.* A paymaster's list of persons entitled to pay, with the amounts due to each; also, the amount necessary, or the money, for distribution to those on such a list.

‖**pay′sage′** (pā′ē·zàzh′), *n.* [F.] A landscape or a landscape picture.

PC (pē′sē′). [patrol craft.] *U.S. Navy.* A fast patrol craft equipped with submarine-detection devices, 3-inch gun, machine guns, antiaircraft guns, and depth charges.

pea (pē), *n.; pl.* PEAS (pēz) or PEASE (pēz) (*see Note below*). [AS. *pise,* pl. *pisan,* fr. *pisa,* fr. L. *pisa,* pl. *pisa,* fr. Gr. *pison,* *pisos.* The vowel may have been influenced by OF. *peis,* fr. L. *pisum.* The final *s* was misunderstood in English as a plural ending.] **1.** Any plant of a family (Fabaceae, the pea family) of herbs, shrubs, and trees, the fruit of which is a true pod or legume. **2.** The round, smooth or wrinkled, edible seed borne severally in dehiscent pods by a vine (*Pisum sativum*) of this family; also, the similar angular seed of a related plant (*P. arvense*). **3.** Any of various leguminous plants or their seeds, resembling the common pea; as, the sweet *pea,* cowpea, etc. **4.** Something like a pea, as in size.

☞ The plural *peas* was formerly used to indicate a definite number, as contrasted with the collective plural *pease;* the tendency now is to use *peas* as plural in all senses.

peace (pēs), *n.* [OF. *pais, paiz* (F. *paix*), fr. L. *pax, pacis.*] **1.** A pact or agreement to end hostilities, between those who have been at war or in a state of hostility. **2.** A state of tranquillity or quiet; esp. **a** Freedom from civil disturbance or war. **b** Public order or security, as provided by law; as, a breach of the *peace.* **3.** Harmony in personal relations; mutual concord. **4.** Freedom from fears, agitating passions, moral conflict, etc. **5.** One who or that which makes or maintains peace. — *v. i.* To become quiet; be silent; — *Obs.,* except in the imperative.

peace′a·ble (pēs′å·b'l), *adj.* Being in or at peace; not disposed to war, disorder, etc.; pacific. — **peace′a·ble·ness,** *n.* — **peace′a·bly,** *adv.*

peace′ful (-fŏŏl; -f'l), *adj.* **1.** *Now Rare.* Pacific; peaceable. **2.** Possessing, enjoying, or marked by, peace; tranquil; also, of or pert. to peace. — **Syn.** See CALM. — **Ant. Turbulent.** — **peace′ful·ly,** *adv.* — **peace′ful·ness,** *n.*

This half page from a dictionary shows the type of information that is given for a word and the abbreviations and symbols used to convey that information.

Verifying Spelling. When you check the spelling of a word:

1. Be sure that you read the letters in their correct order; for example, it is *drudgery*—not *drugdery*.

2. Do not insert letters that are not there; for example, it is *caress*—not *carress*.

3. Do not leave out letters; for example, it is *aghast*, not *agast*.

4. Be sure that you have not found some other word pronounced exactly like the word you seek; for example, the noun *mucus* instead of the adjective *mucous*.

5. See that you have not found some other word spelled somewhat like the word you seek; for example, *ordnance* instead of *ordinance*.

6. When more than one spelling of the word sought is allowed, choose the preferred spelling. Each dictionary has its own method of indicating whether the varying forms are of equal or nearly equal standing, or whether one is distinctly preferable.

7. In looking up compound words, notice whether the word is one solid word (as *baseball*), two separate words (as *dining room*), or hyphenated (as *half-mast*). Be sure you understand how the dictionary you are using indicates hyphens; that is, do not confuse a real hyphen with a hyphen indicating syllable division. Also, do not overlook the extra space between two-word compounds. The spelling of compound words is discussed at greater length in Unit 7.

Verifying Pronunciation. In looking up the pronunciation of a word:

1. Notice how the word is separated into syllables.

2. Notice where the accents fall. Dictionaries differ in the method of distinguishing between primary and secondary accents.

3. Notice how the vowels and consonants are pronounced in the key words at the foot of the pages.

4. Notice whether the word may be pronounced in more than one way.

Reading Definitions. In looking up definitions:

1. Understand how the dictionary presents definitions. Some dictionaries give the meanings in historical order; some give the most common meaning first; some give separate entries for each meaning.

2. Read any illustrative sentences or quotations incorporating the word.

3. Look up the meaning of any word in the definition that you do not understand.

4. Notice any indications of special meanings.

5. Look up any cross references to other words.

Style Books. In your English course, much attention is given to preferred usage in the matters of capitalization, punctuation, quotations, use of figures, abbreviations, italics, and word division. It is almost impossible to carry all this miscellaneous information in one's mind; also, new problems of style are constantly presenting themselves.

The best source of such information is one of the style books prepared for the use of authors and proofreaders, but of equal value to anyone who prepares typewritten copy. A *Manual of Style* (the University of Chicago Press) and the *Style Manual of the United States Government Printing Office* are authoritative.

Secretarial Handbooks. A reliable secretarial handbook is a great timesaver. These handbooks contain information on a wide variety of matters that commonly pass through the secretary's hands. Lois Hutchinson's *Standard Handbook for Secretaries* and Ruth E. Gavin and E. Lillian Hutchinson's *Reference Manual for Stenographers and Typists* are typical of such reference works, as can be seen from the illustration on page 108.

English Grammars. An authoritative English grammar and a handbook on writing are among the most effective of argument settlers. Someone is always asking, "Which is correct, . . . or . . . ?"

The following books are especially useful for quick reference: *The English of Business*, by Hagar, Stewart, and Hutchinson; *College Handbook of Composition*, by Woolley, Scott, and Bracher; *The Century Handbook of Writing*, by Greever and Jones; *Take a Letter, Please!* by Opdycke.

Synonyms and Antonyms. The English language is unusually rich in synonyms—words having approximately the same meaning. Synonyms are seldom identical in meaning, however. To use the precise word to express the shade of thought intended is a real art. The secretary, in transcribing her notes taken from dictation, often has an opportunity to substitute a synonym for a word that is repeated several times and thus avoid monotony.

The study of antonyms—words having opposite meanings—will enrich your vocabulary. The ability to substitute an antonym, a positive word, for a negative used is a reflection of initiative and resourcefulness and is the mark of the better-than-average secretary.

Among the most useful books on synonyms and antonyms are

Capitalization and hyphenization

24 Abbreviations follow the capitalization and hyphenization of the full words for which they stand.

e.o.m.	end of month	a.m.	ante meridian
ft.-lb.	foot-pound	D.A.R.	Daughters of the American Revolution

Typewriter spacing

25 Do not space *before* the period that marks an abbreviation.

26 Leave one space *after* the period if the abbreviation occurs *within* a sentence.

27 When an abbreviation falls *at the end of a sentence*—

    a) If the sentence requires a period, use *only one* period.

        The books were audited by Robert T. Graves, C.P.A.

    b) If the sentence requires a question mark or an exclamation point, leave no space between the period and the other mark.

    c) If the sentence ends with a parenthetical expression that closes with an abbreviation, use this style:

        Please call tomorrow afternoon (we close at 5:30 p.m.).

28 When two or more capital letters represent the abbreviations of *personal names,* separate the letters by spaces. *Mr. L. B. Anders.*

29 Omit spaces within abbreviations that consist of small letters; as *f.o.b., i.e.; a.m.*

30 Never divide an abbreviation at the end of a line, nor separate an abbreviation from a preceding figure to which it applies.

SECTION IX

Helps for the puzzled speller

Basic rule

The basic rule in spelling is: *When in doubt, consult the dictionary.* However, the mastery of a few simple rules will prove a great timesaver. The rules and suggestions that follow should be memorized.

Webster's New International Dictionary, Second Edition, is the authority for the spellings in this and other sections of this Manual. Wherever two spellings are allowable, only the preferred form (the first form) is given here.

When a final consonant is doubled

1 Double the final consonant in words of *one* syllable if:

A page from the *Reference Manual for Stenographers and Typists.*

Fernald's *Standard Handbook of Synonyms, Antonyms, and Prepositions* and Allen's *Synonyms and Antonyms.*

Thesaurus. A thesaurus is a collection of words and phrases arranged according to ideas. Its object is the exact opposite of the object of a dictionary. You refer to a dictionary to find the meaning of a *word* that you have in mind. You refer to a thesaurus to find the word by which to express the *idea* you have in mind. Thus a thesaurus goes one step farther than a book of synonyms. In using a book of synonyms, you must have at least one word in mind; in using a thesaurus, you can start with a vague idea! *Roget's International Thesaurus* is the classic work.

There are two kinds of thesauri. One is arranged alphabetically, and one is arranged by ideas. The alphabetic arrangement, similar to a dictionary, lists the words in a straight alphabet; but instead of giving a definition for the word, it gives a long list of words that can be substituted for it. In the thesaurus arranged according to ideas, the word you have in mind is listed in an alphabetic index in the back; after it, various related idea sections are given with page references. When turning to this, the correct word for the purpose will be found.

Books of Quotations. Even though you may not work for a literary person, a number of occasions may arise when it is necessary to verify the exactness of a quotation, to determine "who said it," or to find a suitable quotation to use in a speech or a report. For all such purposes, a standard book of quotations is invaluable.

In such collections, quotations are classified under topics, according to meaning, the topics being arranged alphabetically. Usually, there is a concordance—a word index showing the quotations in which the principal words occur. Sometimes a useful biographical index of the authors quoted is included. Bartlett's *Familiar Quotations* and Hoyt's *New Cyclopedia of Practical Quotations* are standard works.

Section 2. REFERENCE BOOKS ON BUSINESS CONCERNS AND PEOPLE

You may often have to find the address and telephone number, to check the spelling and form of the name of a concern or of a person, or to obtain data on some person's achievement. Numerous types of directories are available to help in this search. Telephone directories, both regular and classified, are described in Unit 10.

City Directories. A city directory contains, in alphabetic order, a listing of the name, business, and home address of each resident of a town or city. These directories may be used to supplement the telephone directory in finding names of persons who are not telephone subscribers. City directories are not revised so frequently as are telephone directories. In consulting city directories, therefore, remember that they may not be up to date.

Trade and Business Directories. Special directories are available for almost every branch of business. These books usually contain the addresses of plants and offices, names of officers and directors, and the size and output of each concern listed. Rand McNally's *Bankers Directory*, Kelley's *Directory of Merchants, Manufacturers, and Shippers of the World*, Ayer's *Directory of Newspapers and Periodicals*, and the *Hotel Red Book* are representative trade and business directories. It is impossible, of course, to list the innumerable directories available. The head of the reference room of the public library will be able to direct you to the titles you require.

Professional Directories. Directories are also available for the leading professions. In addition to the names and addresses of members of the profession, directories of this type usually include an assortment of information of interest to the particular profession. The *American Medical Directory*, the Martindale-Hubbell *Law Directory*, and the *Educational Directory* are typical examples of professional directories. Here, again, the public library staff will be able to advise and recommend.

City, State, and Congressional Directories. Most cities and states publish lists of the city and state officials. These lists may usually be obtained at a small charge from the city hall or the statehouse, respectively. If such lists are not for sale, they may be consulted at the library.

The *Congressional Directory* contains the names of members of Congress and their addresses; also, the executive personnel of all departments of the Government.

Lists of Prominent Persons. For data on prominent persons in America, no book can compare with *Who's Who in America*, a biennial compilation of brief biographies of many thousand notable men and women whose positions or achievements make them of interest. No eulogies or criticisms are included—simply data on birthplace, age, parentage, education, degrees, occupations, achievements, societies,

clubs, marriage. *Who's Who* is a similar book devoted to English people of note. Many professions and localities issue their own books, as *Who's Who in Advertising*, *Who's Who in New York*, *Who's Who in American Education*.

The *Social Registers* are annual publications telling who's who in society of the larger cities of the United States. For other localities, there are the various *Blue Books*, listing persons of social prominence in the community.

Financial information of interest to investors and financiers may be found in Moody's *Manuals of Investments*. These *Manuals* contain financial ratings, financial statements, and brief histories of the companies listed.

Credit Information. Decisions on the extension of credit to customers or prospective customers are usually the responsibility of the manager of the credit department of a business. The secretary should be acquainted with the source of such information, however.

Mercantile agencies, such as Dun and Bradstreet, Inc., issue books giving the credit rating of businessmen and firms throughout the United States. They also supply special reports when requested. The books and the other services are given only to subscribers.

The lists are arranged according to states and cities. Hence, if the financial rating of Mr. Robert Fife, of Minneapolis, Minnesota, is desired, you should look first under "Minnesota" and then find the city, "Minneapolis." Names of business concerns are arranged alphabetically. Under each name a letter and a figure are given, such as E2 on the illustration on page 112. This symbol refers to a schedule of classified ratings in another part of the book, which must be consulted to obtain ratings.

Two ratings are given, the capital rating and the credit rating. The capital rating indicates the approximate amount of capital invested in the business. The credit rating is the judgment of the agency as to the financial standing of the corporation, firm, or person. In other words, it is an estimate of the ability of a corporation, firm, or person to meet obligations. It is based on information collected by the agency through an organized system of obtaining reliable information. The familiar saying, "That firm has an AA rating," meaning the highest rating given, comes from the symbols used by Dun and Bradstreet.

Credit information may also be obtained through arrangement with

Credit -
MAN'S CONFIDENCE
IN MAN

Dun & Bradstreet, Inc.

MERCANTILE CREDIT REPORTS NECESSARILY DIFFER IN FORM AND IN LENGTH, DEPEND-
ING UPON THE SIZE AND COMPLEXITY OF THE CONCERN REPORTED .... THE POLICY
OF THE AGENCY IS TO PRESENT THE ESSENTIAL INFORMATION AS CONCISELY AS POSSIBLE.

RATING
UNCHANGED

5912
PENN PINES PHARMACY

CD I JUNE 26 195-

BROOKLYN 19 NY
1246 HAZEL ROAD

Miles Gross, Partner   Hannah (Mrs. Miles) Gross, Partner

RATING: E 2

SYNOPSIS

BACKGROUND: Firm formed in April, <u>1946</u>. One partner a pharmacist since 1933.
NET WORTH: $26,865   SALES: $89,232 (Annual)
PAYMENTS: Discount
CONDITION & TREND: Condition sound. Sales increasing and operations profitable.

HISTORY

The style was registered by the partners on April 30, 1946.
This firm was formed in April, 1946. Starting capital consisted of $10,500
in savings, a $3,500 loan from the Teachers Credit Union, and a $3,000 loan from
the partners' families, making a total of $17,000. The loans have since been re-
paid.
Miles Gross is 41, and native born. A registered pharmacist, he graduated
from Columbia College of Pharmacy in 1933. Employed as a pharmacist by Liggett
Drug Co. between 1933 and 1936, and by Ray Drug Co. until this business was started.
Hannah (Mrs. Miles) Gross is 36. She was a New York school teacher prior to
the formation of this firm.

OPERATION-LOCATION

Operates a pharmacy with a soda fountain. Drugs and prescriptions account
for 50% of sales, with the balance equally divided among the fountain, sundries,
and confectionery. Fixtures are new with a twenty-foot soda fountain. Both partners are active and two clerks are employed.
Rents the first floor of a two-story building in good condition. The store
measures about 20 x 50 feet. Location is in a recently developed residential
section.

FINANCIAL INFORMATION

A financial statement at April 30, 195--cents omitted:

ASSETS		LIABILITIES	
Cash on Hand	$ 304	Accts. Pay.	$ 3,724
Cash in Bank	1,872		
Merchandise	14,950		
Total Current	17,126	Total Current	3,724
Fixts. & Equip.	10,913		
Station Wagon	2,464		
Deposits	86	NET WORTH	26,865
Total Assets	30,589	Total	30,589

Net sales from May 1, 195- to April 30, 195- $89,232; gross profit $26,181;
net profit $10,199; withdrawals $3,732. Monthly rent $150. Fire insurance on
merchandise and fixtures $25,000.
Signed: June 26, 195- PENN PINES PHARMACY By Miles Gross, Partner
Received by mail. No accountant indicated.

----0----

After the war, residential construction stepped up in this section with the
result that both sales and profits of this business have mounted steadily. Part
of earnings have been re-invested in the business to finance its steady expansion.

PAYMENTS

HC	OWE	P DUE	TERMS			
2431	2146		10th of Mo.	May 20, 195- Disc.		Sold 3 yrs. to date
340	230		2-10-N30	Disc.		Sold since 1946
250			2-10	Disc.		Sold 3 yrs.
136	136		2-10 Prox	Disc.		Sold yrs. to date
75			2-10-EOM	Disc.		
15			30	Ppt.		Sold 2 yrs.
6-26-5-	(241	29)				

PLEASE NOTE WHETHER NAME, BUSINESS AND STREET ADDRESS CORRESPOND WITH YOUR INQUIRY
The foregoing report is furnished, at your request, under your Subscription Contract, in STRICT CONFIDENCE, by DUN & BRADSTREET, Inc. as your agents and
9R2-3 (27704) *employees, for your exclusive use as an aid in determining the advisability of granting credit or insurance, and for no other purpose.*

Courtesy Dun & Bradstreet, Inc.

A page from a credit-rating book of one of the large mercantile agencies.

credit-reporting bureaus or associations, which are listed in the telephone directory. The credit department of a bank will also obtain
credit information on a person or concern. A charge is made for this
service.

Section 3. BOOKS OF FACTS

Certain questions that arise in the course of a business day can be answered only by reference to the more general types of reference books.

The World Almanac. *The World Almanac and Book of Facts*, published yearly by the *New York World-Telegram and Sun*, is a "must" in any office. It contains information and statistics on an unbelievably varied assortment of interests: a chronology of important events of the preceding year, a list of memorable dates starting as far back as 4004 B.C., population figures and vital statistics, the Declaration of Independence and the Constitution of the United States in full, to mention but a few. Many secretaries make it a rule to look in the *World Almanac* first for any desired bit of information. More often than not the information is there, and much time has been saved.

Atlas. An atlas, keyed with an index, is essential in any office especially when the business extends over a wide territory. This type of book gives an index to cities (their population, too) and provides big maps on which you can readily locate these cities. Loose-leaf atlases are very practical, as revised maps may be inserted at any time. Rand McNally's large *World Atlas* contains statistics in addition to maps and index. C. S. Hammond & Company and J. B. Lippincott & Company also issue many maps and atlases. Offices located in large cities will find many uses for detailed city maps.

Shipping and Postal Guides. Shipping guides, such as *Bullinger's Postal and Shipping Guide* and *Leonard's Guide for Parcel Post, Express, Freight, Rates and Routing* are invaluable in the shipping and mailing departments of a business. These guides supply complete information about postal, freight, and express rates and regulations. They contain the name of every post office, railroad station, boat landing, and United States port, with the railroad or water route on which each place or the nearest communicating point is located. The *Official Airline Guide* gives complete information regarding air travel, air express, air freight, air mail, and related data about air transportation and travel in the United States and all foreign countries.

The *United States Official Postal Guide*, in addition to postal regulations, contains the properly spelled name of every place in the United States where a United States post office is maintained. Form the habit

of using this *Guide* for verifying the spelling of city and town names just as you use the dictionary for looking up the spelling of words.

This unique book contains three classified lists: first, a state list, giving an alphabetic list of all post offices in every state; second, an alphabetic list of all post offices in the country; third, a county list, giving for each county of each state all post offices in that county. If you are sure of the state, but doubtful of the city name, consult the first list; if you are sure of the city name, but doubtful of the state, consult the second list.

Webster's Geographical Dictionary is the final authority for the correct spelling of foreign geographic names.

Encyclopedias. Usually it is necessary to go to a public library when reference to an encyclopedia must be made, as the majority of offices do not have frequent enough occasions to use them to warrant investing in these fairly expensive works. Each of the leading encyclopedias has its place.

The *Encyclopaedia Britannica* is very complete and carries material for literary and general character as well as information on science and business.

The *New Funk & Wagnalls Encyclopedia*, with its annual yearbook that keeps the material up to date, is excellent for quick reference.

The *Columbia Encyclopedia*, in one volume, is intended for desk use.

All encyclopedias have indexes. If no article is found on the subject sought, reference to the index will enable you to find the article in which the material is discussed.

Specialized encyclopedias, containing information on one particular field, are available in the technology rooms of public libraries or in the libraries of technical and professional societies. The *Reader's Encyclopedia*, *Encyclopaedia of the Social Sciences*, and the *Exporters' Encyclopedia* are specialized encyclopedias.

Special Dictionaries, Glossaries, Handbooks, and Catalogues. Almost every special field and almost every profession has its own special dictionary, glossary, or handbook. At least one of these reference books covering the field of the company's business should be in the office library. There will be numerous occasions when some technical point can be checked only by reference to such authorities.

The catalogues of competitors and of allied lines of goods or services will have many uses also.

Dictionaries of the leading foreign languages are valuable in certain offices; and for foreign-trade or export business, they are essential.

Government Publications and Information Service. The United States Government publishes a vast number of pamphlets and books on a great variety of subjects. To obtain information regarding these publications, write the Superintendent of Documents, Government Printing Office, Washington 25, D. C., for a list of the price lists published. When you receive this list, refer to it for the name of the particular price list covering the subject in which you are interested; and then write again, requesting the special price list. From that price list, select the reports and bulletins desired. The price list will contain information regarding methods of ordering and remitting.

In 1934, the United States Bureau of Information was established as part of the Executive Office of the President. This bureau will mail an inquirer the material pertinent to his inquiry or will refer him to the proper source.

News Items. When it is desired to ascertain the exact date of a news item, the *New York Times Index* makes it possible to locate the item. This *Index* will be found in the reference room of the public library.

The *Index* is published monthly and in a cumulative annual volume. References show the date, page, and column of the *New York Times* in which the items listed appeared. Editorials, book reviews, magazine articles, and other material published in that newspaper are also listed. When the date of an item has been located, it is then possible, of course, to refer to other newspapers and periodicals for their reports on the same event.

The secretary should form the habit of reading at least one reliable newspaper every day—and this means reading something more than the "funnies," sporting news, recipes, and fashion notes. Read enough of the reports on world, national, and local events to be intelligently informed on current civic and business affairs. Do not overlook the editorials, for some of the most thoughtful writing on current affairs appears in the editorial columns of the leading daily papers.

Form the habit also of keeping an eye out for items of interest and value to your chief and your company. Clip all items of this nature and mount each one separately on $8\frac{1}{2}$- x 11-inch sheets. Type on this sheet the source and date of the clipping. These sheets may be collected in a loose-leaf scrapbook, similar to the one in the illustration on page 116.

Magazine Articles. Articles that have appeared in about a hundred of the leading current magazines may be located by referring to the *Readers' Guide to Periodical Literature*, which may be found in any public

Courtesy Shaw-Walker Company

You may be asked to keep a scrapbook of clippings of interest to your employer.

library. This is a semimonthly index, which is cumulated quarterly, annually, and at certain longer intervals. Articles are listed under the name of the author, the title, and the subject.

Special indexes cover articles in periodicals for special fields. These indexes are of great value to anyone who is doing research work. Among these indexes are the *Art Index, Bulletin of the Public Affairs Information Service*, the *Business Education Index*, the *Education Index*, the *Engineering Index, Index to Legal Periodicals*, the *Industrial Arts Index*, and *Social Science Abstracts*.

Most offices subscribe to the magazines of special interest to their business or trade and sometimes to some of the more general magazines. In addition, exchange copies and marked copies are often received. In order that all those of the personnel interested in these magazines may have an opportunity to see them, it is well to attach to the cover of each magazine received a slip bearing the names of these per-

sons interested. As each person finishes with the magazine, he crosses his name off and the magazine goes to the next person on the list.

Many executives are too busy to examine magazines as thoroughly as they would like, and they rely on their secretaries to mark and bring to their attention articles, news comments, and advertisements of interest to them and the business. Make a definite place in your at-home reading schedule for the more important trade magazines that go to the desk of your superior. In so doing you not only will be conserving his time but also will be preparing yourself for an administrative position.

Catalogues of Books. It is often necessary to look up certain information regarding books—the correct title, the spelling of the author's name, the name of the publisher, the date of publication, and similar information. The reference room in the public library has various types of catalogues for this purpose.

The *United States Catalog* is an index to all American books in print on January 1, 1928. It is supplemented and kept up to date by the *Cumulative Book Index* (monthly and cumulations), which was enlarged in 1929 to include all books published in English, regardless of the country in which they were published. Books are listed by author, title, and subject. For each book, the price, publisher, binding, paging, size, date of publication, and Library of Congress card order number are given.

The *Publishers' Trade List Annual* contains the catalogues of most of the American publishing houses. In order to find entries in this *Annual*, however, it is necessary to know the publisher of the work.

The *Book Review Digest*, issued monthly, and cumulated at four-month intervals and annually, quotes excerpts from leading reviews of new books.

Books of Etiquette. Despite the informality of the present day, there are still acceptable and unacceptable ways of doing things. Even the most experienced person now and then needs to refer to an authority on certain details of social correspondence, introductions, travel and club etiquette, business gifts, and diplomatic and official customs. A standard book of etiquette is an essential reference book in the business office. *Etiquette*, by Post, is a very complete book. *What Do I Do Now?* by Payne, *Manners in Business*, by MacGibbon, and *Etiquette in Business*, by Carney, will be very useful personally to the secretary.

Secretaries who report board and committee meetings and transcribe minutes should have access to a book on parliamentary procedure. Robert's *Rules of Order* is the standard work.

Section 4. HOW TO USE REFERENCE BOOKS

To be able to use the various sources of information described in this unit to the best advantage, the secretary must cultivate an efficient method of searching for information. Keep in mind these essentials:

1. Be sure that you know exactly what you are looking for and why. Any haziness about either aspect of the problem will only lead to loss of time. If you do not understand the nature of the problem, ask questions. And take your instructions in shorthand.

2. Make full use of the various mechanical aids each reference work offers—index, table of contents, page headings, etc. Get acquainted with the organization and individual features of the leading reference works you consult. Make certain that you are using the latest edition in order to obtain up-to-date information.

3. Do not dawdle over your reading. Read only the sections pertaining to the problem in hand, no matter how interesting the other material is. Later, when you have time, you can go back and read anything that interests you.

4. If you work away from the office—for example, at the library or in the rooms of some technical organization—make accurate, careful shorthand notes on what you find. Any quotations must be exactly copied. Make a careful record of the source of all data, including the author's name, the title of book, the edition, date of publication, and the page.

5. If you are obliged to consult anyone for help in locating materials or information, state your problem clearly and with sufficient detail to make the object of your search clear to that person. Be courteous always. In writing for information, send a stamped self-addressed envelope.

Section 5. OBTAINING INFORMATION FROM NONREFERENCE SOURCES

Use Initiative. Information not readily available in published references may become available to the secretary with initiative. Much

data helpful to the work of her employer may be gathered *in advance* by the alert secretary who understands the problems of the firm and anticipates future needs.

In addition to the clipping scrapbook mentioned on page 115, a secretary can obtain valuable information by means of the following ten steps. The wide-awake secretary must depend on her own judgment and initiative in adapting these suggestions to specific problems encountered on the job.

Be Systematic. You must be systematic! You must record information when you find it in such a way that you can later use it, and file it for future reference. You will find additional and specific discussion of various ways to implement

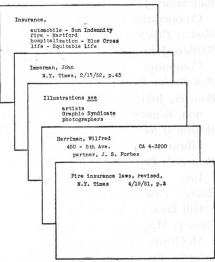

The efficient secretary maintains a quick-reference card file of information of interest to her employer.

the following ten suggestions in other sections of this textbook.

1. Be observant—look around and listen to what you hear.
2. Do not hesitate to use the telephone.
3. Read incoming mail as well as outgoing mail.
4. Refer to correspondence in the files.
5. Write for specific information.
6. Talk to callers.
7. Build a scrapbook—articles, speeches, pictures, graphs, charts, maps.
8. Develop habit of reading newspapers and magazines—make notations.
9. Maintain a card file.
10. Use the library.

Books Referred to in Unit 6 and Additional Reference Sources

Allen, F. Sturges. *Allen's Synonyms and Antonyms*, Revised Enlarged Edition. New York, Harper and Brothers.

American Medical Directory. Chicago, American Medical Association.

American Year Book. New York, American Year Book Corporation.

The Art Index. New York, H. W. Wilson Company.

N. W. Ayer & Son's Directory of Newspapers and Periodicals. Philadelphia, N. W. Ayer & Son.

Ballentine, James A. *Law Dictionary*. Rochester, New York, The Lawyers Co-operative Publishing Company.

Bankers Directory. New York, Rand McNally & Company.

Bartlett, John. *Familiar Quotations*, Twelfth Edition. Boston, Little, Brown and Company.

Book Review Digest. New York, H. W. Wilson Company.

Bouvier, John. *Bouvier's Law Dictionary and Concise Encyclopedia*, Eighth Edition. Kansas City, Missouri, Vernon Law Book Company.

Bulletin of the Public Affairs Information Service. New York, New York Public Library.

Bullinger's Postal and Shipping Guide. New York, Bullinger's Monitor Guide, Inc.

Business Education Index. New York, Gregg Publishing Division, McGraw-Hill Book Company, Inc.

Carney, Marie L. *Etiquette in Business*. New York, Gregg Publishing Division, McGraw-Hill Book Company, Inc.

Columbia Encyclopedia, Second Edition, Revised, Enlarged. New York, Columbia University Press.

Congressional Directory. Washington, D. C., U. S. Government Printing Office.

Dorland, William Alexander Newman. *American Illustrated Medical Dictionary*, Twenty-second Edition. Philadelphia, W. B. Saunders Company.

Dun & Bradstreet Ratings and Reports. New York, Dun & Bradstreet.

The Education Index. New York, H. W. Wilson Company.

Educational Directory. Washington, U. S. Government Printing Office.

The Encyclopaedia Britannica, Fourteenth Edition. New York, Encyclopaedia Britannica, Inc.

Encyclopaedia of the Social Sciences. New York, The Macmillan Company.

Engineering Index. New York, Engineering Index, Inc.

Exporters' Encyclopedia, Annual. New York, Thomas Ashwell & Company.

Fernald, James C. *Standard Handbook of Synonyms, Antonyms, and Prepositions*, New Edition. New York, Funk & Wagnalls Company.

Funk & Wagnalls New Standard Dictionary of the English Language. New York, Funk & Wagnalls Company.

Gavin, Ruth E., and E. Lillian Hutchinson. *Reference Manual for Stenographers and Typists*. New York, Gregg Publishing Division, McGraw-Hill Book Company, Inc.

Greever, Garland, and Easley S. Jones. *The Century Handbook of Writing*, Fourth Edition. New York, Appleton-Century-Crofts Company.

Hagar, Hubert A., Marie M. Stewart, and E. Lillian Hutchinson. *The English of Business*, Second Edition. New York, Gregg Publishing Division, McGraw-Hill Book Company, Inc.

Hotel Red Book. New York, American Hotel Association Directory Corporation.

Hoyt, Jehiel Keeler. *New Cyclopedia of Practical Quotations,* Revised Edition. New York, Funk & Wagnalls Company.

Hutchinson, Lois. *Standard Handbook for Secretaries,* Sixth Edition. New York, Gregg Publishing Division, McGraw-Hill Book Company, Inc.

Index to Legal Periodicals. New York, H. W. Wilson Company.

The Industrial Arts Index. New York, H. W. Wilson Company.

Kelley's Directory of Merchants, Manufacturers, and Shippers of the World. London, England, Kelley's Directory, Ltd.

Leonard's Guide for Parcel Post, Express, Freight, Rates, and Routing. New York and Chicago, G. R. Leonard & Company.

MacGibbon, Eleanor Gregg. *Manners in Business.* New York, The Macmillan Company.

A Manual of Style, Eleventh Revised Edition. Chicago, The University of Chicago Press.

The Martindale-Hubbell Law Directory, 1951. Summit, New Jersey, Martindale-Hubbell, Inc.

Moody's Manuals. New York, Moody's Investors Service.

New Funk & Wagnalls Encyclopedia. New York, Funk & Wagnalls Company.

New York Times Index. New York, New York Times Company.

Official Airline Guide. Chicago, American Aviation Publications.

Opdycke, John Baker. *Take a Letter, Please!* New, Revised. New York, Funk & Wagnalls Company.

Payne, Mildred. *What Do I Do Now?* New York, Gregg Publishing Division, McGraw-Hill Book Company, Inc.

Post, Emily. *Etiquette,* New Edition, Revised. New York, Funk & Wagnalls Company.

Publishers' Trade List Annual. New York, R. R. Bowker Company.

The Reader's Encyclopedia. Edited by William Rose Benet. New York, Thomas Y. Crowell Company.

Readers' Guide to Periodical Literature. New York, H. W. Wilson Company.

Robert, H. M. *Rules of Order,* Revised, 75th Anniversary Edition. Chicago, Scott, Foresman & Company.

Roget's International Thesaurus, New Edition. New York, Thomas Y. Crowell Company.

Social Science Abstracts. New York, Social Science Research Council.

Style Manual of the United States Government Printing Office. Washington, U. S. Government Printing Office.

The United States Catalog. (Supplemented by the Cumulative Book Index.) New York, H. W. Wilson Company.

United States Official Postal Guide. Washington, U. S. Government Printing Office.

Webster's Geographical Dictionary. Springfield, Massachusetts, G. & C. Merriam Company.

Webster's New International Dictionary of the English Language, Second Edition. G. & C. Merriam Company.

Who's Who. New York, The Macmillan Company.

Who's Who in America. Chicago, The A. N. Marquis Company.

Who's Who in American Education. Nashville, Tennessee, Who's Who in American Education, Inc.

Who's Who in New York, Twelfth Edition. New York, Lewis Historical Publishing Company.

Woolley, Edwin C., Franklin W. Scott, and Frederick Bracher. *College Handbook of Composition,* Fifth Edition. Boston, D. C. Heath & Company.

The World Almanac and Book of Facts, Annual. New York, New York World-Telegram and Sun.

World Atlas. (Several editions) New York, Rand McNally & Company.

Some Highlights of This Unit

1. Know the titles (authors if necessary for identification) of six types of reference books on the English language and the kind of information in which each book specializes.

2. Know the titles of ten reference books on business concerns and people. Be able to identify each.

3. Know the titles of fifteen representative books of facts and the type of information each contains.

4. Know the five essentials in the use of reference books.

5. Be systematic and use initiative in recording the information located in nonreference sources.

Questions and Items for Discussion

1. Name five reference books of value to the secretary. Which would you give first place in importance?

2. Describe briefly your idea of efficiency when using reference books.

3. What is a thesaurus and how does it differ from a dictionary?

4. How would you go about obtaining biographical information about a prominent American? a prominent Englishman? a national figure in American politics?

5. What are the necessary steps in obtaining any of the numerous United States Government publications?

6. When was the United States Bureau of Information established, and what service will it render?

7. Your employer has asked you to verify the date of an important news item. What will you do?

8. What reference book would you consult for current information on a national issue?

9. What reference book is indispensable to the credit manager of a manufacturing concern that enjoys national distribution of its product?

Personality Questions and Projects
(Based on Personality Pointer, page 101)

1. Think of someone whom you admire for his or her ability to do the right and graceful thing. Rate this individual, using the questions and items listed in the Personality Pointer for this unit.

2. Think of yourself. Rate yourself critically using the same questions and items as in question 1. You can, if you will, improve yourself. Work on one point at a time.

3. Keep a notebook of magazine and newspaper articles dealing with poise and the factors that it involves.

Secretarial Assignments

1. Give two or more synonyms for each of the following words:

importance   enveloped   pomposity   pacific

2. Your employer has dictated the following quotations from memory. He plans to use them in an address that he will make before a businessmen's club.

a. He that has a merry heart has a continual feast.

b. If you laugh, the world laughs with you.
If you weep, you weep alone.

c. The old order changes, giving place to new;
And God fulfills himself in many ways,
For fear one custom should corrupt the world.

Verify the accuracy of the wording of each one of these quotations. Give the name of the author or—if the author's name is unknown—the source for each. Type the three quotations neatly on one sheet and hand to Mr. Martin.

3. Clip and bring to class some current news items that might be of special interest to two of the following executives:

a. A bank vice-president in charge of loans

b. A corporation lawyer

c. A purchasing agent for a trucking company

d. A general sales manager for a business-machines company

e. A credit manager for a department store

Mount each clipping neatly on a sheet of paper 8½ by 11 inches in size, and type the source and date above each clipping.

4. List ten types of information found in the *World Almanac*.

5. How many books on etiquette are available in your school library? If there are a number, list five titles and the authors.

6. The office manager will dictate an interoffice memo to go to the general manager, Mr. William Wright. Type one original and three carbon copies, making a note on the original that one carbon copy is going to the president, Mr. Arthur K. Redding, and another to the secretary-treasurer, Mr. James L. Stuart. The third copy is for your files. Use Sheet 16 in your Workbook.

For extra copies of interoffice memos that are to be sent to others for their information, it is customary to use white onionskin or a paper of a different color from that of the file copy.

Follow the regular interoffice memo style in working this assignment.

7. The office manager will dictate three letters that you are to set up in semiblock form. Use Sheets 17, 18, 19 in your Workbook.

Use letterheads from your Workbook for the originals. Type an envelope for each letter. Be sure that the envelope address conforms with the style of the inside address of the letter. The enclosures will be taken care of by the Mailing Department.

8. Your office manager has changed one of the letters you have given him. The revised letter will be found in your Workbook (Sheet 20). Retype the letter in accordance with the changes indicated. Because of the revision, a new carbon will be necessary. Address an envelope. Use Sheet 21.

Optional

9. Compose a brief paragraph answering each of the following inquiries that Mr. Martin has given you in the form of pencil notations. Make each of your replies complete, so that he will know what he asked concerning each item. Also give the source of the information.

When you have finished, you will have consulted various references; and you will have written six short paragraphs. Place all this material on one sheet of plain paper.

a. Owen Tucker used "S.J.D." after his name as author of a magazine article. What does it stand for?

b. Lieutenant Charles W. Frost sometimes uses "Lt." in abbreviating his title, sometimes "Lieut." Which is right?

c. The Peasants' Revolt took place during the early years of the reign of Richard II of England. In what year, or approximately, did the Peasants' Revolt occur?

d. When we use "mecca" to stand for a goal, rather than in its literal sense, must it be capitalized?

e. What do the middle initials stand for in the name Samuel F. B. Morse?

f. What state has for its motto, *Sic semper tyrannis?* What's the meaning of *chacun à son goût?* (When foreign accents occur, they should be inserted with pen—never omitted because they are not on the typewriter.)

10. Mr. Martin has put the following note on your desk:

> Please get me a list of twelve hotels, with addresses, in this or near-by cities. See classified telephone directory. This is for the Advertising Department. Send it to them, after checking against the directory for accuracy, and let me have a carbon.

Follow his instructions. In the upper right-hand corner of the original copy, write "Advertising Department—Requested by C. F. Martin," and in the same position on the carbon write "Original to Advertising Department" and the date.

11. It is not so important, in most jobs, to know details of matters not primarily connected with your work as it is to be able to obtain the information by looking in the right places. On a sheet of typewriting paper, type the correct answers to the following assignments:

   a. A visitor remarks, "This office would be Utopia if it had air conditioning." What does "Utopia" mean?

   b. Modern merchandising is no longer conducted on the principle of *caveat emptor.* Explain *caveat emptor.*

   c. "A salesman who doesn't know his merchandise has two strikes on him to begin with." Rewrite without using the slang expression but retaining its meaning.

   d. "The Advertising Department is always right behind the eight ball." Follow the same instructions as in paragraph *c.*

   e. Whose face was said to have "launched a thousand ships and burnt the topless towers of Ilium"?

   f. When did the Pilgrims land in America? Where?

   g. In what year did George Washington become the first President of the United States?

Spelling Demons

colonel	commissioners	conspicuous
colonies	competitors	consulate
combustion	confident	controversy

Job Tips

1. Remember, a librarian is trained in reference work; her suggestions and her assistance can be invaluable to you.

2. The library and files of your community newspaper are helpful sources of local information.

3. Acquaint yourself with the location of the special libraries in your locality; such as, the technical libraries of industrial firms and the extensive legal libraries that many attorneys have.

4. When checking information, remember to record the exact, complete source of the reference.

Personality Pointer

CAN YOU BE PERSUASIVE?

We all have to use persuasion in our dealings with others. Those of us who use it most effectively achieve the greatest power.

Webster's Dictionary defines "persuade" as "to induce one to believe or do something; to argue into an opinion or procedure"; also, "to plead with; urge." The dictionary gives us two points of interpretation. Don't you really think that argument is the *least* effective means of changing people's minds?

It is better to urge than to argue. Persuasion's tool is the appeal, not the threat. By threats, you may make someone do unwillingly what you want him to do, but by persuasion you may make him do it of his own free will.

With the executives in your office, your relationship is simple; you do what you are told and you don't argue.

With your co-workers in the office—those who do about the same work as yours—your relationship is more complex. You must look out for signs of irritation if you are not always tactful or if the other person is nervous or sensitive. You must not try to use force in putting over your idea; it will only make trouble all the way around.

With those who work under your direction, your relationship is also complex. Without blustering or threatening—and also without relaxing your authority—you must get the work done, because it is your responsibility.

Writing Business Letters

Until you become familiar with the policies of the company in which you are employed, you will probably not be called upon to compose letters, reports, or memorandums. Your superior will dictate them instead of asking you to write them. As soon as you have gained his confidence, however, and understand the flow of the work and the organization of routine business, you may be permitted and expected to write many routine letters yourself. Your employer may, at first, wish to sign the letters you have composed; but gradually, as you win his confidence, he will authorize you to send them out over your own signature as "Secretary to Mr. Cummings." The ability to handle this important feature of secretarial work effectively is one of the chief distinctions between a secretary and a stenographer.

Because the business letter is a very powerful means of communication, this unit points out its primary purpose and main characteristics. The fundamentals of good letter writing as they apply to all types of letters are studied in one section. Another section is devoted to the more common types of business letters that are usually dictated to the secretary and the types of letters most likely to be composed by the secretary. One section is concerned with the use of words. The last three sections provide a condensed summary of the basic rules of grammar, punctuation, capitalization, abbreviations, and figures. Illustrations are included to show correct application of the rules. You may also wish to refer again to Unit 4, which considers various letter styles and arrangements.

Section 1. YOU'LL LIKE TO WRITE LETTERS

Purpose of the Business Letter. Basically a letter is the written means used to send a message to the reader. A *business* letter is written because a business transaction makes written communication necessary; for example, it is often used to obtain new business or to create and build good will. You must keep the purpose of a letter in mind when you take dictation, when you transcribe, or when you compose the letter yourself.

Characteristics of the Business Letter. Ordinarily, good letters are not written easily or quickly; neither are they the result of accident. To write an effective letter, you must know what makes a good letter. Your letter will be good to the extent that you can include the following characteristics. A good business letter

1. Is accurate in its statements
2. Reflects the personality of the writer
3. Uses simple, clear, and concise wording
4. Uses language in keeping with the subject and the reader
5. Possesses force because it is the result of planning and clear thinking
6. Is enthusiastic, courteous, and friendly in tone
7. Is grammatically correct
8. Is attractive in appearance and arrangement

Plan the Letter. Nothing constructive can be satisfactorily accomplished without first carefully planning all the details, whether it be of a dress, a house, a menu, a book, or a letter. A letter that is not planned is almost sure to be haphazard, illogical, and confusing.

Suppose you received the following letter. What opinion would you have of the business efficiency of the writer and of the company?

An Unplanned, Confusing Letter

Dear Mr. Hall: Was the paper that was returned to us one week after it went out to you unsatisfactory? This order for 10 reams of our bond paper was shipped on May 4. It came to us on May 2, together with your remittance.

If you wrote us, we should like to clear up this matter as soon as possible and either replace the returned merchandise or credit you for its value. We should appreciate your forwarding us a duplicate copy of your letter as we

are unable to locate any correspondence from you in explanation. There is a return envelope enclosed. Very truly yours,

You will have to read the letter several times to disentangle the thoughts. Study will reveal that the writer is trying to cover these points:

1. The date on which the customer's order was received.
2. The date on which the material was shipped to the customer.
3. The date on which the material was returned to us.
4. An inquiry regarding the reason for the return.
5. Assurance to the customer that we want him to be satisfied and that we will do everything we can to correct whatever the difficulty may be.
6. Request to customer to co-operate with us in accomplishing adjustment.
7. Statement of what we want the customer to do.

Applying this organization to the above letter, the following is the result.

The Revised Letter

Dear Mr. Hall: Your order for 10 reams of our bond paper, together with your remittance, reached us May 2.

This paper was shipped to you May 4—two days after the order was received. On May 11, exactly one week after the shipment went to you, it came back to us.

Was the paper unsatisfactory?

We are unable to locate any correspondence from you in explanation. If you wrote us, we should appreciate receiving a duplicate copy of your letter so that we may clear up this matter as soon as possible and either replace the returned merchandise or credit you for its value.

If you have not written us, won't you please let us know what the trouble is so that we can correct it to your satisfaction. Very truly yours,

Write from the Reader's Point of View. To each person the most important person in the world is himself. This psychological truth is the reason for the frequent repetition in this chapter of the rule, "Write from the reader's point of view." This has been called the "you" attitude—the use of "you" and "your" rather than "I" and "mine" and "we" and "ours." In the following two sentences, the same idea is expressed in two ways.

From the writer's point of view: We have received your letter of November 10 and have referred it to *our* Order Department. They tell *us* that *we* shipped the furniture to you on November 8.

From the reader's point of view: You will be pleased to know that the furniture *you* mention in *your* letter of November 10 was sent to *you* on November 8, in accordance with the information received from the Order Department.

If the reader is known personally to you, it will be comparatively easy to picture what will interest him most in reading your letter.

The more quickly you cultivate the habit of presenting all facts from the *reader's* point of view, the more quickly will you be preparing yourself to write the more difficult types of business letters—such as collection letters and sales letters—in which the failure or success of the letter depends on the way in which you present the facts to the reader.

Keep Your Own Personality Out of Routine Letters. In answering letters for your employer, remember that you are writing *for* him. This does not mean that you should strive to imitate his personal style of letter writing, nor does it mean that you should refer to yourself as the writer. Note that the following letters written by the secretary never once introduce an "I." The only indication of the fact that the secretary has written these letters is the line below the signature, "Secretary to Mr. ----------." Later, should you develop into a correspondent and write sales letters, credit and collection letters, and adjustment letters, you will have an opportunity to inject your personality into your letters. The executive type of letter is greatly strengthened by a reflection of the personality of the writer.

Be Brief. It should be easy to cultivate conciseness in the letters you write because in most cases they will deal with but one matter. Your letter should be just long enough to tell its story, for the reader's time is valuable and not to be wasted by unnecessary words.

Despite the attention that has been given in recent years to achieving directness in business letters, many letter writers still think it necessary to use certain formulalike expressions in business letters. Much of this "jargon" is a survival of earlier days when businessmen felt inferior to the persons of higher rank whom they served and so referred to themselves as "obedient servants" and to letters from their patrons as "favors." The resulting wordiness to cover plain speaking, the over-courteous tone, and the affectations should all be replaced in the modern letter by simple, sincere words that express the real meaning.

The following are some of the commonest of these trite words and expressions, with comments on them or suggested substitutions.

Advise	Do not use for *say* or *tell*. Reserve for real advice.
And oblige	Omit.
As per, per	Use only with Latin words, as *per annum*. Ordinarily, substitute *a* or *according to*.

At all times	*Always.*
At an early date	*Soon.* Or give the specific date.
At this time, at the present time, at the present writing	*Now, at present.*
At your convenience	Be more specific.
Attached hereto	Omit *hereto.*
Beg	Don't be a beggar.
Contents carefully noted	Contributes little.
Due to the fact that	*Because.*
Duly	Usually unnecessary.
Enclosed please find	*Enclosed is.*
Even date	Give specific date.
Esteemed	Too flowery.
Favor	Do not use for *letter.*
Hand you herewith	*Enclosed.*
Have before me	Outworn.
Herewith	Redundant.
In re	*Regarding* or *concerning.*
In the event that	*In case, if.*
Instant (inst.)	Give exact date.
Kindly	*Please.*
Line	Do not use for *merchandise* or *goods.*
Our check in the amount of	*Our check for.*
Our Mr. So-and-So	*Our representative, Mr. So-and-So.*
Party	*Person* except in legal matter.
Proximo	Give exact date.
Recent date	Give exact date.
Same	*It, they, them,* or whatever is meant.
State	*Say* or *tell.*
Take pleasure	*Pleased, are happy, are glad.*
Thanking you in advance	Discourteous.
Ultimo	Use exact date.
Under date of	*On.*
Under separate cover	*By parcel post,* or whatever the means of sending.
Up to this writing	*Previously.*
Valued (letter or order)	Omit.
Via	*By way of.*
We wish to thank you	*Thank you.*
Would ask, remind, say, suggest	Go ahead and say what is to be said without warning.

| Yours received and contents noted | Meaningless. It is to be presumed the letter has been received and read if it is being answered. |

Avoid also the roundabout way of saying things. For example:

Wordy: If it would be to your advantage to have additional copies of this report other than those already in your office, you can obtain them by getting in touch with our Advertising Department.

Concise: If you need additional copies of this report, our Advertising Department will be glad to supply you with them.

Be Courteous. Just because a letter is concise does not mean that it need be curt. In fact, a letter written with proper regard for the feeling of others cannot be discourteous.

Note that the mere introduction of polite words does not make a letter courteous. A letter may be full of expressions like "we are greatly pleased," "we deeply appreciate," and "thanking you kindly" and still lack a friendly tone. For example:

Curt: We must insist on immediate payment.

Courteous: We are counting on receiving your check sometime this week.

The closing sentence, especially, should convey a cordial feeling. (See also page 135.) And remember—never send out a letter written in anger. Hold the letter for at least a day; then reread it, and you will probably tear it up.

Be Positive and Use Pleasant Words. Certain words suggest unpleasant, disagreeable feelings and situations. Such words should be avoided, and words suggesting pleasant feelings should be used in their place. For example:

Avoid	*Use*
complaint	assurance
damage	confidence, confident
delay	co-operation
displeased, displeasure	pleasure
dissatisfied	satisfaction, satisfied
fail, failure	success, successful
inability	
mistake	
neglected	
trouble	
unfortunately	

Of course, difficulties will arise in any business; but they can be acknowledged in a friendly, helpful tone that suggests that a satisfactory solution can be found. This is especially important in the closing sentence of a letter (See also page 135).

Negative: We regret that our mistake has caused you so much inconvenience.
Positive: It was a pleasure to be able to adjust this matter to your entire satisfaction.

Be Wary. Anything that is put in writing becomes a record—an official stand of the person or company sponsoring the letter. Therefore, in writing letters, you must be wary of how far you commit yourself.

Do not quote anyone unless you are positive that you have the right to do so and that the person would approve. The quotation of a person's casual remark may embarrass him or even lead to serious complications.

Do not make a positive claim without modifying it by, "it is our understanding," "we believe," or some similar phrase. An unscrupulous person might insist on the claim's being proved. The writers of advertising letters, particularly, are careful to avoid unconditional claims that their products are the best on the market.

Do not make derogatory remarks about anyone's character. This may lay you open to a libel suit. Writers of collection letters have to be extremely cautious in this regard.

If you are uncertain about the accuracy of any statement you make, and there is no way to verify it, word your sentence so as to avoid making it too positive. Instead of saying, for example, "Mr. Hunt will take up the matter of this price adjustment as soon as he returns," say, "The matter of this price adjustment will be called to Mr. Hunt's attention immediately upon his return."

Paragraph Wisely. In your courses in English composition, you learned that each paragraph should have a topic sentence, which should state the main topic of the paragraph, and that the rest of the paragraph should be a development of that sentence. Business letters, on the other hand, usually deal with but one topic; the paragraphing is mainly an attention-getting device. It also helps the reader grasp each thought quickly. It is still possible, however, to paragraph according to *parts* of a topic.

As most of the secretary's letters are short, it may not be necessary

to paragraph more than once. Numbered items and series of questions or topics are much more effective if each one is paragraphed rather than all run in one paragraph.

Be Grammatically Correct. To hand your employer a letter containing errors in English, whether it is a letter that you have composed or one that you have taken from dictation, is a reflection on your ability. If the worst happens and the letter is mailed with the errors uncaught, they reflect on the dictator and the company as well as on you.

Errors in English fall into two main classes: (1) errors in grammar, and (2) confusion of words. You will find a summary of the rules of grammar most often violated in Section 4 of this unit. For words often confused—words like *principal* and *principle*, which sound exactly alike, and *expect* and *except*, which sound and look somewhat alike— refer to a standard speller or English textbook. (See page 107.)

Try to develop a detective sense of suspicion that here is a construction or a word that *may* be wrong. By constant questioning, checking, and correcting, you will gradually overcome inaccuracies in grammar.

Make Your First Sentence Count. The first sentence of the letter is the most important sentence in the letter—it sets the tone for the entire letter. Do not waste this precious space, therefore, by making some long-winded reference to correspondence received. Instead, go directly to the point and express the subject of the letter. Also, make the sentence show your interest in the reader—again, the reader's point of view. Any reference to previous correspondence can be made indirectly.

Most good letter writers make it a rule never to begin a letter with "I" or "We."

Poor: We have received your inquiry of November 16, which *we* have referred to our Advertising Department.

Improved: You will be pleased to know that the advertising folders *you* described in *your* letter of November 16 are being imprinted for *you* by our Advertising Department and should reach *you* early next week.

Close Your Letter Effectively. Because most letters that the secretary writes are short, often the complimentary closing is the only closing that is really needed. Sometimes, however, a real wind-up sentence is required. It should be carefully framed, for the last words are those that linger in the reader's mind.

One letter-writing authority has advised that the writer review his

reasons for writing in the form of a definite statement to the reader—and *then* his letter is complete.

Perhaps the purpose of your letter, for example, has been to inquire about the delayed delivery of certain goods ordered. Contrast these two sentences:

Weak: We await the favor of an early reply regarding this matter.
Improved: Please write us at once whether you have the goods in stock.

The closing sentence, therefore, should be short, specific, and positive—not rambling, vague, and negative. Above all, avoid the participial ending—"trusting," "hoping," "thanking," etc.—that was so much in vogue a generation ago, for the participial ending is extremely weak.

Weak: Assuring you that your order will have our prompt and careful attention, we are
Improved: Your order will be shipped promptly.

Correct Forms of Address. The standard business forms of address follow. For the special forms for use in correspondence with government officials (national, state, or municipal), the clergy (Protestant, Roman Catholic, or Jewish), the Military and Naval services, professors, doctors, and other persons with titles, consult one of the style manuals listed in Unit 6.

Salutations
1. Impersonal:
   a. A firm consisting of men or of men and women: *Gentlemen.*
   b. A firm consisting solely of women: *Mesdames* or *Ladies.*
   c. Very formal and impersonal: *My dear Sir* or *My dear Madam.*
   d. Formal and impersonal: *Dear Sir* or *Dear Madam.*
   e. Formal letters to government officials: *Sir* or *Sirs.*

2. Personal:
   a. More formal: *My dear Mr.* (or *Mrs.* or *Miss*) *Jones; My dear Doctor* (or *Professor*) *Smith.*
   b. Less formal: *Dear Mr.* (or *Mrs.* or *Miss*) *Jones; Dear Doctor* (or *Professor*) *Smith.*

Complimentary Closings
1. Formal:
   Yours truly,   Yours respectfully,
   Yours very truly,   Yours very respectfully,

2. Informal:

Sincerely yours,	Very cordially yours,
Very sincerely yours,	Fraternally yours,
Appreciatively yours,	Gratefully yours,
Cordially yours,	Co-operatively yours,

The position of the word "yours" in each of these closings may be changed if desired.

Titles of Address

1. For men:
   a. For a man who has no special title or whose title is unknown: *Mr.* (never spelled out).
   b. For young boys (under twelve years of age): *Master.*

2. For women:
   a. Married: *Mrs. Arthur J. Davis.*
   b. Unmarried: *Miss Louise Sloan.* (*Miss* is also used when it is not known whether the woman is married or single.)
   c. Widowed: Ordinarily, her former title, as *Mrs. Henry Ames,* unless she prefers to use her own Christian name, as *Mrs. Patricia Ames.*
   d. Divorced: Follow the woman's preference, which may be ascertained from her own signature.

3. For two or more persons:
   a. Men: *Messrs.,* as *Messrs. John and Albert Shaw, Messrs. Bruce and Barton.*
   b. Women:
      (1) Unmarried: *Misses,* as *The Misses Clark, Misses Clark and Stevens.*
      (2) Married, or one married and one unmarried: *Mesdames,* as *Mesdames Wright and Dunn.*

4. Business titles, such as *Sales Manager, Secretary,* which follow a name, are descriptive or identifying rather than strict titles, and do not affect any preceding title.

> Mrs. Henry Hobart, Secretary
> The Vincent Saw Company
>
> Dr. Donald Carr, Consulting Engineer
> Steel Construction Company

5. *Honorable* is used in addressing persons holding important positions in national, state, and city governments, even after their retirement. *Reverend* is used before the name of a clergyman. Both

titles are preferably preceded by *The*, and either a title or a given name must follow the titles.

6. *Esquire* (always abbreviated *Esq.*) is a courtesy title applied to lawyers and justices of the peace. It always follows the name; and no title, not even *Mr.*, precedes the name.

7. *Jr.*, *Sr.*, *2d*, etc., follow the name and are separated from it by a comma.

Section 2. TYPES OF BUSINESS LETTERS

Letters Usually Dictated to the Secretary. Letters dealing with administrative matters, advertising and sales letters, adjustment letters, and credit and collection letters are examples of letters that are usually dictated. Their composition requires specialized knowledge both of the business and of the technique of letter writing.

The secretary who looks forward to promotion to an executive position constantly observes the executive's letter-writing technique. Also, many excellent books have been written on business letter writing. It is certainly worth your while to familiarize yourself with one of them, so that you may consult it when problems arise.

Letters the Secretary Frequently Composes. The letters that you will compose will probably be of the following types:

1. Letters to make or to cancel appointments
2. Letters of acknowledgment, especially during your employer's absence
3. Letters of transmittal
4. Letters replying to formal invitations
5. Letters of congratulation, thanks, and sympathy

You will find many helpful suggestions and examples to assist you in composing the types of business letters you are most likely to write on the following pages.

1. Letters Making and Canceling Appointments. Suppose that, on a busy day when every minute has been scheduled with appointments, dictation, and conferences, a representative of the out-of-town manufacturer that supplies your company with certain articles drops in to your office on the chance of being able to see your employer. It will be your duty to tell the visitor tactfully that your employer is exceed-

ingly busy and that he cannot be disturbed, but that you will be glad to obtain a definite appointment for him and to notify him by letter as soon as you have been able to schedule it. If you are not sure of the caller's name and address, ask for his card or make an exact notation of the name and address on your memo pad. Also, ask him when he expects to be in town again.

When you consult your employer to learn his wishes, you may be told, "I can see him Monday, the 15th, at 3:30."

In planning the letter you will write the representative, you must be sure to include the time (the day and the hour) and the place. The keynote of the letter will be definiteness; and, naturally, the letter will be short.

See how effectively the following letter incorporates all these features.

 Letter Making an Appointment

Mr. James L. Granville
237 Marshall Avenue
Spokane 14, Washington

Dear Mr. Granville:

If you will call at this office on Monday, April 25, at 2:30 p.m., Mr. Beatty will be glad to confer with you on the matter of public-relations policies in the Spokane office.

Very truly yours,

Secretary to Mr. Beatty

An appointment with a caller in town would doubtless be made by telephone. (See Unit 9.)

Perhaps, however, your employer will feel that he is too busy to make an appointment for the present and will ask you to "put him off."

This assignment is a challenge to your resourcefulness and tact, for you are going to disappoint the recipient of your letter—and no one likes to be disappointed.

You can soften the blow to some extent by giving the reason for the refusal first, somewhat like this:

Letter Refusing an Appointment

Mr. George R. Baker
27 Jefferson Street
Atlanta 3, Georgia

Dear Mr. Baker:

Mr. Montgomery has asked me to inform you that the pressure of matters in connection with the opening of the Macon office makes it impossible for him to see you at the present time.

If, in about four weeks, you still wish to make an appointment, Mr. Montgomery will be glad to arrange one.

Very truly yours,

Secretary to Mr. Montgomery

Again, your employer may suddenly decide to leave that evening for a hurried trip that will take him out of town for several days. This means that all appointments for those days must be canceled. Local appointments can be broken by telephone, but appointments with persons out of town must be canceled by mail or wire.

These letters, too, must be definite—they must give the time and the place of the original appointment. They must, like all business letters, be written with the reader's point of view in mind; that is, they must express regret for the inconvenience caused and extend the courtesy of setting another time for the appointment. For example:

Letter Canceling an Appointment

Mr. Conrad L. Arthur
618 Madison Avenue
New York 22, New York

Dear Mr. Arthur:

Mr. Doyle regrets that he will be unable to keep his appointment with you on Thursday morning, June 22. Because the meeting of the board of directors has been rescheduled, he will have to leave for Chicago two days earlier than originally planned.

If you will set a time after July 1 that will be convenient to you, I am sure Mr. Doyle will be glad to make arrangements to see you.

Very truly yours,

Secretary to Mr. Doyle

2. Letters of Acknowledgment. Many business offices have a rule that all letters must be acknowledged the day they are received. The secre-

tary often has to write a correspondent that his letter has been received but that action on it is being delayed because (1) the employer is absent from the office or (2) not all the necessary information is available for acting on the matter concerned.

In writing letters of acknowledgment, you must be exact—you must mention the date of the incoming letter, the matter with which it deals, and any enclosures. You must give a brief and reasonable explanation of the reason for any delayed action—and, again, your entire letter must be written from the reader's point of view. Remember that the reader is more interested in the action that has been taken on his letter than in the fact that his letter was received. (The fact he is hearing from you shows his letter was received.)

Note how the following letters of acknowledgment observe the cautions just mentioned.

Mr. Bruce R. Dailey
1218 Sixth Street
Milwaukee 6, Wisconsin

Dear Mr. Dailey:

Mr. Horner is at present in New York on a business trip. Your report on new production methods, which accompanied your letter of June 16, has been referred to Mr. Martin Blake, the assistant production manager.

Plans to incorporate two of the suggestions are now being studied, and the whole report will be referred to Mr. Horner as soon as he returns.

Yours truly,

Secretary to Mr. Horner

Mr. George M. Lee
231 Broad Street
Baton Rouge, Louisiana

Dear Mr. Lee:

Mr. MacDonald is very much interested in your letter of February 19 containing suggestions for the newspaper advertising campaign of the Southern Fruitgrowers Association.

When he has completed the preliminary work on another matter now occupying his attention, you will undoubtedly hear from him.

Very truly yours,

Secretary to Mr. MacDonald

3. Letter of Transmittal. Whenever valuable papers such as contracts, specifications, stocks, bonds, mortgages, deeds, and similar important documents are sent by mail, a letter of transmittal should accompany them, even though the recipient is expecting the papers. The carbon copy of the letter thus becomes a permanent record of the transmittal.

Your employer may simply say, "Send this deed to Mr. Ames"; but unless he has dictated the necessary accompanying letter himself, you are expected to write it.

Letters of transmittal should identify the enclosed paper exactly. For example:

Mr. David Lee Pierce
1822 Carson Street
Fort Worth 3, Texas

Dear Mr. Pierce:

Enclosed is the duly executed deed to the property known as Millbank, located south of the fairgrounds near Fort Worth.

Yours truly,

Secretary to Mr. Brown

Letters containing valuable papers should be registered and a return receipt requested.

4. Letters Replying to Formal Invitations. Most executives receive many invitations to formal events—banquets, receptions for distinguished visitors, openings of stores and of exhibits; frequently, too, they are asked to be patrons of notable events. Such invitations are usually engraved or printed.

Many formal invitations bear the notation, "A favor of a reply is requested" or "R.S.V.P.," an abbreviation of the French, *Répondez, s'il vous plaît* (Answer, if you please).

Replies to formal invitations are hardly ever dictated and, of course, are never signed. The employer expects his secretary to be sufficiently informed regarding social custom to be able to write the correct reply from a decision briefly noted on the invitation.

The chief thing for the secretary to remember is to follow the style and the form of the invitation. If it is written in the third person, use the third person in the reply; if it is written in the first person, use the first. Replies are usually written by hand on semisocial or social sta-

Mr. Gregory Brooks
accepts with pleasure
the kind invitation of
The Rockford Lions Club
for Friday, the tenth of March
at seven o'clock.

A formal note of acceptance.

tionery. A popular size for executives, as stated in Unit 5, is the monarch. It is not considered good taste to use a regular business letterhead for this purpose.

No excuse is necessary in declining an invitation, though it is considered gracious to add one. The day and the hour should be repeated in an acceptance, but in a letter of regret only the day need be repeated.

Mr. Gregory Brooks
regrets that a previous engagement
prevents his accepting
the kind invitation of
The Rockford Lions Club
for Friday, the tenth of March.

A formal note of regret.

A standard book on etiquette, which should be a part of every secretary's library, will contain instructions about the preparation of other social letters of this type. (See Unit 6.)

5. Letters of Congratulation, Thanks, and Sympathy. The executive has many occasions to write letters of congratulation to his friends on such happy events as promotions to higher positions, the obtaining of important contracts or orders, the publication of books, their marriages and anniversaries, and similar notable occasions. He may wish to express his personal thanks for some courtesy shown or special

service rendered, to recommend a person for membership in a club, or to resign from a club; and only a callous person would neglect to offer his sympathy when some business acquaintance suffers the loss of a member of his family or meets with some other personal misfortune. The wider the executive's personal contacts, the more of these letters he will write.

The secretary can be of great help to her employer in bringing such events to his attention through news items in the daily papers, office "gossip," or personal contacts.

Letters of congratulation, thanks, and sympathy must be written promptly. They should be brief and, above all, sincere. The choice of salutation and complimentary closing will depend on the degree of friendship between your employer and the person to whom he is writing. Inquire whether he wishes the letter to be written on personal or club stationery. Whether the executive or his secretary composes the letter, the executive will sign it.

Because of the intimate nature of such letters, no standard forms can be given. The following letters illustrate a few typical situations.

Letters of Congratulation

Dear Bob: Your company letterhead, I notice, now bears your name as President.

My heartiest congratulations! You deserve the post, and your company is to be congratulated on having you in it. Sincerely yours,

Dear Bill: Mrs. Brown and I were delighted, indeed, to hear the big news from your home. There is no joy quite like that felt upon the arrival of a son and heir. You all have our best wishes for the years to come. Sincerely yours,

Letter of Thanks

Dear Mr. Rogers: Santa Claus called at our house yesterday and left a note saying I am to have the pleasure of enjoying your magazine for another year.

All the members of our family read this magazine from cover to cover each week and look forward to its coming with a great deal of pleasure.

I want to thank you sincerely for this Christmas remembrance.

I hope the coming year will be a grand year for you personally as well as for your company. Sincerely yours,

Letter Proposing Friend for Club Membership

Gentlemen: It affords me much pleasure to propose Mr. Henry Nichols for membership in the _____ Club. I have known Mr. Nichols since boyhood and consider him well qualified for membership.

He is a graduate of _____ University and is now practicing law in New York City. Yours very truly,

Letter of Sympathy

Dear George: News has just reached me of your misfortune in losing your house through fire. The thought of the beautiful furnishings and art objects that you have spent so much time in collecting being consumed depresses me very much.

May I be of any help to you in this misfortune? Sincerely yours,

Form Letters for Routine Correspondence. Many situations in the business office require correspondence of a similar nature. Much time and money may be saved for the firm if a study is made of these common situations and form letters composed to cover them.

Form letters that have been composed to handle certain situations may be used in various ways:

1. The secretary may type an original copy from the particular form letter selected.
2. It may be advisable to duplicate a form letter in advance. Then it is only necessary to insert the date, correct inside address, and salutation.
3. You may need to prepare form paragraphs—not letters. A form letter may then be prepared by selecting appropriate paragraphs to meet the specific situation. In this way form letters take care of slightly different situations.

Form letters should be classified according to the kind of situation and filed.

Section 3. YOUR USE OF WORDS

The Importance of Words to the Secretary. Words—written and spoken—may be said to be the secretary's stock in trade, for what is shorthand but a system of recording words; typewriting but a means of preserving words; the mail, the telegraph, and the cable but means of transmitting written words; and the telephone and the radio but means of transmitting spoken words?

As a secretary, you will use certain words over and over again; other words you will use only occasionally. You are already acquainted with some of the common business words; you will have to acquire others with varying degrees of effort.

What does being familiar with words mean? It means knowing how to spell them correctly; how to form plurals, compound words, and possessives; how to divide words; when to capitalize words; the meaning of the more commonly used foreign words and of the technical words used in the special business or industry in which you are employed.

Does this sound like a large order to you? It won't if you begin right here to tackle one element at a time.

How to Study Spelling. The foundation of learning to spell is physical —matters of correct seeing, correct hearing, and correct speaking.

In each word you study, first be sure you see it correctly. Look at each letter and note the sequence of the letters in the word. In studying *accommodate*, for example, note that there are two *c*'s and two *m*'s. In other words, photograph the words on your mind's eye.

Next, listen attentively to the correct pronunciation of each word and, vice versa, pronounce each carefully. Do you fail to hear or fail to pronounce whole syllables—as *incidently* for *incidentally?* Or do you fail to hear or fail to pronounce individual letters—as the *n* in *government?* On the contrary, do you insert letters or syllables in words? Do you say *fillum* instead of *film?*

The adoption of one or more of the following methods of practice will speed up your results in overcoming spelling troubles.

1. Write each word you study several times on the typewriter. If some one syllable or group of letters is giving you trouble, capitalize it or underscore it, thus:

```
belIEve          believe
                       ‾‾‾
```

2. Watch for the word in newspapers, in car and bus ads, and in your textbooks. You will be amazed at the repetitions you will find.

3. Keep a list of the words you habitually misspell. Review these words often and check up on yourself and your results.

4. Occasionally, review the rules of spelling in a standard spelling book or in the dictionary.

5. Most important of all, develop the dictionary habit.

COMPOUND WORDS

Some compound words are written as one solid word; others are two separate words; still others are hyphenated. Authorities do not agree on the rules, and practice changes from time to time. An up-to-date dictionary is the only sure guide. The following rules represent the best present-day practice.

Prefixes and Suffixes. When the first element of a compound word is a prefix, as *over*, *sub*, or the last element is a suffix, as *tion*, *ful*, the compound is usually written solid.

Exceptions

1. When the last letter of a prefix is the same as the first letter of the word to which it is being added, a hyphen is inserted.

co-operate   semi-independent   re-enter   pre-existing

When, in adding a suffix, the same letter occurs three times, the hyphen is inserted.

bell-like   shell-less

2. When the second element is a capitalized word, a hyphen is inserted after the prefix.

pro-British   trans-Pacific   anti-American   semi-Diesel   extra-League

3. The prefix *self* is always followed by a hyphen.

self-esteem   self-confidence

4. The hyphen is necessary in some verbs beginning with the prefix *re* to distinguish them from identically spelled words of different meanings.

re-count   recount   re-cover   recover   re-form   reform
re-mark   remark

Compound Titles. 1. Social and military titles consisting of two or more words are not hyphenated.

Secretary of State Acheson   General Manager Moulton

Exceptions

Compound titles containing *ex*, *vice*, and *elect* are hyphenated.

ex-President Hoover   Dean-elect McSwain

2. If a title represents two offices, however, it should be hyphenated.

Secretary-Treasurer Westover

Compound Adjectives. 1. When two or more words are used *before* a noun as if they were but one adjective, the expression is hyphenated.

able-bodied man	light-blue letterhead	time-honored custom
change-of-address card	middle-aged man	top-heavy load
clear-cut distinction	never-to-be-forgotten	twelve-year-old child
double-quick time	event	uncalled-for remark
first-class condition	100-watt bulb	up-to-date method
ill-bred remark	one-way street	well-groomed man
law-abiding citizen	slow-paying customers	would-be promoter

Exceptions

a. Compound adjectives containing an adverb ending in *ly*.

finely drawn distinction rapidly falling barometer

Caution: Some commonly used *adjectives*, however, end in *ly*.

a friendly-appearing person a worldly-looking woman

b. Two-word proper nouns used as adjectives.

New York style Park Avenue shop South American product

2. When a compound adjective *follows* a noun, it is usually not hyphenated.

the plan above described a man well groomed
a method that is up to date

3. When a series of hyphenated adjectives has a common basic element that is omitted in all but the last adjective, a hyphen follows each adjective.

5- and 10-cent store

Compound Verbs. When a verb is built from two or more words, it should be hyphenated.

to dry-clean   to blue-pencil
to hard-finish   to double-check

Compound Numbers. 1. Compound numerals from *twenty-one* to *ninety-nine* are hyphenated.

fifty-two one hundred forty-seven

2. Fractions are hyphenated, the hyphen being placed between the numerator and the denominator unless one element or both contain a hyphen.

one-eighth forty-six hundredths twenty-one thirty-seconds

Note: This rule is based on customary business practice. Webster does not recommend the hyphen in such cases.

FORMATION OF POSSESSIVES

Many errors occur in the formation of possessives. Study the six rules, and their illustrations, given below.

1. To form the possessive of *singular* nouns *not* ending in *s*, add an apostrophe followed by an *s*.

customer, customer's world, world's
month, month's Frank, Frank's

2. If a *singular* noun ends in *s* or an *s*-sound, add an apostrophe and an *s* if a new syllable is formed in the pronunciation of the possessive.

boss, boss's Jones, Jones's
miss, miss's Thomas, Thomas's
fox, fox's witness, witness's

If, however, the addition of *s* would make an *s* ending word hard to pronounce, it is permissible to add only an apostrophe.

hostess, hostess' Frances, Frances'

Note: Some authorities differ on this rule.

3. The possessive of *regular plurals* is formed by adding only the apostrophe after the *s*.

lawyers, lawyers' celebrities, celebrities'
sheriffs, sheriffs' Negroes, Negroes'

Caution: In forming the possessive of a noun ending in *s*, the apostrophe must not be placed *before* that *s*.

Wrong: Burn's, misse's *Right:* Burns's, misses'

4. The possessive of *irregular plurals* is formed by adding the apostrophe followed by *s*.

freshmen, freshmen's   Englishwomen, Englishwomen's

5. Possessive personal pronouns do not require an apostrophe.

they, theirs   you, yours   she, hers
he, his   it, its   who, whose
we, ours

Caution: The possessive pronouns *its, theirs,* and *whose* must not be confused with the contractions *it's,* meaning "it is"; *there's,* meaning "there is"; and *who's,* meaning "who is" or "who has."

6. The sign of the possessive is added at the end of a compound noun.

somebody else's   bookkeeper-secretary's

Division of Words

The point at which a word may be divided at the end of a line is governed by its syllabication and by the appearance on the printed or typewritten page.

Words may be divided only between syllables; therefore, one-syllable words should not be divided.

bruise   search   sound   through   would   Charles

In the past tense, many short verbs are still one-syllable words.

trimmed   scrapped   stripped   hauled   helped

The following rules represent accepted *typewriting* and *printing* practice for the division of words of more than one syllable. If one is in doubt as to the syllabication of any word, the dictionary should be consulted.

1. A one-letter syllable—whether at the beginning or at the end of a word—should not be separated from the rest of the word.

One-Letter Beginning Syllables		*One-Letter Ending Syllables*	
adulterate	obedience	rainy	hysteria
agreeable	idolize	camera	bindery
enumerate	unification	radio	heavy

2. Two-letter final syllables should not be carried over to a second line.

idiomatic   beautify   exceptional   commissioner   interested

3. Four- and five-letter words, even though of more than one syllable, should not be divided.

only   Asia   exit   idea   rabid   carry   ideal

4. When a word begins with a prefix of two or more letters, division should be after the prefix.

Note: In the examples that follow, hyphens represent points of division. Do not confuse these with hyphenated compound words.

dis-similar	with-drawing	super-ficial	con-centrate
sub-ordinate	pre-conceived	mis-addressed	per-pendicular
over-influence	under-value	inter-relate	sub-sidize

5. When a word ends with a suffix of three or more letters, division should be before the suffix.

sudden-ness	tempera-ment	lubrica-tion	comfort-able
treacher-ous	justify-ing	statisti-cal	temper-ance
primi-tive	motor-ist	digest-ible	appar-ent

Exception to Rules 4 and 5. Sometimes, however, division after a prefix or before a suffix would misrepresent the pronunciation—that is, would not coincide with the syllabication.

Prefixes		*Suffixes*	
antic-ipate	signifi-cance	crea-tive	trium-phant
pref-erence	abun-dant	vigi-lance	combus-tible
prel-ude	compe-tence	impenetra-ble	spar-kling

6. When the final letter of a word is doubled because of the addition of *ing, er, est, en,* etc., the division is between the doubled letters.

refer-ring   rob-ber   alot-ted   red-dest   glad-den

Such words should not be confused with words ending in a double consonant, in which the original form is retained.

full   full-est   pass   pass-ing   fulfill   fulfill-ing

7. A single-vowel syllable should not be carried over to a new line

medi-cine   facili-tate   deli-cate   approxi-mate   simi-lar

except with a two-letter syllable in order to make a division possible.

simplic-ity   propri-ety   durabil-ity

8. Compound words, whether solid or hyphenated, should be divided only between the elements of the word.

Solid Compounds		*Hyphenated Compounds*	
inasmuch	inas-much	heart-rending	heart-rending
southwestern	south-western	above-mentioned	above-mentioned
newsstand	news-stand	machine-made	machine-made

Foreign Words and Phrases. A surprising number of foreign words and phrases are used in business. Such expressions as *de luxe, bona fide,* or *esprit de corps* may arise in any line of business; and in law offices innumerable Latin words and phrases occur, as *modus operandi* or *habeas corpus.* The secretary must be alert, therefore, to recognize such words and then must be sure that they are spelled correctly when transcribed. It should be remembered that, usually, the pronunciation of a foreign word, especially of a French word, is no guide to its spelling.

When you have verified the spelling with a reliable word list or dictionary, check to be sure:

1. That the accents *á, à, â,* and *ç* are correctly placed. This is best done by pen after the transcript has been removed from the machine.

2. That adjectives are properly inflected. In many foreign languages, the form of the adjective is changed to agree with the gender of the noun it modifies. For example, in French, you would write *petit fils* (grandson) but *petite fille* (granddaughter).

In printed matter, foreign words that have not been fully adopted into the English language—for example, *carte blanche*—are italicized. Therefore, if you are typing manuscripts that are to be set in type, underscore such words. This will indicate to the printer that the words are to be set in italics. In business correspondence, however, such words are not usually underscored, underscoring being reserved for emphasis.

For the most commonly used foreign words and phrases, refer to your dictionary.

British Spelling. In some offices, secretaries are expected to use English forms of spelling.

The chief variations are as follows: *-our* for *-or;* as in: honour, favour; final *-re* for *-er;* as in: fibre, centre; *-xion* for *-tion;* as in: connexion, inflexion.

The final consonant is doubled before *ed* and *ing;* as in: travelled, cancelling, carburetted.

One *l* is used instead of two in certain words; as: instalment, fulfil, instil.

Miscellaneous: cheque, endorse, offence, programme, acknowledgement, mould.

Geographical Names. Never take a chance on the spelling of a geographical name. If there is the least doubt in your mind about the form of a name, look it up. Costly delays may result from misdirected envelopes, and incorrect mailing lists waste postage.

The authority for the correct spelling of towns and cities in the United States is the *United States Official Postal Guide.* See page 113 for a description of the contents of this invaluable book.

Geographical spelling errors fall into the following groups:

1. Names that are so similar in appearance or in sound that the visual image has never "registered" correctly; for example:

Columbia (which is the capital of South Carolina and occurs also in sixteen other states; which is the last word in the full form of *D. C.;* and which, combined with *British*, is the name of a Canadian province).

Colombia (which is the South American Republic).

Colombo (which is the capital of Ceylon).

Columbus (which is the capital of Ohio and which also is found in eighteen other states).

Then there are Alexander in twelve states and Alexandria in fourteen; and Altona in two states and Altoona in seven; and Mechanicville, New York, and Mechanicsville in five states; and Fort Myer, Virginia, and Fort Myers, Florida; and so on.

2. Names that are pronounced alike but spelled differently; as:

Allegany, New York and Oregon

Savannah, Georgia and four other states

Alleghany, California and Virginia

Savanna, Illinois and Oklahoma

Allegheny, Mountains and River

Belleview, in four states

Worcester, Massachusetts

Bellevue, in twelve states

Wooster, Ohio

Bellview, New Mexico

Matawan, Minnesota and New Jersey

Bellvue, Colorado

Matewan, West Virginia

Belvue, Kansas

Mattawan, Michigan

Belview, Minnesota

3. Names that are sometimes one word but other times two words:

Bel Air, Maryland   Eldorado, in nine states
Bellaire, in four states   La Fayette, in eight states
El Dorado, in two states   Lafayette, in nine states

4. Names in which just the terminations are spelled differently; as:

a. Burgh, burg, and *berg:*
     Pittsburgh, Pennsylvania
     Pittsburg, in nine states
     Newburgh, New York and Indiana
     Newburg, in nine states
b. Ton and *town:*
     Charleston, South Carolina, and in fourteen other states
     Charlestown, in four states
     Charles Town, West Virginia
c. Mor, more, and *mour:*   *d. Mount* and *mont:*
     Dunmor, Kentucky   Fairmount, in seven states
     Dunmore, Pennsylvania   Fairmont, in seven states
     Seymour, Connecticut   Fair Mount, Georgia

5. Names that are properly hyphenated; as:

Wilkes-Barre, Pennsylvania   Winston-Salem, North Carolina

The following names may be called the geographical spelling demons.

Albuquerque	Des Moines	Passaic	Somerset
Asheville	Duquesne	Paterson	Terre Haute
Chattanooga	Eau Claire	Phoenix	Tucson
Cheyenne	Frederic	Prescott	Vermilion
Chillicothe	Gloucester	San Luis Obispo	Wethersfield
Cincinnati	Greenwich	Sioux City	Xenia
Conshohocken	Lorain	Skaneateles	Ypsilanti

A final warning—watch for those names that are duplicated in several states. Some of the most frequently duplicated names are:

	No. of States		*No. of States*
Chester	27	Madison	26
Clayton	23	Marion	28
Clinton	28	Springfield	25
Glenwood	20	Troy	27
Lincoln	23	Washington	27

Also, a vast number of post offices are duplicated in the same state, but with a differentiating *North*, *East*, etc. For example, in Massachusetts there are:

Newton	Newton Lower Falls
Newton Center	Newton Upper Falls
Newton Highlands	Newtonville
West Newton	

Foreign Geographical Names. The names of a vast number of foreign cities are spelled one way in the country itself and another way in English. The United States Geographic Board recommends that the conventional English form be used for the names of *countries*, to facilitate the handling of mail by the postal clerks in the United States up to the time that the mail is loaded on the proper steamer. It also recommends that the names of *cities* be written in the language of the country to which the letter is going, to assure promptness of handling when the letter reaches its destination. Consult *Webster's Geographical Dictionary* for the correct spelling of foreign geographical names.

A few of the more important alternative spellings are:

English Spelling	*Official Name*
Berne, Switzerland	Bern
Beirut, Syria	Beyrouth
Cologne, Germany	Köln
Constantinople, Turkey	Istanbul
Florence, Italy	Firenze
Lisbon, Portugal	Lisboa
Lucerne, Switzerland	Luzern
Milan, Italy	Milano
Moscow, U.S.S.R.	Moskva
Naples, Italy	Napoli
Seville, Spain	Sevilla

Section 4. YOUR USE OF GRAMMAR

In order to write a clear, concise letter, the writer must know the correct use of grammar. Good writing depends on the correct use of English. Your employer expects you to know the rules of grammar and to apply them when you transcribe or write letters.

This section presents the most common errors in sentence structure. The rules are illustrated by examples to show the application. When

you are on the job, however, a standard English grammar or reference manual should be on your desk for ready reference. Keep in mind that you are developing the ability to use correct English, so that the reader will get the message you want him to have.

For definitions of the grammatical terms used in the following rules, as well as for more detailed explanations of the rules, see any standard English grammar, such as those listed in Unit 6.

Subject and Verb. A verb must agree with its subject. Often singular verbs are incorrectly used with plural subjects, or plural verbs are used with singular subjects. The most common reasons for these errors are:

1. The real subject of the sentence is not recognized because an expression containing a word different in number from the subject occurs between the subject and the predicate.

> *Wrong:* The cause of the errors that the new bookkeeper makes *are* his carelessly written figures.
>
> *Right:* The cause of the errors that the new bookkeeper makes *is* his carelessly written figures.

2. The correct number of a collective-noun subject is not recognized. If the group is thought of as acting as a body, the subject is singular; if acting individually, plural.

> *Right:* The committee *is* preparing its report.
> *Right:* The committee *are* all able men.

Expressions of quantity when denoting a definite part are usually singular.

> *Right:* Five dollars *is* too high a price for this hat.
> *Right:* Two times three *is* six.

When fractions are followed by *of* and a singular noun, they are considered as being singular; when followed by *of* and a plural noun, they are considered as being plural.

> *Right:* One-half of the time *was* well spent.
> *Right:* Three-fourths of the girls *were* promoted.

3. The correct number of singular subjects connected by conjunctions is not recognized. Study the six following rules and the illustrations given:

a. Two or more singular subjects connected by *and* take a plural verb.

> *Right:* A new pen and a better quality of ink *are* necessary for this work.

b. Two or more singular subjects joined by *or* or *nor* take a singular verb.

> *Wrong:* Neither he nor she *are* able to go.
> *Right:* Neither he nor she *is* able to go.

c. If one of the subjects joined by *or* or *nor* is singular and the other plural, the verb agrees with the nearer subject.

> *Wrong:* Either one large file drawer or two smaller ones *is* all right.
> *Right:* Either one large file drawer or two smaller ones *are* all right.

d. When the subject consists of two singular nouns joined by *and* and both nouns denote the same person or thing, the verb should be singular.

> *Right:* The secretary and treasurer (meaning one person holding both offices) *was* reading *his* report when the explosion occurred.

e. When the subject consists of two singular nouns connected by *and* and preceded by *each, every, many,* the verb should be singular.

> *Right:* Each name and address in the mailing list *is* correct.

f. The connectives *with, together with, as well as, including* do not affect the number of the subject.

> *Right:* The report, with its addenda, *is* enclosed.
> *Right:* The silk, as well as the lace, *was* delivered in poor condition.
> *Right:* The paragraph, including the headings, *is* to be copied once.

4. Foreign plurals are often not recognized as plurals. (For a list of the most commonly used words having foreign plurals, consult any standard grammar.)

> *Wrong:* The data *indicates* the seriousness of the condition.
> *Right:* The data *indicate* the seriousness of the condition.

5. The fact that some nouns end in *s* in the singular, and hence require a singular verb, is overlooked.

> *Right:* The news *is* encouraging this morning.
> *Right:* Mathematics *has* always been difficult for me.

Right: Politics *interests* him greatly.

6. It is forgotten that *there is* precedes a singular noun and *there are* a plural noun.

Wrong: There *is* too many children for this game.
Right: There *are* too many children for this game.

7. The verb is often erroneously made to agree with the predicate noun instead of with the subject of the sentence.

Right: The chief feature of this edition *is* the attractive cuts.

Mixed Tenses. Three primary tenses are used to indicate *present, past,* and *future* time. Also, three secondary tenses are used to indicate the action or being as *completed* in *present,* in *past,* or in *future* time. Some of the most frequent errors in mixing tenses are given below. Study the illustrations that follow the statement of the rule.

1. Do not use the simple past tense when the perfect is required.

Wrong: I *filed* the correspondence already.
Right: I *have* already *filed* the correspondence.

2. If a narrative is interrupted to refer to a preceding event, the past perfect tense should be used.

Wrong: In his files he kept a collection of advertising copy that he *found* effective.
Right: In his files he kept a collection of advertising copy that he *had found* effective.

Wrong: The clerk *worked* three days before his exact duties were established.
Right: The clerk *had worked* three days before his exact duties were established.

3. Keep a proper relationship between the tense of the verb in the main clause and the tense of the verb in any dependent clause and infinitive.

a. When the subordinate clause expresses a statement that is permanently true, the verb should be in the present tense, even though it follows a verb in the past tense in the main clause.

Wrong: He said that Federal income tax returns *were* due March 15.
Right: He said that Federal income tax returns *are* due March 15.

Wrong: I have always understood that a man's home *was* his castle.
Right: I have always understood that a man's home *is* his castle.

b. An infinitive should be in the present unless it indicates action preceding the action of the main verb.

Wrong: It was wrong for you *to have said* that.
Right: It was wrong for you *to say* that.

4. Conditions contrary to fact or doubtful; wishes; and motions, resolutions, votes of thanks, and similar formal statements are expressed in the subjunctive mood. *Be* and *were* are almost the only subjunctive forms used.

Contrary to fact: If Mr. Ames *were* here, the matter could be settled at once.
A wish: I wish I *were* old enough to hold the position.
In a motion: I move that the sentence *be stricken* from the record.

Troublesome Verbs. In the following paragraphs your attention is called to some of the most troublesome verbs. Review the rules for their correct usage, and study the illustrations.

1. *Shall* and *will* (*should* and *would*).

a. To announce a mere future action or state, use *shall* and *should* with *I* or *we*.

I *shall* be glad to attend to the matter.
I *should* prefer a blue dress.
We *shall* soon celebrate the fiftieth anniversary of the founding of our business.
We *should* appreciate hearing from you soon.

but use *will* and *would* with *you, he, she, it, they.*

You *will* receive the shipment Friday.
You *would* be better off at home.
He *will* accompany his father to the Coast.
He *would* like to go tomorrow.
They *will* be disappointed in your failure.
They *would* never agree to that.

b. To represent a promise, willingness, determination, desire, threat, prophecy, and emphatic assurance, use *will* or *would* with *I* or *we.*

I *will* meet you at ten o'clock. (Determination.)
I *will* go if it does not rain. (Promise.)

We *will* start suit at once. (Threat.)
We *would* never agree to that. (Emphatic assurance.)

but use *shall* or *should* with *you, he, she, it, they*.

You *shall* have the position as soon as it is vacant. (Promise.)
It *shall* be done as you request. (Determination.)
They *shall* be punished for this negligence. (Threat.)
He *should* have the book if he wants it. (Determination.)

c. In *questions*, always use *shall* or *should* with *I* or *we*, whatever meaning is intended.

Shall I close the window?
Should I go by train or by bus?
Shall we join with our competitors in contributing to the Community Fund?
Should we verify the time of the arrival of the plane?

But with *you, he, she, it,* or *they*, use the word that is expected in the answer.

Shall you take your vacation in July? (The answer expected is, "I shall.")
Will he be here soon? (The answer expected is, "He will.")
Shall he be required to pay a deposit? (The answer expected is, "He shall.")

2. Don't and *doesn't.* As *don't* is a contraction for *do not*, it must not be used with a subject in the third person singular. Use *doesn't*.

Wrong: He *don't* like mathematics.
Right: He *doesn't* like mathematics.

3. May and *might; can* and *could. May* and *might* imply permission; *can* and *could* imply ability or power.

Can this watch be repaired? (Ability.)
I *could* start immediately. (Ability.)
May I leave half an hour early today? (Permission.)
He asked whether he *might* go early. (Permission.)

4. Sit and *set. Sit* does not take an object; *set* does.

Please *sit* here.
Please *set* the vase on the table.

The principal parts of these verbs are:

Present	Past	Past Participle
sit	sat	sat
set	set	set

5. *Lie* and *lay*. *Lie* does not take an object; *lay* does. There are two *lie's*—one meaning to utter a falsehood; the other, to recline.

> To *lie* is a confession of weakness.
> I am going to *lie* down a few minutes.
> *Lay* the book on the table.

The principal parts of these verbs are:

Present	Past	Past Participle
lie (falsify)	lied	lied
lie (recline)	lay	lain
lay (place)	laid	laid

6. *Rise* and *raise*. *Rise* does not take an object; *raise* does.

> Gentlemen *rise* when ladies enter a room.
> Please *raise* the window shade.

The principal parts of these verbs are:

Present	Past	Past Participle
rise	rose	risen
raise	raised	raised

7. *Learn* and *teach*. *Learn* means to acquire knowledge; *teach*, to impart it to others.

> I plan to *learn* shorthand next year. Miss Bancroft will *teach* me.

8. *Affect* and *effect*. *Affect* means to influence; *effect*, to cause. *Effect* is also a noun, meaning result or outcome.

> International developments *affect* the stock market.
> We hope to *effect* a settlement next week.
> The stormy weather had a bad *effect* on attendance at the concert.

Pronouns Incorrectly Used. Frequently, errors are made in the use of pronouns. The stenographer or secretary is expected to produce transcripts that are grammatically correct even though the dictator may have made errors in the dictation. You will find the eleven rules concerned with incorrectly-used pronouns an excellent review.

1. *Each, every, everyone, everybody, anybody, either, neither, no one, nobody* are singular. Pronouns referring to these words must be singular in form.

> *Wrong:* Everybody must hold *their* own ticket.
> *Right:* Everybody must hold *his* own ticket.
>
> *Wrong:* Neither of the applicants brought *their* references along.
> *Right:* Neither of the applicants brought *his* references along.

2. *Who* and *whom*. An expression inserted between *who* and its verb does not change the case of the pronoun.

> *Wrong:* The truck driver *whom* they thought was to blame for the accident was innocent.
> *Right:* The truck driver *who* they thought was to blame for the accident was innocent.

3. The object of a verb or of a preposition must be in the objective case.

> *Wrong:* Thank you for the welcome to Mr. Smith and *I*.
> *Right:* Thank you for the welcome to Mr. Smith and *me*.
>
> *Wrong:* He greeted Mr. Jones and *I* cordially.
> *Right:* He greeted Mr. Jones and *me* cordially.
>
> *Wrong:* There has always been a close friendship between you and *he*.'
> *Right:* There has always been a close friendship between you and *him*.
>
> *Wrong:* Some of *we* girls gave her a present.
> *Right:* Some of *us* girls gave her a present.

4. A pronoun that is the subject of a verb must be in the nominative case, even when the verb is understood.

> *Wrong:* Charles is older than *him*.
> *Right:* Charles is older than *he* (is).

5. Two pronouns or a pronoun and a noun connected by any form of the verb *to be* are in the same case, as *to be* does not take an object.

> *Wrong:* It is *me*. Was it *him*?
> *Right:* It is *I*. Was it *he*?
>
> *Wrong:* They proclaimed the winner to be *she*.
> *Right:* They proclaimed the winner to be *her*.

6. A pronoun that refers to a collective noun should agree with the noun in number.

The committee is preparing *its* report.
The committee are not in agreement in *their* opinions.

7. A pronoun that refers to words connected by a conjunction should be singular or plural depending on whether the nouns denote the same person or thing or different persons or things.

The indexer and cataloguer has a large stack of books on *his* table.
The credit manager and the advertising manager have enlarged *their* offices.

8. Guard against using a singular pronoun when it refers to a noun that has a foreign plural form.

The analyses were helpful because of *their* illustrations.

9. A pronoun referring to a singular noun ending in *s* should be singular.

The news is serious in *its* implications.

10. Avoid uncertain reference of pronouns.

Confusing: As soon as the dress comes from the store, hang it on a hanger.
Better: As soon as the store delivers the dress, hang it on a hanger.
Poor: The stenographer's letters often contained errors in spelling, which irritated her employer.
Better: The stenographer's habit of misspelling words irritated her employer.

11. Avoid the intensive pronouns *myself*, etc., unless they are necessary.

Wrong: The comptroller and *myself* will attend the lecture.
Right: The comptroller and *I* will attend the lecture.

Confusion in Adjectives and Adverbs. Six rules to avoid confusion in the use of adjectives and adverbs are given below. Study the illustrations carefully.

1. The modifier following a verb should be an adjective if it describes the subject of the sentence; an adverb if it qualifies the verb.

The process is designed to keep the paper *smooth*. (Describes the condition of the paper.)
The attachment will run the paper through *smoothly*. (Refers to the manner of operation.)

2. A verb that refers to one of the senses, as *taste, smell, look, seem, hear,* usually requires an adjective because the word describes the subject. But if the word describes the verb, an adverb should be used.

> She *looks beautiful* in that gown.
> She looked *carefully* before crossing the street.
> The tainted meat tasted *bad.*
> She tasted the candies *daintily.*
> The radio sounds too *loud.*
> The echo sounded *clearly* across the lake.

3. Some adjectives and adverbs cannot be compared because they are absolute in meaning, as:

always	nearly	round	unanimous
complete	perfect	square	unique
final	perpetual	supreme	wrong
ideal	right		

4. Avoid incomplete comparisons.

> *Faulty:* Stocks are *higher* today.
> *Complete:* Stocks are *higher* today *than* they were yesterday.

5. In comparing one person or thing with the group to which it belongs, the word *other,* as well as the comparative form of the adjective, must be used.

> *Wrong:* Our spring materials are prettier than *any* materials in the city.
> *Right:* Our spring materials are prettier than *any other* materials in the city.

6. An article should be repeated before each noun of a series unless all the nouns refer to the same person or thing.

> *Wrong:* We shall need a letter tray, dating machine, and letter opener.
> *Right:* We shall need a letter tray, a dating machine, and a letter opener.
> *Right:* The aim and purpose of the plan is as follows:

Position of Words. Another indication of poor writing is evident when the position of words is incorrect. Note the illustrations in the three rules in this paragraph.

1. An adverb should be placed as near as possible to the word that it modifies. Notice the difference in meaning in the following sentences.

We only shipped two gross.
We shipped two gross only.
I do not think I shall go.
I think I shall not go.
Do you ever remember seeing him?
Do you remember ever seeing him?

2. An adverb should not be placed between an infinitive and *to*.

Wrong: It is better to *carefully* check each list typed.
Right: It is better to check *carefully* each list typed.

3. Words, phrases, and clauses should be so arranged that there is no doubt about what they modify.

Wrong: When properly oiled and cleaned, no one will consider this type-writer hard to use.
Right: No one will consider this typewriter hard to use when it has been properly oiled and cleaned.
Wrong: The shipping clerk gave the express package to the expressman that was to be sent today.
Right: The shipping clerk gave the expressman the package that was to be sent today.

Miscellaneous. Two other common grammatical errors are called to your attention in this paragraph.

1. Double negatives. The use of two negatives in a sentence results in an affirmative.

Wrong: I can't find no time to do it.
Right: I can find no time to do it.
Wrong: He won't try nothing.
Right: He won't try anything.
Wrong: I couldn't hardly stand it.
Right: I could hardly stand it.
Wrong: They didn't own only one typewriter.
Right: They owned only one typewriter.

2. *Like* and *as* or *like* and *as if*. *Like* takes an object. It should not be used to introduce a subject and a verb. *As* and *as if* may introduce a subject and verb.

Wrong: He does *like* he pleases.
Right: He does *as* he pleases.
Right: This looks *like* a good investment.

Section 5. YOUR PUNCTUATION

Proper punctuation helps to make the meaning clear to the reader. Rules for using the various marks of punctuation are given in this section; study the illustrations given in order to use the punctuation marks correctly.

The Comma. The comma is the most frequently used mark of punctuation. Its purpose is to insure that the meaning of the sentence is absolutely clear to the reader. Some writers and dictators use commas profusely. There are many instances, however, when the comma is essential to the clarity of the sentence. For example:

> Mr. Holley reports the Evanston store is first in total volume of sales for the past year.
> Mr. Holley, reports the Evanston store, is first in total volume of sales for the past year.

The meaning of these two sentences is changed by the use of the comma.

Below are ten rules for the correct usage of the comma. Note carefully the illustrations.

1. Use a comma before the conjunctions *and, but, or,* or *nor* in compound sentences if the second clause is complete with subject and predicate.

> The store will be officially opened today, and we are expecting a large crowd.
> For years we have occupied this site, but we are moving to larger quarters.
> Please send your remittance immediately, or we shall take legal action.
> We cannot send you a new coat, nor can we credit your account.

Exception. If the clauses are very short, the comma may be omitted.

> The door was closed and the shades were drawn.

2. Do not use a comma between independent clauses not joined by a conjunction. Use a period or a semicolon:

> You are the general manager. You are not a salesman.
> You are the general manager; you are not a salesman.
> Our company manufactures locks. We are equipped to supply hardware to dealers in all parts of the country.

Our company manufactures locks; we are equipped to supply hardware to dealers in all parts of the country.

3. Use the comma to set off subordinate, or dependent, clauses and adverbial phrases, especially when they precede the main clause:

Because you have such excellent references, we will place you in our correspondence department immediately.

Although your notebooks are of fine quality, we cannot place an order now.

In answer to your request of June 10, we are sending you a new price list.

If you will call at our office on Thursday, your papers will be ready for you.

4. A nonrestrictive clause (a clause that adds descriptive facts about the antecedent, but that can be omitted without changing the meaning of the main clause) is set off by commas.

Mr. Stewart, who called on you yesterday, is very enthusiastic about your sales for the past year.

That beautiful gold watch, which he valued because of its association, was stolen last night.

He is studying at the state university, where a greater variety of courses is offered than at _____ College.

5. A participial phrase should be set off from the main clause by commas.

Being a close friend of the manager, Mr. Ames could not tell the entire truth.

The man was discharged, indicating that he was not competent to hold the position.

Passing the school the other day, I noticed two new statues at the entrance.

6. Parenthetical elements—that is, expressions neither logically nor grammatically necessary to the structure of the rest of the sentence —and introductory expressions should be set off by commas. These elements may be words, phrases, or clauses.

It will be necessary, therefore, to send another shipment.

Moreover, we cannot extend you further credit.

The stenographer, of course, should be ready for dictation.

We shall all be there, to be sure.

This car, I am convinced, is the best buy at that price.
This material, it is said, will stand rough wear.

7. Words, phrases, or clauses used in apposition should be set off by commas.

Our president, Mr. John Briggs, has the interests of all his employees at heart.

Last July, the month of our annual sale, our profits were far beyond what we had anticipated.

The new ruling, that all employees shall receive three weeks' vacation, will go into effect this summer.

8. Use a comma before the conjunction connecting the last two elements—words, phrases, or clauses—in a series of three or more.

Our department needs more stationery, pencils, and pens.

This summer I am going to the mountains, to the seashore, or on a boat trip.

Mary is majoring in French, Helen is planning to teach commercial subjects, and Edith will do social work.

9. Use commas to set off contrasted words, phrases, and clauses.

She emphasizes the use of clauses, not phrases, in her article.

This salesman, as always, made an excellent record during the past year.

Mr. White was given a different position, not because he had not done his work well, but because he deserved a promotion.

10. A comma is used to separate parts of a sentence that might erroneously be read together.

Most of the members whom I have talked to, do attempt the test.

Whatever you wish, you may have.

Inside, the house was aglow with warmth and friendliness.

A month before, the man could not have given a donation.

The Semicolon. The semicolon is used when the parts of a sentence need a stronger mark of separation than the comma.

1. The semicolon is used to separate two co-ordinate clauses in a compound sentence:

a. Where the conjunction is omitted:

Send our order immediately; we cannot wait any longer.

He is not entirely to blame; the fault is partly yours.

b. When the clauses are connected by transitional expressions:

Please supply the necessary information; otherwise, we cannot discuss the matter intelligently.

c. When either clause contains a comma or commas:

We shall be glad to consider your application; but, as we interpret your records, you have not had sufficient experience.

2. Use a semicolon before an expression that introduces an explanation or an enumeration. Such expressions should always be followed by a comma.

Three states are included in Mr. Anderson's territory; namely, New York, New Jersey, and Pennsylvania.

A great deal of work must be done before you can give the speech; for example, you must read many articles on the subject.

A great many subjects are taught in the commercial course; such as shorthand, typing, bookkeeping, commercial law, business mathematics, and secretarial training.

3. When such items as names and addresses, commodities and their prices, persons with their offices, etc., are arranged in paragraph form, the items should be separated by semicolons, the data within the items being separated by commas.

The officers elected for the ensuing year are: President, Edward Hayes; Vice-President, Frank Donnelly; Secretary-Treasurer, Clyde Brown.

The chairman appointed the following members for the entertainment committee: Robert Stafford, 98 Main Street; Leroy Noble, 164 Ives Avenue; and Howard Aldrich, 273 West Street.

The grocer quoted the following prices: butter, a pound, 79 cents; eggs, a dozen, 80 cents; milk, a quart, 25 cents.

The Period. The following rules govern the most common uses of the period.

1. The period is used at the end of a complete sentence that makes a statement, issues a command, or makes a request.

The date of your birthday has been included in the report.
Tell him that you cannot attend the meeting on August 25.
Will you please send us a copy of the budget.

2. An abbreviation is followed by a period; however, only one period is used if the abbreviation comes at the end of the sentence.

D. W. Arnold (initials in a name)
Please ship the order to Mr. Cansler by express, C.O.D.

3. A period is used to separate a whole number from a decimal fraction; as 12.8%, $14.92.

4. To indicate omissions of words from quoted matter, three or four periods are used, as follows:

Miss Farrelly suggests you dine at "The Pantry" . . . fine food . . . sizzling steaks . . .

5. The period is used after a number or a letter that indicates a division in an outline (*exception:* unless the figure or letter is enclosed in parentheses). For example:

I. Business Books
   1. Secretarial Practice
      a. Author
      b. Publisher
         (1) and so on

Note: The period is not used in the following cases:
   (*a*) After roman numerals, unless used with numbered items.

      Vol. VIII   Chapter X
      Louis XIV   I. Punctuation Marks

(*b*) After display heads.

UNIT III
SECONDARY SCHOOLS AND COLLEGES

(*c*) After items in a tabulated list.

The following persons are members of the group:
   Doris L. Howell
   Don Calame
   Floyd Crank
   Janet Helsel

The Colon. The colon may be thought of as a mark of introduction. It is used in the following cases:

1. To introduce enumerations or concrete illustrations of a general statement.

The secretarial curriculum includes the following courses: shorthand, typewriting, business English, bookkeeping, and office practice.

2. After the words *following, in the following manner, thus, these, two, three.*

> The officers of the club are three:
> President
> Secretary
> Treasurer

3. To introduce long quotations.

> Before Mr. Cox left for the meeting, he said: "I am going to ask Mr. Gerfen, one of the outstanding members of the faculty, to be the main speaker at our next convention."

4. After the salutation in business letters.

> Dear Mr. Herndon: Dear Sir:

5. In expressions of time, in proportions, and in literary references, as follows:

> He leaves on the 7:55 train every morning.
> U.S.C. is a 2:1 favorite in next Saturday's game.
> Hagar, H. A., Marie M. Stewart, and E. Lillian Hutchinson, *The English of Business*, Second Edition. New York: The Gregg Publishing Division, McGraw-Hill Book Company, Inc., 1948.

The Dash. It is sometimes desirable to use a stronger mark of punctuation than the comma, the semicolon, or the colon. In such cases, the dash is used.

1. The dash can show a break or an abrupt change in thought.

> I asked if my purse had been found—and it was there.

2. The dash is used to give emphasis to parenthetical expressions.

> Margaret felt sure of a promotion—though promotions were unusual at that season—because of her excellent work during the conference.

3. Use the dash before credits at the end of quoted matter.

> The business of being a consumer is as important as your pocketbook.
> —*The Consumer's Economic Life.*

4. The dash may be used after run-in sideheads.

> Chief Advantages of the Plan.—There are seven advantages that result. . . .

5. The dash is used to show omissions of letters or figures.

Please report a Miss S— was seen in the vicinity.

6. The dash is often used in sales letters to introduce a summary of particulars.

Here's today's best automobile buy—beauty, speed, economy!

The Exclamation Point. You may use an exclamation point (!) after a word, phrase, or sentence expressing emotion, surprise, command, or irony. It should be used sparingly in business correspondence. A number of examples are given below.

The sign at the railroad crossing read: Stop! Look! Listen!
Congratulations! You have been awarded first prize!
Keep Off the Grass! This means you!

Quotation Marks. Quotation marks are used in the following instances:

1. Enclose the exact words of a speaker or a writer in quotation marks.

The office manager said, "Please type this report in triplicate."

2. The titles of articles and plays are always enclosed in quotation marks. Book titles are enclosed in quotation marks only in typewritten matter that is not to be set up in type. If material is to be sent to the printer for type setting, the titles of books are underscored; this indicates to the printer that the titles are to be italicized.

Have you seen the play, "South Pacific"?

3. Words with special interpretations, humorous words, objectionable words, slang, etc. are enclosed in quotation marks.

We feature several ever-popular "oldies" on our program.

4. Words used aside from their original meaning are enclosed in quotation marks.

First transcribe all letters marked "Rush."

5. Indicate technical words and trade names by enclosing them in quotation marks.

The next step in the process is "justifying" the line.

6. If the quotation consists of more than one paragraph, use quotation marks at the beginning of each paragraph and at the end of the last paragraph.

> "It was a peculiar incident," the old man said. "I was a witness to the whole thing.
>
> "It all happened within a few minutes, but I have remembered it all my life."

7. Commas and periods are *always* placed inside the closing quotation marks.

> "I was there for an hour," she replied.
>
> The name of the play is "Lost in the Stars."

8. If there is a quotation within another quotation, use single quotation marks for the inside quotation.

> The credit manager said, "I suggest that you add the following sentence, 'We must hear from you before December 1.' "

9. The question mark is placed inside the closing quotation mark if only the quoted matter is a question; outside, if the entire sentence is a question.

> What is the meaning of the word "memorandum"?
>
> The teacher asked, "What is your typing speed?"

10. The semicolon and the colon are always placed outside the closing quotation mark.

> The following points were covered in the talk on "Your Health": diet, sleep, exercise, cleanliness.
>
> First he read a chapter from his book, "You and Your Life"; then he asked for our opinions.

The Question Mark. 1. The question mark (?) is used at the end of a direct question.

> What are the duties of a secretary?
>
> You will come with him, won't you?

2. Use a question mark after each question in a series in the same sentence, as:

> Where are the receipts for the barrel of apples? the box of pears? the lug of plums?

3. Use a question mark, enclosed in parentheses, to express doubt or uncertainty, as:

> His explanation (?) was supposed to be a plausible one.
> She gave her age as 21 (?).

The Parentheses. There are two main uses of parentheses:

1. Enclose in parentheses letters, words, or expressions that are independent of the main thought of the sentence.

> A majority of the members (about 60 per cent) were in favor of the motion.

2. Enclose in parentheses letters or numerals that accompany enumerated items.

> Please send carbon copies to the following persons: (1) Harry R. Price; (2) Eldred C. Speck; (3) James F. Giffin.

The Apostrophe. 1. The apostrophe (') is used to indicate the possessive case of nouns.

> The handle of the president's brief case was broken.

2. Use the apostrophe to show omission of letters in contractions.

> Don't leave before one o'clock.

3. Use the apostrophe in typing a quotation mark within another quotation.

> The announcement read: "All mail must be deposited in the 'Outgoing Box' before 4 p.m."

Section 6. YOUR USE OF CAPITALIZATION, ABBREVIATIONS, AND FIGURES

Capitalization. Words are capitalized for emphasis and for clarity. Below are seven basic rules of capitalization, with illustrations of each.

1. Names of the days of the week and the months of the year should always be capitalized, seasons of the year only when they are personified.

> He came back to work on Monday, April 15.
> The snow on the mountains is beautiful in the winter.
> Welcome, sweet Spring!

2. Capitalize proper nouns and proper adjectives.

George	Elizabethan	English	Delaware Water Gap
American	French	Catskill Mountains	Christian
Italy	Hindu	Pike's Peak	

3. Descriptive words that have come to be used as substitutes for proper names or are affixed to proper names should be capitalized.

Swedish Nightingale   Bloody Mary
Holy Writ   Alexander the Great
the Pretender   the Father of our country

4. Words that were originally proper names, but that have developed specialized meanings, should not be capitalized.

roman type   india ink
arabic numeral   manila hemp
paris green   china clay
plaster of paris   pasteurized milk
german silver   brussels sprouts

5. The first word and any titles in a salutation should be capitalized.

Dear Sir: Dear friend John:
My dear Sir: Very Reverend and dear Father:
My dear Friend: Your Excellency:

6. Only the first word in a complimentary closing should be capitalized.

Most cordially yours   Yours very sincerely   Yours truly

7. Capitalize all words except articles, conjunctions, and prepositions in the titles of books, newspapers, pamphlets, documents, periodicals, proceedings, reports, plays, music; divisions of books; subjects of lectures, sermons, paintings; headings of paragraphs, tables, and charts.

Salesmanship for Everybody
Good Housekeeping
Part III. Transportation in the West
Developing Your Personality
Now Is the Time to "Wake Up and Live"! (a speech)
Table VI. Supply and Demand of Most-Used Commodities

Abbreviations. In general, use abbreviations sparingly.

1. Preferably, spell out all titles before personal names except *Mr.*, *Mrs.*, *Messrs.*, and *St.* The title *Doctor* is abbreviated to *Dr.* when a name includes the given name or initials but is spelled out when only the surname appears.

Dr. William L. Crump	Mr. John W. Rau, Jr.
Dear Doctor Charles:	Mrs. Hazel Faulkner

2. Academic degrees, names of religious orders, and such designations as *Esq.*, *Jr.*, and *Sr.* following a personal name should be abbreviated.

James A. Anderson, Ph.D.   Mr. Paul Clifford, Jr.

3. Names of firms should be written in the style which the company uses.

Charles Ilfeld Company	Marshall Field & Company
J. H. Smythe Co.	Pennsylvania Railroad

4. Names of *associations*, *societies*, and *railroads* are often abbreviated. Usually, the spaces between the letters of such abbreviations are omitted; and many times the periods are omitted.

Y.M.C.A.	Young Men's Christian Association
N. E. A.	National Education Association
TVA	Tennessee Valley Authority
A.T. & S.F.	Atchison, Topeka, and Santa Fe

5. The names of *months* should be spelled in full; also, names of *cities*, *states*, *provinces*, and *countries*, even in the addresses on envelopes.

November 2, 1953	Las Vegas, New Mexico
Paris, France	Maywood, Illinois

6. *Street*, *Avenue*, *Place*, and similar designations in names of thoroughfares should be spelled out.

3256 Hartzell Street	2504 Central Park Avenue
333 South Michigan Boulevard	3222 Park Place

7. Abbreviate B.C. and A.D. when these designations are used with year dates; a.m. and p.m. when time is expressed in figures; and *No.* when followed by a number.

456 B.C.	12:01 p.m.	No. 5907
A.D. 1492	8:30 a.m.	

8. Spell out names of common *weights*, *measures*, and *dimensions*.

13 dozen	1 quart	80 degrees
9 cubic feet	6 inches	1,206 miles

9. No period should follow the individual letters in names of *radio* and *television* stations and *chemical symbols* and *formulas*, because these are not true abbreviations; also no period should follow *IOU*, *SOS*, or *ordinals*.

WOR   WGN-TV   Na (sodium)   H (hydrogen)

10. Consult the dictionary for abbreviations.

Use of Figures. In business letters, numbers are often written in figures. A number written in figures is quickly seen by the reader. *Figures* are used to express numbers in the following instances:

1. Write all exact numbers above ten in figures.

There were 16 salesmen at the meeting.

2. If a sentence contains more than one number, write *all* numbers, including those under ten and round numbers, in figures.

She asked for 16 pencils, 2 erasers, and 10 envelopes.

3. Always use figures for all numbers in statistical and tabular work.

$$\begin{array}{r} 2,614 \\ -407 \\ \hline 2,207 \end{array} \qquad \begin{array}{r} 6 \\ +2 \\ \hline 8 \end{array} \qquad 30 \div 6 = 5$$

4. Use figures for the day of the month and the year, house numbers, street names with numbers over ten, and postal zone numbers.

January 16, 1952	East 177th Street
2449 Marcy Avenue	Atlanta 14, Georgia

5. Exact time and an age given in years, months, and days are expressed in figures:

His plane is due at 11:10 a.m.   35 years 3 months and 5 days old.

Note: Commas do not appear in expressions of age, measurements, etc., consisting of several words because the item is considered a single unit.

6. Amounts of money, decimals, percentages and proportions, and weights and measures are written in figures:

> $101.50   10 cents $6   4 francs.   The booket cost $1.50.
> 12.5   0.44   216.897.   The average attendance was 76.4.
> The interest rate will be 4 per cent.
> 5 feet 4 inches   106 pounds   180 degrees Fahrenheit

7. Literary references are expressed in figures:

> Volume I   Unit VI   Section 8   pp. 99-102
> Chapter IX   Column 9   page 37   Article 3
> Appendix II   Figure 5   No. 4   Chart 13

Words are used to express numbers in the following cases:

1. Write out numbers below and including ten when the numbers appear individually in a sentence.

> There are six members in our family.

2. Write out numbers that begin a sentence.

> Five hundred sixteen students are enrolled.

3. Write out round or indefinite numbers.

> It is expected that about three thousand accidents will occur within the next six months.

4. Write out ordinal numbers, except in certain technical work.

> She will take a trip around the world after her eighteenth birthday.

5. Amounts of money in legal documents, followed by the figures in parentheses, are written out.

> The property was sold for ten thousand dollars ($10,000).

6. Spell out fractions standing alone.

> We have had only about one-half of the normal rainfall.

Some Highlights of This Unit

1. To increase your knowledge both of the business and of the technique of letter writing, observe your executive's letter-writing technique and read the many excellent books on business letter writing.

2. Make use of form paragraphs and form letters where the correspondence in your office admits of such uniformity in reply.

3. All good letter writers observe the following fundamentals in writing their letters: (*a*) plan their letter, (*b*) write from the reader's point of view, (*c*) keep their own personality out of routine letters, (*d*) are brief, courteous, positive, (*e*) use pleasant words, (*f*) paragraph wisely, (*g*) use correct grammar, (*h*) make their first sentence count, (*i*) close their letter effectively.

Questions and Items for Discussion

1. Name some types of letters that a secretary may be asked to compose.
2. What information must you be sure to include in your letter when you have been asked to make an appointment for someone to see your employer?
3. What information must you be sure to include in your letter when it is necessary to acknowledge a letter received in the absence of your employer?
4. What will be the correct procedure for you to follow when your employer hands you several valuable business papers and tells you to mail them to Mr. So-and-So?
5. What are the features of a formal invitation that distinguish it from the usual business correspondence?
6. Describe the uses of form paragraphs or form letters in business correspondence.
7. Name and describe the fundamentals of good letter writing.

Personality Questions and Projects
(Based on Personality Pointer, page 127)

1. Your employer is an attorney who has his own office. Just after lunch he told you, "Be sure to remind me to get through those papers in the Benson case; they have to be mailed on the 5:15."

A few minutes later, an old college friend of his came into the office, and they have been having a reunion ever since. You can hear shouts of laughter from the boss's private office. It is Attorney Whelan's own affair how he spends his time, but it is your affair to see that the Benson papers go out. At half past three you reminded him, and he put you off. It is now four o'clock, and those papers will take time to dictate and type.

Choose from the following list the most persuasively worded reminder you can make to Mr. Whelan.

a. "My goodness, Mr. Whelan, when are you going to settle down and get some work done?"

b. "Mr. Whelan, it's four o'clock."

c. "We have just time to get out the Benson papers if we start right now. You wanted them to go on the 5:15."

d. "If you put the Benson papers off any longer, I can't get them done on time."

2. You and Roy Webster are both employed, at the same pay, in the same department. You came into the organization at the same time. The head of the department tells you, "Make three copies of this at once; Roy Webster can stop what he's doing and help you with it."

Choose from the following list what you would say to Roy Webster. Remember you are not his superior, but you have to get the work done.

a. "Will you help me type this?"

b. "You'll have to stop what you're doing and help me. Start typing at the top of this page."

c. "Mr. Farnsworth asked me to tell you that you and I are to get out this job together and that you can stop the job you are on now."

d. "Mr. Farnsworth says you will have to help me with this typing."

3. A new employee has been assigned to help you in her spare time. You must keep her good will, or you may find that she never has any spare time when you have work for her to do. You discover her typing for Mr. Blake, one of the company's salesmen, who gave her some letters although he has no authority to do so. You need her, too.

Choose from the following list the most persuasive way to tell her to do your rush work first.

a. "Will you prepare this copy for the printer, Miss Bowers, as soon as that letter is done? I'll explain to Mr. Blake."

b. "You'll have to stop Mr. Blake's work and go on with this. You shouldn't have accepted any work from him, anyway."

c. "Can't you do my work first and then explain to Mr. Blake later?"

d. "Why didn't you ask me before you started that? Put it aside and go on with this copy for the printer."

Secretarial Assignments

1. Mr. Martin expects to arrive in Chicago on a New York Central train at 9 o'clock in the morning (Central Standard time) on the first Friday of next month. He wishes to discuss certain matters with Mr. Leroy Bedford, a sales representative of the Acme Corrugated Carton Company, before he has to leave Chicago on another train at 1:45 p.m. of the same day. Write to Mr. Bedford, whose office is at 421 South Wabash Avenue, Chicago, asking him to arrange to meet Mr. Martin at 10:30 a.m. in the Chicago office of United Products Corporation. Refer to a calendar for the correct date on which the meeting is to take place. Use Sheet 22 in your Workbook.

2. Mr. Martin will be unable to keep his appointment with Mr. Bedford, because he has had to change his plans and does not know when he can go to Chicago. You happen to know that Mr. Martin is going to Washington to give expert opinion on certain phases of an important labor dispute; also, that he expects to see his brother-in-law, who is in the Federal Bureau of

Investigation. You will, however, avoid giving such information as this to anyone. Write to Mr. Bedford, breaking the appointment and asking him to let Mr. Martin know when he expects to be in New York. Use Sheet 23 in your Workbook.

3. Mrs. J. W. Anderson, who won a prize of $100 in a recipe contest that United Products Corporation sponsored some months ago, wrote your chief, Mr. Martin, on Friday of last week, asking for six copies of a four-color poster on which her winning recipe was featured. Mrs. Anderson lives at 422 North 39th Street, Milwaukee, Wisconsin.

In Mr. Martin's absence, acknowledge the letter, which you are sending at once to the manager of your Chicago office, because Milwaukee is in the territory served by that branch. Use Sheet 24 in your Workbook.

4. Write a letter of transmittal to the manager of your Chicago office, to accompany Mrs. Anderson's letter. (Refer to the preceding assignment.) Mention that it has been the policy of the New York office to accede to such requests because of the good will involved. Each branch manager can make his own decisions on matters like this, however; therefore, do not give the Chicago office any definite instructions about how to proceed. Use Sheet 25 in your Workbook.

5. Mr. Martin has just received the following formal invitation to a reception for the national president of a charitable organization to which he has contributed generously.

To meet
Mr. J. Wentworth Dobbs, III
The New York Chapter
of
Youth Resources
requests the pleasure of your company
on Monday, the twenty-third of February
at four o'clock
at Youth Resources House
121 West Ninth Street

Write a formal acceptance of this invitation for Mr. Martin. Use the monarch-size personal letterhead provided in your Workbook, Sheet 26.

6. The following letter received from a customer of your firm is a shining example of the trite, repetitive letter sometimes produced, even in these days of efficiency, by rather pompous letter writers of the "old school."

Dear Mr. Martin: The writer begs to state that his attention has just been called to your letter of the 14th inst. about a discount of $7.20

that we took the liberty of deducting when recently remitting for a purchase of your valued goods made on the 15th ult.

The total amount of the invoice was $360; and our check, less the discount, was drawn in the amount of $352.80.

It appears to the undersigned that your company is only too willing to enforce a technicality in attempting to deprive us of this discount, in the face of the fact that we have spent thousands of dollars in the past ten years in dealing with your concern. Beg to advise that your attitude is extremely displeasing to the writer; and unless you see fit to allow this discount, we will be forced to take steps to immediately sever our business relations with you.

It is true that the date of the invoice was November 15 and that our check was not mailed until the seventh day of the month immediately following. This was purely an oversight on the part of someone in the employ of the undersigned, and a review of former transactions between your company and ours will serve to indicate to you without a shadow of doubt that it has always been our custom to discount bills according to the terms of sale. In the case under consideration at the present moment, our cashier had the misfortune to be in the hospital; and a number of unpaid bills accumulated and piled up that otherwise would have been paid and taken care of within the customary ten-day period. The bill in question was one of this group.

The writer takes this opportunity to state, in addition, that your company is the only one out of about fifty that has attempted to arbitrarily deprive us of this discount; also, that the undersigned establishment can buy plenty of watches, equal in quality to yours, from competitors in your line of business who are willing and able to meet a customer halfway—and who have come to realize that at all times there exist just exceptions to any business rule.

In closing, the writer would say that if your company continues to insist on payment of the amount in question, a check will be mailed by the undersigned firm; but we beg to add that it strikes us as a small amount to cause the severing of business relations between us.

Hoping to hear from you favorably at your earliest convenience, we remain, Yours truly,

You can omit many unnecessary words and phrases and overworked, meaningless expressions in this letter. Make your revision go right to the point of each sentence, without changing the thought of the original letter. Be careful to correct the two split infinitives that have been included. Use of the third person ("the writer" or "the undersigned") is not in the best literary taste. A man with sufficient authority to write a letter of this kind

can surely dare to identify himself as "I." Type the revised letter on plain paper.

Optional

7. Write a formal note of regret for Mr. Martin, who has a previous engagement for the date on which the reception mentioned in Assignment 5, page 181, is to be held. Use Sheet 27 in your Workbook.

8. Write a letter congratulating Mr. Ward P. Parker, for the past twenty years vice-president in charge of sales for the Appleton-Cromwell Manufacturing Company, on his election to the presidency of his firm. Mr. Martin, who will sign this letter, knows Mr. Parker very slightly; he read about the advancement in the *New York Times*. Mr. Parker's company is a leading customer of United Products Corporation. Use Sheet 28 in your Workbook.

9. Mr. Martin has been elected national president of the Associated Office Managers, a position of considerable honor and great responsibility. He will receive a great many letters of congratulation. You are to write a form letter that can be used to answer them. Use Sheet 29 in your Workbook.

10. Mr. Henry Webster is editor of the *Mercantile Man*, a trade journal to which Mr. Martin has contributed articles about business management. This morning you called Mr. Martin's attention to a news item reporting that Mr. Webster had been taken to Shady Knoll Hospital as the result of an automobile accident. Prepare, for Mr. Martin's signature, a short letter expressing sympathy. Attach to it a note from you to Mr. Martin suggesting the names of two recent books that you think Mr. Webster might like to read. Mr. Martin asked for your suggestion because he is considering sending a gift to Mr. Webster. Use Sheet 30 in your Workbook.

11. A user of one of your company's products, Mrs. Walter F. Baker, has written the following letter, which is more notable for its confusion than for any other characteristic. Persons who write letters hurriedly, without arranging their thoughts in logical order, often produce such letters as this.

Gentlemen: I wish to report an experience I have just had in view of your wide advertising of the mildness of your soap flakes and the safety with which the most delicate fabrics may be washed with them, including wool.

I have a light-tan flannel dress and I washed it in lukewarm water and your flakes and it is ruined and won't you explain how it happened? I have used your soap flakes for washing other fabrics. Now it is quite ruined and I have generally had good results and I am distressed because faded spots are distributed all over the entire surface of the dress, which I noticed when I came to press it.

You advertise that they are safe and I can't understand how this hap-

pened and I am very upset. So please tell me how I can get a new dress out of your company. Yours truly,

Your assignment is to revise this letter, so that it will state the case clearly and intelligently. Mrs. Baker's address is 645 Fourth Avenue West, Seattle, Washington. Use plain typing paper.

12. Your instructor will dictate a letter from the Busy Bee Gifte Shoppe and some information about it. You are to compose a reply to this letter. Use Sheet 31 in your Workbook.

13. Mr. Alexander Formsby, a member of the Board of Directors, passed away last night. Mr. Martin has asked you to prepare a memorial resolution for presentation at the next meeting of the Board of Directors. Mr. Formsby was a civic leader and especially active in the Community Chest organization of White Plains, where he resided. He was also a member of the Rotary Club of White Plains and of the Manhattan Mid-Town Executives Club. He is survived by his wife, Mrs. Edith Formsby; two children, Alexander, Jr., and Mrs. J. Kent Atwell, of Bronxville, New York; his mother, Mrs. Anna L. Formsby, of Little Rock, Arkansas; and a sister, Mrs. Thomas Johnston, of Philadelphia, Pennsylvania. Prepare a suitable resolution, following the style given in your Workbook on Model Form 2.

Spelling Demons

corridor	defendants	deliberately
criticism	deferred	development
cylinder	delegate	diphthong

Job Tips

1. Never do rough-draft work on good stationery. Use scrap paper or some inexpensive paper.

2. When you assume the responsibility for composing a letter, be sure you check (and recheck if necessary) the accuracy of each piece of work.

3. In letter writing, remember that "eye" appeal is an important factor.

4. When writing letters of complaint or grievance, do not use the direct "you" attitude. Keep your statements impersonal.

Personality Pointer

WATCH YOUR MANNER . . . ISMS!

Any peculiar or odd habits of movement, of bearing, or of speech make you conspicuous and place you in an unfavorable light as compared to others.

Only rarely, and in exceptional cases or under special circumstances, is a mannerism deliberately acquired. Actors and actresses intentionally cultivate mannerisms to portray a character part. Comedians make expert use of this affectation, so much so that the mannerism becomes an identifying characteristic.

But for you, a secretary, to take on a mannerism is annoying and irritating to your employer and to those with whom you come in contact.

Meaningless gestures distract attention from the thought you are expressing in speech; toying with jewelry and jingling money interfere with the thought others are trying to express to you; unhappy personal mannerisms do not endear you to your co-workers; grimacing is less than attractive. Affectations usually indicate a measure of conceit, not refinement.

Remember, the best indication of a well-poised secretary is the quiet, unobtrusive, pleasant manner with which you carry out your responsibilities.

Undesirable Personal Habits

1. Sniffing, smacking lips, coughing needlessly, humming, singing, sucking air through teeth, talking to oneself, muttering, making exasperated comments

185

2. Chewing pencil points, finger nails or cuticle, gum, candy
3. Constantly brushing, stroking hair or scratching head
4. Blinking eyes, pulling nose or ear, squinting, stroking chin, grimacing
5. Picking off chipped nail polish
6. Working your foot up and down while taking dictation
7. Ripping paper out of typewriter, slamming down books, papers, and pencils when irritated

Undesirable Social Habits

1. Using expressions such as "swell," "un-huh," "okeydoke," etc.
2. Using and disposing of handkerchiefs or cleansing tissue carelessly and untidily
3. Blowing smoke in another's face
4. Drumming with the fingers, pencil, etc.
5. Taking shoes off during office hours
6. Talking and laughing too much and too loud; giggling
7. Gushing and being overly enthusiastic about simple things
8. Being overbearing about duties and responsibilities

Handling the Mail

Every business constantly seeks ways to do its work faster, better, and at a lower cost. Numerous opportunities to improve the efficiency and decrease the costs of operating the office are offered in the handling of mail.

This unit is divided into four sections, all directly concerned with the efficient and economical handling of mail. You will learn practical ways to handle and to improve the routines concerned with the mail that comes into and goes out from the office. As a secretary, you should have a thorough knowledge of mailing procedures and postal regulations.

The secretary's duties in the smaller offices may include the entire routine from opening the incoming letters to dropping the outgoing letters into a mail box. In the larger organizations, however, the central mailing desk or department takes care of the opening and distributing of the incoming mail and of the collecting, folding, sealing, weighing, and stamping of the outgoing mail.

Section 1. INCOMING MAIL

You now know that the size and the type of the business will determine the procedures used in handling the incoming mail. The general routine is to sort, open, date, check enclosures, classify, route, and distribute the incoming mail.

The Mailing Department. When there is a special mailing department, the incoming mail, which comes into the office in an almost endless stream throughout the day, goes directly to that department

187

Courtesy Pitney-Bowes, Inc.

This electrically operated letter opener cuts off a narrow edge of the envelope and automatically drops the opened letter into the tray at the right side.

to be sorted. The mail clerks send letters addressed to specific departments or persons to them immediately by messengers, who make frequent deliveries of mail throughout the offices. The mail clerks then open the remaining mail, classify it, sort it for various purposes, and deliver it to the proper departments as speedily as possible.

Mail in quantity is usually opened by a mechanical letter opener. This machine strips off a narrow edge from each envelope as the envelopes are fed to the machine by the operator.

Handle Mail with Dispatch. If there is no separate mailing department, and you are the one who receives and distributes the mail, organize your duties so that all the different kinds of mail will be handled with dispatch.

With the exception of the letters marked "Personal" and those marked for the attention of a designated person, official, or department, all mail should be opened and read. Inspect each letter as it is

opened, and see that the enclosures mentioned in it are attached to the letter. If any are missing, note this fact on the letter. When signatures or the return address are missing, attach the envelope to the letter, as the return address may be the means of identifying the writer. In some offices, the practice is to attach envelopes to the letters when important data are missing in the letter. In the case of important documents, the date of mailing may be a valuable item of information, as well as such facts that the letter was sent special delivery, registered, or by air mail.

Before you throw any envelopes away, hold them up to the light to make sure that all enclosures have been removed.

Date and Route Mail. It is important to date all incoming mail. If the letter is to be noted by several persons in the office, stamp it with a rubber stamp. Another method is to attach a "route slip," bearing the names of persons or departments, to the letter. Then place a check mark or a figure against the proper names, to show how the correspondence is to be routed.

In many concerns, the time element is so important that the time, as well as the date, is stamped on incoming mail. An electric clock-dating stamp is used for this purpose (see page 190). Be sure to place the impression of the clock or the rubber dating stamp where it will not render other writing illegible.

If the correspondence indicates that something is being sent under separate cover, record this fact on a special "under separate cover" form. Record exactly what is to come later, so that you can recognize the item when it is received or follow it up if it is not received within a reasonable time.

If you have opened mail by mistake, reseal the envelope with mending tape and write on it plainly, "Opened by mistake."

Your Executive's Mail. Your executive will probably wish his mail placed on the desk in the following order:

1. Telegrams and reminders of appointments for the day
2. Personal mail
3. Regular mail
4. Advertisements
5. Magazines and newspapers

In other words, arrange mail according to its importance, placing the most urgent matters on top, so that they will receive immediate attention.

If other persons have access to the executive's office, a space for his mail should be provided inside his desk; or he should have a mail folder where correspondence may be placed for his attention without risk of its being seen by persons who may come into his office.

If you have been authorized to open his mail and answer part of it, do so according to the procedure already outlined. Letters marked "Personal" of course should always be given him unopened. As you

This machine stamps the "Received" stamp with time and date shown below.

RECEIVED
JOHN WILLIAMS CO.
NEW YORK CITY
JUN 10 7 57 AM

ATT...................................
ANS. ....

Courtesy Simplex Time Recorder Company

open the letters, place in one group those that you will be expected to answer; in another group, those that your executive will answer; and in a third group, all letters that concern other departments. Documents, reports, etc., should be attached to the letters accompanying them. The disposition of mail of an advertising nature, which ordinarily is extensive, will depend on your employer's wishes.

If a letter relates to previous correspondence that is necessary to an understanding of the whole situation, this correspondence should be taken from the files and attached to the letter just received. When correspondence is taken from the file, be sure to prepare an "out card" to take its place in the file. (See illustration on page 359.)

You will be able to answer many of the letters that are of a routine nature, as discussed in Unit 7. Prepare these letters promptly and place them on your employer's desk for signature. If you are permitted to sign these routine letters, your employer may wish to see the carbon copies so that he will know what disposition was made of the various matters.

You may be instructed, on occasions, to sign letters dictated by your employer. If so, sign his name and place your initials below the signature.

Section 2. OUTGOING MAIL

The usual routine procedures for handling outgoing mail are to collect it, check and insert enclosures, fold it, seal the envelope, weigh it, affix the stamps, and finally dispatch it.

Where a business organization has a central mailing desk, a messenger makes the rounds of the office at regular intervals throughout the day, making the last pickup about one hour before closing time. He collects the mail from the "out" boxes in each department and takes it to the central mailing desk. In such a setup, the secretary's connection with outgoing mail stops after she has folded and inserted letters and enclosures in envelopes and put them in the out box.

In some business houses, the procedure is to have mail picked up unfolded and without enclosures, the person at the mailing desk folding and making the proper enclosures from notations on the letters. Mail of a confidential nature is handled according to special instructions issued by the executive concerned.

Your Duties before Releasing the Mail. It is your responsibility, before releasing correspondence for the mailing desk, to check carefully to see that you have

1. Typed the addressee's name and address correctly on both letter and envelope
2. Addressed extra carbon copies to the proper persons
3. Referred to a key number or department number in the letter if such reference is requested in the original correspondence
4. Made proper notations on letters calling for enclosures and noted that all enclosures are in the envelope
5. Placed stamps sent as a remittance in a wax-paper envelope
6. Transferred to carbon copies whatever corrections were made in the original letter, and any other notations required for guidance in completing the transaction
7. Typed labels for bulky materials to be sent under another cover
8. Placed your initials below the employer's signature, if you have signed the letters for your employer
9. Typed, in all capital letters, on the envelope the notation "Special

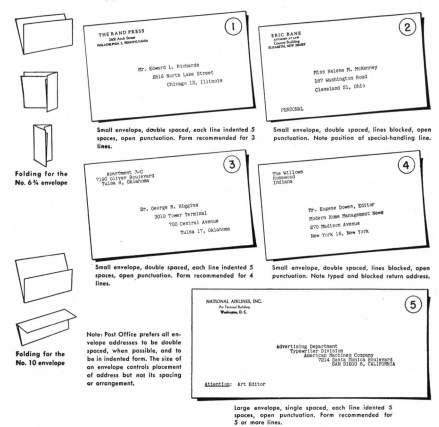

Folding for the No. 6¾ envelope

Folding for the No. 10 envelope

(1)

THE RAND PRESS
2600 Arch Street
PHILADELPHIA 3, PENNSYLVANIA

Mr. Edward L. Richards
2516 North Lake Street
Chicago 13, Illinois

Small envelope, double spaced, each line indented 5 spaces, open punctuation. Form recommended for 3 lines.

(2)

ERIC BANE
ATTORNEY AT LAW
Cowery Building
ELIZABETH, NEW JERSEY

Miss Helene M. McKenney
187 Washington Road
Cleveland 21, Ohio

PERSONAL

Small envelope, double spaced, lines blocked, open punctuation. Note position of special-handling line.

(3)

Apartment 3-C
7190 Oliver Boulevard
Tulsa 8, Oklahoma

Dr. George R. Higgins
3010 Tower Terminal
700 Central Avenue
Tulsa 17, Oklahoma

Small envelope, double spaced, each line indented 5 spaces, open punctuation. Form recommended for 4 lines.

(4)

The Willows
Homewood
Indiana

Mr. Eugene Dowes, Editor
Modern Home Management News
270 Madison Avenue
New York 16, New York

Small envelope, double spaced, lines blocked, open punctuation. Note typed and blocked return address.

(5)

NATIONAL AIRLINES, INC.
Air Terminal Building
Washington, D. C.

Advertising Department
Typewriter Division
American Machines Company
7214 Santa Monica Boulevard
SAN DIEGO 8, CALIFORNIA

Attention: Art Editor

Note: Post Office prefers all envelope addresses to be double spaced, when possible, and to be in indented form. The size of an envelope controls placement of address but not its spacing or arrangement.

Large envelope, single spaced, each line idented 5 spaces, open punctuation. Form recommended for 5 or more lines.

Recommended styles for typing small and large envelopes and correct method of folding letters to fit these envelopes.

Delivery," "Registry," "Air Mail," "Personal," or "Confidential" if any of these special services or handling is desired

10. Marked foreign mail with the notation "Foreign" in the corner where the stamp is to be affixed

11. Marked the envelope with the notation "Attention of . . . . ." if the letter is addressed in that manner

12. Sealed all letters marked "Personal" or "Confidential"

Folding and Inserting Letters. Study the proper method of folding letters and inserting them in small, large, or window envelopes as illustrated on this page. Window envelopes do not require addressing, but mail must be folded so that the address is visible through the window. Be sure all creases are straight and free from smudges. Extra

precautions should be taken by those whose hands have a tendency to perspire.

Sealing Envelopes by Hand. It is recommended that you spread about ten envelopes at a time on the mailing table so that only the gummed flaps are exposed. Then run a moistener over the flaps.

With the right hand, palm facing down, pick up one envelope at a time; pass it on to the left hand, address side against the left thumb and flap down against the palm of the hand, and seal the flap by simply closing the left hand. This operation is repeated, and the envelopes accumulate in the left hand until the unit of ten is finished.

Courtesy Pitney-Bowes, Inc.

A popular scale for weighing mail, particularly air mail.

Weighing Mail. Many popular types of postal scales are used for computing postage on mail. The one pictured on this page is used particularly for air mail.

After the mail has been sealed, sort out and weigh those pieces that seem to be over the 1-ounce limit. Small pencil notations showing the amount of postage required should be made in the corner where the stamp is to be affixed. Postal regulations are discussed in Section 4.

Affixing Stamps. Stamps may be affixed to envelopes by hand, or by a mechanical stamp affixer, or a postage meter machine may be used.

Stamps may be affixed by hand quickly in the following manner. Moisten a complete strip of stamps by drawing the moistener, with one stroke, across the strip. Affix the stamp with the right hand and press it down with the left, at the same time tearing the stamp loose from the strip with the right hand and moving the envelope along with the left hand to expose the next envelope to be stamped.

The hand stamp affixer shown on page 194 is filled with 3-cent

stamps, the amount required on the greater part of the mail. The machine moistens and affixes a 3-cent stamp every time the plunger is depressed. Stamps for odd amounts can be applied by hand.

Precanceled Stamps. Precanceled stamps in various denominations may be purchased for parcel post and circular mailing, but not for first-class mailing. Mail with precanceled stamps affixed does not have to go through the regular canceling routine at the post office. This saves time in delivery.

Courtesy Goldsmith Brothers

Hand stamp affixer.

Automatic Mailing Machines. If the office is equipped with a postage meter machine such as the one shown on page 195, the job of mailing is, of course, greatly simplified. This machine prints postage on the envelope and postmarks and seals it, all in one operation. At the throw of a lever, the machine will print postage on a gummed tab for affixing to packages. The machine can also be adjusted to print a slogan or other advertising message next to the postage mark.

Postage can be printed by this machine in any denomination and for any size, weight, or class of mail, including air mail, special delivery, and other special mail. With a machine of this type, the necessity of buying stamps in many denominations is eliminated. Before the machine can be used, a portable meter must be detached from the machine, taken to the post office, and set for the amount of postage desired, say for $100 or $1,000. Payment for postage is usually made by certified check payable to "Postmaster (Name of Town)." Two visible registers on the machine show in dollars and cents the amount of unused postage on hand, and the amount used to date. The latter register facilitates record keeping and the control of postage.

Automatic mailing machines are extensively used. Recent figures released by the United States Post Office Department reveal that one out of every five letters is dispatched by this means. These machines come in various models, operated by hand or electricity, and require no special skill to operate. Some models can stamp, seal, and stack as many as 250 letters a minute.

An automatic mailing machine eliminates the possibility of stamps becoming detached in transit. As the machine postmarks when it prints the postage, it is unnecessary, just as with precanceled stamps, for the post office to cancel each piece of mail. It also enables the

This desk model postage meter is very popular in small firms. By dialing the stamp value wanted and pressing a lever, this meter prints postage of any value, complete with dated postmark and, optionally, the user's own advertising message. It accounts for postage used and postage on hand in visible, dollar-and-cents registers. A moistening mechanism permits sealing of envelope flaps, and a detachable unit takes care of parcel post postage.

Courtesy Pitney-Bowes, Inc.

office to control its stamp supply and helps eliminate the use of company stamps for personal letters.

Section 3. VOLUME MAILING

Many firms maintain large mailing lists as an integral part of their operations. Frequently these lists consist of the names and addresses of all customers and prospective customers. The lists may be compiled by the firm itself—by its salesmen or by the office force. Mailing lists of all kinds may also be purchased from firms that specialize in this field.

Mailing Lists. Directories of all kinds, membership lists of organizations, school lists, tax lists, newspaper clippings, and the like, are general sources from which names and addresses may be obtained to build mailing lists.

Mailing lists are not of much value unless they are kept up to date. A duplicate set of the names in a mailing list is usually run off on 5-by-3 cards for this and other purposes and filed in the most convenient way. The information necessary for keeping lists up to date may be supplied by the company's own salesmen or obtained from

other sources. Corrections, additions, or eliminations should be made promptly. Every letter or piece of advertising matter that is returned by the Post Office should be checked with the mailing list to see whether a mistake was made. If no error was made, and there is no way of finding the proper address, the card and the stencil should be removed.

In large firms and shipping rooms, this electrically operated, hand-fed postage-meter machine is used. It seals, stamps, and postmarks all classes of mail.

Courtesy Pitney-Bowes, Inc.

Mailing lists may be kept on file cards, on embossed metal plates, or on stencil address plates. When a mailing list consists of more than a thousand names, the use of embossed or stencil plates facilitates the addressing of sales and other promotional literature. The Elliott addressing machine and the Addressograph are high-speed addressing machines pictured here and discussed in the following paragraphs.

Elliott Addressing Machine. Stencil address plates for the Elliott may be prepared on a regular typewriter with the help of a small attachment; thus, the impression obtained from these stencils resembles a typewritten impression.

The stencils are loaded into an addressing machine. The stencils feed automatically into the machine; but the operator must feed the envelopes, wrappers, cards, or tags into the machine and remove them by hand. After the stencils have passed the printing mechanism, they fall back into the tray in the proper order. In the most up-to-date

models, like the one illustrated here, the envelopes and address cards are also fed into the machine automatically.

By punching holes at various points on the rim of the stencil, it is possible to select for printing certain stencils out of the entire list. An attachment on the addressing machine, corresponding to the holes on the stencils, selects the stencils desired for printing, passing the others without making an impression.

This addressing machine automatically feeds envelopes and address cards. It addresses these from the stencils, like the one shown, prepared on a typewriter.

Courtesy Elliott Addressing Machines

It should be mentioned that stencil plates are not usually used to insert names and addresses on forms that should give the appearance of having been typed.

The Addressograph. Permanent metal plates are used with the Addressograph machine for addressing and form-writing work. A metal section is embossed on the electric typewriter keyboard Graphotype machine shown on page 198 and is inserted in a frame that also holds a full index-card imprinted from the embossed section. Classification tabs provide automatic selection of plates as they pass through the addressing machine, so that forms, envelopes, magazines, and mailing pieces may be selectively addressed. Sixty direct classifications and thousands of combinations are available from these tabs, which may be quickly changed.

All Addressograph machines, whether manually or electrically operated, imprint names and addresses through a ribbon. The electrically operated model shown in the illustration on page 199 may

be equipped with an automatic form feeder to address 100 envelopes or mailing pieces per minute. The same machine may also be used for writing other forms, such as payrolls and statements.

Quantity Typing of Envelopes. Frequently, envelopes have to be addressed to a short mailing list that will not be used often enough to

Electrically operated Graphotype with typewriter keyboard. The insert shows the metal address plate, with tabs, embossed by this machine. These plates are filed in the trays at the right-hand side of the machine.

Courtesy Addressograph-Multigraph Corporation

warrant the cutting of address stencils. In this case, type the envelopes.

You can save time and motion, when addressing envelopes in quantity, by inserting a blank envelope and removing a typed envelope at one operation. As soon as you have completed the typing on the envelope you are addressing, insert a blank envelope. As the blank envelope is turned into the machine, the completed envelope will fall out. This procedure—known as chain feeding—saves much time in highly repetitive work of this nature, though it eliminates but one motion.

Section 4. POSTAL INFORMATION

Offices should keep on file the latest *Postal Bulletin,* issued by the United States Post Office, showing changes made in the classification of mail or the rates of postage. These bulletins may be obtained from the local post office. A copy of the latest edition of the *Official Postal Guide* is an absolute necessity in every mailing department. It may

be obtained from the Superintendent of Documents, U. S. Printing Office, Washington 25, D. C.

Air Mail. The swiftest means of carrying letters, securities, perishables, and other merchandise requiring speedy delivery, is the airplane. The greater the distance, the greater the saving in time when air mail is used. The rate on domestic as well as foreign air mail should be ascertained from the local post office. Special air-mail stamps are available, but ordinary stamps may be used if desired.

Air mail comes under the same classifications as ordinary mail, namely: first class, second class, third class, and fourth class.

Air mail may be sent by special delivery, if stamps to cover special-delivery charges, in addition to the air-mail stamps, are affixed. Air mail may also be insured, registered, or sent C.O.D.

Stamped envelopes, carrying a distinctive

Courtesy Addressograph-Multigraph Corporation

The metal address plates, embossed by the Graphotype, are fed into this electrically operated Addressograph, which stamps the addresses on the envelopes.

red-white-and-blue design, may be obtained at the post office. If an ordinary envelope is used, mark it plainly "Air Mail" or use a red-white-and-blue strip. Air mail may be posted in any street letter box, mail chute, or at the post office.

The regulations regarding the classification of mail, as well as postage rates, frequently undergo changes. Your local post office will be able to supply the latest and most up-to-date information on rates. This section, therefore, will not give postal rates or other information

that is subject to frequent change. The four domestic mail classifications, each taking different rates of postage, and the common special services of the Post Office will be discussed.

First-Class Matter. First-class mail includes handwritten or typewritten matter, carbon copies, letters, postal cards, private mailing cards, and all matter partly or wholly in writing, whether sealed or unsealed. A partial list of articles included in first-class mail follows: (*a*) assessment notices, printed, with amount due written therein; (*b*) bills or statements of account produced by any photographic process; (*c*) cards or letters, printed, bearing a written date, which is different from the date of mailing; (*d*) certificates, checks, receipts filled out in writing; (*e*) price lists, printed, containing written figures changing individual items; (*f*) receipts with written signatures; (*g*) unsealed written communications; (*h*) manuscripts, handwritten or typed, unaccompanied by proof sheets thereof;

Courtesy New York Central System

Mail being sorted in the mail car of a train.

(*i*) stenographic or shorthand notes; autograph albums containing writing.

Second-Class Matter. Second-class matter includes newspapers and periodicals bearing notice of entry as second-class matter. No limit of weight is prescribed. The publisher of a magazine pays a special pound rate determined by a periodic, geographic analysis of his entire mailing list. He must file this analysis with the post office whenever requested.

Third-Class Matter. Third-class matter includes printed circulars,

books, catalogues, merchandise, miscellaneous printed matter, and all matter (except first-class and second-class) weighing less than 8 ounces. Facsimile copies of handwriting or typewriting reproduced by a mechanical process—as by the printing press, Mimeograph, Ditto, Multigraph—are treated as third-class matter, provided such copies are presented for mailing at the post-office windows, or other depository designated by the postmaster, in a minimum number of twenty identical unsealed copies. If mailed elsewhere, or in smaller number, they will be subject to the first-class rate. Furthermore, proof-sheets containing corrections and instructions to the printer, manuscripts accompanied by printer's proof, letters and reading matter for the blind including sound reproduction records and Braille writers, merchandise, seeds, bulbs, and plants may be sent as third class when mailed in packages weighing up to and including 8 ounces.

Fourth-Class Matter. Fourth-class mail is known, popularly, as "parcel post" and is used extensively for the shipment of packages weighing from 8 ounces up to 40 pounds. (See pages 427-28.) Fourth-class matter includes all mailable matter in third class weighing more than 8 ounces and not included in first- or second-class matter.

Special Services. The Post Office offers several special services to speed up and insure the safe delivery of mail. These special services are: special delivery, registered mail, and insured mail. The rates for these special services are in addition to the regular postage rates.

Special Delivery. All classes of mail may be sent by special delivery. Special-delivery service is the prompt handling, transportation, and delivery of mail by messenger. All special-delivery mail must be handled and transported in the same manner as first-class mail.

Insured Mail. Third- and fourth-class (parcel-post) matter, mailed at, or addressed to, any post office in the United States and its possessions, may be insured against loss, rifling, or damage. The maximum amount of insurance is $200. The insurance fees are based on the value of the article being sent and rise on a graduated scale with the valuation.

Registered Mail. The registry system provides special safeguards for the transmission of money and other valuable mail to domestic destinations. All mailable first-, second-, and third-class matter for domestic destinations may be registered if the registry fee, in addition to the required postage, is paid.

Return Receipts. A return receipt for registered or insured mail may be obtained on payment of a small fee. The parcel must be marked "Return Receipt Requested."

C.O.D. Fees. Third- and fourth-class matter and sealed matter of any class bearing postage at the first-class rate may be sent C.O.D. be-

tween money-order offices of the United States. The maximum amount collectible on a single C.O.D. article is $200. Consult the *Official Postal Guide* for further information on this service.

Tracing Mail. Mail that does not reach its destination at the expected time may be traced by filling out a form supplied by the Post Office Depart-

In some areas, it is convenient for the Government to use postal busses in addition to railroads.

ment. In general, an attempt to locate a lost unregistered letter or document is futile when no return address is given.

Consult the Postal Authorities. When in doubt as to postal regulations, take your problem to your local post office. The employees or officials there will be glad to help you. If they cannot answer your question, they will write to headquarters in Washington, D. C., to get a ruling.

If, for example, your organization is planning to sponsor a contest, it is most advisable to have some authority at your local post office read all the details and rules of the contest. He will help you frame your specifications so that they will comply with Government regulations.

Some Highlights of This Unit

1. Letters addressed to specific departments or persons are sent to them directly by the mail department; the remaining mail is opened by the clerks, classified, sorted, and delivered to the proper departments as speedily as possible.

2. Inspect each letter to see that enclosures mentioned are attached; if they are not, note that fact on the letter.

3. In some instances it is well to note on the letter such facts as date of mailing (from the envelope), special delivery, registered, or air mail.

4. All communications must be stamped with the date of their receipt and the hour of receipt.

5. Stamps may be affixed to envelopes by hand, by a mechanical stamp affixer, or by using a postage meter machine.

6. Automatic mailing machines are used extensively. They print the postage on the envelope, postmark and seal it.

7. Mailing lists may be compiled by the firm using them, or they may be purchased from firms that specialize in this field. They may be kept on file cards, on embossed plates, or on stencil address plates.

8. The Elliott addressing machine and the Addressograph are types of high-speed addressing machines.

9. Chain feeding of envelopes into the typewriter saves time.

10. The latest edition of the *Official Postal Guide* should be available for use wherever a quantity of mail goes out daily.

Questions and Items for Discussion

1. Explain the use of the routing stamp on incoming mail. Why is it necessary that the mail clerks be well informed regarding the responsibilities of the various departments of the business and be acquainted with the duties of various executives?

2. How can you assist your employer in taking care of his mail efficiently?

3. What are the routine procedures for handling outgoing mail?

4. Name the four classifications into which domestic mail is divided. What is the source of information for the regulations that govern these classifications? Who should be consulted when there is doubt regarding postal regulations?

5. Imagine yourself as a secretary in an office that has no central mailing department. Outline the procedure you would follow in order to facilitate the handling of incoming mail.

6. What provision should be made to check on the receipt of matter being sent under separate cover?

7. What special mailing services does the Post Office provide?

Personality Questions and Projects
(Based on Personality Pointer, page 185)

1. Name actors, actresses, comedians, and other well-known personalities who have identifying characteristic mannerisms.

2. List annoying mannerisms that you have noticed among your acquaintances.

3. Do you have annoying mannerisms?

Thursday

Secretarial Assignments

1. Calculate the amount of postage required for mailing each item listed on Sheet 32 of your Workbook. Fill in the amounts in the Postage column and give the class in which each item belongs.

2. If you have kept all the letters you have transcribed thus far, practice the folding and inserting of these letters in envelopes and sealing the envelopes. After the envelopes have been sealed, figure the postage on each one and write the amount in the upper right-hand corner of the envelope. Follow carefully the procedure illustrated in this text for handling outgoing mail.

3. Use the sealed mail accumulated in the preceding assignment for practice in handling incoming mail. Open the envelopes, check enclosures carefully, clip the envelope to the letter, and stamp the opening time on each letter. If you do not have access to a time stamp, use a small hand dater or write the time in longhand.

4. List several articles that cannot be shipped by mail.

5. The head of the Shipping Department will dictate a letter to you. Use Sheet 33 in your Workbook.

6. There are several efficient methods of sealing and stamping first-class mail. Ask three or four of your office-worker acquaintances how they handle the matter; then make a report.

Optional

7. Ascertain the following rates:
   a. First-class postage to Hawaii. Air mail to Hawaii. Air express on 1 pound to Honolulu from your own city.
   b. First-class postage to Mexico. Air mail to Mexico. Air express on 1 pound to Mexico City from your own city.
   c. First-class postage to Canada. Air mail to Canada. Air express on 1 pound to Quebec from your own city.
   d. First-class postage to Brazil. Air mail to Brazil. Air express on 1 pound to Rio de Janeiro from your own city.
   e. First-class postage to France. Air mail to France. Air express on 1 pound to Paris from your own city.

8. You have instructions to forward first-class mail to your chief during his absence. What would you do with the following pieces of mail?
   a. A letter from a firm on your street, with a 3-cent stamp on it
   b. An advertisement with no stamp, left with your receptionist
   c. Two magazines

   d. A heavy catalogue

   e. A letter from Cleveland, Ohio, with a 3-cent stamp on it

   f. A long envelope, rather thick, on which the prepaid cancellation does not state the amount of postage paid. One end of the envelope is tucked in, not sealed.

   g. A government postal card with 2-cent postage

  9. If you were working in the Mailing Department, what would you do with the following pieces of mail?

   a. A letter addressed to a former employee of the firm whose present address is not known to you

   b. A catalogue addressed to an executive of your firm who is now permanently in your Chicago office

   c. A 3-cent stamped envelope addressed to the same man

   d. A monthly magazine addressed to the same man

   e. An air-mail letter addressed to your firm, marked for the attention of a man whose name is unknown to your Personnel Department

   f. A registered letter addressed to the president of the company, marked "Deliver to addressee only"

   g. A registered air-mail letter addressed to your chief, who can be reached through your Boston office

 10. A number of letters will be dictated to you.

Spelling Demons

dirigible	elimination	evidently
disease	eminent	exhaust
dissatisfied	enrollment	exhibition

Job Tips

1. Be sure to indicate special handling, air mail, special delivery, etc., below the identification data in the letter, as well as on the envelope.

2. If your office does not supply you with a staple remover, purchase one of your own. It is efficient, and it is easy on your temper and fingers.

3. When forwarding mail over an extended period to the same addressee, number the envelopes so that the addressee can know if he has received all of them. Some offices make note of the contents of each numbered envelope in case one should be lost in the forwarding process.

4. Do not delay opening mail that comes to your desk. Such delay slows up business activity.

5. Return incorrectly delivered mail promptly to the postal authorities.

6. Unmailed Government envelopes or Government postal cards that have been misaddressed or damaged may be redeemed at your post office.

Personality Pointer

CAN YOU BE DIPLOMATIC?

In business, as in personal affairs, the ability to get along with your fellow workers, your superiors, and others with whom you come in contact, is a recognized "must."

In the everyday sense we call this ability *tact;* in the larger sense, it is *diplomacy*. Webster says tact "implies delicate and sympathetic perception of what is fit or considerate in dealing with others."

Your ability to do or say the appropriate thing is of immeasurable value to you. Haven't you at some time experienced the satisfaction of knowing that you had done the appropriate thing? Because you were pleasant to someone, he, in turn was pleasant to you—and you could attribute it all directly to your behavior. A chain reaction had been set up!

How do you get along with your family? with your schoolmates? with your other friends? The way you get along with your present associates is an indication of how you may get along with your business associates. Businessmen consider the ability to get along pleasantly with others a very important characteristic. Why?

1. Through the co-operation of others and because of the pleasant atmosphere created, your work is easier to do and will give you greater pleasure and satisfaction.

2. Your associates do better and more work.

3. The physical and mental health of everyone is beneficially affected by the congenial surroundings.

4. Your superiors will note your ability to adapt yourself to office customs and routines and to the personalities of others.

5. Tact is necessary for leadership and a sound future.

Tact is an acquired trait. You must *work* at its development. A few characteristics of a diplomatic person are:

1. He controls his temper—incidentally the modulation and pitch of his voice.
2. He refrains from making snap judgments or acting impulsively.
3. He accepts suggestions and criticism calmly.
4. He is sure of his facts before making a positive statement.
5. He is willing to be helpful.
6. He is willing to share.
7. He gives the other person an opportunity to "save face."

Wherever you may be, whatsoever you may be called upon to do, there is a fitting, considerate manner in which to handle the problem. Seek it!

*read ∫ on
unit*

Meeting the Public

You like people; that is one reason why you want to be a secretary. You enjoy meeting, talking, and working with people. Secretarial work by its very nature inevitably brings you into contact with many persons who transact business with the firm. Since you like to associate with people, you will find this phase of your work intensely interesting. To succeed in this part of your job, however, you must constantly study human nature. Why do people act as they do? What motivates their actions? How can you satisfy their desires? How can you refuse requests when it is not possible to grant them?

To look at this problem another way, one of your main responsibilities is to help your employer secure and maintain the good will of the public served by the firm. As a secretary you occupy a unique position. You must carry out effectively the assignments of your employer and you must also represent him frequently in contacts with the public.

It is the purpose of this unit to help you carry out smoothly, tactfully, and skillfully your duties in receiving callers and handling appointments. Another important way you meet the public, by means of the telephone, is discussed in the next unit.

Section 1. THE EMPLOYER AND PUBLIC GOOD WILL

What Is Good Will? In business, good will is the favorable attitude other persons have toward the firm: the attitude of customers, salesmen, executives, prospective employees, and others.

You will understand your responsibilities in receiving callers and in handling appointments much better if you know why your employer

209

places so much importance on gaining and maintaining the good will of the public. He knows that the success of the firm depends in large measure on satisfied customers who are attracted to make initial purchases and encouraged to become steady customers.

Your Employer Must Depend on Others. Today's executive is a busy man who must delegate responsibilities to his employees. For example, his secretary is given the important role of handling callers from the time they come into his office until they leave. He knows his success is dependent on the work of all employees in the firm—his team. He knows, too, that he must depend on his secretary to create initial good will. He expects his secretary to understand thoroughly his preferences —whom he should see, when he should see them, and how much time should be allotted to them. You are your employer's "right-hand man." You are the secret of his success in building public good will.

The Secretary as a Good-Will Builder. In all offices, large or small, the secretary is a builder of good will for the firm. Since a considerable portion of time is devoted to these duties, the secretary is truly one representative of the firm who impresses the public. The manner in which the caller is greeted frequently influences the attitude he takes when he talks to the executive. Should the executive be out of the office at the moment, the manner in which the secretary receives the caller may determine whether he will wait, return, or not return again.

In other words, the secretary is the liaison officer between the employer and those who wish to talk to him. Sometimes the secretary is referred to as the "office hostess" because this particular phase of her work is essentially that of a receptionist. In larger offices, the general receptionist may handle the initial contact with callers and the secretary then takes care of the caller when he comes to the executive's office. By keeping in mind the fundamental fact that you are a builder of good will, you will have no particular difficulty in performing these duties.

It should not be overlooked, of course, that the manner in which you handle other employees is also important in building the spirit of team work in the firm.

Factors Needed for Success. The many daily opportunities you will have to meet the public will be interesting experiences. You may even consider them the "high spots" in your day. What are those personal qualities and factors that will make you a capable receptionist and an

Courtesy Shaw-Walker Company

The secretary greets callers pleasantly.

efficient liaison officer? You will be expected to rank high in the ten office etiquette factors listed below.

Office Etiquette. The rules of courtesy govern your actions in dealing with the public. Study the following points of office etiquette; they are pertinent to the development of your ability to take care of all callers.

1. A knowledge of basic etiquette
2. An understanding of human nature
3. Poise and confidence in meeting all types of people
4. Patience in handling trying situations that may arise; avoidance of any emotional display
5. Courteous action at all times, whether or not you are able to grant the request of the caller
6. Diplomacy, fairness, and tactfulness in your treatment of each caller
7. A friendly smile, a cheerful attitude, and a sense of humor

8. Maintenance of a businesslike atmosphere in the office whenever visitors are present
9. Politeness, alertness, tolerance, at all times
10. Omission of any gossip about other employees or your visitors

Section 2. RECEIVING CALLERS

Your attention is now directed to suggestions that will help make the receiving of callers an enjoyable duty. The satisfactory performance of your duties of receiving callers will be measured by the extent to which you follow these suggestions.

If you have a genuine liking for people and are not afraid to talk with persons who are strange to you, you will have little difficulty with this part of your daily routine. A liking for people is necessary, because you should be sympathetic and without prejudice when dealing with those who present themselves at your desk. You must be free from timidity, too, because your employer is depending on you to treat callers in the same manner as he himself would treat them if he were receiving them. You will be able to do this part of your work more effectively if you learn to classify callers quickly.

Here again you are faced with the reality that you represent your employer. Your voice and manner of speech, your concern for the comfort of the caller, your office "housekeeping"—all these affect the attitude of the caller toward your employer.

It is important to remember names. It means a great deal in building good will if you will develop the ability to remember names. A new customer, for example, is very much impressed when the secretary can call him by name on his second visit.

There is little excuse not to remember the names of salesmen or customers who are regular callers. These persons deserve every courtesy from you. On the other hand, be careful not to let your attitude toward them become careless or flippant because you do know them well.

The names of important callers, whom your employer will see under any circumstances, should be catalogued in a card file. Keep this card index in a convenient place, where you can consult it when necessary. After some experience, you will recognize these callers immediately.

Some callers may use devious methods to obtain the favor of the secretary. If you possess good judgment, you can easily weed out this type of caller as well as the caller who is unimportant.

Perhaps the most difficult group for the secretary to deal with is the one made up of the unwelcome callers, such as peddlers, solicitors, aggressive salesmen, and insistent applicants. With these callers the secretary has to be firm without losing her temper.

Take care of the caller yourself at once if possible. In some instances perhaps you can redirect him to subordinates who can handle the situation as well as, or even better than, your employer. By using tact, you will be able to obtain the necessary information to classify the caller quickly, so that he will be impressed not only by your courtesy and attentiveness but also by your businesslike disposition of the matter. Never leave a caller unattended.

There are those callers whose business is legitimate but who are strangers to you. You must find out the purpose of their calls. Then you can decide whether to handle the matter yourself, whether to refer it to someone else, or whether to let the caller interview your employer. This group includes prospective customers, new salesmen, applicants for a position, or persons asking for a favor. Your employer's friends or members of his family and business associates make up another group of callers.

Approach each caller with a smile, no matter what his status, and exhibit an active interest in him. Obtain enough information from the caller to enable you to give his business adequate attention.

Summary. You will be considered proficient in handling callers when you:

1. Have the ability to classify callers according to the importance of their business
2. Have the initiative and ability to obtain needed information from the caller in order to make intelligent decisions
3. Remember names of visitors, friends, and customers
4. Maintain a systematic record of callers, either in a register or in an alphabetic card file
5. Are able to detect flattery when used to obtain information from you— "apple polishing"
6. Give a caller immediate attention when he enters the office
7. Are clear and concise in giving information to callers, but tactful in the kind of information given
8. Are helpful to those callers whose request you cannot immediately grant

Section 3. HANDLING APPOINTMENTS

Closely related to the duty of receiving callers is the duty of handling appointments. After you have determined the nature of a particular caller's business, an immediate interview with your employer

MARCH
S M T W T F S

						1
2	3	4	5	6	7	8
9	10	11	12	13	14	15
16	17	18	19	20	21	22
23 24	25	26	27	28	29

30 31

FRIDAY

11

APR. 1952

MAY
S M T W T F S

					1	2	3
4	5	6	7	8	9	10
11	12	13	14	15	16	17
18	19	20	21	22	23	24
25 26	27	28	29	30	31

APRIL
S M T W T F S

	1	2	3	4	5
6	7	8	9	10	11	12
13	14	15	16	17	18	19
20	21	22	23	24	25	26
27 28	29	30

FRIDAY

11

APR. 1952

APPOINTMENTS

9:00
9:30 *Mr. Raymond*
10:00
10:30 *Advertising Conference*
11:00
11:30
12:00 *lunch - Mrs. Martin*
1:00
1:30
2:00
2:30 *Mr. Pritchard*
3:00
3:30
4:00
4:30
5:00
Evening

Call up on Mr. R's letter ''/21
February promotions

contract for refrigerators

102   FRIDAY, APRIL 11, 1952   264

This appointment schedule lists actual appointments on one side and, on the other side, acts as a reminder for certain things to be taken up in connection with these appointments.

may be granted; or, it may be necessary to make an appointment with your employer at a later time.

You will have considerable responsibility in scheduling of appointments, in keeping a record of the appointments made, and in handling certain aspects of the interview. You should also remember that your employer may occasionally need to meet persons away from his office. You would be expected to handle the scheduling of these appointments.

Your employer may ask you to interview callers to relieve him of

this necessity. It is your responsibility to know definitely his wishes regarding all types of callers.

Persons who call by appointment naturally have precedence over other callers. It is essential, therefore, to keep a careful record of all appointments for the day. Refer to it the first thing on arriving at the office in the morning. A memorandum of his appointments for the day should be submitted to your employer early in the day. (See illustration on page 214).

At the end of the day, your appointment record should show which appointments were kept and which were not. If you are informed of the results of meetings, you can make suitable notations in your appointment record. These appointment records are part of your permanent files. They may prove to be valuable for reference in the future.

You will be of great assistance to your employer if you can anticipate his needs during his interviews. For example, see that the furniture is arranged, if the appointment is for a group of persons; get all necessary papers from the files and place them on his desk, and do any other thing you can to add to his convenience.

Telephone Message
FOR *Mr. Martin*
DATE *9/15*   TIME *10:45*
WHILE YOU WERE OUT
M *iss Harrison*
FROM *Wiley & Smith*
PHONE No. *Pe. 6317*

✓ TELEPHONED	PLEASE PHONE
RETURNED YOUR CALL	WANTS TO SEE YOU
CAME TO SEE YOU	✓ WILL CALL AGAIN

MESSAGE: *reference to insurance contract*

J. P.

FORM 5054   TAKEN BY

The message should be complete and written legibly.

When your employer is absent from the office or is in conference and does not wish to be disturbed, callers will frequently leave messages for him. (See illustration given above). When your employer returns to the office, deliver the message at once. The message must be complete and exact with all details such as date, time, names, and so forth. Always treat these messages with extreme care and do not depend on your memory. As soon as you have written down the message, place it on your employer's desk where he will see it immediately upon his return. An efficient manner of handling such messages is to

use a printed form. These forms should be readily available near the telephone.

Occasionally callers overstay the time reasonably allowed for a scheduled appointment. Your employer will work out with you a tactful method for terminating the conference in such instances.

Summary. The suggestions given below are essential in the handling of appointments and will help you in the performance of this responsibility.

1. Understand and be considerate of your employer's preferences in granting appointments.
2. Be diplomatic in refusing appointments, giving the reason whenever possible.
3. Confirm important appointments by telephone or by letter.
4. Keep a daily calendar of your own which duplicates your employer's appointments.
5. Anticipate the pertinent data needed by your employer for a specific appointment.
6. When necessary, cancel appointments at once by telephone or by letter, rescheduling a new appointment if desirable.
7. Anticipate your employer's schedule of appointments in advance.
8. Be tactful in terminating conferences when persons overstay a reasonable time.

Section 4. TYPICAL SITUATIONS WHEN RECEIVING CALLERS

You cannot learn how to receive callers simply by reading printed instructions. You must practice under the critical guidance of your instructor until you feel sure that you are qualified to handle situations similar to those described below.

It is suggested that you first read this section. Then, adapting the conversations, if necessary, you and your fellow students should carry on similar conversations in the classroom, repeating the demonstration until your instructor is satisfied that your attitude and conversation with callers will meet business standards.

The secretary should be able to classify all types of callers quickly. The following conversation illustrates how Miss Jackson, an experienced secretary, greets well-known callers who always come on legitimate business.

MISS JACKSON. Good morning, Mr. Ross. How are you today?

MR. ROSS. Good morning, Miss Jackson. May I see Mr. Martin for a few minutes?

MISS JACKSON. I think so, Mr. Ross. Just a moment. (*Into phone.*) Mr. Martin, Mr. Ross is here and would like to see you for a few minutes. (*Pause.*) You may go right in, Mr. Ross.

*   *   *   *   *

There are those callers whose business is legitimate but who are strangers to the secretary. Miss Jackson receives such callers courteously.

MISS JACKSON. Good morning.

MR. ANDREWS. I'd like to see Mr. Martin, please.

MISS JACKSON. Do you have an appointment?

If the secretary asks a question like, "What do you wish to see him about?" the caller is put on the defensive and will be less willing to state his business than if the question suggests that he may be an expected caller.

MR. ANDREWS. No, I haven't. I'm Mr. Andrews, of the Acme Company. Here's my card. I met Martin at the Rotary Club meeting last Tuesday, and he told me to drop around when I was up this way.

MISS JACKSON. Just a moment, Mr. Andrews. I'll see if Mr. Martin is free. (*Into phone.*) Mr. Andrews, of the Acme Company, is here. He met you at the Rotary Club last Tuesday, and you invited him to drop in for a visit. Will you see him now? (*Pause.*) Mr. Martin will be glad to see you, Mr. Andrews. His office is just through that doorway.

If the secretary is not sure that the caller is welcome, she may use the device of speaking to Mr. Martin over the phone as though it were someone other than Mr. Martin on the other end. For example, "Mr. Andrews, of the Acme Company, is here to see Mr. Martin. He met Mr. Martin at the Rotary Club last Tuesday. Mr. Martin suggested that he call." This device gives Mr. Martin a chance to consider whether he wishes to see the caller, or to refuse to see the caller, and to tell Miss Jackson what reason to give. He may give Miss Jackson instructions as to how to handle the call herself.

*   *   *   *   *

Courtesy Shaw-Walker Company

The receptionist telephones the executive to find out whether he will see a caller.

In the next conversation, Miss Jackson shows a member of the office staff the same courtesy she would to someone outside the company.

MISS JACKSON. Good morning, Miss Turner.

MISS TURNER. Good morning, Miss Jackson. I have those reports ready for Mr. Martin. Is he available now?

MISS JACKSON. I'll see. (*Into phone.*) Mr. Martin, Miss Turner of the Accounting Department has the reports ready to show you. Will you see her now? (*Pause.*) Thank you. (*To Miss Turner.*) You may go right in, Miss Turner.

*   *   *   *   *

Perhaps the most difficult callers to deal with are peddlers, persistent solicitors, and overly aggressive salesmen. With these callers Miss Jackson is firm but never loses her temper.

MISS JACKSON. Good morning.

MR. FISHER. I want to see Mr. Martin, please.

MISS JACKSON. Is he expecting you?

MR. FISHER. No, but he'll be glad to see me.

MISS JACKSON. May I have your card, please?

A caller's business card usually bears his name and title, and the name and type of business that he represents.

MR. FISHER. Oh, just tell him Fisher is here.

MISS JACKSON. Does Mr. Martin know you, Mr. Fisher; and what do you wish to see him about?

MR. FISHER. No, young lady, he doesn't know me—and my business is personal.

MISS JACKSON. I'm sorry, sir; but without knowing the nature of your business, I am not permitted to announce you to Mr. Martin.

MR. FISHER. O.K. I want to give your boss a wonderful chance to invest in some gilt-edge securities. I'll take only a few minutes of his time.

MISS JACKSON. Mr. Martin makes all his investments through his broker, Mr. Fisher. I don't believe he'd be interested.

MR. FISHER. You're keeping your boss from hearing about a sure thing. But maybe you'd be interested in it yourself. Now here's the idea—

MISS JACKSON. No, I'm not making any investments just now. Thank you. Good day.

* * * * *

The secretary must keep complete and accurate appointment records. This necessitates knowing the employer's plans for the day and his wishes regarding his time schedule.

MISS JACKSON. Good morning.

MR. WINTERS. Good morning. I'm Winters, of the National Printing Company. I have an appointment with Mr. Martin at 10:30. I'm a little early.

MISS JACKSON. Yes, Mr. Martin is expecting you; and I'm glad you *are* early, Mr. Winters. I'll tell Mr. Martin you're here. (*Into phone.*) Mr. Martin, Mr. Winters is here a few minutes early for his 10:30 appointment. Shall I send him right in? (*Pause.*) Thank you. Please go right in, Mr. Winters. You know the office, of course.

Miss Jackson knows that Mr. Winters is expected at 10:30 because his appointment is recorded on her appointment sheet for the day. She is glad that he arrived early for his appointment because she sees that Mr. Martin has another appointment at eleven and, with this extra time, Mr. Winters's visit will not be hurried; or, Miss Jackson may wish to hurry Mr. Winters through so that Mr. Martin can take care of others matters before his eleven o'clock appointment.

MISS JACKSON. (*Answering phone ring.*) Mr. Martin's office, Miss Jackson speaking.

MR. SAUNDERS. This is Jack Saunders, of Imperial Products. Will I be able to see Mr. Martin if I come in about eleven? He told me to come in sometime today.

MISS JACKSON. I'm sorry, Mr. Saunders; but Mr. Martin has an appointment at eleven. He won't be free until after the noon hour. Could you come in about 1:30?

When arranging new appointments, Miss Jackson must be sure that the time set will be convenient for both persons. She knows that 1:30 is convenient for Mr. Martin and asks if it is convenient for Mr. Saunders.

MR. SAUNDERS. All right. Tell him I'll be in around 1:30.

* * * * *

When referring a caller to another department, the secretary should make the transfer without causing annoyance to the caller. See how Miss Jackson handles such a situation.

MISS JACKSON. Good morning.

MR. MARSHALL. Good morning. (*Handing over a card.*) I'm Marshall, of the Portland Contracting Company. I'd like to talk with Mr. Martin, please.

MISS JACKSON. Is he expecting you, Mr. Marshall?

MR. MARSHALL. No. I'd like to see him about the roofing contract on your new warehouse.

MISS JACKSON. Is your company one of the bidders?

MR. MARSHALL. Yes. I want to make another checkup on the specifications.

MISS JACKSON. In that case, Mr. Marshall, I believe you should see Mr. Black, who has all the specifications. He's in the Legal Department. If you'll wait just a moment, I'll call him and tell him you're here. (*Dials phone.*) Mr. Black, this is Miss Jackson. Mr. Marshall, of the Portland Contracting Company, is here to talk about the specifications on the roofing contract on the new warehouse. (*Pause.*) All right. Thank you. (*To Mr. Marshall.*) Mr. Black is in his office; and he can see you right now, Mr. Marshall. His office is 531, on the fifth floor.

Some Highlights of This Unit

1. An employer expects his secretary to understand thoroughly his preferences regarding callers—whom he should see, when he should see them, and how much time should be allotted to them.

2. Be sympathetic, free from timidity, and without prejudice when dealing with others.

3. Learn to classify callers quickly; remember names and catalogue important ones.

4. Handle tactfully, but firmly, known peddlers, solicitors, aggressive salesmen, and insistent applicants.

5. Take care of the caller yourself at once, if possible, and never leave a caller unattended.

6. From strangers who are legitimate callers obtain enough information to enable you to give their business adequate attention.

7. A secretary can be of great assistance if she will arrange in advance the chairs and all pertinent data needed for a conference.

8. See that messages left for your employer are written down neatly and are delivered promptly—the message must be complete and exact.

Questions and Items for Discussion

1. Why should the person who meets callers be well informed about the business?

2. What are some of the advantages of a secretary's maintaining a card index of important callers?

.3. Into what three groups may office callers be classified?

4. Should all callers be treated with the same degree of courtesy? Justify your answer.

5. What is meant by good will, and why is it important to a business?

6. Describe what is meant by office etiquette in regard to callers.

7. Describe an appointment memorandum and its use.

8. How may a secretary be helpful in terminating an appointment that goes beyond the scheduled time?

Personality Questions and Projects
(Based on Personality Pointer, page 207)

1. Assume that you are employed as confidential secretary to an attorney, Vincent Varick. You have as your assistant a young man named Wallace Chester. He does typing and filing, runs errands to the courthouse, and takes care of outgoing mail. You have authority to give him his working instructions, and you are responsible to Mr. Varick for the accuracy and efficiency of his work. (Authority almost always carries responsibility with it.) You must take the blame if Wallace makes mistakes.

Because there is so little difference in your ages, Wallace sometimes rebels at taking orders from you. It is your duty to keep things running smoothly, without bothering Mr. Varick, without angering Wallace, and without relaxing your own hard-earned authority as Mr. Varick's assistant.

One hot summer afternoon, while you are both busy, Mr. Varick telephones to ask for the papers on the case of Bridges *vs.* Trimmer. Wallace, none too willingly, gets the folder from the file and gives it to you. After checking to see that the file is complete, you tell him pleasantly, "Mr. Varick has to have this at the courthouse right away. Will you take it to Room 302, please?"

"Listen, I can't do two things at once," grumbles Wallace. "You gave me all this copying to do, and I'm not through with it."

Choose from the following list the most effective and tactful reply.

a. "Say, who's boss around here anyway?"

b. "I'll tell Mr. Varick on you if you don't do what I say."

c. "You can finish the typing later; this errand is more important."

d. "Well, all right. I'll take it over there myself."

2. In another case, Wallace has made a serious mistake, because he used his own judgment when he should have asked you. As a result, you will both have to work about an hour overtime to retype the legal papers he prepared incorrectly. You want to prevent the recurrence of such a situation.

Choose from the following list the most effective but tactful advice to give Wallace.

a. "Don't ever hesitate to ask me when you are in doubt; you know I'll be glad to tell you how Mr. Varick wants things done."

b. "Hereafter, ask me, or I'll have to ask Mr. Varick to let you go."

c. "If you can't get things right by yourself, you might ask me."

d. "I'll bet you will know better than to do a stupid thing like that again."

3. This time, Mr. Varick himself has made a mistake. You want to suggest that you are not to blame (you have been having enough trouble!), without making him angry. "Just how did *this* happen?" he inquires coldly, giving you an accusing glance over his spectacles.

Choose from the following list the most effective, tactful reply to give Mr. Varick.

a. "I did it exactly the way you told me to."

b. "I'm sorry—it's all my fault—I should have known you were wrong when you gave me those instructions."

c. "Wallace did it."

d. "I understood you to say that it should be done that way, but you were very busy that day."

4. Another attorney, James P. Murphy, with whom Mr. Varick is working on a very important case, has dictated material full of legal terms all morn-

ing, with Mr. Varick's permission. He wants the transcript at once. Mr. Varick calls you in and says, "Old Harrison wants to change his will again and sign it tonight. We'll have to get at it right now."

You can't do both, but you don't want to seem unwilling to do either one. Choose from the following list the most tactful way to ask which job comes first.

   a. "But I've got half a notebook full of dictation from Mr. Murphy; and that's important, too."
   b. "Too bad Wallace doesn't know shorthand so he could take some of this load off my shoulders."
   c. "Mr. Murphy dictated all morning and wants it transcribed right away. Shall I let his work go while we do Mr. Harrison's will?"

5. Mrs. K. Forbes Pennington, a wealthy client, sails into the office and demands that you announce her at once to Mr. Varick. She has no appointment, and he is in consultation with another client in his private office. You have definite instructions from him not to disturb him for any reason whatever. You can't even get him on the telephone. But remember, Mrs. Pennington, with all her faults (one of them is a tendency toward hysterics), is an important client.

Choose from the following list the most tactful reply to Mrs. Pennington. Remember your obligations to your employer as well as to the client.

   a. "I have strict orders not to disturb Mr. Varick; but if he had known you were coming, he wouldn't have given them. Won't you let me make an appointment for another day?"
   b. "You'll have to come back some other time, Mrs. Pennington. He's busy."
   c. "I'm sorry, he's out of town today."
   d. "His receiver is off the hook, so I can't ask him; and he told me not to bother him."

Secretarial Assignments

As Mr. Martin's secretary, you are called upon to receive the callers who come to his office to see him. Mr. Martin has asked that you always find out the name of the caller and the purpose of the call before announcing the caller to him.

1. A caller comes in and asks to see Mr. Martin but does not tell you who he is. You have not seen him before. After some questioning on your part, you find out that he is Mr. Philip Porter, the New York representative of the Consolidated Furniture Company of Chicago. Their products have just

recently been put on the market, and Mr. Porter wants to talk over a sales-promotion plan with Mr. Martin.

   a. Write down your conversation with Mr. Porter and what you tell Mr. Martin over the telephone when announcing Mr. Porter. Mr. Martin will see Mr. Porter in about five minutes.

   b. What would you do if Mr. Martin does not tell you he is ready to see Mr. Porter after the five minutes have elapsed?

2. Miss Garner, from the Collection Department, asks to see Mr. Martin. She has some statistical data that Mr. Martin asked for. You announce Miss Garner to Mr. Martin over the telephone. Mr. Martin tells you to take the data and any further message Miss Garner may have, as he is busy at the moment. Miss Garner says that there is no message regarding the data. She believes that all the information is in the papers that she leaves with you.

   a. Write down both sides of the conversation with Miss Garner and your conversation with Mr. Martin.

   b. What will you do with the papers Miss Garner leaves with you—keep them on your desk until Mr. Martin calls for them, put them with other materials that you intend calling to Mr. Martin's attention within a short time, or take them in to Mr. Martin immediately?

   c. On one of the call slips from your Workbook, Sheet 37, record the result of your conversation with Miss Garner. This message is to be attached to the papers left by her.

3. A peddler comes in and insists on seeing Mr. Martin. The rules of the office building are that no peddlers are allowed in the building without a permit. When you refuse to let the man see Mr. Martin because you know Mr. Martin would not be interested, the man tries to sell you something. You finally get rid of him by asking to see his permit and telling him that the building regulations require that peddlers without permits are to be reported to the building management immediately. The peddler leaves.

   a. Write down your conversation with the peddler, beginning with your refusal to let him see Mr. Martin. Always remember, in cases of this kind, that courtesy should govern every action in the office.

   b. If you had to put in a call to the building management about this peddler, what would you say?

4. Mr. Martin is interested in discussing further the matter of the new consignment of electric stoves about which he spoke to Mr. Brown over the telephone. He asks that you write the representative, Mr. Horace Balsam, Electric Products Corporation, Newark, New Jersey, making an appointment for next Friday at 10 a.m. Enter this appointment on the appointment sched-

ule in your Workbook, Sheet 36 and write the letter. Use Sheet 34 in your Workbook.

5. Write a short letter to Mr. Henry Forbes, of the Turner Publishing Company, Dover, New Jersey, and ask him if he will call next Friday at 11:30 a.m. Use Sheet 35 in your Workbook. Enter this appointment in the schedule in your Workbook, Sheet 36.

6. Complete the appointment schedule for Mr. Martin for Friday, using the following data:

Enter an appointment with Mr. J. T. Gray, of the Utica Express Company, Utica, New York, for 4 p.m. Friday. There has been some difficulty regarding shipments to three of the company's distributors in Utica—the Lincoln Supply Company, Johnson & Keyes Company, and Leverson Brothers. Mr. Gray wishes to discuss the matter with Mr. Martin and make recommendations for improving deliveries.

The president of the company, Mr. John J. Redding, has called a conference for 1:30 p.m., Friday. Mr. Stuart, the treasurer, will also participate. Some changes have been suggested for the organization of the Billing and Accounting Departments to facilitate handling of data between the departments. The president has called the conference to study the suggestions proposed.

Enter an appointment for 3 p.m., Friday, with Mr. Charles T. Smith, of the Mail Equipment Company, who wishes to demonstrate some machine devices for use in the Mailing Department. These devices are designed to handle both incoming and outgoing mail with more efficiency.

Enter a luncheon appointment at twelve o'clock Friday with Mr. Charles Slade, manager of Williams & Company, our Washington, D. C., dealer.

Place the schedule on the office manager's desk.

Optional

7. Ask a relative, friend, or neighbor who is employed in an office about his experience in meeting callers. Write up two or three of the most interesting ones in dialogue style. Use these "scripts" in the classroom.

Spelling Demons

existence	franchise	haphazard
familiar	grammar	hygiene
feminine	granary	illegal

Job Tips

1. To discourage prying eyes when you are typing confidential matter, casually roll the typed material back into the typewriter or place some correspondence over the material while you converse.

2. Don't hesitate to refer to your who's-who card file in front of the caller—he will be flattered to have his name listed.

3. Watch out—don't be a nagging "office wife." Just because you know office routines and feel secure in your job, don't become officious.

# Personality Pointer

HOW DO YOU SPEAK?

Now that you know the importance of a voice pleasing to the ear, you have to consider how to combine this pleasing voice with effective speech. Some rules for forming effective voice and speech habits are:

1. Speak in a well-modulated voice.
2. Enunciate all words distinctly.
3. Express thoughts clearly; use good judgment in choice of words.
4. Avoid making statements too positively.
5. Look directly into the eyes of the person to whom you are speaking.
6. Show animation and interest in your face.
7. Let your eyes rather than your lips express your laughter when speaking; laughter should not interfere with the clearness of your words.
8. Let your voice and manner of speaking be a reflection of your best personality, avoiding obvious affectations.

People are inclined to judge your mental capacity by your conversation. If you present your thoughts vaguely, you will give the impression of having vague thoughts. Use a clear and logical manner of expression, and you will give the impression of having a brain that functions effectively. You've heard the descriptive words "scatter-brained," "nitwit," "slow thinker," "ponderous thinker," "smart as a whip," "bright as a dollar." Aren't these characteristics revealed mainly through speech or manner of speaking?

Your home environment, your social standards, and your education are revealed in your choice of words, the grammar you use, and your manner of speaking. You very readily imitate the mannerisms of those

227

with whom you constantly associate. You adopt their standards of speech. Realizing this, you will choose your associates carefully or try to overcome such objectionable speech mannerisms as you may have acquired from your environment up to this time.

Success in this phase of personality development, as in all its phases, is based on consideration for the responses and feelings of those with whom you come in contact. Remove the annoying characteristics of your voice and manner of speaking, and you will make a favorable impression on those about you.

y-t

P 248

UNIT 10

Using the Telephone and Telegraphic Services

You have now studied that part of your work in an office that will take up much of your time—taking dictation, transcribing, writing letters on your own, and sending out the mail. This unit will discuss two other very important phases of your work—using the telephone and various types of telegraphic services.

Section 1. THE TELEPHONE

When you meet the public, whether face to face or by means of a telephone conversation, *you* are representing the company—no matter what your job may be. The outsider will not only judge your company by what you do and say; but he will also classify you as to your cultural background, training, and efficiency. With this in mind, you will be careful to treat persons outside your company in such a way as to cause them to say, "I like dealing with that company; every employee is courteous and considerate." You must be absolutely sincere in your attitude of helpful and courteous service. Any insincerity or artificiality will react most unfavorably against both you and your firm.

Telephoning is one of the most frequently performed of the many secretarial duties and one of the most important ways of meeting the public.

Telephone Voice, Courtesy, and Techniques

The telephone company employs persons with a good "telephone personality" as telephone operators. Their experience has proved

229

that "the voice with a smile wins." This well-known saying refers to the kind of voice one likes to hear over the telephone—the kind operators are trained to use to indicate their desire to serve you courteously. Because you will use the telephone very often as a secretary, you must be conscious of your own telephone personality and seek to improve it. The suggestions in this section will help you become skillful in the use of the telephone.

Courtesy New York Telephone Company

The "Voice with a Smile" is best heard when the lips are about a half inch away from the mouthpiece.

Your Telephone Voice. Talking with persons by telephone is very much like talking with them face to face. When you are talking to a person face to face, however, you can use gestures and facial expressions to help convey your meaning and invite a favorable response. But in a telephone conversation you have to depend on the tone of your voice and your manner of speaking to convey the exact expression you wish the listener to receive.

A cheerful voice and clear, distinct enunciation are essential factors in good telephoning. A low, well-controlled voice carries better and is more pleasant than one that is pitched high. Your voice should not be raised above normal; if anything, talk in a lower tone than you are accustomed to use in speaking—and speak slowly. Speak directly into the telephone, *with your lips about half an inch from the mouthpiece.* Speed, accuracy, and understanding depend on talking directly into the transmitter.

So that all numerals and letters may be clearly understood, telephone operators pronounce numerals and certain troublesome letters as follows. You will notice that the suggested ways of saying several of

the numerals do not agree with dictionary rules. To avoid confusion with other numerals, however, experience has shown that these are the easier and surer ways to pronounce numerals over the telephone. For spelling out names, see the alphabetic word list on page 238.

Numeral or Letter	Sounded as	Principal Sounds
0	oh	Round and long O
1	wun	Strong W and N
2	too	Strong T, and long OO
3	th-r-ee	A single roll of the R, and long EE
4	fo-er	Strong F, long O, and strong final R
5	fi-iv	I changing from long to short, and strong V
6	siks	Strong S and KS
7	sev-en	Strong S and V, and well sounded EN
8	ate	Long A, and strong T
9	ni-en	Strong N, long I, and well sounded EN
10	ten	Strong T and N
J	jay	Strong J, and long AY
R	ahr	Strong R
M	em	Short E, and strong M
W	dubble-yoo	Full value given to every syllable
F	ef	Short E, and strong F

Your Telephone Speech. Good telephone speech means you will be easily and correctly understood. It also means that you will make the good impression that brings a pleasant response.

One of the great advantages of using the telephone is the saving of time. This advantage is lost unless your conversation is to the point and concise. Avoid sounding curt, however. Avoid, too, all cheapening slang expressions, such as, "alrighty," "O.K.," and "yep." Avoid the impression of haste. Over the telephone it is more important to speak unhurriedly, as well as distinctly, than when face to face.

Some very good practice sentences are given below. Read them aloud, slowly enough to give every sound its proper value and to be conscious of your mouth action. They will give all-around exercise to your vocal apparatus and at the same time some mighty useful ideas to carry about with you.

1. For distinct enunciation, every word, every syllable, every sound, must be given its proper form and value.
2. Think of the mouth chamber as a mold, in which the correct form must be given to every sound.
3. Move your lips more noticeably.

4. The teeth should never be kept closed in speech.

5. As your voice is the most direct expression of your inmost self, you should be careful, through it, to do yourself full justice.

6. You may know what you are saying, but others will not, unless you make it clear to them.

7. Through practice, we can learn to speak more rapidly, but still with perfect distinctness.

8. Good speech is within the reach of everyone, through conscientious practice.

9. The courtesy of face to face conversation, where the smile plays such an important part, can be expressed over the telephone only through the tone of voice and a careful choice of words.

Your Telephone Manners. In addition to your voice and your speech, your telephone manners are most important. By following the simple rules of courtesy, you can develop a pleasing telephone personality. The telephone company has outlined these rules as follows. While they were written for telephone company employees, they apply equally to the secretary who uses the telephone. They are discussed in some detail in the remainder of this unit.

1. Answer promptly.
2. Greet the caller pleasantly.
3. Identify yourself properly.
4. Explain delays.
5. Leave word where you're going.
6. Ask questions tactfully.
7. Take the message.
8. Signal the operator slowly.
9. Know the number.
10. Allow time to answer.
11. Ask if convenient to talk.
12. Speak in a natural tone.
13. Visualize the person.
14. Say "Thank you" and "You're welcome."
15. Listen attentively.
16. Use the customer's name.
17. Speak directly into transmitter.
18. Apologize for mistakes.
19. End the call properly.
20. Replace receiver gently.

INCOMING CALLS

Identify Yourself. When your executive's telephone rings, answer it promptly. Avoid answering with such words as "Hello" or "Yes." Let the caller know he has reached the right telephone. Your bell rings. You answer, "Mr. Dawson's office" or, if appropriate, "Mr. Dawson's desk, Miss Smith speaking." The calling person will usually respond by giving you his name. If he does not do so, say, "May I tell

him who is calling?" Your procedure after that will depend on the circumstances.

Transferring Calls. Frequently, calls made to some particular person may be handled much better by another department or by someone who is familiar with the particular matter about which inquiry is made. Say to the caller, "Mr. Brown is in the Accounting Department, will you hold the line a moment, please?" or "I'm sure Mr. Brown in the Accounting Department can answer your question. I'll have your call transferred."

Attract the attention of the switchboard attendant by signaling slowly, depressing and releasing the plunger or switchhook to the count of one-two, pause, one-two, pause. Ask her to transfer the call to the person or department desired. Relay the request, if possible, so that the caller won't have to repeat what he has already said.

If the call has come to your telephone or extension through an error on the part of the telephone operator, don't let the caller find this out by a sign of annoyance in your voice or by any words of criticism of the operator. A criticism of any one employee, as you know, is, from the customer's standpoint, a criticism of the firm.

Your Policy in Handling Calls. Your policy in handling incoming calls for your employer will depend entirely on his wishes in the matter. If the busy executive personally answered every ring of the telephone, he would hardly have time for anything else. Many executives prefer to have all calls answered by their secretaries, so that they will be relieved of calls that can be answered satisfactorily by a secretary.

Classify Callers. It is necessary to classify your telephone callers so that important customers will receive special attention, frequent callers will be instantly recognized, and undesirable callers will not be allowed to be annoying. In the following situations the trained secretary would handle specific telephone calls somewhat like this.

1. Your chief may not be in the office. Say, "Mr. Collins is not in the office at the moment. May I take a message for him?"

2. He may be busily engaged and has instructed you that he is not to be disturbed. Say, "Mr. Collins is engaged at the moment. May I call you back as soon as he is free?" or "May I give him a message?"

3. If he is in but has left you no special instructions, say, "Just a moment, please; I'll see if he is available." You may then speak with him directly if he is in the same office or through the secretarial telephone installation or the Dictograph installation (see page

242) and dispose of the call as instructed. With either of these instruments, you can talk with your chief without the calling person hearing the conversation.

4. Where one telephone is used by both your employer and yourself, and a caller has given you his name, you can place your hand over the transmitter and announce that Mr. Customer is calling. If your employer signals that he is ready to receive the call, you turn the telephone over to him without further conversation. He will then go ahead as if he personally had answered the telephone in the first place. If he does not wish to receive the call, he will so instruct you.

5. If the caller is evasive, saying, for example, "My call is personal" or will not give his name, and if you have no instructions about the handling of personal calls, you should excuse yourself and convey the nature of the call or the circumstances to your employer. Then proceed as instructed. The frank statement that, without the required information, you are not at liberty to connect the calling party is sure to be irritating to everyone and many times may embarrass your employer.

Much of your success in handling these situations will depend on your attitude toward the caller. If you are friendly and reflect a ready-to-serve spirit, you will be more likely to get the information desired. And remember at all times that there is an exception to every rule. One of the most severe tests of secretarial ability is to recognize the exception when it occurs.

Answering Requests for Information. Many of the calls you will receive will be requests for information. Make sure that in answering these requests you don't reveal confidential information. Give the caller only the information that you have permission to give. But never hesitate to give him that information and to give it cheerfully and promptly.

Answer every question directly. This necessitates your understanding exactly what the caller wants. A misunderstanding of the question may cause you to give out incorrect information. Many firms follow the practice of sending confirming letters when important information has been given over the telephone, especially where prices or agreements are concerned.

Obtain Information if Possible. Sometimes it is necessary to look up information in the files or elsewhere while the caller holds the wire. If this will require more than a minute or two, get the caller's telephone number and say you will call back as soon as you have obtained

the information. If you find that you cannot answer the inquiry, try to ascertain where the caller can obtain the desired information. This "one step farther" marks the successful secretary.

Terminating the Call. Always terminate a call when the business involved is completed. Do not prolong the conversation by needless words. Hang up your receiver quietly.

Personal Calls. Avoid incoming and outgoing personal calls at the office except in case of necessity. If any relative or friend has a tendency to forget your instructions regarding personal calls, you must remind him that the violation of this business rule is endangering your status.

OUTGOING CALLS

Many times a day you will pick up your telephone to initiate outgoing calls. You can systematize this part of your work just as you do your dictation and transcription.

Telephone Directories. You will recall the discussion of various types of directories that may be used by the secretary (see Unit 6,

---

Forecast and Temperature—Call WE ather 6-1212   Caigen—Conklin

culating Company 481W165 ..AT water 9-0269
np and Trail Outfitters 381 4Av AU dubon 3-0523
np Information Bureau 35W103 .BR yant 9-1093
hd D Company 44CooperSq ...CO rtlandt 7-6224
dle Craft Inc 68FirstSt .....CO rtlandt 7-6061
nvas Specialty Co 49E96 ....CO rtlandt 7-3858
pitol Chemical Corp 15PkRw .BU tterfield 8-1625
pitol Furniture Co 306W100 .CH ickering 4-2461
avan Co 239CentPkW ....CI rcle 6-2781
bon Engineering Co
         1150CentPkW .CO rtlandt 7-5340
rburator Exchange Co
         160W77.BO wling Green 9-5654
d Case Co 146CentPkW .....ED gecomb 4-3821
rdcrafts Inc 1265Bway .....EL dorado 5-4367
rlsbad Restaurant 4700Bway ..EN dicott 2-4905
hival Inc 333WEndAv ......CO rtlandt 7-5258
pet&Rug Inst 520 8Av ......CO rtlandt 7-4947
and Dog Hospital 107W86 ....WO rth 2-5655
tral Co Inc 60Wall ....LO ngacre 3-5077
tral Woodwork Co 340E57 ..CO rtlandt 7-4640
tified Milk Co 250W103 .....LO rraine 7-5589
in Stores Co 8W19 ....MO nument 2-6128
r Caning Co 254 4Av ......CO rtlandt 7-3552
r Co of America 225Bway .....PL aza 3-6856
hois Co Inc 262W107 ..BO wling Green 9-7573
ndelier&Co 151E92 ....CO rtlandt 7-3779
art Co Inc 201W108 .....PE nnsylvania 6-7169
art for Business Inc 175W72 RH inelander 4-7725

Check Service Inc 176W87 .....CO rtlandt 7-4264
Checker Co Inc 1150PkAv .....CO rtlandt 7-3858
Cheese Distributing Co
         3495Bway.SA cramento 2-8124
Chelsea Co 118E28 ....SC huyler 4-8947
Chemicals Inc 180MadAv ....HA nover 2-3788
Chemists Service Inc 180MadAv ..HA nover 2-6469
Chicago Watch Co 910WEndAv ..TR afalgr 4-9462
Childrens Hat Co 163W79 ....WO rth 2-1817
Chime Mfg Co 821 6Av ....CO rtlandt 7-4125
Chimney Corp 76W86 ,.........HA nover 2-4079
China Imp Co 651W188 ......UN iversity 4-9925
Chinaware Assn 128CPkS .....WA dsworth 7-9962
Chlorine Products Co 254W34 ...AT water 9-0269
Chromium Co 67W44 ....AU dubon 3-0523
Cigar Imp Co Inc 235W4 ....BR yant 9-1093
Cin-Made Corp The 225CentPkW CO rtlandt 7-6224
Circle Co Inc 100Gold ....CO rtlandt 7-6061
City Light Co 255W88 ....BU tterfield 8-1625
Classified Inf Co 237Lafyet ...CH ickering 4-2461
Cleaners Inc 1234HenryHudsonPkwyE CI rcle 6-2781
Cleaning Co Inc 52Wm ....CO rtlandt 7-5340
Collegiate Cap Co 200W57 .BO wling Green 9-5654
Colonial Art Co 140E40 ....ED gecomb 4-3821
Colonial Inn 225 5Av ....EL dorado 5-4367
Colonial Institute 20W22 ......EN dicott 2-4905
Colonial Restaurant 152Mulbry .CO rtlandt 7-5258
Colonial Service Co 80Brd ....CO rtlandt 7-4947
Columbia Uniform Corp 261Bway LO ngacre 3-5077
Comfort Cap Co 2272 3A CO rtlandt 7-4640

Courtesy New York Telephone Company

Section of an alphabetic telephone directory.

pages 109-112). You also should be familiar with the various telephone directories in your office. Keep close at hand the directories that you use often. If you need additional directories, the telephone company will be glad to supply you with them.

Dyers—Educational

Dyers–Industrial (Cont'd)

WESTERN DYE WORKS INC
Dyers All Types Buttons, Novelties
234W39 --------------- LOngacr 3-6629
Wilson Button&Novelty ColoringCo
105E28 MUryhil 9-2992
WONDER-AGE DYE WORKS INC
GARMENT
DYEING to the TRADE
EXPERT BATHROOM MATS,
COTTON GOODS
Chenille Dyers and Finishers
21Morton Bklyn --------- EVrgrn 9-4643
WORTH DYEING & FINISHING CO INC
45W15 --------------- WAtkns 5-2650
(SEE ADVERTISEMENT PAGE 510)
YORKTOWN DYE CORP
SPECIALISTS
HOSIERY DYERS & FINISHERS
Dyehouse 506E79 --------- TRaflgr 5-4270
Finishing 434Delancy ------- ORegn 5-4294

Dyers–Textile

See "Dyers–Industrial"; also "Textile Dyers"

Dyes & Dyestuffs

(See also Colors & Pigments)
AMERICAN COLOR & CHEMICAL CO
627Greenwich --------- WAtkns 4-2211

Courtesy New York Telephone Company

Part of a page from the classified
section of a telephone directory.

In smaller cities, there may be but one telephone directory that includes both alphabetical and classified listings. In larger cities, telephone directories are generally issued in two sections: (1) the alphabetical directory, and (2) the classified directory. In large metropolitan areas there may be, in addition, a suburban directory that covers the municipalities in the suburban area of the large city.

The *alphabetical telephone directory* contains the name, address, and frequently the business connection of each subscriber, followed by the name of the central office and the telephone number. It is arranged alphabetically by the surname of the subscriber. When there is more than one subscriber with the same surname, the arrangement continues alphabetically by given names or initials. Notice that, in the illustration following, a listing consists of surname, initials, designation, address, central office, and telephone number.

Hogan's Market 16 E. Jay......MAin 9-9118
Holly B T 94 High...........ADams 8-7738

In finding names, you will save time by referring to the index reference printed in bold type at the top of the directory page. This reference gives the first and last names appearing on the page.

The telephone directory also contains much other valuable information, such as rates and definite instructions for telephoning.

The *suburban telephone directories* give, for suburban towns and vil-

lages, the same kind of information as is given in the city telephone directory.

The *classified telephone directory* contains the name, address, and telephone number of every business subscriber, listed under a classified heading that is descriptive of his business. This classified directory will be found of great convenience—

1. When you want to buy something.
2. When you want to find a dealer of a trade-marked product.
3. When you have forgotten a business firm's name. For example, suppose you want the radio man on West Main Street. Simply turn to the "Radio" classification. Here you will find the radio concerns. Then all you have to do is to look for the address that is familiar to you.
4. When you have forgotten part of a name but remember the address. For example, suppose you want a laundry and all you remember is that the firm has the word "Individual" in its name. First, turn to the "Laundries" section on the *L* pages. Here you will find the laundry companies. A brief look through the addresses listed will reveal the company you are looking for.
5. Even when you know the name, the classified directory will help you.

Suppose you want to telephone Smith the plumber. It is usually easier to find the Smith you want among the few Smiths listed in the "Plumbers" section of the classified directory than in the long list of Smiths in the general alphabetic directory.

Lists of Frequently Called Numbers. Your executive and you call a few numbers very often. These numbers should be listed. An alphabetic index of all frequently called or otherwise important numbers, kept near your telephone, will prove useful to anyone who may substitute for you at any time. Such a listing is particularly important to the secretary herself when placing long distance calls that may not be called too frequently.

This index should include addresses also. Your employer may also like to have a copy of this list, even though he usually places his calls through you.

Obtaining Numbers Through "Information." When you need to call a number that is not listed in your telephone directory, call "Information." On dial telephones, a special number is assigned to the Information operator. This special operator will provide the number desired if you will give her the name and the address of the person or firm. Also call Information for numbers in nearby towns, but not for numbers reached by calling the Long Distance operator.

Should a person or a firm have a nonpublished telephone number, the Information operator will not give you the number. Nonpublished numbers are the telephone numbers of businesses or individuals who, for one reason or another, do not wish their numbers given to anyone except by themselves.

Enunciate carefully when talking with Information, because a mistake of *b* for *d* when you have asked for a Mr. Darnley's number, for example, will result in her telling you something like this: "There is no Mr. Barnley on South Main Street." Be sure to write down numbers obtained from Information for future use.

Memorize the following alphabetic word list and also keep it in a handy place. Use it to spell names to Information or anyone else when accuracy of spelling is important. This list is commonly used by telephone operators.

A	as in *Alice*	J	as in *James*	S	as in *Samuel*
B	as in *Bertha*	K	as in *Kate*	T	as in *Thomas*
C	as in *Charles*	L	as in *Louis*	U	as in *Utah*
D	as in *David*	M	as in *Mary*	V	as in *Victor*
E	as in *Edward*	N	as in *Nellie*	W	as in *William*
F	as in *Frank*	O	as in *Oliver*	X	as in *X-ray*
G	as in *George*	P	as in *Peter*	Y	as in *Young*
H	as in *Henry*	Q	as in *Quaker*	Z	as in *Zebra*
I	as in *Ida*	R	as in *Robert*		

Toll Calls. A toll call is a call to any telephone outside the local service area. The charge made is in proportion to the distance involved, the type of service, the time of day or night that the call is made, and the time taken for the conversation. There are two types of toll calls: station-to-station calls and person-to-person calls.

Station-to-station calls are calls on which you ask the operator for the desired telephone only, and not for a particular person nor for a particular private-branch-exchange (PBX) station. Generally, these calls are handled more rapidly and at lower rates than person-to-person calls. A charge is made if anyone at the called station answers.

Person-to-person calls are calls on which you ask the operator to call a particular person to the telephone or to reach a particular PBX station. The rates are somewhat higher than the station-to-station rates, but there is no charge if the desired person or extension station is not reached.

Procedure for Making Out-of-Town Calls. To determine which out-of-town calls should be placed with the local operator and which with

"Long Distance," consult the information pages of your local telephone directory.

On a nondial telephone, give the local operator the details of the call, or ask for "Long Distance." On a dial telephone, dial "Operator," or the code for "Long Distance." (Your directory will tell you which procedure to follow in each of these cases.) Give the details of the call clearly and at a moderate speed, so as to give the operator time to record the information you give her.

The following examples show how to give the details of the various kinds of out-of-town calls:

Station-to-Station Call. Called Number Known. Asbury Park 1-9971.

Collect Station-to-Station Call. Called Number Known. Collect. Albany 3-6522. (Operator will ask name of calling party.)

Station-to-Station Call. Called Number Not Available. St. Louis, Missouri. Anyone at Read's Warehouse, 2100 Broad Street.

Person-to-Person Call. Called Number Known. Albany 6-5241. Miss Ann Warrick.

Person-to-Person Call. Called Number Not Available. St. Louis, Missouri. Read's Warehouse, 2100 Broad Street. Mr. James.

Give your telephone number when the operator requests it.

Reversing the Charge. (Calling "Collect.") The charge for a call may be reversed upon the request of the calling party and with the consent of the party called. A salesman, for example, often reverses the charges for toll calls to his firm.

Classification of Outgoing Calls. Your outgoing telephone calls will generally fall into three classes: (1) calling a person with whom your executive wishes to converse; (2) telephoning a message as instructed by him; (3) obtaining information desired by him.

More and more executives are making all their calls themselves instead of having their secretaries "get so-and-so on the telephone." If the practice in your office, however, makes it necessary for you to place calls of Class 1, you will save your executive's time and the time of other busy persons by making sure that he is ready to talk when the called person answers. When you make a call for your executive, and you are answered by the called person's secretary, avoid arguments about who is to be "put on the line" first. If your executive initiates the call, he should be on the telephone when the called person answers.

In making a call of Class 2, put through the call as usual; and, when

the response is received, give the message, prefacing it with, "This is Mr. Brown's secretary. Mr. Brown has asked me . . ." and so on.

In making a call of Class 3, place the call as usual. Identify yourself. Know exactly what information you desire and ask for it courte-

ously. State your request clearly and briefly. Get all the information at one time so that you will not need to make repeat calls. And don't forget to thank the giver of the information.

Telephone Instruments. Two kinds of telephone instruments are in use—the manual telephone and the dial telephone. In some cities

Courtesy Illinois Bell Telephone Company

A standard dial telephone.

a combination of the two systems is used, making it necessary to master the technique of both.

How to Use the Manual Telephone. Give the number in the following manner:

The Directory Number	As Pronounced
9970	Nine-nine (pause) seven-oh
CI rcle 6-2781	Circle-six (pause) two-seven (pause) eight-one

The first two letters indicate the central office symbol used in dialing.

If you hear the operator pass your call to another operator incorrectly, say "No," and give the correct number again. In a short time you should hear either the ringing signal, an intermittent bur-r-r-ing sound denoting the ringing of the bell, or the "busy" signal, a rapid buzz-buzz-buzz (quicker and louder than the ringing signal). If you hear the "busy" signal, hang up the receiver, without waiting for a report from the operator, and repeat the call a little later. To call back the operator, move the receiver hook up and down *slowly*. Do not hang up the receiver until you are ready for the operator to disconnect the call.

How to Use the Dial Telephone. Lift the receiver from the hook and listen for the dial tone, a steady humming sound that indicates that the line is ready for use. Once the dial tone is heard, the receiver should be kept off the hook until the call has been completed. If the hook is

pressed down while one is dialing or talking, the line is disconnected, and it is necessary to start again.

See the information pages of your telephone directory for exact information on dialing. In localities where there are many central offices, it is necessary to dial a letter code (usually the first two let-

ters of the central office name) in addition to the figures. For the directory number ELdorado 5-4367, for example, you would dial E-L-5-4-3-6-7. To do this, simply place a finger in the hole containing the letter *E* and move it to the right until your finger strikes the dial stop. Remove your finger, and the dial will return to its normal position, without forcing. Then proceed to the next letter and to the succeeding figures.

Courtesy Illinois Bell Telephone Company

A Dial PBX Cord Switchboard.

If the dial should slip during the dialing process, hang up the receiver for a few seconds; then remove it and redial the number. If the line is not busy, you will hear the bur-r-r-ing sound that indicates that the number is being rung. If the line is busy, you will hear the buzz-buzz-buzz sound.

OPERATING THE SWITCHBOARD

PBX Board. Telephone service in many firms involves the use of a private branch exchange, commonly called a PBX. A PBX is a switchboard through which connections are made between trunk lines to the central office and extension telephones in the offices of the firm. Extension users may also communicate with each other through this

switchboard. PBX's are furnished by the telephone company to meet the individual firm's requirements. They vary in size from the small cordless boards with a capacity of three trunks and seven extensions to the large cord boards with capacities for over one hundred trunk lines and several thousand extensions.

Switchboard Operation. Any PBX requires an attendant to operate it —a person who is thoroughly competent to operate it in such a manner that telephone calls may pass through the PBX accurately, with the minimum of delay and with the maximum of courtesy. The mechanics of establishing connections at a PBX are easy to learn. The operator, however, must have not only the technical know-how, but also a sound service perspective and a broad knowledge of the organization that will enable her, with the help of extension users, to route calls with skill and assurance to their proper destination.

If you, as a secretary, are called upon to operate the switchboard at times when the regular attendant is off duty, it is advisable for you to call on the telephone company for training. The company is prepared to give you individual training under the guidance of an experienced instructor, so that you may be able to handle your firm's telephone calls in a businesslike and pleasing manner.

Special Communication Systems

Dictograph. The Dictograph is a means of communicating between offices in a business organization. It is a variation of the telephone

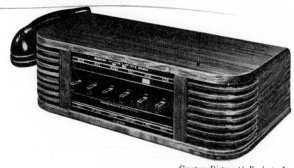 extension system, the difference being that it is an independent system, thus leaving the switchboard clear for incoming and outgoing calls. Instant contact can be made with any and all departments at the same time by the pressure of a key.

Courtesy Dictograph Products, Inc.

A Dictograph with telephone attachment.

A conference may be held and business involving several departments may be dispatched quickly without requiring anyone to leave his desk. The loud-speaker that is built into the Dictograph makes it unneces-

sary to hold a receiver to the ear. An earpiece receiver or French-telephone hand set can be attached for privacy.

Teletypewriter. The teletypewriter is, in appearance and operation, somewhat similar to an ordinary typewriter. Messages typed on one machine are instantly and accurately reproduced on any other teletypewriter to which it is connected.

Teletypewriter Exchange (TWX) service is furnished by the telephone company on substantially the same basis as telephone service, except that communication is typewritten instead of oral.

Teletypewriter Exchange stations are connected to

Courtesy Western Union Telegraph Company

A teletypewriter.

central offices and through these central offices communication may be established with other teletypewriter stations similarly connected in the same city or in any other city.

During the connection of two teletypewriter stations, communication may be carried on in either direction but not in both directions simultaneously. This permits a two-way communication service.

Teletypewriter Private Line (TWPL) service is also available. A teletypewriter at one location is permanently connected with one or more teletypewriters at other locations. Typewritten messages may then be sent directly from one machine to the other machine, or machines, without requiring central office connections.

TelAutograph Telescriber. The TelAutograph telescriber is used for transmitting handwriting instantly over the wire. A message written on a transmitter will be instantly reproduced on a receiver located in another department, building, or city. A message sent in this way

furnishes a permanent record on rolls of paper. The TelAutograph is used in many large institutions, such as banks, factories, hospitals, hotels, insurance offices, and railroad offices.

Typical Telephone Conversations

A series of typical secretarial telephone conversations follows. You cannot learn how to use the telephone properly by merely reading

printed instructions. You must practice telephoning under the critical guidance of your instructor until you feel sure that you are qualified to handle all the customary telephone situations that confront the secretary. Study the manner in which these secretaries handle difficult situations. The comments will point out to you the important points in each conversation.

Courtesy TelAutograph Corporation

A TelAutograph Telescriber.

Speak unhurriedly, enunciating your words distinctly.

JANE WILSON. (*Speaking rapidly.*) This is Jane Wilson calling. I had an appointment with Mr. Martin at ten o'clock, but I'll never be able to make it. I was a little late starting, and traffic was slow this morning. Will you tell him I'll be there at 10:30?

MISS JACKSON. I'm sorry, I'll have to ask you to repeat what you said, and will you please speak a little more slowly?

JANE WILSON. (*Normal tone, slow and distinct.*) I'm sorry. This is Jane Wilson calling. I had an appointment with Mr. Martin at ten o'clock, but I'll not be able to make it. The traffic was quite slow this morning. Will you tell him I'll be there at 10:30?

* * * * *

Miss Jackson obtains the necessary information from a caller who is reluctant to give it.

MISS JACKSON. Mr. Martin's office. Miss Jackson speaking.

MR. ADAMS. May I speak to Mr. Martin, please?

MISS JACKSON. Who is calling? (*The "please" is implied by the voice.*)

MR. ADAMS. This is Adams of the Modern Furniture Company.

Miss Jackson. Oh, yes, Mr. Adams. One moment, please.

Miss Jackson. Mr. Martin has gone for the day. May I help you?

Mr. Adams. No, I'll call back tomorrow.

Miss Jackson. Are you calling regarding an order, Mr. Adams?

Mr. Adams. No, I'm with the Modern Furniture Company. Mr. Martin is interested in some new fireproof files. I'll call back tomorrow.

Miss Jackson. Thank you, Mr. Adams, I'll tell Mr. Martin to expect your call.

*   *   *   *   *

Sometimes your executive is too busy to take a call at the time it comes in.

Miss Jackson. (*Bell.*) Mr. Martin's office, Miss Jackson speaking.

Mr. Scott. This is Ted Scott, of the Walker Motor Company. I'd like to talk to Mr. Martin.

Miss Jackson. One moment, please, Mr. Scott. (*Pause.*) I'm sorry, Mr. Scott, but Mr. Martin is going to be busy for a few minutes and would like to call you back as soon as he is free. May I have your number, please?

Mr. Scott. I'll be in the office for just a half hour. Ask him to call as soon as possible. My number is Columbus 2-0611.

Miss Jackson. Columbus 2-0611. I'll have Mr. Martin call you as soon as possible. Thank you.

*   *   *   *   *

Notice how tactful Miss Jackson is in transferring a call that should be handled in another department.

Miss Jackson. Mr. Martin's office.

Telephone Voice. I'd like to speak to Mr. Martin about prices on floor lamps.

Miss Jackson. Mr. Brown handles prices on floor lamps. Would you mind holding the line just a moment? I'll have the call transferred.

Telephone Voice. I thought Martin was in charge. Who's Brown?

Miss Jackson. Mr. Brown is in charge of the Household Furnishings Department. I am sure he can take care of the matter quite satisfactorily.

Telephone Voice. All right, I'll talk to Brown.

Miss Jackson. One moment, please. (*Signals operator.*)

Telephone Operator. Yes, please.

Miss Jackson. Will you transfer this call to Mr. Brown in Household Furnishings? ("*Please*" *is implied in the voice.*)

*   *   *   *   *

In the following conversation, Miss Jackson shows that it is possible to withhold confidential information without giving offense.

Mr. BEACH. May I speak to Mr. Martin? This is Roy Beach, of the Acme Company.

Miss JACKSON. Mr. Martin is out of town for a few days, Mr. Beach. May I help you?

Mr. BEACH. Yes. You might tell me who's going to get the contract on the new warehouse job.

Miss JACKSON. I understand they are going to open the bids next Monday, Mr. Beach. We won't know until then.

Mr. BEACH. Well, confidentially, which firm does Mr. Martin favor?

Miss JACKSON. The bids are being received on a strictly competitive basis, Mr. Beach. But if you would like to talk with Mr. Martin, I'll be glad to have him call you when he returns.

Mr. BEACH. No, thank you. I guess I can wait until the bids are open. Thanks anyway. Good-by.

* * * * *

If someone has been told to wait on the wire, he should not be kept waiting for any great length of time.

Mr. THOMAS. How many bids were received on the last printing contract, Miss Jackson?

Miss JACKSON. Will you hold the line just a moment, Mr. Thomas? I'll have to refer to the files. (*Pause.*) Mr. Thomas, I find that particular file is on Mr. Martin's desk, and it will take a few moments to get it. Do you wish to wait, or shall I call you back?

Mr. THOMAS. Better call me back, Miss Jackson. I'll be in the Comptroller's office.

Miss JACKSON. Thank you. I'll call you there.

* * * * *

A secretary has to make long-distance calls. Miss Jackson will ask her switchboard attendant to put through a station-to-station call for her.

Miss JACKSON. Operator, will you please get Springfield, Illinois, Lincoln 724.

Or Miss Jackson may put through the call herself.

Miss JACKSON. Operator, will you please give me Long Distance. (*Pause.*)

LONG-DISTANCE OPERATOR. Long Distance.

Miss JACKSON. Springfield, Illinois, Lincoln 724, please.

LONG-DISTANCE OPERATOR. Your number, please?

Miss JACKSON. Caledonia 5-3421.

This is how Miss Jackson puts through a person-to-person call. She is talking to the long-distance operator.

MISS JACKSON. I wish to place a person-to-person call. Springfield, Illinois, Lincoln 724—Mr. John Spencer or his secretary.

* * * * *

When Mr. Martin is ready to talk with Mr. Scott, of the Walker Motor Company, whose call was postponed because Mr. Martin was in conference, he asks Miss Jackson to get Mr. Scott on the phone.

MISS JACKSON. (*Lifts phone.*)
TELEPHONE OPERATOR. Yes, please.
MISS JACKSON. Columbus 2-0611, please.
WALKER OPERATOR. Good morning. This is Walker Motor Company.
MISS JACKSON. May I speak to Mr. Scott?
SECRETARY. Mr. Scott's office.
MISS JACKSON. Mr. Martin, of United Products Corporation, wishes to speak to Mr. Scott.
SECRETARY. One moment, please.

While his secretary tells Mr. Scott who is calling, Miss Jackson turns the call over to Mr. Martin. Mr. Scott picks up his phone and says, "Hello, Martin."

MR. MARTIN. Hello, Scott, I hope I haven't delayed too long in answering your call.

* * * * *

Extreme care must be taken when delivering messages over the telephone so that there will be no possibility of misunderstanding. Miss Jackson makes such calls in this way.

MISS JACKSON. Mr. Redding, this is Miss Jackson of Mr. Martin's office. Mr. Martin has been called into conference but would like to meet you for luncheon today at 12:15 in the Grill Room of the Hotel Commodore. Will that be satisfactory?
MR. REDDING. Yes, Miss Jackson, I think I can make it. Tell Martin, though, that if I'm late, he should go ahead and order. I'll be there promptly if possible.
MISS JACKSON. Thank you, Mr. Redding. I'll deliver your message.

* * * * *

Even the most efficient telephone operators will at times dial the wrong number. This should never be the occasion for anger or impatience. Notice how the three persons concerned in this wrong-number call handle the situation.

MISS JACKSON. Will you get me Capital 6-5100, please?

FIRST OPERATOR. Capital 6-5100.

SECOND OPERATOR. Merchants National Bank. Good morning.

MISS JACKSON. Oh, I'm sorry. We must have dialed the wrong number. Will you excuse it, please?

SECOND OPERATOR. Certainly.

FIRST OPERATOR. Yes, please.

MISS JACKSON. Operator, we must have dialed the wrong number. Will you try Capital 6-5100 again, please?

FIRST OPERATOR. I'm sorry, Miss Jackson. I'll try it again.

Section 2. TELEGRAPHIC SERVICES

Several types of telegraphic service are provided to meet the varying needs of business for the transmittal of important messages. A description of the different types of messages follows.

KINDS OF SERVICE AVAILABLE

Telegram. A full-rate fast service. Telegrams have precedence over all other messages. The initial rate is based on the first 15 words; words in excess of the first 15 are charged for at a reduced rate. If additional words are necessary for clarity, however, the sender should not hesitate to use them. A telegram that is not understood can cause delay and add the additional expense of an extra, and unnecessary, exchange of telegrams to clear up the misunderstanding.

Day Letter. A deferred day service. The initial rate on day letters is based on a minimum of 50 words, making the word rate for long messages lower than the word rate for the full-rate fast service. Each additional 5 words are charged for at a still lower rate. As the time between transmission and delivery of a day letter is from one to two hours, allowance must be made for time-zone differences to insure delivery on the day intended before the closing hours of the office of the addressee. For example, a day letter sent from San Francisco at 3 p.m. might not reach New York until one or two hours later, which would be either 7 or 8 p.m. Eastern Standard Time. A night letter is

often more economical than a day letter for getting a long message to the addressee the following morning. See the time zone map on page 418.

Night Letter. A low-rate overnight service. Night letters may be filed up to 2 a.m. for delivery the following morning. The initial rate is for a minimum of 50 words. Additional words are charged for in groups of 5. As more words are used, the rate is progressively lower.

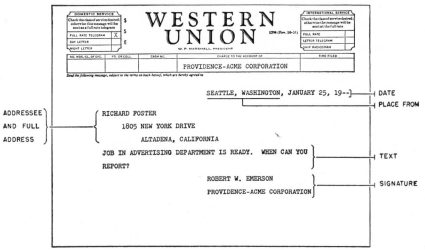

Courtesy Western Union Telegraph Company

A full-rate telegram, correctly typed, with the parts of the telegram identified.

Greeting Messages. Greetings sent for such holidays as Christmas, Easter, Thanksgiving, Mother's Day, Father's Day, and St. Valentine's Day will be delivered on special holiday blanks and in special holiday envelopes at no extra charge to the sender. These messages are charged at the regular rate.

Miscellaneous Services. The telegraph company will provide messengers to run errands and do other odd jobs for a nominal fee.

How to Construct a Telegram. In preparing telegrams or other forms of telegraphic communications, observe the following details:

1. Mark the type of service wanted, under "Class of Service Desired," on the blank telegraphic form.

2. Be sure that the date and a full, correct, and verified inside address are typed in the proper places. Check carefully the spelling of all proper names.

3. Word the message so that it is clearly understood. Leave out un-

necessary and unimportant words, but put in enough words to make the message clear.

4. Avoid contractions and abbreviations.

5. Spell out "East," "West," "North," "South," etc.

6. Do not count punctuation marks as words.

7. Never divide any word by a hyphen at the end of a line.

8. Indicate in the lower left corner whether or not the message is to be sent "Paid," "Collect," or "Charged." Some blanks provide a space at the top for indicating that a message is to be charged.

9. Consult the telegraph company for the latest rates on messages.

A telegraphic communication may be written or typed in the usual way, or it may be written entirely in capital letters. The illustration on page 249 shows a correctly typed telegram.

Carbons and Confirmation. Three copies of a telegram generally are required—the original, or "ribbon" copy, is sent to the telegraph company; another is filed; and the third is mailed, if desired, as a "confirmation" to the addressee. A fourth copy of a charge telegram will be required by the accounting department for use in checking the telegraph company's bill at the end of the month. Additional copies may or may not be needed. It is advisable to have several sets of blanks, with carbon sheets inserted between them, ready for instant use.

Words Counted. The following rules govern the counting of the words to determine the cost:

1. Only the words in the body of the message are counted. The place of origin, date, name, and address of the addressee, and signature of the sender are sent free. There is, however, a charge for the sender's address. Punctuation marks are not counted.

2. Dictionary words from the English, German, French, Italian, Dutch, Portuguese, Spanish, or Latin languages are counted as one word each regardless of length.

3. Proper names from any language are counted according to the number of words and initials they contain as they are normally written. Two or more initials may be written together as a letter group. Examples:

A. B. C. Letter Company. . . . . .5 words
ABC Letter Company. . . . . .3 words
St. Louis. . . . . .2 words

Van Dorne. 2 words
O'Connor. 1 word
John L. Sullivan. . . . . 3 words

4. Abbreviations of single words count as full words.

5. A common abbreviation or a trade term, such as *O.K.*, *a.m.*, *p.m.*, *f.o.b.*, *C.O.D.*, and *S.S.* is counted as one word.

6. Numerals are counted at the rate of one word for every five characters, and may consist of the following characters or combinations of characters:

    a. The arabic numerals themselves; as, *47800.*

    b. Arabic numerals with any of the twenty-six letters of the English alphabet; as, *4780a* or *4B780.*

    c. Arabic numerals with any of the punctuation marks [. , : ; - ? """ ()]; as:
    40,780 . . . . 1 word (comma is not counted)
    485,000 . . . . 2 words

    d. Arabic numerals with other characters [$ / & % # ' (for feet or minutes) and " (for inches or seconds)]; as:
    4780'; *47,800".*

Note that the character ¢ does not appear in group *d.* This sign cannot be transmitted in telegrams. The word "cents" should be used.

7. Ordinal numbers consisting of figures and ordinal affixes (*d*, *st*, *th*) are counted at the rate of five characters or fraction of five characters to the word for the entire group. For example, *3d* is counted as one word; *1287th* is counted as two words.

Delivery Report. In some cases, a report of the delivery of a message is important. If a report is desired, type the words "Report delivery" in a conspicuous place at the top of the telegram. This request will be answered "collect" by the office of destination.

"Repeat Back." Occasionally, a message is of such great importance that it is desirable to have it repeated back from the receiving operator so that it may be checked for errors. When a message is to be repeated, the words "Repeat back" are typed at the top. An additional charge is made for this service.

Payment for Telegrams. Telegraph service may be paid for in any one of three ways:

1. At the time the message is sent. Cash may be required of an infrequent telegraph user.

2. Through charge accounts. Charge accounts are carried by the telegraph companies, particularly for heavy users. A charge account is run on a monthly basis. Also, a person who uses the telephone service for delivering telegrams to the telegraph office may pay for the telegraph service at the end of the month together with his telephone bill.

3. By the one receiving the message. A telegram paid for in this way is sent "collect."

How to Place Telegrams. There are several ways in which telegrams may be placed with the telegraph office.

1. Directly from an office of the telegraph company. The telegraph company maintains a large number of branch offices to facilitate the handling of messages delivered to it by patrons.

2. By telephone. Rapid typists are employed by the telegraph company for speedy reception of messages dictated over the telephone.

3. Messenger boys and call boxes. In large cities, the telegraph company maintains a messenger service. Business offices are supplied with call boxes for summoning messengers. By simply turning a knob or pulling down a lever, the call is registered automatically in the nearest office of the telegraph company; a messenger is sent immediately.

4. Tie lines. Tie lines are direct wires provided by the telegraph companies, when the volume of business justifies, to connect the offices of patrons with the telegraph operating room for the handling of messages. Tie lines in patrons' offices are operated by the patrons' employees.

Sending Money by Telegraph. Money may be transmitted by telegraph to any point in the United States. Money may be transmitted by cable or radio to foreign countries. A telegraphic money order is simply an order that a person pays for at a telegraph office. That office communicates with the desired telegraph office, authorizing the second office to pay to the designated person the amount of the order. A money-order charge and a telegraph toll charge must be paid. The money-order charge is based solely on the amount of money to be sent. The toll charge varies according to the number of words in the message and the destination.

OTHER TELEGRAPHIC SERVICES

The Teleprinter. The teleprinter facilitates the accurate and speedy exchange of messages between patrons' offices and the telegraph com-

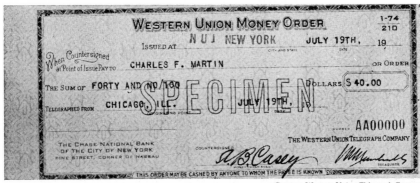

An application for a telegraphic money order with message.

A telegraphic money-order check.

pany. The installation of the teleprinter is desirable where there is a large volume of messages. The teleprinter is operated like a type-writer. When a key is struck on a teleprinter located in the patron's office, the letter is simultaneously recorded on a paper tape in that

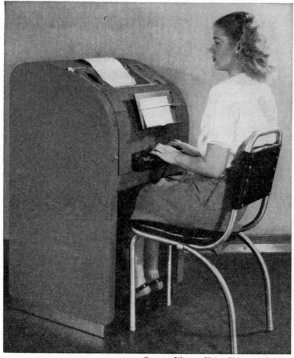

Courtesy Western Union Telegraph Company

A teleprinter.

printer and on the tape of a corresponding machine in the telegraph company's main operating room. A company operator immediately transmits the message to its destination. A reversal of the operation serves to send messages directly to the patron's office. In this manner, the interval between the time the message leaves the sender's office and its receipt by the addressee is reduced to a minimum.

Code is often used, as in this message from one branch office of an airlines company to another branch:

RETEL ULNY 1 ON 4 10 10 NO SPAC 21 19 JGNY TNX

Key: Regarding your telegram about a seat between Montreal and New York I have a seat on trip 4, October 10; but I have no space available on trip 21, October 19, from Niagara Falls to New York. Thank you.

The tape on which messages are typed by the teleprinter is gummed on the under side so that, when moistened, it may be affixed to telegraph blanks provided for that purpose.

Telemeter service provides a fast direct service for companies or persons that exchange a considerable volume of communications. The service is charged for according to the number of words exchanged. The minimum monthly charge is for 25,000 words.

High-Speed Telegraph System. A new ultra-modern national communication system of fifteen high-speed message centers, each serving

Courtesy Western Union Telegraph Company

Operators in a high-speed message center speed the messages along to the destinations indicated on the tapes.

as a funnel for all telegrams to and from one to five states, was completed in 1950. This system inaugurated a new era of telegraph service in the United States, by which telegrams flash automatically from origin to destination without manual retransmission at any point.

When a telegram is sent by an operator from the point of origin at any place in the nation, it flashes to one of the new high-speed centers. A big electrical brain in the center connects incoming messages with the proper outgoing lines and transmits them automatically to their destinations at the speed of 186,000 miles per second. The telegram is received in the distant city in printed form ready for delivery. This system eliminates the old one in which messages arriving at central

offices were sorted by clerks and carried to operators who retransmitted them on their way, often to another relay point.

To interconnect the fifteen high-speed message centers and provide direct circuits between them and other cities, the telegraph company has installed about 2,000,000 channel miles of carrier circuits. Carrier

Courtesy Western Union Telegraph Company

A convenient Desk-Fax for sending and receiving telegrams.

systems permit the transmission of as many as 288 telegrams simultaneously over a single pair of wires, or more than 2,000 simultaneously over the company's microwave radio-beam system.

Facsimile Telegraphy. Facsimile is the newest and fastest growing modern telegraph method. The most widely used facsimile machine is the Desk-Fax, with which the businessman or his secretary can send and receive telegrams by merely touching a switch within arm's reach. Thousands of these tiny machines, which speed service by eliminating the time required for messenger pickup and delivery, have been installed in business offices in many cities. They provide immediate and direct connections with the local telegraph office, where the messages are flashed over the new high-speed national network to their destinations.

Another type of facsimile machine, the Telefax, is used to send and receive messages between local telegraph offices and some hotels, office buildings, universities, and public places. To transmit a telegram by this method, the sender turns the machine on by means of a push button or key; when a panel reading "Deposit Telegram" is lighted, he drops the telegram into a slot in the box. The slot immediately closes to prevent insertion of another telegram before the first one has been transmitted. In the machine, the telegram is automatically wrapped around a revolving cylinder. An electric eye scans the message and flashes electrical impulses over the wire. At the distant end, the arriving impulses produce a picture of the sent mes-

sage ready for immediate use on Teledeltos, an electrosensitive recording paper.

Still another use of facsimile is the Telecar, an automobile equipped
with facsimile recording apparatus, similar to the Telefax, which receives telegrams automatically by radio while the car is cruising in its
assigned area. While the telegram is being received, the Telecar starts

A TELEFAX

Left: The receiving ma-
chine with a telegram
being removed from cabi-
net.
Right: The sending ma-
chine.

Courtesy Western Union Telegraph Company

on its way to the address to deliver it. The Telecar also picks up telegrams in its area and transmits them by radio to the main telegraph
office. Telecars may replace the present system in cities in which
messengers travel from telegraph offices to suburban areas to deliver
telegrams.

INTERNATIONAL COMMUNICATIONS

Telegrams are sent by overland telegraph wire or radio beams.
Cablegrams are sent by means of submarine cables laid across the floor
of the ocean. Cablegrams are used for fast communication between
countries separated by large bodies of water. A cablegram is more
rapid than a letter and less expensive than a telephone conversation.
Messages may also be sent to foreign countries by radio. The classes of
service are the same as those for telegrams, with the addition of ship-
to-shore service. Radio messages are accepted for ships at sea and from
ships at sea.

Cablegrams may be filed with the telegraph company in the same
manner as telegrams. Customers may specify the cable company of
their choice by simply writing on their message the word "via" fol-

lowed by the name of the company that is to send the message. Cablegram messages are typed on the same forms as telegrams. The class of service desired is checked on the right-hand side in the box headed "International Service." (See illustration on page 249.)

Mexico, Canada, and Alaska are in the domestic class of telegraphic service and do not come under the international communication classifications. The rules and regulations applying to domestic telegrams apply to these countries, with this exception: the count of five numerals to a word is not allowed in Canada, where each figure and sign is counted as one word and each group of letters written together is counted at the rate of one word for each five letters or fractions of five letters.

Courtesy Western Union Telegraph Company

The interior of a telecar, showing the removal of a telegram from the Telefax radio receiving machine.

All Central and South American countries are in the same classification; and all messages to them are governed, therefore, by the international rules that are discussed below.

There are two classes of public message international service—full rate and international letter telegrams. A third category, press, is available only for reporters and publishers of public information.

Full Rate. The full-rate classification is the standard, fast service for international messages. Full-rate messages may be written in any plain language that can be expressed in roman letters, or in secret language.

The minimum charge is for five words. Plain-language words are counted at the rate of fifteen letters to the word, and code and cipher at five letters or five figures to the word.

International Letter Telegram. The international letter telegram is a reduced-rate service for international communications written in plain language only. The language employed may be any one of the authorized languages. For example, cable letters are accepted with the understanding that they will be delivered generally on the day after filing. The indicator LT must appear before the address and is charged for as one word. The cable-letter rate is one-half of the full rate, with a minimum charge for twenty-two words. Registered code addresses may be used in the address or signature.

International Code Addresses. A business house that does an extensive foreign business nearly always has a registered international code address, usually consisting of one word, such as "Socony," for "The Standard Oil Company of New York." Unregistered addresses should not be unduly shortened, as government lines abroad hold senders responsible for incorrect or insufficient addresses and will accept corrections or amplifications only by paid-service message at the full rate. While the name of the place of destination and the name of the country, state, or county are counted as one word each, irrespective of how composed, the names of streets and of persons in addresses are counted at fifteen letters or fractions thereof to a word.

Code and Cipher. In code and cipher systems, one word is used to represent a phrase or sentence. The A B C, Western Union, Bentley, and other codes are generally used by businessmen whenever the saving of expense, rather than secrecy, is the chief consideration.

The code books give full information about coding and decoding methods. Anyone may purchase these books from the publishers. During national emergencies, the Government may limit the use of code.

EXAMPLES OF CODE WORDS

Word	*Meaning*
Abhor	Draw with bill of lading attached.
Chasm	For your private information only.
Lucky	Your instructions are having every attention.
Ketch	Until further orders.

Distinction Between Code and Cipher. Note the distinction between the following terms:

Plain language is that which makes intelligible sense in the language used.

Code words may be formed of real words or artificial words. Each five letters or fraction thereof in one group constitutes a chargeable word.

Cipher language is formed of groups of figures or letters having a secret meaning; or of words, names, expressions, or letters not complying with the conditions of plain language or code language. Cipher language is used by governments and others for secrecy.

Sending Money. Cable and radio money orders are accepted in normal times for payment by the cable and radio companies in almost every country in the world. As the rates for this service are subject to change, information about rates should be obtained direct from the cable or telegraph companies when this kind of service is required.

Courtesy United States Lines

Radiograms may be sent to and from ships at sea. Large liners, like the "America," have well-equipped radio rooms.

Some Highlights of This Unit

1. Speak directly into the telephone with your lips about half an inch from the mouthpiece.

2. Make your telephone conversation to the point, but avoid sounding curt.

3. In handling incoming calls:
   a. Answer promptly
   b. Identify yourself
   c. In transferring calls, signal the operator slowly and, if possible, relay the request
   d. If the call is for your employer, handle it according to his wishes
   e. Mentally classify callers quickly

4. In handling requests for information, do not reveal confidential information, but never hesitate to give cheerfully and promptly information which you have permission to give.

5. In securing information for a caller:
   a. Obtain the information promptly
   b. Take the caller's number, if it will take some time to obtain the information, and call back as soon as possible
   c. Try to ascertain where the caller can obtain the desired information if you cannot obtain it for him

6. Avoid incoming and outgoing personal calls at the office except in case of necessity.

7. Keep an alphabetic index of all frequently called or otherwise important numbers.

8. Call "Information" for numbers not listed in the telephone directory.

9. Memorize the suggested alphabetic word list for use in spelling names to "Information" or anyone else when accuracy of spelling is important.

10. A toll call is a call to any telephone outside the local service area, either station-to-station or person-to-person.

11. A private branch exchange (PBX) connects the central office by one or more trunk lines to the private extension telephones distributed throughout a firm's offices.

12. The Dictograph system is a means of communicating between offices in a business organization independent of the telephone switchboard.

13. Money may be transferred by telegraph, by cable, and by radio.

14. The TelAutograph transmits handwriting between the respective offices where the transmitter and the receiver are located.

Questions and Items for Discussion

1. What are the similarities between talking to a caller on the telephone and talking to him face to face? What are the differences?

2. Why is a pleasing telephone personality a personal asset?

3. How would you handle an incoming telephone call for your employer, received under the following circumstances:

    a. When he was not in the office

    b. When he had given instructions that he was not to be interrupted

    c. When he was in the office

4. Name some situations in which a classified telephone directory or the classified section of a general telephone directory could be of help.

5. Describe in their proper sequence the details of making a long-distance telephone call.

6. What is meant by "reversing the charges"? When may the charge for a toll call be reversed?

7. Why would a business be interested in having an unlisted telephone number in addition to those numbers that are listed?

8. Describe the TWX service provided by the telephone company.

9. Describe briefly the following telegraphic services: (*a*) day letter; (*b*) night letter.

10. Of the various classes of telegraphic service, which one has precedence over all the others?

11. Under what conditions might it be better to send a night letter from New York to an addressee in San Francisco rather than a day letter?

12. Distinguish between a telegram and a cablegram. For sending a message to an addressee in Rio de Janeiro, which service would you use?

13. Name another means of transmitting messages to foreign countries.

14. On what basis will you make your decision as to the manner of sending a message by telephone, letter, or wire? If you are in doubt and do not wish to trust your own judgment, with whom would you consult: your employer, the telephone company, the post office, or the telegraph company? Explain your answer.

15. Distinguish between code and cipher.

Personality Questions and Projects
(Based on Personality Pointer, page 227)

1. How does a person reveal his cultural background through speech?

2. Name some peculiarities of speech that can be attributed to place of birth, geographic location, home environment. When are these peculiarities undesirable?

3. What do the following contribute to attractive manner of speech: college education; dramatic training; world-wide travel; extensive reading; attendance at public lectures; radio listening; vocabulary study? Explain your answers.

4. These expressions describe a manner of speaking. Which ones apply to you?

Rate of Speaking: Responsive to ideas to be expressed. Rapid. Methodical. Slow.

Vocabulary: Sparkling. Limited. Colorless.

Grammar: Flawless. Faulty. Careless.

Facial Expression: Animated. Stiff. Needs muscular control. Blank.

Attitudes Reflected in Speech: Understanding. Friendly. Positive. Negative. Aggressive. Offensive.

5. The following situations emphasize the importance of careful speech. Write your solution to each in your notebook. After a few days, reread the situations and your answers. Ask yourself whether you have employed tact, good grammar, and effective words in your answers. Read your answers aloud and reflect the proper attitude in your voice and manner of speaking. Here are the situations.

When Anne Sumner was in high school, and during vacations from college, she used to work in the office of a small electric-light company.

She soon learned that the work of dealing with the public consisted largely of reciting various company rules, all necessary and all unpopular. And she learned that one of the rules was that she must not tell anyone, "You'll have to" do such-and-such a thing.

Every customer wanted to be an exception, and no customer could be. The customers really did have to do certain things, and Anne had to see that they did them; but she was not permitted to tell them so outright.

One of the rules was this: The company would not send a man to connect an electric meter until the new customer had signed a connecting order. That entailed a visit to the office. In addition to signing the order, the customer had to deposit $5 with the company (as a guarantee that bills would be paid) or else persuade a property owner to sign the order with him, as his guarantor.

Assume that you are doing the work Anne did, in the same office. Most of the time, no one else is in the office.

a. A haughty voice informs you, "Mrs. Beverley Houston speaking. I wish to have the electric service connected immediately at 312 Avondale Street."

Break the news to her, in less than twenty-five words, that you must have a signed contract before service can be given.

b. She replies, in apparent surprise, "Why, I can't possibly visit your office! I'm busy supervising the moving men. You'll have to send the order over here if you want it signed."

Answer Mrs. Houston courteously, but remember the company rule. You cannot take the contract to her. Your office is only three blocks from 312 Avondale Street.

c. An authoritative masculine voice informs you next, by telephone, "This is Beverley Houston. I understand you refused to connect the current when my wife telephoned you a few minutes ago. I want to talk to your manager."

The manager is out; inform Mr. Houston of that fact. (Keep calm, cool, and collected. Make your words and your voice sound sympathetic, whether you feel that way or not.)

d. "All right," snaps Mr. Houston. "Send the contract over to my office and I'll sign it."

You have no way of sending the contract.

Try to persuade him to come to your office himself. You know his office is less than a block away.

e. "Very well," he answers coldly. "I'll be there shortly. Meanwhile, *will* you send the man to my house *immediately?* There's no necessity for you to be so fussy about details, you know."

Answer tactfully and pleasantly. You must refuse to send a lineman until Mr. Houston has signed the contract.

Secretarial Assignments

In order to get the full benefit from these telephone assignments, you should read each solution aloud, with appropriate vocal expression and in the presence of someone who will criticize wording and expression.

1. You are in the midst of typing a long legal document. You must finish the job within a limited time. The telephone has been ringing unusually often, causing you to interrupt your work to answer it. You finally say to yourself, "If that telephone rings again, I'll scream!" and it rings again. The caller is a very important client, Dean Elder, who wants to speak to Mr. Martin. Mr. Martin is in and will talk with Mr. Elder. Write down both sides of the conversation between yourself and the caller, beginning with your answer to the telephone ring.

2. Mr. Martin has gone for the day. He told you that he is expecting a telephone call from Mr. William Rader, of the Petroleum Corporation. You are to find out from Mr. Rader where Mr. Martin can reach him by telephone tomorrow morning and at what time.

When you receive Mr. Rader's call, he says that he will not be at a telephone where Mr. Martin can reach him tomorrow morning. You suggest, then, that Mr. Rader call Mr. Martin on the telephone in the morning at ten.

a. Write down both sides of the conversation between yourself and Mr. Rader, beginning with your answer to the telephone ring.

b. Write out a memorandum of this call to place on Mr. Martin's desk, using one of the call slips from Sheet 37 of your Workbook.

3. You receive a call for Mr. Martin from one of his best friends, Jim Raseley, from Baltimore, Maryland. You know that Mr. Martin would be glad to talk with Mr. Raseley; but the president of the company is with Mr. Martin, and you think it better not to disturb him with this call.

You ask Mr. Raseley whether Mr. Martin can reach him later by telephone. Mr. Raseley replies that he is in town between trains, for about three hours, and that he will be at the Athletic Club, Main 6000, for about half an hour.

a. Write down both sides of the conversation between yourself and the caller, beginning with your answer to the telephone ring.

b. Make a record of this call on one of the call slips on Sheet 37 in your Workbook and place it on Mr. Martin's desk.

4. About fifteen minutes after the situation described in Assignment 3, Mr. Martin is free; and you remind him about the call from Jim Raseley. Mr. Martin asks you to get Mr. Raseley at the Athletic Club.

Write down both sides of the conversation from the time you call the Athletic Club until you connect Mr. Martin with Mr. Raseley.

5. The operator has referred a call to your extension by mistake. The caller wants to speak to Mr. Black in the Legal Department.

Write down both sides of the conversation with this caller, in which you explain the mistake and ask the operator to transfer the call to Mr. Black.

* * * *

The following matters have come up requiring telegraphic responses by your office manager. Write the telegrams from the following instructions, making one original and three carbon copies of each. Use the telegraph blanks on Sheets 38 and 39 of your Workbook for the originals; make carbons on plain paper. Have all telegrams charged to your company's account.

6. A telegram has been received from one of your dealers, Mr. J. W. Linden, 72 Liberty Street, Utica, New York, in which he states that the floor samples of sun lamps he ordered have not yet been received and that he is receiving calls for them daily. Send Mr. Linden a full-rate charge telegram explaining in as few words as possible that the lamps were shipped to the wrong address by mistake but that a second shipment correctly addressed was forwarded by express yesterday and should arrive in a few days.

7. A telegram has been received from another dealer, Mr. H. L. Bridges, 7261 South 18th Street, Philadelphia, asking if there has been any recent change in price in your Model T—008 refrigerator. Send him a full-rate charge telegram telling him that it still sells for $290 but that a 5 per cent increase in price may go into effect next month.

8. On Monday, one of your representatives, Mr. Frank Barton, wires

from Charlotte, North Carolina, that the executives of the company's southern sales agency are planning a meeting in that city for Wednesday and Thursday, on which days he should be in Baltimore.

Mr. Barton wants to know whether he should extend his stay in Charlotte until after the meeting.

Send Mr. Barton a night telegram at the Colonial Arms Hotel in Charlotte asking him to stay over until after the meeting. State also that arrangements are being made from your office for another representative, Mr. Arthur Lyons, to take care of the Baltimore calls. Instruct Mr. Barton to proceed to Lynchburg, Virginia, after his Charlotte visit.

9. Send a telegraphic money order for $250 to Mr. Arthur Lyons, who is staying at the Pittsburgher Hotel, Pittsburgh, Pennsylvania, with a message asking him to fly to Baltimore tomorrow morning (Tuesday). Tell him that a letter with further instructions will be waiting for him at the Hotel Lord Baltimore, Baltimore, Maryland. Use Sheet 40 in your Workbook.

10. Mr. Martin asks you to prepare a cablegram in code to send to Mr. H. W. Potter in London. Mr. Potter's code address is "Claridge." You are to tell Mr. Potter that all prices are advanced 10 per cent until further notice. Your company's code name is "Unipro." Use the form on Sheet 41 in your Workbook.

Select the code words for your message from the following list taken from the Universal Trade Code. Remember that you pay for each word in the address, message, and signature. Reduce your message to as few words as possible.

ageyb	all	loiez	raised all prices (of)
agfes	all are (is)	klehf	9 per cent
aghee	all or any part (of)	klemk	10 per cent
agikj	all will be	klero	11 per cent
leorw	can raise price-s to	imtit	not until further notice
loaja	price-s raised (on)	imuku	official notice (of)
loasv	price-s rising	imvir	until further notice
loelx	price-s will be raised (by)	imxau	without notice (of)
lohyi	raise-s all prices (of)		

11. Mr. Martin received the following radiogram from Mr. Arthur Dodds who is on his way to Panama, traveling on the S.S. "Washington":

CHARLES MARTIN
UNITED PRODUCTS CORPORATION
500 MADISON AVENUE
NEW YORK CITY
CURTIS REPRESENTATIVE ON BOARD. HAS CONTRACT BEEN APPROVED?

DODDS

Mr. Martin asks you to prepare a radiogram telling Mr. Dodds that the contract was approved today and that he is to proceed as planned. Use the radiogram blank in your Workbook, Sheet 41.

Optional

12. Mr. Martin is out of the office. You are in the midst of transcribing a reference letter regarding John Stephens, a former employee in your department. The letter is in answer to a request from a company where Mr. Stephens is now making application.

You receive a telephone call from Mr. Stephens in which he asks whether you have received the inquiry from the other company; whether Mr. Martin has answered the inquiry; and, if so, what he said in the letter.

Mr. Martin has given you no instructions, but you know that such matters are confidential. You tell Mr. Stephens tactfully that the inquiry was received. Of course, you cannot tell him what Mr. Martin said in his reply.

  a. Write down both sides of the conversation, beginning with your answer to Mr. Stephens's ring.
  b. Make a memorandum of Mr. Stephens's call to place on Mr. Martin's desk. Use one of the telephone message slips in your Workbook, Sheet 37.

13. Mr. Brown, of the Household Furnishings Department, calls and asks what the decision was regarding the new consignment of electric stoves. You ask Mr. Brown to hold the line a moment while you ask Mr. Martin. Mr. Martin says, "I'll have to get in touch with Black of the Legal Department first. Just a moment, I'll get Black on the other wire." Mr. Martin gets Mr. Black, but you see that the conversation is going to be longer than you thought it would be; so you return to your telephone and ask Mr. Brown whether you may call him back when Mr. Martin gets the information. Mr. Brown says that will be satisfactory.

Write down what you would say to Mr. Brown, beginning with your request that he hold the line a moment.

14. Mr. Martin asks you to put through a person-to-person call to Mr. George Ames, of the Chicago office. The Chicago office number is Park 6281. Your number is Caledonia 5-3421.

What will you say to the long-distance operator?

15. The secretary is often asked by her chief to get a particular person on the telephone for him. All unnecessary conversation on the secretary's part should be avoided, and the time involved should be reduced to a minimum. This is such a call as it is sometimes made:

TELEPHONE VOICE. Mr. Johnson's office, Miss Forbes speaking.
CALLING SECRETARY. Mr. Martin, of the United Products Corporation, would like to speak to Mr. Johnson.

TELEPHONE VOICE. One moment, please. (*Buzzes Mr. Johnson's telephone.*)
CALLING SECRETARY. Mr. Johnson, Mr. Martin, of the United Products
Corporation, is calling. One moment, please. (*Buzzes Mr. Martin's
telephone or hands the telephone to Mr. Martin.*)

   a. How would you change this conversation to eliminate unnecessary
   steps?
   b. How would this situation be handled if Mr. Johnson had answered the
   telephone instead of his secretary?

   16. A new typist in your office transcribed a telegram at your typewriter,
using the shift lock. Just as she finished typing, she was called away to take
dictation; and you offered to complete the sending of the telegram. This is
the result:

JOHN KENNEDY
UNITED PRODUCTS CORPORATION
__NORTH MICHIGAN AVENUE
CHICAGO, ILLINOIS

ORDER &'(%B DATED MAY #L SHIPPED JUNE __ TO
BARKER BROTHERS __ L# ATLANTIC PLACE JERSEY CITY
TOTAL $#L$.(" TERMS TWO TEN NET #).

By typing the same thing without using any capitals, you can quickly
decode this confusing message. Type it properly and count the words for
the straight telegram. Sign Charles F. Martin's name. Use Sheet 42 in your
Workbook.

Spelling Demons

illiterate	independence	irrevocable
immigrant	inhabitant	judgment
incidentally	intercede	justifiable

Job Tips

   1. In an effort to prevent a telephone caller from hearing your comments,
do not place the transmitter against your chest while speaking to someone in
the office. The calling party can hear you plainly! Sometimes covering the
transmitter with your hand is also inadequate to close off aside comments.

   2. In answering an unlisted business telephone, do not follow the usual
custom of identifying yourself or your business. Answer the phone by saying,
"Hello."

   3. When a telephone call to your employer seems to be of a very personal
nature and you should be in his office when it comes in, be courteous and
leave the room quietly while he converses.

4. *Never* make comments pertaining to a telephone call until the receiver has been *securely* replaced.

5. If your employer comes to your desk to dictate a rush telegram and you have a transcript in the typewriter, the following procedure can be used on some typewriters and with some stationery: Roll the transcript backward until only an inch or so is left in front of the platen. Now drop a telegraph blank against the paper table and behind each of the carbons—add additional carbons, if necessary. Roll all material to proper typing position on the telegraph blank. Type the telegram as it is dictated to you. Then, roll all material backwards again. Remove the telegraph blanks and any extra carbons. Position the transcript, and continue with your transcribing.

# Personality Pointer

WHAT DO YOU SAY?

When you are a member of a conversational group, what do you say and how do you say it? This question is important to you, because the answer in most instances is an indication of your cultural background, social behavior, and your work status.

Culture has to do with the finer things of life. Webster defines the word as "the enlightenment and refinement of taste acquired by intellectual and aesthetic training"; *refinement* is defined as "to free from dullness, earthiness, to improve or perfect as by pruning or polishing, to free from what is coarse, vulgar, inelegant."

The "training" is the persistent will "to do." "Intellectual and aesthetic growth" come about through the reading of good books covering a great variety of subjects and perhaps specializing in a few; by attending lectures, concerts, plays, symphonies, the ballet; by becoming acquainted with art collections and historical museums; by traveling; by attending evening classes; by associating with worthwhile persons, and so on.

You cannot afford to be unfamiliar with the daily happenings in your local community, the nation, and the world as chronicled in the daily papers and the weekly news periodicals. Include in your reading some magazines and digests of general nature.

What you say and how you say it will reflect the "enlightenment and refinement" you have acquired through the program you carry out.

271

Reports, Tabulations, and Other Forms of Business Writing

In addition to the writing of business letters, your secretarial duties may also include many other forms of business writing. While they are of great importance in modern business offices, you will probably not be called upon to execute these duties as frequently as you will write letters. For example, the drawing up of legal papers is a relatively infrequent transaction in most offices.

A section of this unit is devoted to the development of reports and manuscripts with helpful guides to their mechanical perfection. One section will discuss the preparation of graphs and charts. Another section will describe those legal papers most frequently encountered in the office. The last section will give you information about other important forms of business writing such as the typing of cards, labels, advertising copy, publicity releases, digests, summaries, and the like.

As you study this unit and complete the secretarial assignments for it, you should realize that your value to your employer increases immeasurably to the extent that you can carry these responsibilities to their successful conclusion. They require you to "think"; they are not the routine duties of the stenographer.

Section 1. REPORTS AND MANUSCRIPTS

Secretaries may be called upon at one time or another to help in the preparation of reports and manuscripts. Most executives have occasions for issuing reports and bulletins, composing articles for house

272

organs and trade journals, writing speeches for conventions and dinners, and preparing advertising copy. Some executives also write books. Except for advertisements, all these forms of writing are longer than the ordinary business letter.

The secretary's editorial duties include helping with the gathering of the material, the reading of proof, and the actual transcribing and typing of the dictated manuscript. This phase of your secretarial position can be intensely interesting and can offer you an unusual opportunity to display initiative and creative ability.

DEVELOPMENT OF THE SUBJECT MATTER

Subject Matter. The purpose of an administrative report is to summarize past action on some situation and, usually, to make a recommendation for a future course of action. A report, for example, may be from a subordinate to an executive, from one department head to another, or from a corporation to its stockholders.

In length, reports vary all the way from one page—in which case the report usually resembles a letter or an interoffice memorandum—to a volume large enough to be bound. Because of the factual nature of the report, its language must be clear and direct. Attempts at "fine writing" are entirely out of place.

Manuscripts of articles and books, however, may deal with almost any subject and may run to any length. The literary style will vary with the author's individuality and the subject matter.

Preparation of First Drafts. Writers have their individual methods of preparing manuscripts. Some write them first in longhand and revise the copy before having it typed. Others prepare complete outlines and dictate sections from the outlines. Almost all copy is revised more than once before reaching its final form.

In retyping revised pages containing numerous transposed sections, the secretary will often find it much easier to cut the sections apart and pin or paste them in proper order than to try to follow a complicated plan of inserts and transpositions.

Styling. A manuscript may be clearly expressed and artistically and neatly typed and still be very crude from an editorial point of view. The critical reader will receive a very poor impression of the working methods of the author if the niceties of style are disregarded; for example, if the same or similar words are capitalized sometimes and

written in small letters other times, if a certain term is abbreviated in some cases and spelled out in others, if numbers are expressed in figures in some cases and in words in others, or if the "saltcellar" method of punctuation is used. The poor impression won't be the author's fault at all—it will be his secretary's.

The fundamentals of correct English and style are discussed in Unit 7. Consult this section frequently. The secretarial handbooks, manuals, and English grammars listed in Unit 6 give more detailed information.

The most practical way of making sure that you will maintain a consistent style is to note on a sheet of paper or in a notebook representative illustrations of various style features as they arise. Reference to this sheet will save much time.

Spelling problems are easily settled by the simple rule of invariably choosing the first, or preferred, spelling given in a dependable dictionary.

Outlines. The development of an outline for the report or manuscript to be prepared is a timesaving and effective procedure. Moreover, much report material lends itself to presentation in outline form; that is, in the form of headings with subheadings. The steps are usually numbered and indented according to the following scheme:

I. Elements necessary to formation of a contract:
  A. Agreement:
    1. Reality of assent:
      a. Mistake:
        (1) As to existence of subject matter:
          (*a*) Illustration.

It is seldom necessary, however, to make subordinations so detailed.

In outlining, remember that all ideas that are parallel should be expressed in parallel form; that is, in a series of nouns, of phrases, of clauses, etc.

Parallel: Reasons for decline in sales of machine:
    1. The public is spending its money on increased taxes.
    2. The weather has been unseasonable.
    3. The machine is out of date.
          or
    1. Increased taxes.
    2. Unseasonable weather.
    3. Out-of-date model.

Faulty: Reasons for decline in sales of machine:
1. The public is spending its money on increased taxes.
2. Unseasonable weather.
3. Out of date.

Quotations. The opinions of authorities are often quoted in both reports and manuscripts. The secretary is frequently asked to locate and verify quotations. This operation should include a check on the exact spelling of the author's name and the title of the work being quoted, with the page reference and, if a periodical, the date of issue.

In typing quotations, remember:

1. Brief quotations—those consisting of three or four lines—should be run in on the same line as the text matter that introduces them, and they should be enclosed in quotation marks. If the quotation itself contains quotation marks, these should be changed to single quotation marks (made by striking the apostrophe key).

2. Quotations consisting of more than four or five lines should be typed as single-spaced separate paragraphs. Quotation marks are not needed in such cases.

3. Quotations must be copied exactly as they appear in the original —in capitalization, punctuation, spelling, and paragraphing.

4. Passages from copyrighted publications must not be quoted without written permission from the publisher and copyright owner. Infringement of copyright is a serious offense, and the offender is liable to prosecution by the copyright owner.

Footnotes. References to authorities for statements or assertions in the text matter, sources of quotations and of further material, and extraneous comments are placed in footnotes. A mark of reference is placed directly after the word, sentence, or number in the text that is to be explained; and the same reference mark is placed before the corresponding footnote.

Footnotes should always be single spaced. About footnotes, remember:

1. The reference marks may be asterisks (other symbols, such as the # sign, being used for a second footnote on a page) or superior figures, made by the use of the variable line spacer.

2. Usually footnotes are numbered consecutively through a report or through a chapter.

3. As you type the mark of reference, estimate the number of lines each footnote will require and allow sufficient space at the bottom of

the page. If you use carbon sheets that bear line numbers at the right-hand side, you can tell at a glance when you are approaching the point where you should type the footnote. Otherwise, you can use a ruler and measure down from the top of the sheet, to determine how much space you have available.

4. References to other publications must be consistently arranged. Such references are especially important in manuscripts of reference works. The following order is standard:

> *a.* Author's name, with Christian name or initials first. (The name need not be repeated if it is mentioned in the text.)
> *b.* Name of publication or of article in a periodical. (The name of the publication or the periodical should be underscored, which indicates it is to be italicized by the printer.)
> *c.* Place of publication, name of publisher, and date of publication.
> *d.* Reference to volume and page.

Here are some representative footnotes:
Reference to a Book:

Fred T. Wilhems, *Consumer Living* (New York, The Gregg Publishing Division, McGraw-Hill Book Company, Inc., 1951), p. 334.
Reference to a Magazine Article:

Harold Schneider, "The Crosspatch Guide to Letter Placement," *Business Education World*, September, 1951, p. 25.

5. When there are two consecutive references to the same work on the same page, the word *"Ibid.,"* (an abbreviation for the Latin, *ibidem*, meaning "the same") may be used for the second footnote.

[2] *Ibid.*, p. 215.

Tables. Statistical matter is an important part of most reports and of many manuscripts. Such material is best presented by means of tables. The secretary has a rare opportunity to show her combined talents in arranging tabulated material: skill in the operation of the typewriter, understanding of artistic balance, and—if she helps with the compiling of the data—mathematical dexterity.

In addition to understanding the mechanics of tabulation, which are more fully discussed on pages 288-292, you will need to:

1. Understand what the table is intended to show. If you are given a rough draft of the table, read the column headings, noting which are amount columns, which are percentage columns, and which columns

contain other quantities. This study will help you to establish the proper relationship between column widths and between main and subordinate column heads.

2. Decide whether the arrangement first planned is the best. For example, the first of the illustrations on this page shows a table that has many more column heads than sideheads, making the table wide

COMPARATIVE STATISTICS ON GREAT LAKES

Great Lakes	Length (Miles)	Breadth (Miles)	Maximum Depth (Feet)	Area (Square Miles)			National Boundary (Miles)
				U. S.	Canada	Total	
Superior.....	350	160	1,290	20,710	11,110	31,820	282.8
Michigan.....	307	118	923	22,400	......	22,400	.....
Huron........	206	101	750	9,110	13,900	23,010	260.8
Erie........	241	57	210	4,990	4,950	9,940	251.5
Ontario......	193	53	774	3,560	3,980	7,430	174.6

Two tables based on the same information. Which do you find easier to read?

COMPARATIVE STATISTICS ON GREAT LAKES

Statistics	Superior	Michigan	Huron	Erie	Ontario
Length (miles)............	350	307	206	241	193
Breadth (miles)...........	160	118	101	57	53
Maximum depth (feet).......	1,290	923	750	210	774
Area (square miles):					
United States............	20,710	22,400	9,110	4,990	3,560
Canada.................	11,110	......	13,900	4,950	3,980
Total..................	31,820	22,400	23,010	9,940	7,430
National boundary (miles)..	282.8	......	260.8	251.5	174.6

and short. In the rearranged form, the column heads and sideheads have been reversed, thus making the table narrower and more easily read. A table thus revised should be carefully checked to be sure no errors were made in the revision process.

3. Center the title of the table over the table, usually in all capital letters. If the title is too long for one line, it should be broken where there is a division of thought. No period is necessary after a heading.

Poor: CRUDE PETROLEUM PRODUCTION BY CHIEF
STATES OF THE UNITED STATES

Better: CRUDE PETROLEUM PRODUCTION
BY CHIEF STATES OF THE UNITED STATES

4. For suggestions on arranging financial statements, see Section 2.

5. Place footnotes to tables immediately below the table, as in the table on page 279, not at the bottom of the manuscript page.

6. Remember that neat ruling adds a great deal to the appearance of a table and makes a table with many columns more easily read. For methods of ruling, see Section 2.

7. Avoid using worn carbon paper in typing tables. Change the carbon sheet often enough so there will be no doubt about any figure, even on the last copy made.

8. Check all tables carefully after typing, preferably with someone else. The person who did *not* type the table should read from the original copy. It is easier to read down the columns than across. Any obscure figures should be verified by the person who compiled the table. Where totals are given, the safest check is by addition. All corrections must also be made on the carbon copies.

Graphic Charts. Since many reports contain statistical material, the secretary should be able to construct simple forms of graphs. Graphs are discussed in detail on pages 292-296. Graphs intended for illustrations in books should be prepared by trained draftsmen.

GUIDES TO MECHANICAL PERFECTION

In this section you will learn much about the many items that must be considered by the secretary to insure the mechanical perfection of the reports and manuscripts prepared in the office.

Paper. Reports are intended to look impressive; therefore, they are usually typed on a good quality of bond paper. Manuscripts of articles, books, or bulletins, which are eventually set in type, need not be typed on such high-quality paper. Never type the original copy of a report or manuscript on onionskin paper; it is not strong enough.

If a report is to be bound in a loose-leaf binder, punched paper should be used, thus saving the time of punching the sheets later. It will be necessary to know, however, whether the binder is to be a two-ring or a three-ring style.

Spacing and Margins. Manuscript copy should always be typed double spaced. The first draft should have extra-wide margins to allow space for changes and additions. The following table gives good standards for margins of final drafts.

MINIMUM MANUSCRIPT MARGINS
(In inches)

Margin	Bound at Top	Bound at Side	Unbound
Top margin:			
First page *..............	3	2	2
Other pages..............	2	1	1
Side margin:			
Left.....................	1½	2	1½
Right...................	1½	1	1½
Bottom margin.............	1½	1	1¼

* The first page of each chapter and of the preface, table of contents, index, or appendix.

The right margin should be as even as possible. If any page is short —for example, because a full-length table follows on the next page— write the word "More" below the last line on the short page.

Numbering the Pages. Every page of a manuscript should be numbered. If a report or a manuscript is to be bound at the top, the page numbers should be placed at the bottom of the page, as nearly as possible in the same position on the sheet. If the report or the manuscript is to be unbound or bound at the left, the page numbers should be at the top of the pages, each in the center or at the upper right corner. No period need follow a page number.

Headings. Most reports and manuscripts contain various headings, which are introduced to make the relationship of the material clear. It is therefore necessary for the secretary at all times to follow the trend of thought in order that co-ordinate headings may be displayed in the same style.

Remember these points about headings:

1. Headings indicating the principal divisions of a report or of a chapter are usually centered in all capitals. If still further emphasis is desired, such headings may also be spaced out and underscored.

2. Subordinate headings may be written flush with the margin or indented, written in the margin, or inserted in a space allowed in the body of the paragraph, as shown in the illustration on page 280.

3. More white space should be allowed above a center head than below it.

UNIT XI

REPORTS, TABULATIONS, AND OTHER FORMS OF BUSINESS WRITING

In addition to the writing of business letters, your secretarial duties may also include many other forms of business
writing. While they are of great importance in modern business offices, you will probably not be called upon to execute
these duties as frequently as you will write letters. For
example, the drawing up of legal papers is a relatively infrequent transaction in most offices.

Guides to Mechanical Perfection

In this section you will learn much about the many items
that must be considered by the secretary to insure the mechanical perfection of the reports and manuscripts prepared.

Paper. Reports are intended to look impressive; therefore, they are usually typed on a good quality of bond paper.
Manuscripts of articles, books, or bulletins, which are eventually set in type, need not be typed on such high quality
paper. Never type the original copy of a report or manuscript
on tissue or onionskin paper; it is not strong enough.

Headings of different weight in a manuscript.

4. Unless a heading is in question form, no mark of punctuation is needed after a center head or a subordinate head that is not run in. A run-in paragraph heading, however, should be followed by a period.

5. An attractive appearance is obtained by typing the leading headings in color.

Title Page. A report, bulletin, or manuscript requires a title page. Your typing course covered the planning and arranging of such pages. Points to be kept in mind may be summarized as follows:

1. The title should be placed somewhat above the center of the sheet and displayed by the use of all capitals, spacing between letters, and underscoring.

2. If the title is too long to go on one line, it may be placed on two or more lines, the breaks coming where there is a division of thought.

3. For a report, the name of the person or the department submitting the report, together with the date, is usually centered near the bottom of the page. For a manuscript, the name of the author, with his titles or connections, is usually centered about halfway down the page.

4. Punctuation should be kept to the minimum. No periods should be used at the ends of lines.

Copyright. Some authors prefer to copyright their books and pamphlets rather than to follow the more usual custom of having the publisher attend to the copyrighting.

In any copyrighted book, the following notice must appear either on the title page or on the reverse of the title page, preferably on the latter.

Copyright (date), by
(Name of proprietor of copyright)
All rights reserved

To copyright a book, write the Register of Copyrights, Washington, D. C., requesting an application form. State whether the book is being published for the first time in the United States or whether it is a revised edition of a former publication.

Fill out the application blank and send it, with two copies of the printed book and a certified check or a money order for $4, to the Register of Copyrights.

Table of Contents. In a table of contents, the chapters or sections of a report or book are listed in the order in which they appear, each item being followed by the number of the page on which the chapter or section begins. The table of contents, therefore, cannot be prepared until the manuscript is completed.

Order of Material. When the manuscript of a report has been completed, the typed copy should be assembled according to the following conventional sequence:

Title page	Text
Letter authorizing the report	Conclusions
Letter of transmittal	Recommendation
Table of contents	Appendix
Synopsis	Bibliography
Introduction	Index

The title page should give the title of the report, the person or committee for whom it was prepared, the name of the compiler, and the date on which the report was submitted.

For shorter, less formal reports, the letter authorizing the report, the letter of transmittal, the synopsis, and other items may be omitted, according to the wishes of the compiler.

For manuscripts of books, the following is the standard order of the material:

Title page	Introduction
Copyright	Chapters I to end
Dedication (if any)	Appendix
Preface	Bibliography
Contents	Index

Indexing. The making of the index to a book, whether historical, biographical, scientific, or technical, is more of a job than most persons realize. The author is the person best fitted to make the index because he knows the content of the book thoroughly. Often, however, he does not have the time to do so, or for some other reason will assign the task either to a professional indexer or to his secretary. If the secretary is asked to make the index, she should consult the indexes of a few standard works in the same field, to see how fully they are indexed and the type of headings included. She should also study one or more of the reference books on indexing.

Indexes are prepared on 5 x 3 cards with one entry to a card. These cards are alphabetized and numbered before being sent to the printer.

Binding. When all the material that makes up the report has been assembled in proper order (see page 281), the report is ready for binding. The style of binding depends on the thickness of the report and the handling it will receive.

Covers may be made of heavy art paper, which may be purchased at a stationery store. Ordinary Manila file folders are also suitable for covers. Loose-leaf binders are especially desirable for long reports or for those that are to receive hard wear.

Pages may be fastened together by one of several devices:

1. Wire staples, put on by a stapling machine, are suitable for short reports—those not longer than about fifteen pages.

2. Metal eyelets may be inserted through holes punched in the paper and clamped in place by a special attachment.

3. Ordinary paper fasteners, the style having a head and two separable ends, which are bent back on the under side, have the advantage of making it easy to separate the pages of the report.

4. Tape or cord may be passed through punched holes and tied in a neat, flat bow. This method of binding has the advantage of permitting the report to lie flat while open.

Gummed reinforcements may be bought to outline punched holes and prevent paper from tearing.

The title of the report should appear on the cover. If the cover material is flexible enough to go into the typewriter, the title may be typed directly on it. If not, it may be typed on a small slip of heavy paper and pasted neatly on the cover.

Illustrations. Illustrations are an extremely important part of many articles and books. The illustrations may be in the form of photographs, drawings, charts, etc. Here are some points to remember in submitting illustration copy to the printer.

1. Copy for photographs must be *original* photographs, not halftone illustrations that have been printed in other publications. Such prints do not reproduce satisfactorily.

2. Do not paste or mount photographs or other illustrations on the same page with the matter that is to be set in type, for illustrations are handled separately—by draftsmen, artists, and engravers.

3. Indicate, either on the back of the illustrations or on a separate sheet of paper, the wording of the legends or captions that should be used for the illustrations. Never write instructions or legends on the face of the illustration copy.

Caution: In writing on the backs of photographs, do not press hard enough to show through on the face of the photograph, as such marks reproduce.

4. In preparing sketches, outline drawings, charts, etc., for reproduction, use black or India ink only, as blue ink does not photograph without the use of special, expensive color screens.

5. Have any charts or drawings containing ruled lines and lettering prepared by a mechanical draftsman, unless you are expert in the use of ruling pen, triangle, and T-square.

6. In preparing illustration copy on the typewriter, see that the "color" (the impression) is even and the type faces sharp.

7. Photographs or drawings should be at least half as large again as the final form, for better results are obtained when illustrations are reduced in size in the photoengraving process.

Type. Most secretaries, sooner or later, find it necessary to know something about the commonly used type faces. Any executive may have an occasional leaflet, circular, or price list to be set in type; and the secretary to an advertising or sales manager or a publishing-house executive is sure to need the information. The accompanying illustrations of the most commonly used styles and sizes of type will give some idea of the variety of effects obtainable.

Type faces are divided into main groups, or families, such as Roman, Gothic, Script, and Old English. Some are simple and very easy to read; others are more complex. Type, by its structure, is made to suggest certain qualities. Such faces as Bodoni may suggest ruggedness; Caslon may suggest delicacy. The skillful advertiser will attempt to have his message set in a face that combines attractiveness, readability, and a relation to the product.

Sizes and Styles of Type

This line is set in 10-point type.

This line is set in 12-point type.

THIS LINE IS SET IN CAPITALS (OR CAPS).

This Line Is Set in Caps and Small Caps.

this line is set in small caps.

This Line Is Set in Caps and Lower Case.

This line is set in italic.

This line is set in boldface.

Manufacturers of type have agreed on a uniform standard of measurement called the "point system." A point measures $\frac{1}{72}$ of an inch. Thus, 36-point type is $\frac{1}{2}$ inch high; 18-point is $\frac{1}{4}$ inch high; 72-point is 1 inch high. Text matter is usually set in 8, 10, or 12 point. For headlines, 12, 18, 24, 36, and 48 point are most used. Light-faced type may be used for text, and bold-faced, or heavy, type for headlines and signature.

Galley and Page Proof. Before a book is printed, the printer sends two kinds of proof to the author: galley proof and page proof. The galley proof is the first proof sent. On this the material is set up in long sheets about the length of a newspaper column and in the width that has been selected for the printed page. This galley proof is cor-

rected by the proofreader and the author and returned to the printer. After the printer has made the indicated corrections, he divides the galleys into page lengths and "pulls" page proof. The page proof shows exactly what the printed book or report pages will show: the headings at the top of each page, illustrations, if there are any, and page numbers. This page proof is again corrected by the proofreader and author and returned to the printer. Usually, no other proof is sent to the author.

Proofreading. The secretary to a person who writes books or articles is almost always expected to read the proofs of the author's works. As the secretary is usually familiar with the manuscript, in most cases having typed it, she is the logical person to read the proof.

Proofreading is anything but a mechanical task. It requires great concentration, accuracy, a quick eye for inconsistencies of all kinds, and "an infinite capacity for taking pains."

The proofreader may read the proof alone, verifying figures, proper names, and unusual terms by referring to the manuscript. If the subject matter is of a technical nature, however, and contains a great many tables, numbers, and scientific terms, the proofreading should be done with a copyholder; that is, someone should read aloud from the manuscript while the proofreader follows the proof.

The copyholder should:

1. Spell out all unusual proper names, other unusual terms, and common personal names that are spelled in more than one way, as Reid, Reade, Reed.

2. Enunciate *s*'s distinctly and indicate the possessive clearly.

3. Read all punctuation marks.

4. Read figures efficiently; that is, read 5428 as "Five-four-two-eight," not, "Five thousand four hundred twenty-eight." Also read decimals by saying the word "point" to indicate the decimal point; as "Point o-o-four-seven" for .0047.

5. Read dollar signs, per cent marks, other symbols, italics (indicated by underscoring), capitals, and paragraphs.

6. Read any notations on the copy regarding type or indention.

7. Read at an even pace, and give the proofreader time to make his corrections.

Miscellaneous Hints. 1. Be sure the author's name and address and the approximate number of words in the article appear on the first page.

PROOFREADER'S MARKS

∧	Make correction indicated in margin.	⌣	Lower to proper position.
Stet	Retain crossed-out word or letter; let it stand.	////	Hair space letters.
. . . .	Retain words under which dots appear;	*w.f.*	Wrong font; change to proper font.
Stet	write "Stet" in margin.	*Qu ?*	Is this right?
X	Appears battered; examine.	*l.c.*	Put in lower case (small letters).
=	Straighten lines.	*s.c.*	Put in small capitals.
√√√	Unevenly spaced; correct spacing.	*Caps*	Put in capitals.
//	Line up; i.e., make lines even with other matter.	*C.&s.c.*	Put in caps and small caps.
run in	Make no break in the reading; no ¶	*rom.*	Change to Roman.
no ¶	No paragraph; sometimes written "run in."	*ital.*	Change to Italic.
out see copy	Here is an omission; see copy.	≡	Under letter or word means caps.
		=	Under letter or word, small caps.
¶	Make a paragraph here.	—	Under letter or word means Italic.
tr	Transpose words or letters as indicated.	∼∼	Under letter or word, bold face.
ℐ	Take out matter indicated; dele.	⫟/	Insert comma.
ℨ	Take out character indicated and close up.	;/	Insert semicolon.
¢	Line drawn through a cap means lower case.	:/	Insert colon.
		⊙	Insert period.
⊚	Upside down; reverse.	/?/	Insert interrogation mark.
◠	Close up; no space.	(!)	Insert exclamation mark.
#	Insert a space here.	/=/	Insert hyphen.
⊥	Push down this space.	⋎	Insert apostrophe.
⊡	Indent line one em.	⋎⋎	Insert quotation marks.
⸢	Move this to the left.	⋎	Insert superior letter or figure.
⸥	Move this to the right.	∧	Insert inferior letter or figure.
⌐	Raise to proper position.	C/Ɔ	Insert brackets.
		(/)	Insert parenthesis.
		$\frac{1}{m}$	One-em dash.
		$\frac{2}{m}$	Two-em parallel dash.

Reproduced from *How Divide the Word* by permission of the copyright owners, Southern Publishers, Inc., Kingsport, Tenn.

2. Supply the exact wording the author wishes used to describe his position or his title. Also, give his academic degrees.

3. Keep a carbon copy of the article, with all corrections on it. (Submit the original, not the carbon, to the publisher.)

4. Do not submit the same article to more than one publisher at a time. Wait until a definite refusal is received from one house before sending the manuscript to another house.

How to Correct Proof

l.c. It does not appear that the earliest printers had any method of correcting errors before the form was on the press. The learned The learned correctors of the first two centuries of printing were not proof readers in our sense; they were rather what we should term office editors. Their labors were chiefly to see that the proof corresponded to the copy, but that the printed page was correct in its Latinity / that the words were there, and that the sense was right. They cared but little about orthography, bad letters, or purely printers' errors, and when the text seemed to them wrong they consulted fresh authorities or altered it on their own responsibility. Good proofs, in the modern sense, were impossible until professional readers were employed, men who had first a printer's education, and then spent many years in the correction of proof. The orthography of English, which for the past century has undergone little change, was very fluctuating until after the publication of Johnson's Dictionary, and capitals, which have been used with considerable regularity for the past 80 years, were previously used on

the miss or hit plan. The approach to regularity, so far as we have, may be attributed to the growth of a class of professional proof readers, and it is to them that we owe the correctness of modern printing. More errors have been found in the Bible than in any other one work. For many generations it was frequently the case that Bibles were brought out stealthily, from fear of governmental interference. They were frequently printed from imperfect texts, and were often modified to meet the views of those who published them. The story is related that a certain woman in Germany, who was the wife of a printer, and had become disgusted with the continual assertions of the superiority of man over woman which she had heard, hurried into the composing room while her husband was at supper and altered a sentence in the Bible, which he was printing, so that it read Narr instead of Herr, thus making the verse read "And he shall be thy fool" instead of "And he shall be thy lord." The word not was omitted by Barker, the king's printer in England in 1632, in printing the seventh commandment, He was fined £3,000 on this account.

Reproduced from *How Divide the Word* by permission of the copyright owners, Southern Publishers, Inc., Kingsport, Tenn.

5. Enclose sufficient postage for the return of the article in case it is rejected, but do not stick these stamps on an envelope.

6. Indicate the end of the article by typing "End," #, or "30," [1] centered, below the last line on the last page.

[1] This arbitrary symbol originated with newspaper reporters, who used it to indicate the end of each report being telegraphed to their papers.

7. Small manuscripts should be sent by first-class mail. Heavy manuscripts may be sent by insured express. Manuscripts cannot be sent by parcel post except when accompanied by printer's proof.

Section 2. CHARTS, GRAPHS, AND TABULATIONS

You have learned much about the writing of reports and manuscripts in Section 1. It will be helpful, too, for you to learn all you can about the preparation, meaning, and use of tables, graphs, financial statements, payrolls, and other business records that are used in business. Of course, the amount of this work that you may be called upon to do will depend mainly on the size and type of organization that employs you.

TABULATION TECHNIQUES

Before studying the following paragraphs, which are concerned with the mastery of tabulation technique for the arranging of tables for financial and statistical reports, review the discussion of tables on pages 276-278.

INCREASE IN NUMBER OF DEALERS STATE OF OHIO		
City	1951	195-
Akron	3,416	3,425
Cincinnati	1,116	1,175
Cleveland	2,236	2,321
Columbus	1,206	1,292
Dayton	1,005	1,692
Sandusky	430	503
Toledo	950	976
Youngstown	1,304	1,353
Zanesville	694	749

A table prepared by means of the diagram method described on next page.

Let us take a practical problem in tabulation and follow through the planning process with pencil and paper. Here is the material we are going to set up attractively on an 8½- by 11-inch page. We shall use a typewriter with pica type.

Horizontal Centering. All tables must be planned to assure artistic placement with a minimum of time spent in typing. Many methods of planning are in use, but the simplest and most reliable under most circumstances is the diagram method. (See illustration.) The correct settings of margin and tabulator stops and the center points for all headings are computed but once and recorded on the diagram. In order to construct the diagram—

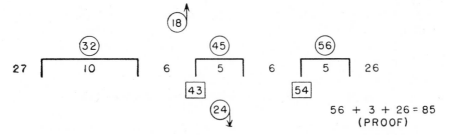

56 + 3 + 26 = 85
(PROOF)

1. Draw three brackets representing the three columns in the table.

2. Count the number of characters and spaces in the longest line in Column 1—ten. Write "10" in the first bracket. Do likewise for Cols. 2 and 3—five each.

3. Spacing between columns should be uniform—2 to 6 spaces. Let us decide on 6 spaces. Insert "6" between each pair of brackets.

4. To find the total width of the table, add the numbers from left to right: $10 + 6 + 5 + 6 + 5 = 32$ spaces.

5. To determine right and left margins (RM and LM)—pica spacing:

$$\text{Available across paper width } (8\tfrac{1}{2} \text{ in.}) \quad = 85 \text{ spaces}$$
$$\text{Width of table (see ¶4)} \quad = 32 \text{ spaces}$$
$$85 - 32 = 53 \text{ spaces remaining for margins}$$
$$53 \div 2 = 26\tfrac{1}{2} \text{ spaces, or 27 spaces in LM (Col. 1)}$$
$$26 \text{ spaces in RM (Col. 3)}$$

Note. For elite spacing: $102 - 32 = 70 \div 2 = 35$ LM and RM

6. To determine tab stop settings—pica spacing: Add horizontally—

$$27 \text{ (LM)} + 10 + 6 = 43 \text{ tab stop (Col. 2)}$$
$$43 + 5 + 6 \quad = 54 \text{ tab stop (Col. 3)}$$

Note. Write the appropriate tab stop setting in a square suspended from the proper bracket.

7. Set these stops at—

LM. 27	RM. 59
Col. 1 tab stop. 43	(54 + 5) or at
Col. 2 tab stop. 54	extreme right—unused

8. To determine column centers from which to center column headings: Start at left margin.

$$27 + (\tfrac{1}{2} \times 10) \quad = 27 + 5 = 32 \text{ (Col. 1 center)}$$
$$32 + 5 * + 6 + (\tfrac{1}{2} \times 5) † = 43 + 2 = 45 \text{ (Col. 2 center)}$$
$$45 + 3 * + 6 + (\tfrac{1}{2} \times 5) † = 54 + 2 = 56 \text{ (Col. 3 center)}$$

* Spaces remaining in the column (bracket) after column center
† Disregard remaining fractions

Note. Write the appropriate column center in a circle above each bracket.

9. Prove the accuracy of your plan-diagram:

(a) Add LM + bracket widths + between-column spaces + RM. The total should be 85 pica spaces for 8½-in. paper; 102 elite spaces for 8½-in. paper.

$$27 + 10 + 6 + 5 + 6 + 5 + 26 = 85 \text{ spaces (PROOF)}$$

(b) Better still, add last column center + spaces remaining in that column + RM. The total should be as in (a) if all column centers and tab-stop settings have been computed accurately.

$$56 + 3 + 26 = 85 \text{ spaces (PROOF)}$$

Vertical Centering. A short table such as our example will look better double spaced than single spaced on a full-sized sheet. Allow an extra line space to separate the heading from the table.

10. To determine vertical placement—top and bottom margins:

Number of typed lines in table   = 12
Number of blank line spaces in table = 12
12 + 12 = 24 total line spaces in table

Since 6 lines can be typed in each vertical inch, a sheet 11 inches long will hold $6 \times 11 = 66$ line spaces.

66 − 24 = 42 blank line spaces remaining
42 ÷ 2 = 21 blank line spaces for each (top and bottom) margin

Suggest 20-22, 19-23, or 18-24 (the last) to place table higher on page for more artistic effect.

Note. Insert "18" above and "24" below the diagram, each encircled plus an arrow.

Typing the Table. Having completed your plan-diagram, you need only insert the paper with its left edge at zero on the writing-line scale, straighten it, line up the top edge of the paper with the top edge of the writing-line scale—then work from the diagram.

Headings. If the left edge of your paper is at zero on the scale, the horizontal center of the sheet, usually used for centering main and subordinate headings, will be at 42(pica) or 51(elite). Having turned in the sheet to the 19th line space, center the carriage as above, back-space once for each two letters or spaces in the first line of the heading; then type the heading from the point reached in the backspacing operation.

In centering column headings, set the carriage on the proper line space at the column center shown in your diagram, and repeat the

backspacing operation. Then type the heading. The handy diagram permits you to type each line from left to right without misgivings, centering headings and items accurately by following the diagram.

When column headings are long, means must be found to prevent them from destroying the essential value of the table, which is the

NOTABLE TALL BUILDINGS

Building	Location	Stories	Height in Feet
Board of Trade	Chicago	44	605
Cathedral of Cologne	Cologne	--	512
Chrysler	New York	77	1,046
Eiffel Tower	Paris	--	984
Empire State	New York	102	1,250
Pyramid of Cheops	Egypt	--	450
RCA	New York	70	850
Taj Mahal	India	--	210

Table A: Centered column headings.

AUTOMOBILE TOURING MILEAGE

City	Asheville	Atlanta	Birmingham	Charleston	Columbia	Jacksonville
Asheville, N. C....	...	209	365	295	173	440
Atlanta, Ga........	209	...	161	306	225	327
Birmingham, Ala....	365	161	...	467	386	465
Charleston, S. C...	295	306	467	...	122	267
Columbia, S. C.....	173	225	386	122	...	309
Jacksonville, Fla..	440	327	465	267	309	...

Table B: Vertical column headings.

compactness of its form. Several lines and abbreviations, as well as the division of words into syllables, are often used. Numbers or letters, such as 1, 2, 3, or A, B, C, with footnote explanations of their meanings are preferred in some instances. Less frequently, the headings are typed in after the rest of the table has been completed by reinserting the long left edge of the paper and typing in the headings slanting or vertical to the horizontal line of the table. The first letter of each heading is typed closest to the first entry in each column—all first

letters in a straight horizontal line across the sheet or the headings centered with respect to one another. The vertical style is easiest to type, but the slanting style is much more readable, which accounts for its growing use. All styles other than horizontally typed headings should read up. (Note Tables B and C.)

SLANTED COLUMN HEADINGS

Branch	January	February	March	April
Chicago	3	5	5	2
Detroit	2	6	11	9
Albany	5	8	7	3
San Jose	4	4	5.	3

Table C: Part of a table with slanted column headings.

Rulings. *Horizontal* rules in tables can be inserted, as the table is being typed, by using the underscore key and the variable line spacer. If *vertical* rules are desired, it is best to hand-rule them with a ruling pen (not an ordinary pen) and India ink after the table has been removed from the typewriter rather than attempt to use any of the characters on the typewriter. Ruled lines should be rather light. Tables A, B, and C are illustrations of ruled tables.

GRAPHIC PRESENTATIONS

Graphs. Statistics presented in the form of tabulated figures are not easy to follow. For example, in a long column of five-figure amounts, $99,000 would not catch the eye any quicker than would $10,000. In order to obtain a comparison, the reader's eye must run up and down the column to determine which figure is the highest, the next highest, and so on. If the same figures were represented by bars in a bar graph, however, the reader could pick out the highest figure at a glance. (See illustrations.)

In other words, graphs present a more vivid picture of comparative information than do tables. For this reason, they are used extensively in business to show the relationships existing between various statistical data. Any information that is presented in tabulated form may be presented in the form of a graph. In fact, graphs are usually constructed from tabulated information.

The various types of graphs are: simple bar graphs (both horizontal and vertical), line graphs, rectangular and block graphs, circle graphs, and pictograms. A secretary is expected to know how to plot the first two types—the bar graphs and the line graphs. The other types are usually planned by experts. (See graph and pictographs on page 296.)

Many simple graphs of the horizontal-bar type can be prepared on a typewriter. Suppose, for example, your employer wishes to see a graph of the payroll in his company. The yearly salaries are:

Office manager.............$7,500   Stenographers.............$2,400
Accountants............... 5,100   Shipping clerks............ 3,000
Bookkeepers.............. 3,000   File clerks................ 2,100
Secretaries................ 3,300   Telephone operators........ 2,700

Bar Graphs. A horizontal bar graph may be prepared on the typewriter as follows:

1. Draw eleven vertical rules equally spaced and, below each, type, vertically, 0, $750, $1,500, etc., to $7,500.

2. As the first horizontal line of the chart, type "Office manager" at the left of the 0 line. Then, starting at the 0 line, strike the small *m* until you reach the vertical line, $7,500.

3. Continue for each item, double spacing between items.

Other characters or combinations of characters may be used instead of small *m;* for example, small *x*, small *w* struck over *m*, or small *m* and small *n* struck over each other. Bars should be made dense.

Two sets of figures for each item can be represented by the use of a black ribbon for one bar and a red ribbon for the other, or by making one bar blacker than the other.

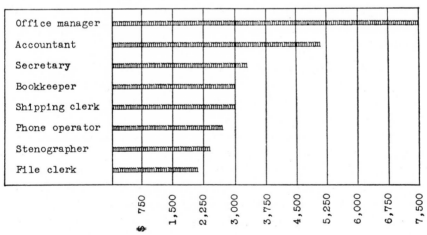

A horizontal bar graph prepared on a typewriter.

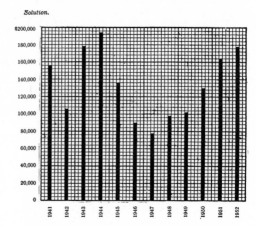

1941................	$156,000
1942................	106,000
1943................	178,000
1944................	194,000
1945................	136,000
1946................	90,000
1947................	78,000
1948................	98,000
1949................	102,000
1950................	130,000
1951................	164,000
1952................	178,000

A vertical bar graph with typed explanation.

Line Graphs. Again, suppose your employer wishes to have a line graph (see page 295) prepared showing the net profits of your company for a ten-year period. The following table gives the figures:

1943....................	$ 94,000	1948....................	$ 56,000
1944....................	112,000	1949....................	62,000
1945....................	168,000	1950....................	74,000
1946....................	126,000	1951....................	92,000
1947....................	78,000	1952....................	116,000

A line graph is plotted by pen and ink as follows:

1. If possible, use graph paper, which may be purchased at any stationer's. A substitute may be prepared by ruling evenly spaced columns vertically and horizontally so as to form a checkerboard.

2. The year dates are typed, vertically, against the vertical rules; the amounts, starting at $180,000 and decreasing by $10,000 each time, against the horizontal rules.

3. For each year on the horizontal scale, locate on the vertical scale the amount representing that year. Place a dot at the intersecting point.

4. Connect the dots by straight lines. (The plotting may be done first lightly in pencil, then checked for accuracy, then ruled with ink.)

STATISTICAL RECORDS

Financial Statements. The mechanical arrangement of accounting statements, such as profit and loss statements and balance sheets, fol-

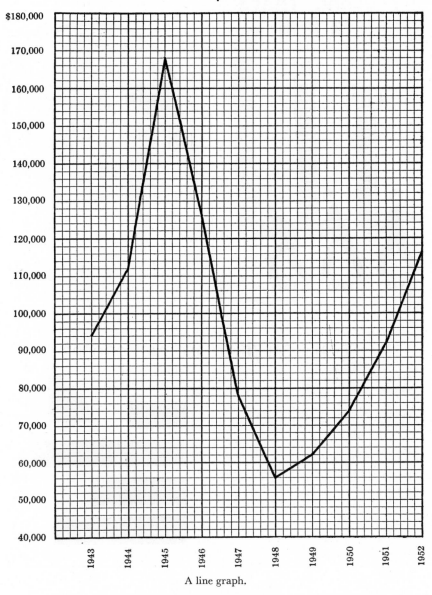

A line graph.

lows a set plan of indention, capitalization, and position of subtotals and grand totals. Co-ordinate items should be uniformly arranged. Dollar signs should appear before the first number in each column, before each total and subtotal, and before each number that starts a new section. All dollar signs in a column should be at the same line.

FEDERAL TAXES

PER PERSON

$ 253 $ 315 $ 400

1949   1950   1952

graphic syndicate

WHAT AMERICANS WORK FOR
BASED ON PERSONAL INCOME

FOOD
72 DAYS

CLOTHING
26 DAYS

TAXES
34 DAYS

SAVINGS
10 DAYS

OTHERS
26 DAYS

HOUSING
HOUSEHOLD
47 DAYS

TRANSPORTATION
23 DAYS

RECREATION
12 DAYS

250 DAYS · 1 WORK YEAR

graphic syndicate

Top: A circle graph.

Left: A pictograph.

RETAIL SALES BY INCOME GROUPS

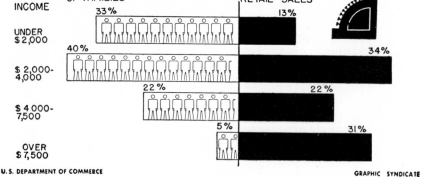

ANNUAL INCOME	PERCENT OF FAMILIES	PERCENT OF RETAIL SALES
UNDER $2,000	33%	13%
$ 2,000-4,000	40%	34%
$ 4,000-7,500	22%	22%
OVER $7,500	5%	31%

U. S. DEPARTMENT OF COMMERCE

GRAPHIC SYNDICATE

A pictograph.

In most offices the style for such reports has already been established in previous statements, and the typist need only follow the style of the last similar report typed. Before making any change in the form or style of a financial statement, you should consult the accountant who compiled it. (See statements on opposite page.)

296

CLARK ELECTRICAL APPLIANCES
PROFIT AND LOSS STATEMENT
Month of March, 19--

Net Income from Sales:
Merchandise Sales.........................	$2,198.50	
Less Sales Returns........................	17.00	
Net Income from Sales....................		$2,181.50

Cost of Merchandise Sold:
Merchandise Inventory, Mar. 1..............		$ 688.00	
Merchandise Purchases.....................$2,344.50			
Less Purchases Discounts.................. 21.47			
Net Cost of Purchases....................	2,323.03		
Cost of Merchandise Available for Sale.....	$3,011.03		
Less Merchandise Inventory, Mar. 31........	1,727.50		
Cost of Merchandise Sold.................		1,283.53	
Gross Profit on Sales.......................		$ 897.97	

Operating Expenses:
Rent......................................	$ 70.00	
Salaries..................................	300.00	
Advertising...............................	22.40	
Delivery Expense..........................	18.00	
Telephone and Electricity.................	25.00	
Miscellaneous Expense.....................	8.00	
Cash Short and Over.......................	.65	
Depreciation Expense......................	27.00	
Supplies Used.............................	19.20	
Insurance Expired.........................	3.00	
Losses from Bad Debts.....................	43.75	
Total Expenses........................		537.00
Net Profit on Sales........................		$ 360.97

CLARK ELECTRICAL APPLIANCES
BALANCE SHEET
March 31, 19--

Assets

Current Assets:
Cash......................................	$1,389.56	
Accounts Receivable......................	1,892.50	
Merchandise Inventory....................	1,727.50	
Total Current Assets................		$5,009.56

Fixed Assets:
Office Equipment.........................	$1,101.34	
Store Equipment..........................	1,966.66	
Total Fixed Assets..................		3,068.00

Prepaid Expenses:
Supplies Inventory.......................	$ 5.00	
Prepaid Insurance Premiums...............	30.00	35.00
Total Assets........................		$8,112.56

Liabilities

Accounts Payable.........................	$1,485.70	
Notes Payable............................	150.00	
Total Liabilities.....................		$1,635.70

Net Worth

T. J. Clark, Proprietorship, Mar. 1.....	$6,165.89	
Add net profit for March................	360.97	
	$6,526.86	
Deduct withdrawals during March.........	50.00	
T. J. Clark, Proprietor, March 31.....		6,476.86
		$8,112.56

Top: A statement of profit and loss.   *Bottom:* A balance sheet.

If the report is to be typed in both red and black, one of two methods may be used.

Method 1. Type as usual until you come to a part that is to be in red. Insert slips of paper between the carbon sheets and the carbon copies. Switch the ribbon lever to red and proceed with your typing. After you have finished typing the original, remove all the copies from the typewriter; then insert the carbon copies in the typewriter one at a time, and type in the sections that are to be in red.

Method 2. Type all the sections that are to be in black; then substitute red carbon paper for the black. Switch the ribbon lever to red and type in all the sections that are to be in red.

Section 3. LEGAL PAPERS

There is an old adage that runs: "He who acts as his own attorney has a fool for a client." This is particularly true of the legal aspects of

Courtesy Shaw-Walker Company

The secretary in a law firm often has a great deal of responsibility and must meet a high standard of accuracy.

business matters. Consequently, it is usually good business to employ an attorney whenever a situation arises in business that requires legal services. The secretary, however, should know the rudiments of business law and understand the meaning and use of the more common legal and business forms. In this chapter, these forms are described in legal phraseology so that you may become familiar with the legal terms you will encounter. Consult a business law text for any terms that you do not understand.

LEGAL PAPERS MOST FREQUENTLY ENCOUNTERED

Contract. A contract is an agreement between two or more parties legally competent to act. (See illustration on Model Form 4 in your Workbook.) It must pertain to lawful subject matter, and there must be legal consideration and mutual agreement between the parties.

Almost every business transaction resolves itself into a contract. Many contracts may be oral and need not be in writing. It is good practice and custom, however, for important contracts to be in writing, in order that they may become part of a record setting forth clearly and definitely the obligations of the respective parties. To reduce a contract to writing tends to obviate misunderstandings, ambiguities, or dissension at a later date, when time or some other element may make witnesses and memories unreliable. Furthermore, a written contract best preserves the rights of heirs, executors, administrators, successors, and assigns.

Verboseness should be avoided in any contract. The sole purpose of the contract should be to set forth the meaning and the intent of the parties thereto; and the four essential elements—competent parties; legal subject matter; legal consideration; and mutual agreement, or meeting of minds—should be clear, definite, and precise, so that there can be no possibility of vagueness or misunderstanding as to the obligations arising from the contract.

Important contracts are signed and "acknowledged" before a notary public, who indicates in an acknowledgment, which is made a part of the instrument, that the parties who signed such contract appeared before him and acknowledged that they signed the document.

Contracts are not limited to individuals. A corporation may be a party to a contract, for a corporation represents a legal entity and, by virtue of its charter granted by the state, has power and authority to contract and to perform other acts in connection with its objects and

---

𝔖𝔱𝔞𝔱𝔢 𝔬𝔣 New York

City 'of New York }-ss.:

𝔈𝔬𝔲𝔫𝔱𝔶 𝔬𝔣 New York

On the   19th   day of   June   , nineteen hundred and --

before me came. ` ALFRED ROSS, of 455 West 85th Street, in the Borough of

Manhattan, City, County, and State of New York , to me known and known to me

to be   the individual   described in, and who executed, the foregoing instrument, and

he   acknowledged that   he   executed the same.

_____

NOTARY PUBLIC

Individual acknowledgment.

purposes with the same force and effect as if it were an individual.

If a corporation is a party to a contract, however, it is important that it be duly authorized by its board of directors or other governing body to enter into such agreement, and that the officer or officers who execute the contract for and in behalf of the corporation be invested with the authority so to do. For that reason, the officer who executes a contract in behalf of a corporation swears before the notary public that he is an officer of the corporation, that he signed the instrument by the order and direction of the board of directors of the corporation, and that the corporate seal was affixed thereto by like order.

Lease. A lease is a form of contract creating the relationship of landlord and tenant. (See Model Form 3 in your Workbook.) The subject matter of a lease usually concerns itself with the possession of lands and/or buildings for a definite period of time in return for compensation to be paid by the tenant to the landlord in the form of "rent."

While there are printed forms for leases, it does not necessarily follow that a lease or, as a matter of fact, any other contract must be made on printed forms. Many leases contain provisions peculiar to themselves and the particular subject matter thereof. Printed forms for leases are used chiefly because such printed forms contain essential and desirable elements of such a contract, including standard provisions that should be covered by the lease.

Ordinarily, a lease should include the following data: the names and addresses of the parties thereto; the subject matter thereof; the term for which it is to run; the purposes for which the premises are to be used; the amount of rental to be paid; a provision relating to expense for repairs and maintenance of the premises; compliance by the tenant with all statutes, ordinances, rules, etc., of the Federal, state, and city governments; notice to be given in the event of fire; a provision pertaining to assignment of the lease; permission for the landlord and his representatives to enter the leased premises at all reasonable hours for the purposes of inspection and the making of necessary repairs or alterations; various damage provisions in case of default in the payment of rent and reoccupation of the premises by the landlord; that there shall be no encumbrances placed about the premises, nor signs without proper authority; limitation of the landlord's liability; that security be provided for the payment of rent; and that the lease shall be subject and subordinate to mortgage liens, payments of special assessments, etc.

To the foregoing provisions may be added such others as may be mutually agreed upon between the parties. If printed forms are used, "riders," or additional clauses, may be attached to the documents in order to set forth fully all the terms of the contract and the intent of the parties thereto.

Bill of Sale. A bill of sale is a formal instrument made for transferring title in goods or chattels from one person to another. (See illustration on Model Form 5 in your Workbook.) A bill of sale is another form of contract and must contain all the elements of a contract. It is important that a bill of sale describe specifically the articles to be sold and that it contain clauses for the protection of both the buyer and the seller, stating that the seller has capacity to act, that he is the owner of the goods that he desires to sell, and that he will indemnify the purchaser for any loss that might arise by reason of the claim of an outsider against the merchandise sold.

In other words, in addition to selling and transferring the seller's interest in the property sold to the purchaser, the bill of sale should contain definite representations that the seller is the sole owner of the property and has a right to sell the same and that there are no liens or other encumbrances against the property sold. Otherwise it may merely be a transfer of the seller's interest in the property, which subsequently may prove to be limited.

Deed. A deed is a contract, or instrument, in writing, duly executed and delivered, that conveys or transfers real estate. As a contract, it must contain all the essential elements of a contract. The party transferring ownership, or title, to the real estate is called the "grantor," and the party to whom it is transferred is called the "grantee."

Among other things, a deed provides for the specific designation of the parties, the consideration involved, a full and complete description of the property conveyed, whether or not there are any liens or other encumbrances on said property, that the grantor has a good right to convey the same, that the grantee shall enjoy the benefits thereof, and that the grantor will warrant the title thereof unto the grantee.

A deed should be recorded in the county clerk's office or the recorder's office in the county where the property is located, so that it becomes a part of the public record and is notice to the world that the property has been conveyed and names the person or persons to whom such conveyance was made.

While it is well for a businessman or a secretary to know what a deed is, an attorney should prepare the instrument, for he has the facilities for ascertaining whether or not there are any liens or encumbrances against the property to be conveyed and for having the title to the property guaranteed by a title guaranty company.

Chattel Mortgage. A chattel mortgage is a conveyance or transfer of an existing right in personal property. The principal object of a chattel mortgage is security, to afford some means of protection for the performance of an act that is to be performed, and concerns itself solely with chattels that are personal property.

A chattel mortgage contains all the elements of a contract and may be given to secure payment of an indebtedness. It remains in full force and effect until the performance of the condition named therein. The chattel must be fully described, and the place where it is stored or kept must be stated in the document. The document usually contains provisions to the effect that, in case of default in the payment of the indebtedness or in the performance of the obligation, the chattel may be sold and disposed of at public or private sale for the best price that can be obtained; that out of the money obtained thereby, the indebtedness or obligation, plus all charges and disbursements in connection with the same, including counsel fees, may be retained by the mortgagee; that the overplus, if any, shall be given to the mortgagor; but if any

deficiency shall remain, then the mortgagee shall agree to pay such deficiency. Usually, the document contains an affidavit by the mortgagor stating the true consideration of the mortgage; that he is competent to contract; that he is the sole and lawful owner of the chattel

---

State of New York. } ss.:
County of __New York__ }

_____ JOHN ALLEN, of 25 East 37th St., New York 16, New York
do_es_ hereby certify that_____he is_____ the owner and holder of a certain mortgage
of personal property, dated the_____20th_____ day of_____April_____ 19 ==___made by
Fred Burger of New York City,_____to__John Allen, aforesaid_____
to secure the payment of__Three Hundred Dollars ($300.00)_____
filed on the_____21st_____ day of__April_____19 ==___in the office of__the Register
of the County_____of_____New York_____and that the interest
of the mortgagee claimed by virtue of said mortgage is that_____he_____hold   the same as security for
the payment of the sum of__Three Hundred Dollars ($300.00)_____
with interest____thereon from the 20th day of April, 19--,_____
which still remains due and unpaid thereon.
    Annexed hereto is a true copy of the aforesaid mortgage.

Dated, New York, April 21_____19 ==__

Statement to continue lien of chattel mortgage.

---

described in the mortgage; that there are no mortgages, liens, or encumbrances affecting said chattel; that the same is free and clear; and that he has the sole right to execute the chattel mortgage.

It is usually necessary that the chattel mortgage be filed in the clerk's office of the town or city where the mortgagor resides or where the property is located. Generally, to be effective, the mortgage must be renewed within the thirty days preceding the expiration of each and every term of one year after the filing thereof. The mortgage may be renewed and continued in effect by filing a statement to continue the lien of chattel mortgage, in which statement the owner and holder of the mortgage declares that the indebtedness remains due and unpaid. A true copy of the mortgage is attached to this statement. See illustration on Model Forms 6 and 7 in your Workbook.

Waiver. A waiver may be defined as the relinquishment of a legal claim or right. A common use of a waiver occurs in conducting the business affairs and transactions of a corporation, where it becomes necessary for the board of directors to meet often or from time to time

to consider and act upon the policies and operation of the corporate business.

The bylaws of a corporation usually provide for the calling of directors' meetings and for the giving of appropriate notice thereof to the directors. Such notice must be given in accordance with the bylaws of the corporation in order to make the meeting proper, valid, and binding.

In the ordinary course of business, however, problems involving the operation of corporate business arise that must be discussed and acted upon immediately by the board of directors. If notice were given in accordance with the bylaws, the corporation might suffer loss through its inability to take advantage of favorable opportunities in the interim necessary for the sending of the notice and the holding of the meeting.

To obviate this delay, the board of directors may waive their right to the notice and sign a waiver of notice as evidence of their voluntary relinquishment of their right thereto. This permits the meeting to be held at the time and place designated in the waiver of notice.

The foregoing is merely one example of the use of a waiver in business; but it may be, and is, applied to any instance where a person relinquishes a known right or privilege to which he is entitled. Of primary importance are the contents of the waiver, which should set forth exactly what it is that is being waived. It is not good practice to make or sign a general waiver, for by so doing a person may be giving up some right to which he is entitled, but which he did not mean to surrender by the execution of the waiver. In the latter case, litigation may ensue in order to determine the real intent and meaning of the waiver.

Affidavit. An affidavit is a statement in writing that is sworn to by the person making the statement, before some person who has authority to administer oaths, such as a notary public. A person may make an affidavit only with respect to facts known to him of his own knowledge, and not acquired by hearsay or upon information and belief. Affidavits are used in business for various purposes.

A form of affidavit much used by corporations is an affidavit of mailing. This affidavit, which is filed with and made a part of the corporate records, pertains to the mailing to stockholders of notices of annual meetings, etc. The affidavit names the persons responsible for

the mailing, puts on record the date of mailing, and is proof that the bylaws of the corporation have been complied with.

Power of Attorney. A power of attorney is an instrument that authorizes a person to act as the attorney or agent of the party granting the power of attorney. (See illustration on Model Form 8 in your Workbook.) The agent to whom the power of attorney is delivered has it as his property and evidence of the authority under which he acts.

It is important that the power of attorney be specific and not general, otherwise it would give the agent unlimited authority to act for the principal. It should set forth clearly, distinctly, and definitely just what the agent has power to do and should leave nothing to ambiguity.

Bylaws. Bylaws are rules adopted by a corporation for its internal government and management and usually include provisions as to the following: the date of the annual meeting of the stockholders of the corporation and the manner in which it shall be conducted; a quorum sufficient for the purpose of the meeting; organization of stockholders meetings and voting privileges; the order in which the business to be transacted at a meeting is to be considered; inspectors of election and how they shall be appointed or elected; the number of directors of the corporation and how to fill vacancies on the board of directors if any should exist from time to time; the place where directors meetings should be held; special meetings of the board of directors and how notice thereof shall be given; a quorum at such meetings and the order in which they shall be conducted; power or removal of the board members; how action may be taken by directors and stockholders if no meeting is held and ratification thereof; the duties of the officers of a corporation in detail; regulation of the powers of the officers; execution of contracts; execution of vouchers and negotiable instruments; bank accounts and banking and other depositories; shares of stock; stock certificates and how to make transfers thereof; appointment of stock registrars; the closing of transfer books; determination of record dates; the payment of dividends; the corporate seal; fiscal year for the corporation; and amendments to the corporate bylaws.

Agenda. An agenda is an outline of the things to be done and the business to be transacted in a corporate meeting. An agenda should be prepared carefully, for it serves as a guide to the presiding officer in the orderly course of a meeting and eliminates the possibility of omis-

sions that might occur through inadvertence or reliance on memory and knowledge. See Model Form 10 in your Workbook.

The bylaws of a corporation may set forth the procedure to be followed; but where no such provision is made, a simple outline of the subject matter to be discussed should be made. As an agenda is merely a sketch or a plan of procedure, it may assume the form most convenient for the persons who are to use it. An orderly arrangement, however, should be observed. The following headings are suggested:

1. Opening of meeting
2. Reading of minutes of previous meeting
3. Reports of officers and committees, if any
4. Unfinished business
5. New business
6. Good and welfare
7. Closing of meeting

Minutes. Minutes are official records of the proceedings of a meeting, such as a meeting of the stockholders or directors of a corporation. Minutes actually constitute memoranda to show what took place at such meetings and by what means authority was given or bestowed to transact certain business.

Usually, minutes contain the following information: the time and place of the meeting; a statement as to the persons present; the name of the person who acted as chairman of the meeting and of the one who acted as secretary; a statement to the effect that a waiver of notice, signed by all the directors, was duly presented; and then a recitation, in chronological order, of the events or business that took place at the meeting, mentioning the person who introduced each subject and the disposition thereof.

When the board of directors of a corporation decides upon a matter of policy or a specific procedure, the decision becomes official by means of a resolution duly made, seconded, and carried. The secretary enters all such resolutions in the minutes, making a note of all essential details.

Minutes, when transcribed, are signed by the chairman and the secretary of the board and are placed in the minute book of the corporation, which contains the official records of the corporate meetings. Copies are often given each member of the board for his own files.

Notice. A notice is an instrument, executed by an authorized person,

that conveys information concerning a fact to the one who is to be notified. A notice need not follow a standard form and, as a matter of fact, may be embodied in a letter. It is of paramount importance, however, that a notice be explicit in its information about a definite fact, so that the person to whom it is addressed may be properly apprised of the fact.

Notices are used to inform stockholders and directors of the times

---

Know all Men by these Presents,

That I Alfred White, of 475 East View Drive, Brooklyn, New York

do hereby constitute and appoint Allen Pawling

Attorney and Agent *for me, and in my name, place and stead, to vote as my proxy* at any election *of the* stockholders of the FRY PRODUCTS CORPORATION, *according to the number of votes that I should be entitled to vote, if then personally present.*

In Witness Whereof, *I have hereunto set my hand and seal this*

first *day of* March, *nineteen hundred and* ------

Sealed and Delivered in the Presence of

A proxy.

and places for annual and special meetings and of the nature of the business to be transacted at such meetings. These two forms of notices are usually provided for in the bylaws of the corporation and must be complied with in order to hold valid meetings.

Notices are also used for pointing out compliance or noncompliance with the terms of a contract or agreement; for notifying of payment or nonpayment; and for stating an intention to do or not to do certain acts set forth in such notice. Various forms of collection and credit letters likewise are considered to be notices.

Proxy. A proxy is a document by which one person is authorized to act or vote for another. It is generally used in connection with corporate affairs, particularly with reference to stockholders meetings, where, because of the wide area of distribution of stockholdings, it is not always feasible for stockholders to be present in person. If the

stockholder does not desire, or is unable, to attend the stockholders meeting personally, he may appoint someone to represent him at the meeting and vote for that person by proxy.

Stockholders are the owners of a corporation, and each stockholder is entitled to vote and participate in its management to the extent of the number of shares of its capital stock that he owns. The stockholders vote for the management as represented by the board of directors, who, in turn, elect the officers of the corporation.

It is customary, particularly where a contest for corporate control appears imminent, to receive and for various coalitions to send out proxies with the name of the agent or representative imprinted thereon, thus leaving merely the execution of the proxy to the stockholder.

· Generally, a self-addressed, business reply envelope, requiring no postage, is enclosed; and the stockholder is requested simply to sign the proxy and return it in the envelope provided for that purpose.

Other Common Legal Papers

Guaranty. A guaranty is a collateral promise or agreement made by a third party to secure the fulfillment of an agreement in case of the default of the party who is primarily liable therefor. The party signing the guaranty is called the "guarantor." A guaranty may be a part of an original contract and have the same consideration; or it may be a separate and independent contract, in which case it must contain all the elements of a contract.

Guaranties are used extensively in business to protect creditors. A firm is often loath to do business with a newcomer, on credit, unless it is satisfied as to his financial responsibility and standing. If the firm is not satisfied, a demand is usually made for references as to the applicant's past business performances. If the applicant's record proves unacceptable, a guaranty may be demanded as a condition precedent to the granting of credit. The guarantor should be a man of business standing and prestige acceptable to the proposed creditor.

Release. A release is also a form of contract; it is the giving up or relinquishing of a claim or right by one person to the person against whom such claim might be enforced. If the intention to release is apparent and the parties are identified, no particular form is necessary.

All the elements of a contract must be contained in a release. The party signing the release, called the "releasor," for a valuable con-

sideration, gives up any claim that he might have or that might exist in his favor "from the beginning of the world to the date of these presents." When properly executed before a notary public and delivered to the party to be released, a release is evidence of the satisfaction of a debt, that the releasor has been fully satisfied, and that no claim exists against the party so released up to the date of the release itself.

The most common form of release is a general release. A release, however, may tend to be a special release and thus be applicable only to certain obligations and rights that are mentioned therein. See Model Form 9 in your Workbook.

Will. A will is an instrument that makes legal disposition of one's property, to take effect after death. Because a will may also be referred to as a testament, the person making a will is commonly referred to as a "testator." The document sets forth the "will" of the testator and what he "wills" to be performed.

Everyone should make a will; otherwise, any property, the title to which is vested in him at the time of his death, will be distributed in accordance with the laws of the state.

A will should be signed in the presence of witnesses, who affix their signatures and addresses to an attestation, or witness clause.

Usually, a will should provide for the payment of all just debts and the funeral expenses of the testator before any distribution is made of the property. The testator may name in his will the executor or executrix who shall see that the terms of the will are carried out. He may also designate that such executor or executrix may serve in that capacity without the necessity of posting a bond for the good and faithful performance of his duties.

After a person dies, his will is usually probated in the surrogate's court or in some court of similar jurisdiction. After the payment of the decedent's debts, a distribution of the property is made in accordance with the will.

Certificate of Incorporation. When it is desired to incorporate a business and to obtain a charter to do business as a corporation, a certificate of incorporation must be filed with the secretary of state of the state under the laws of which the corporation is to be formed.

A certificate of incorporation usually sets forth the following information: the name of the proposed corporation; the purposes for which it is to be formed; the amount of its capitalization or capital stock;

where the principal office of the corporation shall be located; the duration of the corporation; the number of members on its board of directors; the names and addresses of the directors at the inception of the corporation, who shall act as such until the first annual meeting of the stockholders of the corporation; the names and addresses of each subscriber to the certificate of incorporation and a statement of the number of shares that each agrees to take in the corporation; a statement that all the subscribers to the certificate of incorporation are of full age; a statement as to the citizenship of the subscribers; and the designation of the secretary of state or some other person as the agent of the corporation upon whom may be served the process in any action or proceeding against the corporation.

The powers of the corporation are set forth in the certificate; and, outside of the powers mentioned therein, the corporation has no authority to act. Usually, a photostatic copy of the certificate of incorporation is filed in the office of the county clerk of the county where the principal office of the corporation is located. It is important to note that, if a corporation deals outside the state of its incorporation, it is highly desirable, and in some states essential, that it qualify to do business in such outside state in order that it may be fully protected by law with respect to any contract into which it enters.

Certificate of Doing Business under an Assumed Name. If a person desires to conduct a business under a firm name or style other than his own name, but does not wish to incorporate his business, he must file with the clerk of each county in which such business is to be conducted a form known as the "certificate of doing business under an assumed name."

This certificate sets forth the name under which the business is to be conducted, the true full name of the person or persons conducting it, with the residence and business addresses of such person or persons.

This certificate, which is usually mandatory under the penal laws of individual states, is designed primarily for the protection of the persons who have transactions with the person conducting the business.

The certificate becomes a public record when it is filed with the county clerk and becomes available for inspection by anyone who wishes to know who the actual persons are who are conducting the business.

Assignment. Generally speaking, an assignment is a transfer to another of any property, real or personal. The term usually refers to

---

𝕱𝖔𝖗 𝖁𝖆𝖑𝖚𝖊 𝕽𝖊𝖈𝖊𝖎𝖇𝖊𝖉,   I, Frederick Saxton

hereby sell, assign and transfer unto   Francis Smith

one bond of the Salbrite Corporation

for Two Hundred————————————————————($ 200   ),

No. 85   herewith, standing in my name on the

books of said Salbrite Corporation and do hereby irrevocably constitute and appoint

Francis Smith   attorney to transfer the said bond on the books

of the within named company, with full power of substitution in the premises.

Dated New York, Feb. 5, 19--.

In presence of

Assignment separate from certificate.

written transfers. In business, assignments may be used in connection with the transfer of shares of capital stock from one person to another or in connection with the transfer of rights that may be represented by accounts receivable, or otherwise. An assignment is a simple form and contains the elements of a contract.

On the reverse side of every stock certificate there is a printed form of assignment, which is to be executed at the time that the shares of stock represented by the certificate are sold or otherwise disposed of. Many times, however, it becomes desirable to execute an assignment separate from the stock certificate, particularly where the stock may be pledged as collateral security for a loan.

Summons. Generally, a summons is the first paper in the institution of a legal action. It is the instrument whereby the party against whom the action is brought, called the "defendant," is summoned to appear at the time and place specified therein to answer the complaint made against him by the party instituting the action, who is called the "plaintiff."

A summons usually contains: the name of the court in which the action is instituted, the address of the court, the name of the plaintiff, the name of the defendant, a summons to answer the complaint within a specified time, and the name and address of the attorney for the plaintiff.

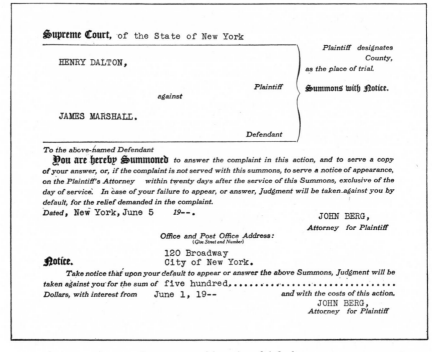

A summons with notice of default.

The service of a summons means only that an action is being instituted against the defendant named therein; but the defendant will be given his right to be heard and an opportunity to answer the complaint made against him. In his "answer," the defendant may set up defenses as to the cause of action specified in the complaint; may deny it entirely; may interpose a counterclaim, or offset, to the complaint of the plaintiff; and may ask for judgment dismissing the complaint and awarding him costs and disbursements made necessary in the defense of the action.

Litigation may be tried either by a judge alone or by a judge and a jury. If a question of fact exists, the defendant has a right to demand a trial by jury.

The language of the summons, designating a time within which to answer the complaint, is not intended to mean that the action will come up for trial at the expiration of that time, but that the defendant has a limited time to answer the complaint and cause a copy of his answer to be served upon the plaintiff's attorney. When properly filed,

Endorsement pursuant to Civil Practice Act § 403-a: The Witness is bound by this Subpoena to appear at the trial, bearing or examination and at any adjourned date thereof.

The People of the State of New York

TO   RICHARD HALL, of 423 West 118th Street, New York 27, New York

GREETING:

We command you, *That all business and excuses being laid aside, you and each of you appear and attend before one of the Justices of our Supreme Court at a* February *Term,* Part II *of said Court, to be held in and for the County of* New York at County Courthouse
60 Center Street
New York 3, N. Y.

on the 15th *day of* February 19-- *at* 10 *o'clock, in the forenoon, and at any adjourned date to testify and give evidence in a certain action now pending in the Supreme Court, then and there to be tried between*

Lloyd Jones   *plaintiff*

and

William Brown   *defendant*

on the part of the said Lloyd Jones . *and for a failure to attend you will be deemed guilty of a contempt of Court, and liable to pay all damages sustained thereby to the party aggrieved, and forfeit* FIFTY DOLLARS *in addition thereto.*

Witness, *Honorable* James Lee *one of the Justices of said Supreme Court, at* the County Courthouse *the* 10th *day of* February 19 --

......Peter Marks.......
Clerk

PHILIP SMITH
Attorney -for
41 Broadway
New York 6, New York

It is hereby stipulated that, the above matter having been adjourned to the 10 day of March 19 --, the undersigned Witness is hereby excused from attending on said date but agrees to remain subject to the call of the attorney for the plaintiff

Dated February 15, 19--   ......RICHARD HALL.........*Witness*

......PHILIP SMITH.........*Attorney for*

A subpoena with notice of adjournment.

the action then takes it place upon the calendar of the court to be reached for trial as expeditiously as possible.

Failure on the part of the defendant to answer the complaint of the plaintiff may cause the plaintiff to proceed to obtain judgment against the defendant by default for the amount asked for in the complaint. In other words, a plaintiff has a right to institute litigation for the enforcement of his claim, and a defendant has a right to answer the complaint and to be heard in court. If the defendant does not answer the complaint and ignores the summons, it is presumed that he does not have any defenses to the litigation; and the plaintiff may then proceed to obtain a judgment in accordance with the laws provided for in such case.

Subpoena. A subpoena is often confused with a summons. A summons institutes litigation, while a subpoena is used *after* litigation has commenced. A subpoena commands the attendance of a witness to

give evidence at the time and place therein specified, and provides for a penalty if the order is not complied with. In other words, a subpoena compels the attendance of a witness to testify in behalf of either the plaintiff or the defendant, whichever one causes the subpoena to be served, concerning his knowledge of the action to be tried.

A subpoena is an order of the court. The failure to heed it carries a severe penalty. It is an instrument by which litigation is expedited, because it makes available to both sides a means by which any person who has knowledge that might prove of value to either the plaintiff or the defendant may be commanded to come to court to testify.

Legal and Business Terms of Latin Origin

a posteriori	ā′pŏs tē′rĭ ō′rī	From effect to cause
a priori	ā′prĭ ō′rī	From cause to effect
ad valorem	ăd và lō′rĕm	According to the value
caveat emptor	kā′vĕ āt ĕmp′tŏr	Let the buyer beware
de facto	dē făk′tō	Actually
de jure	dē jōō′rĕ	By lawful title
del credere	dĕl krĕd′′ĕr ĕ	Of trust, credit (Italian origin)
et al.	ĕt ăl	And others (Abbreviation for *et alii*)
ex officio	ĕks ŏ fĭsh′ĭ ō	By virtue of an office
ex post facto	ĕks pōst făk′tō	From what is done afterwards
habeas corpus	hā′bĕ ăs kôr′pŭs	A writ to produce a person before a court or judge
in re	ĭn rē	Concerning
ipso facto	ĭp′sō făk′tō	By the fact or act itself
modus operandi	mō′dŭs ŏp ĕ răn′dī	Manner of operation
per annum	pĕr ăn′ŭm	Annually
per capita	pĕr kăp′ĭ tà	For each person
per diem	pĕr dī′ĕm	By the day
per se	pûr sē	By itself
prima facie	prī′mà fā′shĭ ē	At first view
pro forma	prō fôr′mà	As a matter of form
pro rata	prō rā′tà	Proportionately
pro tem.	prō tĕm′	Temporarily (Short for *pro tempore*)
proximo (prox.)	prŏk′sĭ mō	In the next month after the present

status quo	stā′tŭs kwō	The state in which; the existing condition
ultimo (ult.)	ŭl′tĭ mō	In the month preceding the present
versus (v. or vs.)	vûr′sŭs	Against

Section 4. OTHER FORMS OF BUSINESS WRITING

It is now quite apparent to you that the functioning of a modern business office involves a variety of different kinds of business writing. In this section you will study briefly a number of other forms of business writing that are often a secretarial responsibility. Of course, the particular position and department will determine the frequency any of these numerous writing duties will be performed.

Typing Advertising Copy. The secretary is often called on to type copy that is going to the printer to accompany advertising layout.

Layouts are usually prepared by professional advertising writers, who indicate on the layout the points at which the copy is to appear. The copy is keyed by letters or numbers to agree with the layout. The illustration on page 316 shows a layout, with the copy.

Publicity Releases. Information about new products, sales, financial standing, changes in boards of directors, new appointments to important positions, and other facts that a concern wishes to announce are commonly sent to the names on its publicity mailing list. Lists may differ according to the purpose of the release.

Such reports are called "publicity releases." They are usually mimeographed on sheets containing the company name and address and bearing a heading "For immediate release," "For release on (date)," "For release at will," etc.

Press Clipping Service. Concerns and persons receiving a good deal of publicity often subscribe to a press clipping service. For a minimum monthly charge, or at a certain rate for each clipping, such services will clip write-ups on any subject the customer specifies from the newspapers in any territory selected. The names and addresses of such clipping bureaus may be found in the classified telephone directory.

Often, it is the secretary's duty to mount clippings in a scrapbook or on loose-leaf sheets for convenience in filing. The date and the source should be noted against every clipping. If library paste is used in mounting, use it sparingly, to avoid wrinkling, and apply it evenly.

Wipe off any excess paste that may appear, so that pages will not stick together. Rubber cement does not cause wrinkling.

The Preparation of Speeches. As the secretary to a man who makes speeches, you can be of great help to him in many ways.

1. You may help in gathering ma-

Courtesy J. Walter Thompson Company

An advertising layout with keyed typewritten copy and indicated size and style of type.

terial. The facts in a speech on a technical subject must be supported by statistics and authorities. An inspirational or general-interest speech usually contains quotations. After-dinner speeches and toasts must have their humorous stories.

2. You will prepare the notes from which your chief will speak, in the form that he personally prefers: (*a*) the complete typewritten copy, as if the speech were an article; (*b*) in outline form, but with any statistics or quotations included in full; (*c*) in card form, each topic,

and perhaps certain key sentences, such as the opening and closing sentences, on a separate card.

3. You should estimate the length of time required to deliver the speech. Count the number of words. From your knowledge of your employer's dictating rate, you can estimate the approximate time required to deliver the talk. This is especially important for radio speeches, which must fit the allotted time exactly.

4. If the daily newspapers will report the speech, you should prepare a typed summary, including excerpts of special significance, and either mail copies of the summary in advance of the talk or arrange for their distribution to reporters at the place at which the speech is delivered.

Digest and Summaries. Digests of reports or of correspondence are often necessary in order to conserve the time of a busy executive or to place summarized data in the hands of several members of the organization. Usually, these summaries are made by the secretary.

The summary is used in several ways:

1. Its main purpose is to present in brief and organized form the content of a mass of correspondence or other material.

2. Your employer may be going away on an extended trip. He may wish a summary of correspondence received during his absence forwarded from day to day. In such cases, you will answer the letters that you can, or at least acknowledge them, and then will forward to your employer a summary of the salient points brought out in the correspondence.

3. A series of letters may have been written dealing with some remote transaction, and a digest will be needed in order to refresh your employer's mind concerning all the attending circumstances.

4. A summary may be needed for use in conference, so that it will not be necessary for every member of the conference to wade through a mass of details.

5. The summary may be used to bring to the attention of your employer the essential facts of a magazine or newspaper article, a report, a booklet, a book, etc.

General Characteristics of Summaries. Summaries should be brief, but they must include elements essential to an understanding of the entire situation. The statements must have continuity. Put the summary in your own language, using quotation marks wherever they seem to be necessary or when you wish to include statements the brevity and

clearness of which cannot be improved by condensation or expansion.

The method that you will use in handling summaries will depend largely on their purpose and your instructions. You must be sure that you understand the instructions thoroughly. Your employer will frequently state the purpose of the digest and leave the details to you if he has learned to rely on your judgment. With your employer's point of view in mind, the making of a digest will be greatly simplified. It is better to err on the side of making it exhaustive rather than too condensed.

In making a preliminary study for a summary of more than one letter, it is first necessary to bring together all correspondence relating to the subject and to arrange it in chronological order, with the answers attached to the original letters. The problem will be a little more complicated if correspondence with several different firms or persons is involved. Read through each letter and the answer, if any,

The Letter as Written

THOMAS HALL, INC.
1418 Block Avenue
Chicago 4, Illinois

June 15, 19—

Mr. John Ramsey
  6843 Allen Street
    Chicago 5, Illinois

Dear Mr. Ramsey:

We wish to establish a suggestion box for the general office, the Sales Department, and the shop of our company.

The purpose of the suggestion box, of course, would be to invite suggestions from our employees for improving commodities, methods of manufacture, sales methods, etc.

It occurs to us that you may have helpful information on the method of inaugurating and conducting such a system, especially the best method of compensating employees for suggestions adopted.

Do you know whether: (1) other concerns of the same type as ours have operated suggestion boxes successfully; and (2) a permanent committee is necessary to approve the suggestions and make the awards?

If it is inconvenient for you to comply with this request now, let us know to whom we may write for the information. Your advice in this matter will be greatly appreciated. Yours truly,

R. J. Smith

The Summary

Letter from R. J. Smith, of Thomas Hall, Inc., 1418 Block Avenue,
Chicago 5, Illinois, June 15, 19—.

Subject: Suggestion box for general office, Sales Department, and shop of
company.

Asks our help in establishing a system whereby employees may make suggestions for improvements of various kinds and may be compensated for
suggestions adopted.

Would like to know what success similar concerns have had with suggestion
boxes and whether suggestions must be approved by a permanent committee.

Asks for name of someone who can give them this information if we are
unable to do so.

to get a comprehensive understanding of the whole proceeding. This
reading, which may be done quite rapidly, naturally will give a background for the summary. In the first reading, underscore statements
that you judge are vital. Upon a second reading, the summary as a
whole should begin to arrange itself logically in your mind.

Summaries of correspondence are usually arranged on the chronological plan, or according to the sequence of events. Statements of the
contents should be condensed to the fewest possible words, giving only
the barest facts in order to save the time that otherwise would be consumed in reading through a mass of details that, while they bear on
the subject, yet are not absolutely essential to an understanding of
the facts. Begin with a statement of the subject, as, for example, "Summary of correspondence between McLoughlin Co. and Morris &
Vandervere. Subject: Steel Contract." Give the date of each letter, as
this may have an important bearing on the situation.

Summarizing Reports. The same general plan may be followed in
summarizing reports. In formal reports, the facts are usually carefully
organized and the language is exact. Nevertheless, many reports are
prepared hurriedly and, while giving all the important facts, may be
wordy and not arranged in logical order. The first step, therefore, is
to find out whether the report is arranged logically and, if it is not, to
reorganize the material for your summary. For example, the report
may deal with many different subjects or phases of a subject and may
embrace such features as finance, physical property and plants, transportation, and foreign fields, which may or may not have been treated
fully under the proper topic head.

Salesmen's reports are often of vital interest to an executive. Generally, such reports have to be written so hurriedly that they lack organization. They usually are in the form of a narrative and often are incomplete. It will be necessary to read through the report to abstract the essential factors. Omitted data, names and addresses of customers, prices, and other information obtainable from the files may be supplied by you in making up your summary.

Summarizing Books. In summarizing books, the secretary will be greatly assisted by referring to the table of contents, which lists in order the subjects treated. In addition, subtitles often appear. Your employer may express a desire for specific information on one point only and care nothing for the rest of the book.

March 15, 195-

Gentlemen:

Will you please send a copy of the Evening Division Bulletin of the School of Commerce to the persons listed below. These young people are employed in our Personnel Department.

Miss Alma Patzke
303 Grand Avenue
Chicago 16, Illinois

Miss Katherine Rapp
915 Second Street
Skokie, Illinois

Very truly yours,

FOSTER SUPPLY COMPANY

CWF:mmf

14 March 195-

Dear Mr. Schoonmaker:

This is to acknowledge and thank you for your payment of $48.50, which is the balance of your account.

Whenever we can be of further service to you, please feel free to call upon us.

Yours very truly,

ACI:s   CHARLES ILFELD COMPANY

Postal cards, typed vertically and horizontally.

Labels. Labels are used to serve as a means of identification and as addresses for items to be shipped. Labels may be entirely blank, or be lined, or contain printed information plus blank lines to be filled in. Accuracy in typing the information on the label is of first importance. It is essential to understand and to follow the directions given for filling in blanks. Use the variable line spacer to insure that the typing will be just above the lines. Sometimes more than one copy of a label is made by the use of carbon paper or a duplicating process (see page 342).

Cards. Government postal cards are used for brief messages when it is not deemed necessary to write a letter. Postal cards, for example, are frequently used for notices, inquiries, acknowledgments, and announcements. Double postal cards are used when it is desired to re-

ceive a quick reply; the message is typed on one card and the other card is to be detached and returned to the sender.

The length of the message determines the spacing used. The message may be typed vertically or horizontally. In either style it should be well balanced on the card. The inside address may be omitted as it is on the face of the card. Use the style of address on the front of the card that you would use on an envelope.

Use the card and label holder to hold the card snugly against the cylinder and to insure clean copies.

Some Highlights of This Unit

1. In carrying out editorial duties, remember that:
   a. A consistent style should be maintained.
   b. An outline is timesaving.
   c. All quotations should be verified and the specific rules for using and typing quotations should be followed.
   d. All footnotes should be consistent in placement and styling.
   e. Arrangement of statistical matter in tables is a challenge to intellectual, artistic, and manual abilities.

2. Achievement of mechanical perfection in preparing a manuscript for the printer requires a knowledge of many technical details as well as a mastery of typewriting technique.

3. Charts, graphs, tabulations, payrolls, and other reports require specific attention to detail. Skill in preparing such reports comes about only through planning and doing.

4. A secretary should be acquainted with common legal terms and the more common legal and business papers.

5. Other forms of business activity that are often a secretarial responsibility are: (a) typing advertising copy; (b) preparing publicity releases—usually in mimeograph form; (c) filing, or mounting, press clippings; (d) helping in the preparation of speeches; (e) preparing digests and summaries; (f) preparing labels; (g) sending messages and notices by postal cards.

Questions and Items for Discussion

1. Name some of the forms of business writing other than letters that the secretary may be called upon to help prepare.

2. In typing or preparing the manuscript for a report, how may the secretary be sure that she will maintain a consistent style with respect to capitalization and hyphenation?

3. In an outline, how must ideas on the same plane be expressed? Illustrate.

4. Four suggestions are given regarding the typing of quotations. What are they?

5. Name some ways in which the secretary can be helpful to an employer who is called upon to make speeches.

6. Explain what is meant by the statement that "proofreading is not a mechanical task."

7. What is the correct procedure to follow when it is desired to copyright a book or other work?

8. Describe the preliminary work you would do in planning a three-column table showing the population increase of five cities. (You may refer to the *World Almanac* for the figures.)

9. What types of graphs should the secretary know how to plot? Which can be prepared on the typewriter? For which should she use pen and ink?

10. Why are graphs used extensively in business for displaying comparative statistical data?

11. State briefly the purpose for which each of the following legal forms is drawn: contract, lease, waiver, proxy, power of attorney.

12. (*a*) Name the four essential elements of a contract. (*b*) Why should important contracts be in writing? (*c*) Why is it possible for a corporation to enter into a contract?

13. Why is it important for a stockholder to sign and send a proxy when he cannot attend a stockholders meeting?

14. Why is it not good practice to sign a general waiver?

15. Name some of the probable duties of a secretary in connection with the taking of minutes.

Personality Questions and Projects
(Based on Personality Pointer, page 271)

1. Discuss the following questions:
   a. Does a person reveal his culture through social behavior? How?
   b. Is it possible to cover up the lack of culture by acquiring polished manners?
   c. Can you distinguish between a thin veneer of charm and genuine social adaptability?

2. On the scale in your Workbook, Sheet 43, you will be able to rate your cultural background. Note the definitions carefully, then check the point on the scale that describes you most accurately as you are today.

Secretarial Assignments

1. Your office manager will dictate the letter to Mr. Lyons. Type one original and two carbon copies. The extra carbon is to be sent to Mr. Barton

in Charlotte. Address envelopes to both representatives and mark them "Air Mail." Use Sheet 44 in your Workbook.

The following matters concern the preparation of reports, rough drafts, tabulations, etc. Read the instructions carefully before beginning each assignment.

2. Retype the two pages of rough draft of a manuscript that you will find in your Workbook on Sheet 45. Follow carefully the instructions given in this unit regarding the preparation of manuscripts. Make one carbon copy. Use plain paper.

3. Type the following statistical material in tabular form. Refer to the instructions in this unit for the arrangement of such tables. Prepare a footnote to indicate which figures refer to women only. Make one carbon copy.

SALARY POSSIBILITIES IN GREEN COUNTY

Monthly salaries for secretaries ranged from $150 for a beginner to a maximum of $225, with a median of $200. For accountants, beginning salary was $175; top salary, $250; median, $225. Stenographers usually started at $155, with the highest salary $175 and $168 as the median. Bookkeepers began at the same salary as stenographers but worked up to $200 top, with $175 as median. For general office clerks, highest salary was the same as the beginning salary for accountants, and lowest salary was $110, the median $155. Median for both office clerks and typists referred to statistics *for women only* and was $155. Maximum for typists was $160; the beginning salary, $150.

The beginning salary for machine calculators was the same as for secretaries, but the highest salary for machine calculators was $175; the median, $160. Machine bookkeepers, who began $10 above the machine calculators, reached the top salary of $185, and a median of $178. Messengers began at $130, reached a high of $155, and had a median of $145.

4. Read the proof given on Sheet 46 of your Workbook, using the proofreader's marks shown on page 286 of this book to indicate all errors in the proof. If practicable, make corrections in red ink or with red pencil.

5. Mr. Martin has had an inventory taken of the stationery now in the department's stock room. A rough draft of the inventory is given on Sheet 47 of your Workbook. Type the inventory neatly on plain white paper. Make one carbon copy.

6. The stock of interoffice stationery is running low. Mr. Martin tells you to write a memo to Mr. Alan Brown, who buys all the company supplies, asking that he have a new supply of 10,000 interoffice memo sheets printed. Use Sheet 48 in your Workbook.

7. Following the style of the graph shown on page 293 of your text, pre-

pare a bar graph on the typewriter for Mr. Wright showing the total sales made last month by each branch office of the United Products Corporation. Here are the figures.

UNITED PRODUCTS CORPORATION

Sales for the Month...................19—

Office	Amount
New York.....................	$820,256.13
Chicago.......................	730,493.22
Boston........................	540,176.70
San Francisco.................	620,442.50

8. The board of directors has called a special meeting and wants complete sales records.

Send a day letter for Mr. Wright to the office managers of the Boston, Chicago, and San Francisco offices, requesting them to wire their sales figures for the month just ended. Prepare an interoffice memo to the New York office manager. Use Sheets 49 and 50 in your Workbook.

9. Mr. Martin has just received the following letter from Mr. Marshall Peterson, president of the Peterson-Worden Iron Works, Escanaba, Michigan, dated February 15. Mr. Peterson is a personal friend of Mr. Martin.

Dear Charlie: My Aunt Mary, whom you know well, has been having some trouble with your company. She ordered a bedroom set a couple of years ago, after saving money for it these many years, and a pretty fancy piece of merchandise it turned out to be. It may not be in the best of taste, but it's what she wanted, and it means a lot to her.

Now she has received one of the most unpleasant letters I have ever seen, written by your company, signed with the initials J. Q. L. I can't believe that one of *your* correspondents would ever write such a letter, let alone mail it.

Believe me, Charlie, if you were not a friend of mine and a devoted admirer of Aunt Mary, I should be writing you a letter right now that would absolutely burn you to a crisp. Where on earth did you get J. Q. L., and why? Sincerely, Marshall Peterson.

"Find out what in the world went wrong here," Mr. Martin tells you. "Write me a digest of the whole affair. See who this J. Q. L. is and send him in here. The lady's name is Mrs. William Peterson, by the way."

You find in the files the following original complaint, dated January 2, from Mrs. William Peterson, and a carbon copy of the shockingly unwise reply, dated January 7, that went out to her from someone in your company.

Gentlemen: About two years ago I bought a complete bedroom suite from you, costing about $269. I had to wait a month for it because it

was ordered with a special finish on the wood. That was inconvenient; but the set finally came, so I was willing to forget about it. Now, however, the varnish is beginning to peel off the top of the bedside table and the top of the dresser where the boudoir lamps stand. Considering the price I paid for this furniture, I certainly do not feel that I got my money's worth, and I want the set replaced or else the whole set refinished. Yours truly, Mrs. William Peterson.

Carbon Copy of the Reply

Mrs. William Peterson, R.F.D. 2, Rice Lake, Wisconsin.

Dear Madam: We are sorry to hear that the bedroom set is giving you trouble. You really must remember, however, that it is two years old, and you can hardly hold us responsible for the wear and tear to which you have subjected it. Setting lamps down on finished wood is bound to scar it after a time. Besides, $269 is not a great amount of money to pay for a bedroom set; so of course you did not get absolutely first-quality goods and must expect it to wear out. We do not now have access to the details about the special finish you got, but suggest that it would be better to be satisfied with the regular finish of our furniture when you place further orders, as it is tested for durability.

We will send a man to see you from our retail store in Oshkosh, Wisconsin. He will let you know what, if anything, we can do for you. Very truly yours, Adjustment Department, By J. Q. L.

In addition to this correspondence, you learn from the Adjustment Department that the correspondent, J. Q. L., was John Q. Larrimer, who was employed by your company in January and recently discharged. It is highly unfortunate that carelessness on someone's part ever permitted Mr. Larrimer's reply to go out.

Write for Mr. Martin a digest of the correspondence and add to it a statement identifying J. Q. L. Use plain paper.

* * * *

Mr. Alan Brown, the head of the Legal Department and also of the Purchasing Department of the company, is in need of some additional secretarial assistance, and you are transferred from the Accounting Department to Mr. Brown's department for the time being.

10. The company is in need of additional working capital for the purpose of expanding the business. Mr. Brown has gone to the bank, the Union Trust Company, and applied for a personal loan of $5,000. The loan was granted on the condition, however, that Mr. Brown deposit with the bank, as collateral security therefor, a certificate for 250 shares of the no-par-value common capital stock of the National Industries Corporation, bearing num-

ber 35, together with an assignment thereof separate from the certificate. The collateral and the assignment are to be returned to Mr. Brown upon the repayment of the loan. Prepare the assignment to be delivered to the Union Trust Company. Mr. Brown will get the stock certificate out of his safe deposit box. The transaction occurred on Monday of this week. Use Sheet 51 in your Workbook.

11. The company needs another delivery truck in order to expedite, and reduce the cost of, deliveries of merchandise. Upon inquiry, Mr. Brown ascertained that by paying cash therefor he could effectuate a substantial saving. Consequently, he purchased from Mr. Donald Ramsey, an automobile dealer, a small 2½-ton Fidelity truck, Model No. K, bearing Motor No. K-376943, and paid $1,750 therefor. Mr. Ramsey asks us to prepare a suitable bill of sale for execution by him in view of the fact that we use our own legal forms. Date the bill of sale for Monday of this week. Use the form on Sheet 52 and follow Model Form 5 in your Workbook.

12. United Products received a check for $200, dated March 11th, from one of the company's customers, Mr. B. A. Smith, of 123 Broadway, New York City, in full payment for invoice No. 781 of January 31st, with the request that its receipt be acknowledged. Prepare a letter acknowledging the receipt thereof. Use Sheet 53 in your Workbook.

13. We are informed that Mr. Joseph Goodberry, a wholesale grocer with his place of business at 142 Walnut Street, Philadelphia, Pennsylvania, was liquidating his business. As a result, Mr. Goodberry had certain fixtures for sale that could be used by the company. Inasmuch as Mr. Brown found it impossible to be present at the sale, he asked you to represent the company in the purchase of certain of the fixtures and equipment. You will need a power of attorney. Prepare the proper power of attorney for Mr. Brown to sign on behalf of the company. Follow Model Form 8 and use Sheet 54 in your Workbook.

14. Mr. Charles Barnet called on Mr. Roy Brown with reference to Apartment 23, consisting of five rooms, vacant on the second floor of The Melville, 82 West 67th Street, New York City, owned by him. Mr. Barnet stated that he had been shown through the apartment by the superintendent of the building, and that, when he expressed his satisfaction with the apartment, the superintendent asked him to call on Mr. Brown.

Mr. Barnet informed Mr. Brown that he was desirous of renting the apartment for a period of one year from the first of next month, and said that the rental of $1,800 quoted by the superintendent was satisfactory. He stated that the apartment would be occupied by himself, his wife, and their three children.

Mr. Brown was favorably impressed with Mr. Barnet's appearance, checked his references, and agreed to lease the premises to him.

Prepare the lease in accordance with the terms outlined above. Follow Model Form 3 and use Sheet 55 in your Workbook.

Optional

15. Your chief is to be in the hospital during this week and will not be able to do any reading. He needs to know what has been going on in the world.

From the newspapers, make a daily summary and a concise report for each of the following matters every day this week. A brief paragraph on each topic will be sufficient.

a. Foreign news
b. United States governmental activities
c. News of labor unions
d. Nature and quantity of department-store advertising
e. Local business and political news
f. Sports news, especially national championship contests

16. The rough draft included in your Workbook, Sheet 56, is to be re-typed, single space, for inclusion in a long report. It is to be page 74 in that report, and is to be headed "Increase in Use of Automobiles."

17. Your teacher or someone assigned by him will dictate some letters.

18. Your company has engaged the accounting firm of Clyde Birch and Company to go over the books at the close of the year. The auditors have just completed their work, and you have been asked to make a copy of the balance sheet, with three carbons, from the figures they have given you. The balance sheet appears in your Workbook, Sheet 57.

The auditor will dictate a letter to you, which is to be submitted along with the balance sheet to the president, the treasurer, and the general manager of your firm. Use Sheet 58 in your Workbook.

19. Today Jack Phillips, of Trenton, New Jersey, called on Mr. Brown. Mr. Phillips is a customer of United Products Corporation and is indebted to the company in the sum of $500 by reason of purchases made several months ago. Mr. Phillips stated that, due to business reverses, he was in dire financial distress—unable to pay his obligations—and thought that he would be compelled to go out of business unless he could effectuate an arrangement to compromise and settle certain of his obligations. He inquired of Mr. Brown whether our company would be willing to accept the indicated sum, and avoid litigation, the result of which might be doubtful in view of Phillips's precarious financial situation. Mr. Phillips paid the $250 and asked Mr. Brown to give him a general release. You are to prepare the general release. Follow Model Form 9 and use Sheet 59 in your Workbook.

20. Mr. Brown arranged for a loan for the corporation from John Price of 250 Broadway, New York City, in the amount of $1,000. As part of the

collateral to be deposited therefor, Mr. Price demands a chattel mortgage on certain equipment consisting of the following: 3 walnut executive desks, 5 four-drawer steel filing cabinets, and 2 guard safes. Using today's date, prepare the chattel mortgage that Mr. Brown is to deliver to Mr. Price. Follow Model Forms 6 and 7 and use Sheets 60 and 61 in your Workbook.

21. You have been called upon to work in the office of the secretary to the president of the corporation while he is on vacation. One of your first assignments it to prepare an agenda for a proposed meeting of the board of directors of the corporation to be held November 15, 19—, at 2 p.m., at the offices of the corporation.

With regard to the procedure to be followed and the subject matter to be taken up at the meeting, your employer gives you the following information:

As president of the corporation, I act as chairman at all meetings of the board of directors and shall call the meeting to order. The secretary of the meeting shall then note whether a quorum is present and record the names of the persons. After that, the secretary will present a Waiver of Notice of the time and place of holding the meeting, which shall be signed by all the directors and shall be ordered to be affixed to the minutes of the meeting. Next, the minutes of the meeting of the board of directors, which was held October 20, 19—, shall be read and then approved by the directorate.

There will be reports presented and read to the meeting in order that the directors may be fully apprised of current proceedings. The treasurer will present and read the Balance Sheet of this corporation for the fiscal year ending October 31, 19—, and then the chairman of the Executive Committee will read the report of his committee on the survey of defense orders, together with the recommendations of that committee pertaining thereto. The chairman of the Finance Committee will then read to the meeting the report of his committee with reference to the advisability and possibility of long-term financing to take advantage of defense orders. After the reading of these reports, I should like to have a discussion thereon and further explanations thereof if any requests are made therefor.

Thereafter this meeting will continue the discussion started at the last meeting of the board of directors in connection with obtaining a contract for and providing machinery and equipment to the Western Shipbuilding Company.

The question of the advisability and the need for this corporation to expand its plant facilities in order to benefit from defense orders should also be discussed, together with the possibility of, and the procedure to be followed in, obtaining such orders, as well as the problem of pro-

curing sufficient skilled labor to enable the corporation to execute such orders expeditiously and in accordance with specifications.

Before closing the meeting, I shall call for suggestions that might be beneficial to our corporation; and if any are forthcoming, we shall give them consideration.

If no further business is to come before the meeting, I shall then call for a motion to adjourn, either subject to call or to a day to be decided by the board of directors.

Prepare the agenda required, following Model Form 10 in your Workbook.

Spelling Demons

knowledge	legacy	minimum
laboratory	legitimate	misappropriate
lacquered	mantel	misdemeanor

Job Tips

1. When preparing several carbon copies, place an envelope over the copies before inserting them into the typewriter. This prevents the paper from fanning. Don't use this envelope for mailing purposes—it is likely to have smudge marks from the carbon. Save it for this purpose alone.

2. *Never* run stapled material into the typewriter even though this may be possible. The staple may damage the platen.

3. To make a correction on material bound at the top, first run a sheet of paper into the typewriter as usual. When the paper is an inch or so above the line indicator, place the page of the bound material, on which the correction is to be made, between this sheet of paper and the platen. Roll all the material backward to the error and correct.

4. It is wise for the inexperienced legal secretary to consult the dictator before making any changes whatsoever in the dictation.

5. In making copies of legal papers, copy them exactly (errors and all) as in the originals. Usually the word *sic*, placed in brackets, is used to indicate that an expression, spelling, or the like, exactly reproduces the original.

Personality Pointer

ARE YOU SPOTLIGHTED?

Watch some people walk! Some of them slouch, some of them drag, some of them scurry, some of them barge—but a few of them hold themselves easily erect and move with a grace that attracts your eye.

Do others watch you? You may be blessed with a natural grace of movement; but, if you are like the great majority of people, you must acquire good carriage consciously.

Correct posture and ease of movement come from constant attention to how to stand, how to walk, how to sit, how to carry out the physical motions of everyday activity. A gym class one day a week, or 15-minutes-a-day exercising, or dieting or stuffing (as the case may require) is not the cure for posture. Granted the foregoing may help, but it will not insure the spotlight on you.

Figure faults, in the normally constructed body, grow out of carelessness and thoughtlessness. Good posture is a habit—a routine matter—that must be practiced all your waking hours. You must have the will to persevere.

Physical vigor is a prerequisite of good posture and carriage. That means you must get adequate sleep and must eat properly before any amount of attention to purposeful "posture" exercise will have any telling effect.

Duplicating Processes and Equipment

The duplicating of form letters, staff bulletins, production schedules, price sheets, and many other forms and records is one of the frequent and important activities of the business office. Office managers are ever on the alert to improve the methods of duplicating the varied materials used extensively in the office.

There are many types of duplicators. The stencil process (mimeograph), the gelatin process, and the direct-process (liquid) are widely used. The secretary should be familiar with the duplicating devices described in this unit and know how they may be utilized efficiently in the office.

Section 1. STENCIL DUPLICATING

MIMEOGRAPHING

Mimeographing is a practical and inexpensive means of duplicating. Some organizations use the mimeograph mainly for duplicating tens to thousands of copies of letters, announcements, and reports. Others use it on a more extensive and elaborate scale, employing color and illustrations. It is possible to turn out mimeographed work that compares well with printed material, considering its low cost.

It is not necessary for a secretary to become expert in mimeographing, but it is necessary for a secretary to know well the requirements of this type of duplicating that is used in most offices.

The Mimeograph Principle. You should understand what mimeographing actually is; that is, the principle that is employed to produce copies with a mimeograph.

332

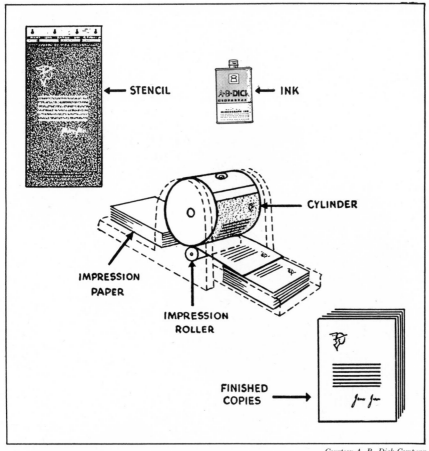

STENCIL ← INK

CYLINDER

IMPRESSION
PAPER

IMPRESSION
ROLLER

FINISHED
COPIES →

Courtesy A. B. Dick Company

Equipment used in the mimeograph process.

The mimeograph principle consists of four important parts: the *stencil*, the *ink*, the *impression roller*, and the *mimeograph itself*. It is through the meeting of the stencil, the ink, and the impression paper in the mimeograph that copies are made.

In order to bring these elements together, the mimeograph has a cylinder and an impression roller. After a stencil has been stencilized, it is placed on the outside of the cylinder over the ink pad; and the ink is poured into the cylinder. As the paper is fed, sheet by sheet, between the cylinder and the impression roller, the pressure causes the ink to flow through the openings in the stencil and deposit itself on the paper.

Stencilization. Since proper stencilization is so necessary to achieve good mimeographed copies, certain steps must be followed.

1. It is helpful to type the material on paper first in order to be sure that it is properly spaced. After this is done, the material can be positioned accurately on the stencil sheet according to the stencil guide marks.

2. Clean the type face of your typewriter with a stiff bristle brush.

A mimeograph showing the stencil in position on the cylinder and the paper ready to receive the impression.

Below: Several types of styli, a burnisher, stencils, correction fluid, and cleaning brush.

Courtesy A. B. Dick Company

3. Disengage the typewriter ribbon by setting the ribbon control lever on the "white" or "stencil" position.

4. Be sure that the cushion is placed between the stencil sheet and the backing as instructed on the stencil carton.

5. Insert the stencil in the typewriter and straighten it. Observe the stencil boundary lines as you type the material.

6. Strike the type keys with a firm, staccato stroke in order to push aside

sufficient stencil coating from each character. For *capital* letters, use a firmer stroke. For punctuation marks, such as the period and the comma, use a lighter stroke.

7. To correct an error on most stencils, apply a thin but complete coat of correction fluid to *each* letter using vertical strokes. Several brush strokes over each letter may be used if one stroke follows the other immediately. Some stencils require burnishing before the correction fluid is applied. This is accomplished by lightly rubbing the glass rod burnisher over the incorrect letter. This is done to return stencil coating, pushed aside by the type, to the typed opening. After burnishing the error, apply correction fluid as described above.

8. Let the correction fluid dry from 30 seconds to a minute.

9. Using a slightly lighter than normal stroke, type in the correct letter or letters. *Do not strike the letters heavier when retyping.*

10. Check your stencil by holding it up to the light. In this way you will be able to see how clear your copies will be by the degree of whiteness you have achieved. If sufficient stencil coating has been pushed aside, the letters will stand out clearly.

The Mimeoscope Illuminated Drawing Board. The Mimeoscope illuminated drawing board, together with many different sizes and styles of styli and lettering guides, is used to make ruled forms, illustrations, and lettering. It is an illuminated drawing board consisting of a frame that holds a piece of translucent glass, lighted from beneath. The newest models are lighted by a fluorescent tube. An important part of all Mimeoscope illuminated drawing boards is the flexible writing plate. This is a translucent, flexible plastic sheet that is grained on both sides. It is placed be-

Courtesy A. B. Dick Company

Using a Mimeoscope as an aid in adding illustrations to a stencil.

tween the Mimeoscope glass and the stencil sheet. The grain of the writing plate permits the stylus to push the stencil coating aside without injury to the base tissue of the stencil. In this way it helps you to produce clear, clean-cut lines.

Styli can be obtained for many different kinds of work—straight or curved lines, short lines and circles, signatures, lettering, dotted lines, shaded lines, or shaded areas. For shaded areas, screen plates are also used.

Running the Job. With the stencil fully prepared, the job is ready to be mimeographed. While most mimeographs operate on essentially the same principle, variations in the different models make it impossible to set down specific rules that will apply to all of them. The instruction book that is supplied with each mimeograph describes in detail the operation of that particular model.

Section 2. LIQUID DUPLICATING

Another widely used means of duplicating is that known as the direct-process or liquid method. It is similar to the gelatin method, described in Section 3, in that a carbon-typed page is used as the master copy. All originals must be typed or drawn through this carbon paper; no special ribbons, inks, or pencils are used in this process. In this method the copies are reproduced by means of a liquid as will be explained later. The direct-process method has two primary advantages over the gelatin method:

1. It produces a larger number of copies, up to 500.
2. The originals can be reused as many times as necessary until a full quota of copies has been obtained.

Making the Master. The preparation of the master copy is essentially the same for both the gelatin and the liquid methods. The following method is recommended for typing the original if you do not have a master unit set.

1. Place a sheet of backing paper (celluloid or heavy card stock) on a flat surface.
2. Place a sheet of special carbon paper over the backing sheet with the carbon surface *facing up*. This produces a *negative master* which is necessary for liquid duplicating. (*Note:* In the gelatin method, place the sheet of special carbon paper with the carbon surface *facing down*.)

3. Over the carbon paper place a sheet of direct-process master paper. (*Note:* In the gelatin method, place the master paper under the carbon paper and on top of the backing sheet.)

4. Insert the set of papers into the typewriter. (*Note:* In the gelatin method, place a sheet of plain paper on top of the carbon paper, inserting the pack into the typewriter in the usual manner—making a positive reproduction.)

Courtesy Ditto Incorporated

Arrangement of papers in the typewriter for typing a direct-process master copy.

If a master unit set is used (available from the manufacturer), the master copy sheet and the carbon paper are already assembled with a tissue paper between to protect the master from smearing. This tissue sheet must be removed before typing.

The original, or "master," is prepared exactly as you would write or type a letter. Drawings are made by using a hard pencil or ball point pen. A deposit of dye is placed on the sheet by writing, typing, or drawing through direct-process carbon paper. This carbon comes in purple, red, green, and blue. All these colors may be applied to the same original and all will reproduce in the one operation.

Making Corrections. If errors are made, follow one of these methods for making the needed corrections:

1. Use an erasing shield to isolate the error from the rest of the copy. Rub out the error with a blockout pencil. Place a piece of new carbon paper (clip from the corner) over the error and type in the correction.

2. Isolate the error with an erasing shield, and with a razor blade or knife carefully scrape away as much carbon as you can without damaging the paper. Remove remaining carbon with an Artgum eraser. Then type in the correction as stated above.

Running the Job. Masters prepared as explained above are attached directly to the rotary drum of the duplicator. (See illustration on page 338). As the copy sheet is fed through the machine the paper is

slightly moistened with a special duplicating liquid. When this moistened surface of the copy sheet comes into contact with the master, it dissolves a tiny amount of the carbon deposit, producing a clear, sharp, and legible copy.

Section 3. OTHER DUPLICATING PROCESSES

Gelatin Duplicators. An older but an economical and satisfactory duplicating method is the gelatin method. It is particularly adaptable when a limited number of copies—up to 100—are required. The gelatin duplicator is extensively used for the reproduction of accounting statements, reports, interoffice bulletins, price sheets, reports to salesmen, and for schoolwork. Many of the large industrial organizations use the gelatin method for the reproduction of their order and billing copies.

Courtesy Ditto Incorporated

A direct-process liquid duplicating machine.

Making the Master. While the preparation of the master copy for the gelatin and the liquid methods is essentially the same (see page 336) in principle, you will note the differences as described in the following paragraphs. The original, or master copy, for the gelatin-type of duplicator is made by typing through a special ribbon or special carbon paper or by writing or drawing with special pencils or special fluid inks.

Ordinary bond paper may be used for the master as well as for the copies, although the special papers available will produce better re-

sults. Pencils, fluid inks, and typewriter ribbons are used in producing the masters exactly as you would use ordinary pencils, inks, and ribbons. The same procedure as in liquid duplicators is recommended for gelatin duplicators when carbon paper is used. Remember, in the gelatin method, to place the sheet of special carbon paper with the carbon surface *facing down* on top of the master paper; also, place a regular piece of typing paper over the carbon paper so that you can see what you are typing. Insert the pack in the regular manner into the typewriter.

Making Corrections. In order to make corrections in masters, use an erasing shield to avoid smearing. Press a plastic cleaner against the letter to be erased. This removes excess dye and prevents smearing. Use an ordinary typewriter eraser to remove all vestige of the impression. Type over

Courtesy Ditto Incorporated

A flat-bed gelatin duplicator.

the same spot, being sure to use an unused place in the carbon sheet when you do so.

Another method of correcting an error is to block out the error by obliterating it with a special wax blockout pencil. You can then type directly over the corrected area.

Running the Job. A master produced as just described can be reproduced on any gelatin or hectograph duplicator, like the one above. While each machine operates a little differently, the fundamental principles are these:

1. The typed or handwritten master is transferred to the gelatin roll or film, which is fastened to the machine. The gelatin quickly absorbs the ink impression exactly as it appears on the master copy.

2. Blank sheets are fed across this impression, transferring an exact copy to each sheet.

All the ink mediums described above—including pencils, inks, ribbons, and carbon paper—are available in several colors, the most common being purple, red, green, and blue. All the colors may be used on the same original, and all will reproduce simultaneously.

The Multilith Process. The Multilith process is a simplified office adaptation of the commercial "offset" printing process. In the offset process the original copy is photographed and transferred to a grained metal sheet from which many thousands of impressions can be produced. The Multilith method of duplicating faithfully reproduces words, lines, and pictures.

A Multilith-process duplicator equipped with automatic paper feeder. This machine may be operated electrically or by hand.

Courtesy Addressograph-Multigraph Corporation

Illustrated on page 340 is one model of the Multilith process machine. Copy is duplicated at the rate of 70 to 100 copies per minute. Paper may be fed by hand or automatically. Larger equipment is also available. The duplicating medium used is a Multilith master. Furnished in either blank form, or with required forms processed upon it in reproducing ink, the paper master is easily composed with a typewriter, pen, pencil, tabulating machine, Addressograph, or any other writing machine or instrument. Corrections are made by simple erasure. These paper masters have the ability to reproduce themselves by transferring all the subject matter to other masters.

The Multilith process also utilizes a metal duplicating master which can be photographically prepared to produce thousands of copies of business forms, stationery, letters, bulletins, and illustrated promotional material in one or more colors.

Because of the ever increasing requirements of business for highly legible copies to guide the flow of work, the adaptation of the Multilith process to this field has resulted in the simplification of business procedures and methods.

The Multigraph Process. By means of a machine called the Multigraph duplicator, letters can be produced that look like typewritten letters. The copy to be duplicated is set up in typewriter-style type with the aid of a composing tool, known as a fork, and a typesetter. The operator uses the grooved fork to remove typewriter type, one character at a time, from an alphabetically arranged type holder called a typesetter. This composing fork is long enough to hold an entire line of type. The operator slides the line of type from the fork into the groove on the Multigraph duplicator and covers it with an inked fabric ribbon. These ribbons are available in six colors and

Courtesy Addressograph-Multigraph Corporation

Typesetter and composing fork.

in several degrees of inking. Impressions are produced by feeding paper between the type drum and a rubber platen roller. A signature device attached to the Multigraph will sign letters, in any one of eight colors, as they are duplicated. A hand-operated Multigraph and an electrical model are shown here.

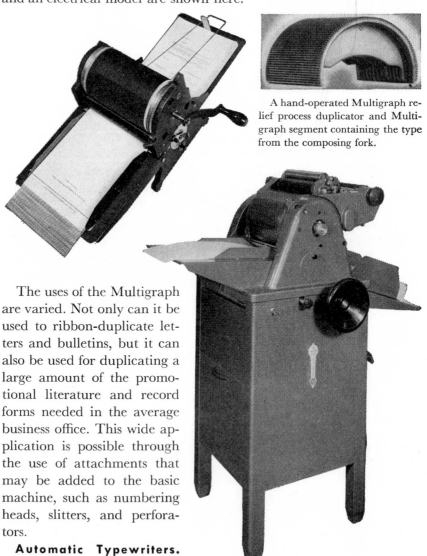

A hand-operated Multigraph relief process duplicator and Multigraph segment containing the type from the composing fork.

The uses of the Multigraph are varied. Not only can it be used to ribbon-duplicate letters and bulletins, but it can also be used for duplicating a large amount of the promotional literature and record forms needed in the average business office. This wide application is possible through the use of attachments that may be added to the basic machine, such as numbering heads, slitters, and perforators.

Automatic Typewriters. Form letters may be actually *typed* on a high-speed automatic typewriter, controlled

Courtesy Addressograph-Multigraph Corporation

Electrically operated Multigraph relief process duplicator.

by a perforated record similar to a player-piano music roll. The operator may use the automatic typewriter as a standard machine for ordinary typing. The machine can be stopped at any point to allow the operator to type in the date, inside address, salutation, or to insert the recipient's name or any special word, thus personalizing the letter. One operator may keep as many as four of these machines in operation at one time.

Courtesy Elliott Addressing Machines

This machine will duplicate messages on postal cards and in a second operation place a different address on each card.

Postal-Card Duplicators. Postal cards containing brief duplicated messages are widely used in business. For example, a card with a duplicated message can be used to announce that shipment of an order will be delayed a number of days, pending receipt of new stock.

Some organizations have occasion to duplicate so many postal cards that it pays them to purchase a special machine for such work. The duplicator pictured above is both a postal-card printing machine and an addressing machine. The message is typed, drawn, or traced on a stencil, from which as many as 5,000 impressions can be made. One simply loads the feeder with blank postal cards, turns the hand crank, and the machine automatically duplicates the advertisement or message on each card. Then by loading the machine with address stencils, turning the cards over, and rerunning them through the machine, the cards are addressed. This can be done at the rate of 125 cards a minute.

The Vari-Typer. The Vari-Typer, as its name implies, is a machine that can produce typed material in a wide variety of type styles and sizes.

It has a keyboard similar to that of a typewriter. As the machine is electrically powered, all impressions on paper are uniform regardless of the touch of the operator.

Courtesy Vari-Typer

Inserting the type font in a Vari-Typer.

The accompanying illustration shows how a type font or plate, of which over 300 are available, is inserted in the machine. Each type font contains ninety characters, including the complete alphabet, figures, marks of punctuation, and symbols. Two fonts are held in the machine at one time, and to change from one to the other is a simple operation. With this variety of type styles and sizes, headings, sideheads, and other important data can be given proper emphasis.

There are two types of machines: the Standard and the DSJ (differential space justifier).

The Standard machine is similar to the typewriter as far as spacing of characters is concerned, each character taking up the same amount of space. An even right-hand margin can be obtained by a simple adjustment on the machine, condensing or expanding the space between the characters within words. On the DSJ an even right-hand margin is obtained by a similar adjustment condensing or expanding the space between the words. The characters on this machine are built proportionately, similar to type.

Vertical spacing can also be adjusted. On the Standard machine there are 9, 6, 4½, 3⅗, and 3 lines to the inch; additional line spacing of 12, 10, 8, 7, and 6.6 lines to the inch can be obtained.

The DSJ machine is designed for both differential and standard

spacing. It therefore has the same vertical line spacing as the Standard machine or can be adjusted to printers' point-size measure.

The Vari-Typer is used for original copies and also for preparing masters for the mimeograph, direct process, Multilith, and other duplicators.

The Justowriter. The Justowriter is an office machine that will produce typed copy with an even right-hand margin. Lining up an even

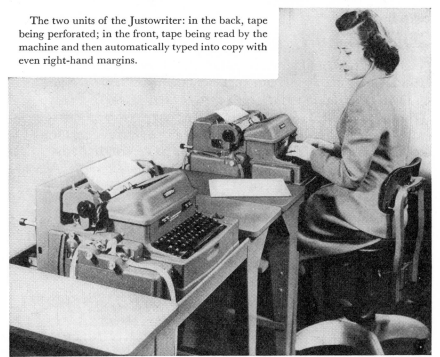

The two units of the Justowriter: in the back, tape being perforated; in the front, tape being read by the machine and then automatically typed into copy with even right-hand margins.

Courtesy Commercial Controls Corporation

right-hand margin is called justifying. For certain kinds of copy to be reproduced by photo-offset, for certain stencils and masters produced for mimeograph and duplicating machines, perfectly typed, clear copy with justified right-hand margin is desirable.

The Justowriter is the only machine that will produce an even right-hand margin in one manual typing operation. The Justowriter consists of two companion units, a recorder and a reproducer. Each is basically a proportional spacing, electrically powered machine with a standard typewriter keyboard. With very little training, any typist

who can operate an electric-keyboard machine can operate the Justowriter. It operates like this:

An operator types on the recorder unit the information to be justified. As in any normal typing operation, a visible copy of the information she typed appears in the platen of the typewriter. When typing, the operator automatically perforates a thin paper tape with the information that is to be justified. Special controls on the machine perforate into the tape the necessary codes for lining up the right-hand margin.

The operator inserts the tape she has perforated into the reproducer. She inserts into the platen of the typewriter the copy paper, pushes a button, and automatically the machine types at the rate of 100 words a minute, and automatically the machine justifies or lines up the right-hand margin.

Photographic Duplication. There are occasions when exact photographic copies are needed of legal documents, insurance applications, specifications, or other important documents. Various machines, such as the photostat, are now on the market that reproduce by a photographic process. Transcripts of school records are often duplicated in this manner.

Microfilming is another duplicating process that is increasing in use, particularly because of its advantage as a method of filing.

Some Highlights of This Unit

1. Stencil duplicating (mimeographing) is an inexpensive method of duplicating, particularly for large-size runs, and may employ color and illustrations.

2. The mimeograph principle consists of four important parts: the stencil, the ink, the impression roller, and the mimeograph itself.

3. In the gelatin method of duplicating, a "positive" master copy is made by the use of pencils, inks, typewriter ribbons, or carbon paper.

4. The Multigraph reproduces letters that look like typewritten letters, the copy having been set up in typewriter-style type on a form.

5. A high-speed automatic typewriter may be used as a standard machine for ordinary typing; but it is primarily used for typing form letters automatically, the operation controlled by a perforated record.

6. The postal-card duplicator, by means of stencils, duplicates the message on each card and, on a rerun, addresses the cards.

7. The Justowriter produces typed copy with a justified right-hand margin.

8. Copies also may be duplicated by the photographic process and by microfilming.

Questions and Items for Discussion

1. Under what conditions do you type a rough draft of copy that is to be stenciled?

2. Describe some of the methods by which a duplicated letter can be personalized.

3. If you owned a business in which a duplicating machine was used constantly, would you have one person operate the machine and run all the jobs or would you have each typist run whatever stencils or master copies she typed?

4. Your employer has given you a sales bulletin to be sent to the branch managers and fifty sales representatives. Your office is equipped with various up-to-date duplicating machines. What type should you use for this job?

5. Outline the proper procedure for preparing a stencil for duplicating.

6. Describe styli, lettering guides, and screen plates and their uses.

7. What method of duplicating necessitates the use of a "negative" master copy? How is this negative master copy prepared?

8. What are the two primary advantages of the direct-process over the gelatin process of duplication?

9. Distinguish between the Multigraph and the Multilith.

10. What is a Vari-Typer? What kind of material is produced by it?

11. What is meant by justified right-hand margins?

12. Name two other processes by which material may be duplicated.

Personality Questions and Projects
(Based on Personality Pointer, page 331)

1. Practice these simple exercises to limber your muscles.
   a. If your abdominal muscles are not firm, try this.
   Lie flat on your back, with your legs straight and together, with your arms extended to the side from your shoulders. Without bending your knees, lift your legs together until they are at right angles to the floor. Then, lower them slowly, toes pointed. Don't cheat and let them down quickly when they get near the floor—that is when the exercise does the most good. Do this only a few times at first, gradually increasing the number of times to fifteen.
   b. Improve the looks of your thighs by this exercise.
   Lie flat on your back. Prop your hips up in the air by supporting them with your arms. Extend one leg at a time in a bicycle motion, being careful of two things: (1) Keep your legs reasonably close together, and (2) make your leg motions opposite motions—one leg

should be extended while the other is bent. Don't hurry the exercise; do it rhythmically.

    c. Slim your waist by this exercise.

    Stand straight with your feet about a foot and a half apart and arms extended to the side at shoulder level. Without bending your knees, touch your left foot with your right hand. Return to position. Touch your right foot with your left hand. Return to position. Do this rhythmically.

    d. Now to limber up your knees and legs.

    Stand straight with your feet together. Extend your arms toward the front at shoulder level as you raise yourself on your toes. Next, bend your knees lowering yourself until you are almost sitting on your heels, but keeping your balance and your back straight! Now return to arms-extended on-toes position. Last return to starting position. This exercise can be done on the count of four.

2. Compile a selected bibliography of the very fine books which are now available on the subject of posture and carriage. Some of the recent reference books on modeling should be included.

3. Set yourself the goal of reading one of these books a week.

Secretarial Assignments

    1. Your office manager will dictate an announcement that is to be duplicated on white paper. First, type the message attractively on a sheet of paper just as it is to appear when duplicated. Then, retype it on a mimeograph stencil, making whatever adjustments in placement may be necessary. Run fifteen or twenty copies.

    If no duplicating machine is available, type the announcement four times, making one original and three carbon copies at each writing.

    2. Address small standard-sized envelopes in block style to the following dealers (do not type a return address; assume it is printed on the envelope):

Johnson Electrical Supply Company, 1219 Market Street, Newark 3, New Jersey

Electrical Accessories, Inc., 400 East 40 Street, New York 18, N. Y.

E. Montgomery Electric Company, 21 Maiden Lane, New York 10, N. Y.

Robert Willard & Company, 127 Pine Avenue, Baltimore 6, Maryland

J. W. Linden Company, 72 Liberty Street, Utica 14, New York

Fiske & Maxwell, 474 East State Street, Rochester 8, New York

Travis Electric Appliance Company, 4112 Chestnut Street, Philadelphia 19, Pennsylvania

Davis & Davis, 986 Capitol Avenue, Albany 15, New York

Emerson & Negren Fixture Company, 78 Fourth Avenue, Plainfield, New Jersey

Syracuse Electric Company, 434 New York Avenue, Syracuse 20, New York

R. J. Kennedy Company, 19 Broad Street, Newark 11, New Jersey

Electrical Supplies Distributors, 78 North Fourth Avenue, Baltimore 21, Maryland

Hobson, Cellars & Jones, 1349 19th Street, Philadelphia 14, Pennsylvania

Fold duplicated announcements and insert properly into envelopes. Do not seal.

3. Duplicate on a direct-process type of duplicator the following bulletin to the sales staff of the New York office of your company.

From: New York Office   Date————

To: All Salesmen, N. Y. Territory

Bulletin No. 17

CONGRATULATIONS to Herb Westbrook, Albany, who filled his quota on the 17th of last month and exceeded it 37% by the end of the period! The One Hundred Percenter gold pin has gone to Herb on loan for a month. . . . The point is that after a man has won this pin about four or five times, it leaves a mark on his lapel. From then on, he has to keep earning the pin in order to avoid having to buy a new suit!—SALES DEPARTMENT.

SAMPLES of the New Design A-140 were mailed to all salesmen a few days ago. These were single samples, sent for your convenience and preliminary inspection. As soon as the first finished run comes in from the Niagara plant, you will get a dozen samples for real study. . . . Let us repeat that it's poor business to try to tell a shipping department manager how fast and easily A-140 works if you can't work it properly yourself. For both durability and attention value, A-140 is the best we have had yet. Don't gyp yourself by not knowing how to work it.—PRODUCTION DEPARTMENT, Plant 5.

PLEASE ACCEPT no more orders for merchandise of any kind to be shipped to any of the Straight & Lee stores until further notice from the home office. Confidential information indicates that these people are having some financial difficulty. Therefore, avoid soliciting their business, and, if you receive unsolicited orders, communicate with this department.—CREDIT DEPARTMENT.

HAVE YOU SENT in your Hundred Best Prospects? Our mailing list is being prepared as fast as these names come in. The big mailing, with samples and personalized letters, is due to go out the first of next month. This is about the best new-account open-upper any salesman

ever had, so it is to your advantage to co-operate. Be sure to include street addresses in towns big enough to need them. These samples are too expensive to lose.—ADVERTISING DEPARTMENT.

Type the master copy and then run off fifteen copies. No envelopes need be addressed. The bulletin must go on one page.

4. Mr. Martin will dictate a form letter to you to be used in answering inquiries regarding certain items of merchandise sold by your company. Set up this letter, including a suitable letterhead, on the Multigraph or prepare a master copy for the Multilith. Run on plain white paper 20 copies without any date, inside address, or salutation. These parts of the form letter will be filled in later on the typewriter to fit the individual inquiry that is being answered.

Alternate assignment: If a Multigraph or a Multilith is not available, type four original copies of the form letter without date, inside address, or salutation. Use the company's regular letterheads. Use Sheets 62, 63, 64, 65 in your Workbook.

5. Fill in dates, inside addresses, and salutations on four of the form letters prepared in Assignment 4 and send them to the following four customers from whom you received inquiries today. Match color of ribbon and style of type as nearly as possible with the equipment at your disposal. In business, the matching should be perfect.

Miss Irma Erickson, 23 Harvard Street, East Orange, New Jersey
Mrs. F. S. Mansfield, Box 46, Penfield, New York
Mrs. Jackson White, Deevers Lane, Bound Brook, New Jersey
Mr. Alexander Appleby, Heathcote Lane, Wyncote, Pennsylvania

Optional

6. Your instructor will dictate a bulletin containing some instructions for making corrections on a stencil. Transcribe this, single space, on a sheet of plain paper. The instructor may assign another student to type a stencil for this bulletin. Enough copies should be run so that each member of the class, and the instructor, will have one.

7. Your instructor will dictate a letter that you are to set up in perfect form for multigraphing. Type it in your best style when you transcribe it; then recopy it if you see any possibility of improving the appearance. Use Sheet 66 in your Workbook.

Five hundred copies of this letter are to be printed on the addressing Multigraph. The Multigraph operator will set it exactly as you specify. This means that every unwise choice you make in arranging the letter or in dividing words will be repeated 500 times!

The names, addresses, and salutations will be filled in automatically when the letters are run on the addressing Multigraph. Be sure to leave room for the fill-ins. Put at the top the date of the first Monday of next month; if you omit the date, the Multigraph typesetter will omit it, too.

8. Mimeograph or duplicate by direct process some bulletin for one of your school offices. Keep a copy to show your future employer the kind of duplicating you can do.

9. Your instructor will dictate some additional letters. These letters are to be set up without addresses or salutations because they will be filled in automatically by the use of plates when they are run on the Multigraph.

10. Design an attractive program cover for some real or imaginary school production. Use a mimeoscope to reproduce the design on a stencil. Run off several copies on the mimeograph to check the quality of your work.

Spelling Demons

mosaic	necessary	occurred
mutilate	notoriety	opposite
mysterious	occasion	pageant

Job Tips

1. If the burnishing tool that comes with correction fluid is lost, the error on the stencil may be rubbed lightly with the back of your fingernail. Do not use the edge of your nail.

2. Simple rulings can be made on a stencil while it is still in the typewriter. Place the stylus on the line indicator against one of the card fingers (or within the card finger); draw a horizontal line by moving the carriage from right to left; draw a vertical line by turning the platen, after the variable line spacer has been released. Be careful not to wrinkle the stencil.

3. It is frequently desirable to file stencils. Special absorbent folders are available for this purpose. Some stencils can be cleaned by holding them under running water for a time and then drying them. Ask the salesman who sells stencils how they may be cleaned.

4. Correction tape is available in one-, two-, and three-line widths for use in correcting master copies for liquid duplicators. The tape is gummed on the back and can be cut to fit over the typographical error.

Personality Pointer

WHO IS YOUR BOSS?

It is important, in most organizations, to be able to recognize the various shades of authority and to know just who is supposed to give you orders. When you are a beginner, almost anyone and everyone may give you instructions. The grace with which you accept instructions, correction, and even criticism may be a determining factor in your progress.

An employee who assumes a sullen attitude when she is told to do something gets no satisfaction from her action, and she endangers her own position. On the other hand, a timid soul who is afraid to consult her own boss for advice when someone else gives her an assignment will not only be imposed upon by everyone but will also be unable to give her own superior adequate attention.

You must remain friendly with the entire staff, if possible, and still get your work done.

Filing Procedures

As in the case of handling the mail, stenographers and secretaries have responsibilities in connection with the classifying and filing of business information. The secretary should have a thorough knowledge of filing procedures and equipment whether the organization is large or small. Large organizations probably will have a central filing department supervised by a file operator or supervisor, an increasingly important position.

In this unit you will study the fundamentals of filing. The basic alphabetic indexing rules are given and illustrated. You will learn the complete filing routine. Charge, transfer, and follow-up methods are also considered. Other filing systems and equipment are considered in the next unit.

Section 1. PURPOSE OF FILING

The work of the office revolves around the use of business letters, papers, cards, records, or other original materials. Nearly every business transaction is initiated by correspondence of one type or another. For example, correspondence may be received through the mail: an order, an inquiry, a telegram, or a bill; it may be interoffice correspondence; it may be a penciled memorandum from an executive to his secretary. In most instances these papers are necessary for the completion of the transaction. They cannot be replaced should they be lost or destroyed; therefore, they must be filed.

Purpose of Filing. Modern filing systems are the solution to two problems: (1) the storing of important data over a period of time, and

354

Courtesy Remington-Rand Inc.

These girls are working in a well-equipped filing department where daily filing routines are handled efficiently with the aid of vertical files, a sorting tray, and a Multisort.

(2) the arranging of the filed materials so that they can be located with dispatch when needed. Filing, then, is simply a system of properly classifying business data and records and of making sure they are readily accessible when needed.

The tremendous volume of correspondence, plus the greatly increased use of accounting and other records, so vital in today's business operations, make it imperative that accurate and up-to-date files be kept. Filing must be done accurately, quickly, and neatly, for errors in filing are costly. Filing requires the ability to classify and to make decisions for all important papers that must be retained regarding the same transaction. It is evident that the filing system used in the office must be the most systematic and accurate that can be devised for the particular firm.

Filing may be compared with other conveniences with which we al-

ready are familiar: for example, the dictionary is a filing system for words; telephone and city directories are filing systems for names; and public libraries are filing places for books.

Vertical Files. The vertical file, because of its convenience, flexibility, and expansibility, is the best receptacle for storing correspondence. In the drawers of vertical filing cabinets, correspondence and

Courtesy Shaw-Walker Company

A vertical file showing the upright position of the folders.

other data are filed on edge, behind guides and in folders, thus bringing together *all* papers to, from, or about one correspondent or about one subject. A typical vertical filing cabinet is shown here.

An alphabetic card file is a type of vertical file. It is used when the information to be filed is more satisfactorily kept on cards.

Methods of Filing. The four basic methods of filing are the alphabetic, numeric, subject, and geographic. Each of these methods will be described in the remainder of this unit and in the next unit.

1. *Alphabetic filing* is the method by which material is filed by the name of the person, firm, or organization. This is the most widely used method.

2. *Geographic filing* is the method by which material is filed by the name of the place (city, state, county, etc.). It is adaptable whenever it is possible to group according to location.

3. *Subject filing* is the method by which material is filed according to the name of the subject that properly identifies the papers.

4. *Numeric filing* is the method in which the correspondence is assigned a numbered folder; this number also appears on a card. The card is filed by any one of the other filing methods. The numeric method is an indirect method inasmuch as it is necessary to consult a card file for the number of the folder before the correspondence can be located.

Alphabetic Correspondence Filing. The use of the term "alphabetic filing" for only that method that calls for the filing of correspondence by name of person, firm, or organization must not be misunderstood. Filing is done by alphabetic sequence in all four methods.

As has just been pointed out, in one case the correspondence is filed alphabetically by name of person or firm; in another case, by name of place; and in still another, by name of subject. Even the numeric method, which employs any one of these three methods, through an indirect process, comes under the classification of alphabetic filing.

The filing method chosen depends on the nature of the business. By far the most widely used method is alphabetic filing. Since every office files business correspondence, most of the references to the materials to be filed as illustrative of filing procedures will be references to business correspondence.

The arrangement of folders and guides for each of the four methods of filing is described fully in Unit 14.

Section 2. ALPHABETIC INDEXING AND FILING

The most important operation in any method of filing is that known as "indexing," which is a mental process. It is imperative that filing be done according to definite and uniform procedures; therefore, you should be thoroughly familiar with the rules given in this unit. These indexing and filing rules enable you to make the two necessary basic decisions:

1. Determine under whose name the correspondence should be filed.
2. Determine the alphabetic order of that correspondence among other names (and consequently the order of that correspondence among other correspondence).

While the rules discussed and illustrated in this unit are advocated by authorities on filing, an individual firm may find it advisable to vary from them in some degree. In any case, however, remember that it is essential that a particular firm consistently follow the rules for alphabetic indexing adopted by the firm.

Determine Name under Which to File. The first step in indexing is to decide under what name in a piece of correspondence the correspondence is to be filed. Although in most cases original correspondence is filed under the sender's name (the name in the letterhead) and

Southern Fruitgrowers Association

1301 Davis Street · New Orleans 2 · Louisiana

March 10, 195-

United Products Corporation
500 Madison Avenue
New York 22, New York

Gentlemen:

Thank you for your letter and order of
March 8. We are sending the grapefruits out
this afternoon.

We are sorry we do not carry the kind of
oranges that you describe but are quite certain that the Citrus Fruit Association, which
is in San Francisco, California, would have
them. We are writing them today, and you
should hear from them in about a week.

Very truly yours,

SOUTHERN FRUITGROWERS ASSOCIATION

DKT:da

David K Thomas

ELH
3/11

3/17

LETTER PROPERLY MARKED FOR FILING

The vertical line indicates the letter has received proper attention and is ready for filing;
the underline in the signature shows where the correspondence is to be filed; the underline
in the body of the letter calls for a cross reference; the notation in the lower right-hand
corner means that the correspondence is to come up for attention March 17.

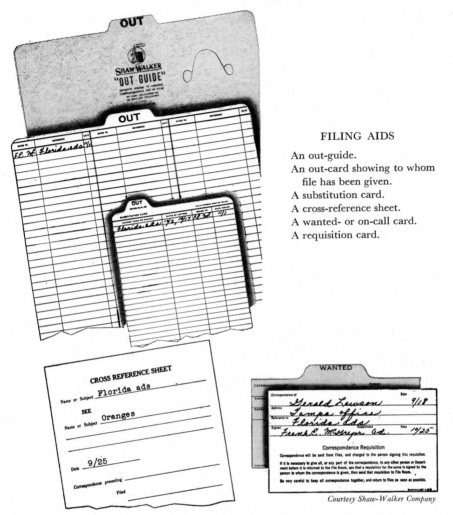

FILING AIDS

An out-guide.
An out-card showing to whom
    file has been given.
A substitution card.
A cross-reference sheet.
A wanted- or on-call card.
A requisition card.

Courtesy Shaw-Walker Company

carbon copies under the receiver's name (the name in the inside address), there are instances where correspondence should be filed, or at least cross-referenced, under the name of a person, a place, or a subject mentioned in the *body* of the letter.

The file operator must use her judgment, asking herself where she will look for the correspondence when it is needed. If she is not sure under which of two names to file, a cross reference, like the one shown in the illustration above, should be made. The name or subject to be cross-referenced is placed at the top of the sheet, and the name under which the correspondence is to be filed is placed after "See:"

Here are some general rules to help determine the correct name under which to file.

1. Correspondence that can be filed under more than one name is indexed and filed under the most important name and cross-referenced under the other names.

2. A letter on company business to or from an employee of a firm is indexed and filed under the name of his firm, but it may be cross-referenced under the name of the employee.

3. A personal letter addressed to an employee of a firm is indexed and filed under the name of the employee.

4. If interoffice correspondence is written about no particular name of individual, firm, or subject, it is filed under the name of the department or official title of the person from whom the correspondence is received. All correspondence to, from, or about one name or one subject (including branch office, interdepartmental and intradepartmental correspondence) is indexed and filed under the name of the individual, firm, or subject about which the correspondence is written.

5. There are a few special subjects, such as Applications, under which correspondence is usually filed regardless of the name of the correspondent. Some organizations, however, require cross references under the names of individual applicants.

Letter A

April 24, 19—

Mr. Charles A. Blake, Principal
Westfield Central School
140 Bleeker Street
Denver, Colorado

Dear Mr. Blake:

I wish that we could encourage Mr. Howe to send his manuscript to us, but we have two publications in production at the present time that duplicate in many ways the plan of his book as described in the résumé that you sent us.

From a study of the content and plan of Mr. Howe's book, I feel sure that it has considerable merit; and, if we were in the market for an advanced economics book, we should be glad to examine it.

Thank you for calling this manuscript to our attention.

Cordially yours,
William Warren
General Editor

As a concrete example of the decision to be made in determining the correct name under which to file a letter, examine Letter A. Letter A is the carbon copy of our letter to Mr. Blake. Although the letter is addressed to Mr. Blake, it refers to Mr. Howe's manuscript. The proper thing to do in this case is to file the correspondence under Mr. Blake's name (not under the Westfield Central School, as it is not business pertaining to that school) and file a cross-reference sheet under Mr. Howe's name.

Letter B

United Products Corporation Interoffice Memorandum
   To: Shipping Department
   Subject: Order for Refrigerators

                                           May 2, 19—

Mr. Harper:

When Mr. Powell was in the office yesterday, he placed an order for twenty refrigerators, Model 49-a, to be sent to the R. B. Stewart Company, 123 Jackson Avenue, Cleveland, Ohio.

Ten of the refrigerators are to be delivered on May 15 and the remaining ten on May 31. Send these shipments under our usual terms.

                        D. Shultes
                        Sales Manager

Letter B illustrates original correspondence about refrigerators to be sent to a specific person or firm. It should therefore be filed with other correspondence about this person or firm, in this case under R. B. Stewart Company. As the letter might be called for under Mr. Powell's name, or under the subject "Refrigerators" (if a subject file is used), cross-reference sheets should be filed under the last two titles.

Determine the Alphabetic Order of a Name. In the second step of the indexing process, the alphabetic order of a name among other names is determined.

To ascertain the relative order of two names, compare each letter in the two names, beginning with the first letters, until you have arrived at a point of difference. For example, in determining the correct alphabetic order of *Jones* and *Johns*, compare *J* with *J*; *o* with *o*; *n* with *h*. Here is a point of difference. As *h* comes before *n* in the alphabet the name *Johns* is indexed before the name *Jones*.

Similarly, in indexing the place names *Springfield* and *Springdale*, *Springdale* comes first, because *d* comes before *f*. Again, in indexing

the names of the subjects *Accounting* and *Accountants*, *Accountants* comes first.

Names are not always so simple as those just presented. In filing thousands of pieces of correspondence, names more complicated in construction are sure to be encountered. As a guide in determining the correct alphabetic order of all names, certain rules for alphabetic indexing have been devised. The function of these rules is twofold:

1. To break up or to consolidate the parts of a name into correct indexing units.

2. To determine the order in which each unit of the name is to be considered in comparing it with other names.

Take, for example, the name *Arthur N. Vane-Bell*. First, break it up or consolidate it into correct indexing units:

Arthur   N.   Vane-Bell

The question of whether or not to consider *Vane-Bell* as one unit or as two units is answered by indexing Rule 3 (page 364), which states that hyphenated surnames of persons should be considered as one unit.

Second, determine the order in which each unit of the name is to be considered. Indexing Rule 1 (page 363) states that the surname of a person is considered first; the first name, or initial if the first name is not written out, is considered second; and the second name, or initial, is considered third. Thus in indexing a piece of correspondence from *Arthur N. Vane-Bell* by name of person, the name is seen in the mind's eye as:

First Unit	*Second Unit*	*Third Unit*
Vane-Bell	Arthur	N

Similarly the name, *Robert E. Van der Henst* is seen as:

VanderHenst	Robert	E

and *William C. Vandergrift, Jr.* as simply:

Vandergrift	William	C

(*Jr.* is not considered, except when two names are otherwise identical.)

By *mentally* comparing the first units of each name, *Vane-Bell, Van*

der Henst, and *Vandergrift,* letter by letter, you will find that the three pieces of correspondence should be filed in the following order:

> Vandergrift, William C. (Jr.)
> Van der Henst, Robert E.
> Vane-Bell, Arthur N.

These examples show the necessity of following definite indexing rules in order to insure consistency in filing. Consistency in filing makes for easy finding, which, after all, is the main purpose of filing. If we did not expect to refer to correspondence, we should not take the trouble to arrange it in any particular order. In fact, there would be no reason for keeping the correspondence at all!

The following rules for alphabetic indexing, set down by the Library Bureau Division of Remington Rand Inc., have been widely accepted in the business world.

General Rules. Arrange all names in A-Z order, comparing each letter in the *first* unit in each name *first.* If the first units are identical, consider the second units. If both the first units and the second units are identical, consider the third units. A shorter unit must be filed before a matching longer unit, *provided* it is spelled the same to its extent.

An old library rule emphasizes this point. The rule is, "Nothing before something," or "Ends first, filed first." For example, *Brown* comes before *Browne.*

Names of Persons

Basic Order of Units

1. Consider surname as the first unit, the given name or initial as the second unit, and the middle name or initial as the third unit.

Name	*1st Unit*	*2nd Unit*	*3rd Unit*
Walter H. Saunders	Saunders	Walter	H
Irving M. Savage	Savage	Irving	M
J. Ida Savage	Savage	J.	Ida

Surname Prefixes

2. Surname prefixes, such as *De, de, d', Le, L', M', Mac, Mc, O',*

St., *van*, *von*, etc., are considered as parts of the surname and not separately.

Name	1st Unit	2d Unit	3d Unit
Louise C. La Brant	La Brant	Louise	C
Howard B. MacHale	MacHale	Howard	B
A. Henry McAdams	McAdams	A	Henry
Mary E. St. Clemens	SaintClemens	Mary	E

Hyphened Surnames

3. Hyphened surnames of persons are considered as one unit, and the hyphen is disregarded.

Name	1st Unit	2d Unit	3d Unit
L. Emmett Holt-Mann	HoltMann	L	Emmett
Jean C. Holtmeier	Holtmeier	Jean	C
Alan J. Holt-Nagel	HoltNagel	Alan	J

Abbreviations

4. Abbreviations in names of individuals are considered as if written in full.

Name	1st Unit	2d Unit	3d Unit
J. W. Rau	Rau	J	W
Jas. W. Rau	Rau	James	W
John W. Rau	Rau	John	W

Titles

5. Titles or degrees of persons, whether preceding or following the name, are not considered in indexing. The title is usually placed in parentheses after the given name or initials when typing the name on index cards.

Name	1st Unit	2d Unit	3d Unit
Mrs. Laura J. Dorr	Dorr	Laura	J
Louis M. Dorrance, Ph. D.	Dorrance	Louis	M
Dr. Leland R. Dorrell	Dorrell	Leland	R

Exception: Titles, including both foreign and religious titles, followed by a name not recognized as a surname are indexed as written.

Name	1st Unit	2d Unit	3d Unit
Brother David	Brother	David	
Madame Frances	Madame	Frances	
Sister Mary Clarita	Sister	Mary	Clarita

Designations

6. Abbreviated designations (Jr., Sr., II, etc.) appearing as part of a name are *not* considered an indexing unit, except when two names are otherwise identical. When typing such names on index cards, the abbreviated designations should be enclosed in parentheses at the end of the name.

Name	1st Unit	2d Unit	3d Unit
Samuel Steel, Sr.	Steel	Samuel	
Edward Steele, Jr.	Steele	Edward	
Ralph Steelton II	Steelton	Ralph	

Names of Married Women

7. The legal name of a married woman is her married surname, which is the one considered in indexing. When typing index cards, the husband's name may be given in parentheses below the woman's legal name. In filing, the husband's name may be cross-referenced.

Name	1st Unit	2d Unit	3d Unit
Mrs. Kenneth H. Johns (Ada)	Johns	Ada	

The cross reference should read:

Johns, Kenneth H. (Mrs.)
See: Johns, Ada (Mrs. Kenneth H.)

Addresses

8. When the same name appears with different addresses, the arrangement of those same names is alphabetic by city or town. If the name of city is the same, then the arrangement is alphabetic by state.

If it is the same name, the same city, the same state, then arrangement is alphabetic by street.

Name	1st Unit	2d Unit	3d Unit	4th Unit
Carl Cummings, Austin, Texas	Cummings	Carl	Austin	
Carl Cummings, Dallas, Texas	Cummings	Carl	Dallas	
Carl Cummings, Evanston, Illinois	Cummings	Carl	Evanston	
Charles Foster, 12 W. Delaware, Chicago, Illinois	Foster	Charles	Chicago	Delaware
Charles Foster, 18 E. Ohio, Chicago, Illinois	Foster	Charles	Chicago	Ohio

Company Names or Titles

Basic Order of Units

9. Names of firms, corporations, and institutions that *do not embody full names* of persons are indexed as written.

Name	1st Unit	2d Unit	3d Unit
R. & H. Upholstery Co.	R	H	Upholstery
Radler Bros.	Radler	Brothers	
Radner Products Co.	Radner	Products	Company

10. When names of firms, corporations, and institutions *do embody full names* of persons, consider the surnames of the persons as the first unit; the first names or given names or initials, as the second unit; the middle names or initials, if any, as the third units; and the rest of the titles in sequence.

Name	1st Unit	2d Unit	3d Unit
Ernest F. Koenig & Co.	Koenig	Ernest	F
Emil Koeppel & Son	Koeppel	Emil	Son
M. A. Koerber Bros.	Koerber	M	A

Hyphened Names

11. Hyphened firm names that *do not embody full names* of persons are considered as separate units in indexing.

Name	1st Unit	2d Unit	3d Unit
Hanson-Brian Inc.	Hanson	Brian	Incorporated
Hanson-Whitney Machine Co.	Hanson	Whitney	Machine
Hapag-Lloyd Travel Service	Hapag	Lloyd	Travel

12. When hyphened firm names *do embody full names* of persons and the hyphened words are the surnames of those persons, such hyphened surnames are considered as one unit.

Name	1st Unit	2d Unit	3d Unit
John Hillers-Thompson Co.	HillersThompson	John	Company
E. C. Hilliard-Matthews Co.	HilliardMatthews	E	C

Compound Names

13. Names that may be spelled either as one word or as two words are indexed as one unit. In filing, cross-reference when necessary.

Name	1st Unit	2d Unit	3d Unit
Hy Grade Meat Market	HyGrade	Meat	Market
North East Ledger Inc.	NorthEast	Ledger	Incorporated
South East Displays Co.	SouthEast	Displays	Company

14. Compound geographic names and location names are indexed and filed as two or more units in the order given, except when the first part of the name is not an English word.

Name	1st Unit	2d Unit	3d Unit
Los Angeles Baking Co.	Los Angeles	Baking	Company
New York Coal Co.	New	York	Coal
North Carolina Home Industries	North	Carolina	Home
St. Louis Power Co.	Saint	Louis	Power

Possessives

15. When a word ends in apostrophe *s* (*'s*), it is indexed as if the *'s* were not there. When a word ends in *s* apostrophe (*s'*), it is indexed as it is spelled.

Name	1st Unit	2d Unit	3d Unit
Hay's Co.	Hay	Company	
Clara C. Hayes	Hayes	Clara	C
Hays' Art Shop	Hays	Art	Shop

Numbers

16. Names that include a number are indexed as if the numbers were spelled out in full. The entire number is considered as one unit.

Name	1st Unit	2d Unit	3d Unit
46th St. Theatre	Fortysixth	Street	Theatre
4200 Hotel	FortytwoHundred	Hotel	
4th Ave. Terminal	Fourth	Avenue	Terminal

Abbreviations

17. Abbreviations are indexed and filed as if they were spelled out in full. An initial or a letter, as a unit of filing, when not a known abbreviation, precedes all other names beginning with the same letter.

Name	1st Unit	2d Unit	3d Unit
Wm. E. Sainsbury	Sainsbury	William	E
Henry R. St. Armand	SaintArmand	Henry	R
Salinger Hat Co.	Salinger	Hat	Company
Schnurer Bros. Inc.	Schnurer	Brothers	Incorporated

Words Disregarded

18. Words such as *and*, *&*, *of*, *the* are disregarded in indexing. They are usually enclosed in parentheses. If the firm name begins with the article "The," it is written in parentheses at the end of the name. When "The" appears in the middle of the name, enclose it in parentheses when writing the name, but disregard it in indexing and filing.

Name	1st Unit	2d Unit	3d Unit
The Hotpoint Co.	Hotpoint	Company	
Houghton The Artist	Houghton	Artist	
House of the Rothchilds Inc.	House	Rothchilds	Incorporated
Houston & Brown	Houston	Brown	

Addresses

19. When firm names are identical, they are filed according to the alphabetic order of the city and state in the address. If city and state are alike, they are filed according to the street address.

Name	1st Unit	2d Unit	3d Unit	4th Unit
Faulkner's, 3313 Culver, Chicago, Ill.	Faulkner's	Chicago	Illinois	Culver
Faulkner's, 1810 Davis, Chicago, Ill.	Faulkner's	Chicago	Illinois	Davis
Faulkner's, 2500 Sheridan, Chicago, Ill.	Faulkner's	Chicago	Illinois	Sheridan
Cox's Television, Glenview	Cox's	Television	Glenview	
Cox's Television, Skokie	Cox's	Television	Skokie	
Cox's Television, Winnetka	Cox's	Television	Winnetka	

Miscellaneous Names

Governmental Agencies

20. Names of *Federal* departments are indexed and filed under "United States Government," followed by (1) name of department, (2) name of bureau, (3) name of division. The words "Department of," "Bureau of," and "Division of" are disregarded in indexing and are put in parentheses.

Name	1st Unit	2d Unit	3d Unit	4th Unit
U. S. Dept. of Commerce	United	States	Government	Commerce
U. S. Dept. of Defense	United	States	Government	Defense
U. S. Marine Corps	United	States	Government	Navy

21. Names of *state* and *local level* departments are indexed and filed by name of location, followed by the name of the department, division, or institution.

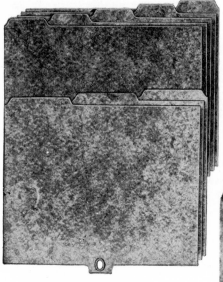

File guides with tabs in various sizes
and positions.

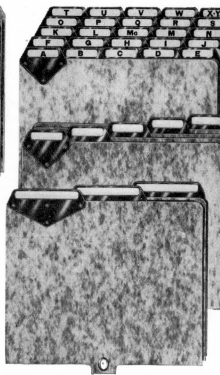

Metal tab file guides in various sizes
and positions.

File folders showing different tab
positions $\frac{1}{5}$, $\frac{1}{4}$, $\frac{1}{3}$, $\frac{1}{2}$ cuts.

Heavy-duty expansion folders.

Courtesy Shaw-Walker Comp.

Name	1st Unit	2d Unit	3d Unit
State of New York Department of Education,	New	York	State
State of California Board of Examiners,	California	State	Education
Chicago	Chicago	City	Examiners

Banks

22. In indexing names of banks, consider first the city and then the name of the bank, with the state at the end of the title in parentheses.

Name	1st Unit	2d Unit	3d Unit
Second National Bank of Buffalo, N. Y.	Buffalo	Second	National
Peoples First National Bank of St. Louis, Mo.	Saint	Louis	Peoples
Tucson Trust Co. of Tucson, Arizona	Tucson	Trust	Company

Exception: If there are very few bank names to be filed, disregard this arrangement and follow rule for indexing names of firms which do not embody complete names of individuals. (See Rule 9.)

Other Organizations

23. Names of hotels, schools, libraries, and other institutions should be indexed and filed under the distinguishing word. If there is no distinguishing word, as in Public Library of Schoharie, file by name of town.

Name	1st Unit	2d Unit	3d Unit
Boston Public Library	Boston	Public	Library
University of Denver	Denver	University	
Hotel Shelton	Shelton	Hotel	

Note: When typing names for a card index, write in parentheses those words ordinarily not considered in the mental operation of in-

dexing, as *the, Jr., Sr., II, Capt., President,* and other titles. *Example:*

> Houghton (The) Artist
> Steele, Edward J. (Jr.)

Section 3. ALPHABETIC FILING PROCEDURES

In addition to a knowledge of the basic alphabetic rules for filing, you should understand the complete filing routine described below:

1. Inspecting Correspondence. As you come to each piece of correspondence, glance quickly to see whether the release signal adopted by your office appears on the correspondence so that you will be sure that it is ready for filing. The release signal may be a line drawn through the paper or the initials of the person who has given the correspondence proper attention.

2. Reading Correspondence. Read the correspondence to determine the name of the person, place, or subject under which it is to be filed.

3. Indexing. Indexing of correspondence is the process of determining the name or subject or other heading under which correspondence is to be filed in the system used. This is done simultaneously with

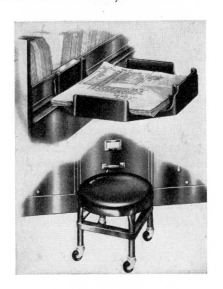

Courtesy Shaw-Walker Company

A file shelf to hold the correspondence during the filing process and a stool to work at lower drawers conveniently.

Above right, a sorting tray.

reading. The functions or official duties of the department and way in which correspondence will be called for will determine the indexing heading.

4. Coding. Coding is the placing of symbols or captions (numbers, letters, or subjects) on papers to be filed, at the time of indexing, thus indicating for all time the caption determined upon. The simplest form of coding is underlining the indexed name or subject.

5. Sorting. After you have gone through all the correspondence, inspecting each piece for a release mark, reading it to pick the name under which to file it, underlining that name, cross-referencing and making out follow-up sheets, the next step will be to divide the correspondence into smaller groups to facilitate filing.

Beside the table or desk at which you work, you should have some sorting device, such

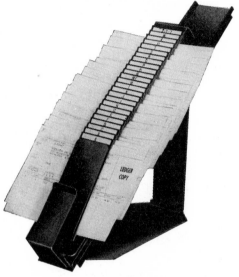

Courtesy Remington Rand Inc.

A Multisort.

as the tray on page 372. The sorting tray contains about 10 per cent of the alphabetic, numeric, geographic, or subject guides of the actual file. Where files consist of a considerable number of drawers, the most practical method of sorting is to break the filing down into the same number of groups as there are drawers. The guides in the sorting tray in that case should correspond to the labels on the front of each drawer.

A sorting device, placed on the table, is shown on this page.

6. Filing. Move the sorting tray close to the files. Working with one group of correspondence at a time, determine the proper folder for each piece of correspondence and the proper place in that folder.

7. Cross-Referencing. If a piece of correspondence comes under more than one classification, make a cross reference for any other heading under which that particular piece of correspondence might be looked for.

8. Preparing Follow-ups. If the writer has indicated on the correspondence that he wishes the letter returned on a certain date, prepare a follow-up sheet to be filed in a separate file arranged by months and days. Letter B, on page 361, for example, should have follow-up sheets made for May 15 and May 31.

Miscellaneous Pointers. Folders should be raised from the file a few inches before placing correspondence in them to be sure that the correspondence falls to the bottom of the folder. Material should be filed with headings to the left and reading matter facing the front of the folder.

Section 4. CHARGE, TRANSFER, AND FOLLOW-UP METHODS

Charge Methods. It is often necessary that correspondence be taken from the files. Several methods that are used in such instances are described in this section. A *requisition card* should be made out and signed by the person requesting material from the files. The requisition card is the charge for material borrowed. It may be attached to an out guide or a substitution card, or it may be filed in a follow-up file. When filed in the follow-up file it becomes the "on-call" card. When placed in the pocket of the out guide or attached to the substitution card, it is placed in the file where the paper or folder has been removed. This procedure will help insure the return as well as decrease the possibility of losing valuable records. Also, it enables any person who may wish materials not in the files to know where they are.

There are several charge forms that may be used. At the time the material is removed from the file, a *substitution card* is put in its place in the folder. This card identifies the papers removed, the date they were removed, the name of the person who took them, and the date they are to be returned. If an entire folder is removed, either an *out guide* with the essential information recorded on it may be substituted for the folder; or an *out folder* with a substitution card may be placed temporarily in the file to take the place of the regular folder. Sometimes the regular folder is retained in the file and the contents of the folder transferred to a special *carrier folder*. When certain desired papers are not in the files, *on-call cards* are used to insure prompt delivery of the papers to the person requesting them. (See page 359 for illustrations of these charge forms.)

Transfer Methods. Sooner or later most correspondence becomes in-

active, its place in the files serving no useful purpose but taking up useful space. To solve this problem, it is customary in business offices periodically to remove inactive correspondence from files to make room for future correspondence. There are two methods of transfer: periodic and perpetual.

Periodic Transfer. There are three commonly used plans for "transferring correspondence" periodically.

Plan 1. Under Plan 1, at fixed intervals, usually on January 1 and July 1 of each year, the entire file of correspondence is transferred to a less expensive set of cabinets, located, perhaps, in a storeroom. The guides are usually not transferred, less expensive ones being used in the transfer files. New folders are then prepared for the file cabinet just emptied. The one disadvantage of this method is that the more recent correspondence must be referred to frequently, necessitating many trips to an inaccessible transfer file.

Plan 2. The disadvantage of Plan 1 is overcome in many offices by keeping the latest transfer correspondence in a duplicate set of files beside the current file. Under Plan 2, at the appointed time transfer correspondence of the duplicate file is sent to the storeroom files, and the space just emptied is utilized for the correspondence of the ensuing

Directions

For attaching labels to folders and guides

1. After typing strip of labels use desk sponge, two blotters and a glass rod or pencil.

2. For easier separation fold labels on perforations before tearing.

3. Draw label across sponge while pressing with glass rod to assure even moistening.

4. Moisten other end of label in a similar manner.

5. Place label (gummed side up) on a blotter.

6. Lay folder tab on label with top edge at center of wide color strip along folding score.

7. Slip second blotter under projecting half of label.

8. Swing blotter toward you while pressing label down on front of tab.

9. The above method assures firm sealing and even alignment.

Courtesy Remington Rand Inc.

period. The cabinets containing correspondence that up to this time was considered current automatically become the transfer files.

Usually the two upper drawers are used for active papers, and the two lower drawers are used for inactive or transferred papers, when four-drawer files are used.

Plan 3. Under Plan 3, the file operator goes through every folder individually and removes for transferring only the correspondence that has been inactive for a certain period—say, for six months. The disadvantage of this plan is that it takes a great deal of time to sort the active from the inactive correspondence.

If it is feasible to have a duplicate set of files, the most practical plan of all is Plan 2 because it embodies two good features: (1) correspondence is transferred as one unit; (2) correspondence most recently transferred is in an accessible location.

Perpetual Transfer. Sometimes it is difficult to define arbitrary periods of transfer. Perpetual transfer is the removal of obsolete, closed, or dead papers at irregular intervals from the current file to the transfer file. In law, contract, or job files, for instance, papers usually accumulate under a given subject for an indefinite time. Such papers should be transferred as a unit when an individual case, job, or contract has been completed.

Follow-Up Methods. In the discussion of the complete filing routine (see page 372), the importance of preparing follow-ups was indicated. Your attention is now called to several methods used in follow-up procedures.

When the volume of correspondence is large, a *card tickler file* is often used to keep track of materials that have been charged out until they are returned. *Date folders* are another follow-up device which serves the same purpose.

If the volume of correspondence to be followed up is not large, the secretary may find the use of a *pending folder* quite satisfactory.

Some Highlights of This Unit

1. The vertical file, because of its convenience, flexibility, and expansibility, is the best receptacle for storing correspondence.

2. The four basic methods of filing are the alphabetic, numeric, subject, and geographic.

3. Folders should be raised a few inches from the file before placing correspondence in them in order to be sure that the correspondence falls into the bottom of the folder.

4. Material should be filed with headings to the left and reading matter facing the front of the folder.

5. A requisition card should be made out by the person requesting material from the file.

6. Should matter not be in the file when a requisition is received, an on-call card is placed in the file.

Questions and Items for Discussion

1. Mention two problems solved by the modern systems of filing.

2. Name and describe briefly the four methods of filing correspondence.

3. Differentiate between indexing and filing.

4. In filing, what is meant by a "unit"? Illustrate.

5. Name the eight steps that constitute the alphabetic correspondence filing procedure.

6. Name and describe three charge forms that may be used when correspondence is removed from the files.

7. Describe the three commonly used plans for periodic transfer of inactive correspondence to inactive files.

8. Describe three follow-up procedures.

Personality Questions and Projects
(Based on Personality Pointer, page 353)

1. Assume that you are the newest employee in the accounting department of a large organization. You were hired by the personnel manager, introduced to the head of Accounts Receivable, and handed over to a young man named Ralph Digby, who was told to get you started heading up statements. Mr. Digby put you to work, after introducing you to Oscar Henderson, whose machine is next to yours.

While you are typing, a bustling woman who acts as if she had a great deal of authority approaches you and says, "Just hold this adding-machine tape for me, please, while we check."

Choose from the following list the most suitable reply you might have made to the woman.

a. "I'll have to finish my own work first."

b. "Are you my boss?"

c. "Will it take very long? I was told to head up statements."

d. "You'll have to ask Mr. Digby if it's all right."

e. "Is it all right for me to stop what I'm doing?"

2. Realizing that your function in any office is to help get the work done, you help check the tape and plan to find out later whether you should continue to take instructions from her.

When an opportunity arises, you ask Mr. Digby what you should do when

similar situations occur in the future. The reason you ask Mr. Digby is that, although he may not have authority to decide, he will feel flattered to think that you suppose he has. Don't go over anyone's head in minor matters. You need all the friends you can keep.

Choose from the following list the most suitable wording for your inquiry.

   a. "Mr. Digby, I'm puzzled. Is it all right for me to stop the work you have given me when someone else tells me to do something?"
   b. "That woman came along and made me check a tape. Should I do things like that for people?"
   c. "Do I have to take orders from everybody around here?"
   d. "I'm way behind—I had to help check a tape, and it put me back. Oh, dear! Maybe somebody could help me catch up?"

Mr. Digby's answer would depend on the customs of that office. Whatever petty jealousies exist, stay out of them yourself by leaving decisions to be made by your superior.

3. Oscar Henderson, who works beside you, turns out to be a likable chap, but lazy. You have been in the office long enough by this time to realize that you and Oscar do the same work and take orders from the same people.

One day Oscar remarks affably, "The boss told me to go help Esther. Finish posting this for me, will you?"

You have your own work—plenty of it—and the job he wants you to do will take at least two hours.

Choose your answer from the following.

   a. "Since when are you giving me orders?"
   b. "I doubt if I'll be able to get to it this afternoon. My own work will keep me busy all day."
   c. "I'll ask Mr. Digby if he wants me to help you."
   d. "Loafing again, eh, Oscar?"

Secretarial Assignments

The following assignments have to do with the filing of cards taken from the mailing list of your company. The names have been arranged in groups to give you training in applying the indexing rules studied in this unit. Type all names on 5-by-3 cards or on slips of paper of that size, following this model:

> Robert C. Marshall
> 10 Locust Street
> Wheeling, West Virginia

1. Arrange the cards for the following names alphabetically, applying the first rule for alphabetic indexing. Put a rubber band around these cards or slips and hold for use in Assignment 3.

Rule 1

Robert C. Marshall, 10 Locust St., Wheeling, West Va.
Alexander J. Marsky, 227 Wills St., Oklahoma City, Okla.
Alexander Servis, 94 Prescott Dr., Jersey City, N. J.
Otto J. Sheeân, 14 Craft Ave., Minneapolis, Minn.
Tabby J. Springate, 90 Landing Rd., Detroit, Mich.
Allan Smithson, 355 Fifty-First St., Canton, Ill.
Henry J. Sackett, 463 Logan Sq., Caldwell, Ill.
J. Cameron Myall, 932 School St., Alton, Ill.
Harry E. Mally, 209 Shore Rd., Alden, Ill.
Harold C. Mally, 25 Palmer Ave., Andover, Ill.

2. In the same manner, type cards for each of the following lists of names and addresses; then arrange the cards alphabetically within each list. Be sure to apply all the rules learned previously as well as the rule that each list illustrates. Place a rubber band around these cards and keep them to use in Assignment 3. When you have finished this assignment, you will have twenty-two packs of cards ready for Assignment 3.

Rule 2

Francis C. St. Andrew, 92 Weston St., Chicago, Ill.
Gregory Saint George, 1224 Green St., Chicago, Ill.
William N. McAllister, 21 Roxbury Rd., Abington, Ill.
Homer R. McDowell, 29 Robin St., Belleville, Ill.
Martin J. McDowel, 41 Pine Ave., Belleville, Ill.
H. Oscar McDowell, 306 Ridgewood Ave., Belleville, Ill.
William S. MacAdam, 126 Swan St., Bismarck, N. Dak.
William R. Macadam, 45 Montrose Ave., Portland, Maine
Kenneth M'Donald, 873 Pershing Ave., Albuquerque, N. Mex.
Louis C. McVaine, 23 Winton Pl., Cleveland, Ohio

Rule 3

William S. Minton, 182 Monroe Ave., Brattleboro, Vt.
Charles L. Shaff, 528 Roselle Rd., Dallas, Tex.
Bernard Minton-Steel, 30 Webster Dr., Reno, Nev.
Jane Smith-Webber, 469 Jackson Blvd., Canton, Ill.
Albert M. Silversmith, 44 Carbery Lane, Bloomington, Ill.
John Henry Silver-Smith, 81 Winston Rd., Bloomington, Ill.
George L. Matkins-Grant, 104 Overland Ave., Lynchburg, Va.
Gertrude A. Matkins, 69 Clayton Ave., Newport News, Va.
Bertram P. Shaffer, 394 Mosby Rd., Brownsville, Tex.
Robert O. Shaff-Berry, 252 Cottage Row, Corpus Christi, Tex.

Rule 4

Wm. H. Mears, 13 South Euclid, Waco, Texas
Geo. O. Mears, 21 Schiller, Brownlee, Montana
Jas. Mears, 5408 Burgess, Scranton, Pennsylvania
Edw. C. Sorrell, 647 Adams, Clinton, Iowa
Robt. T. Sorrell, 3428 North Riley, Eau Claire, Wisconsin
Jasper Mear, 2714 Northview, Billings, Montana
Chas. B. Sorrell, 1213 Bacon, Boulder, Colorado
Edwin Sorell, 232 Langley, Clinton, Indiana

Rule 5

Madame Sophie Maurée, 12 Northwood St., Concord, N. H.
Mayor Henry Maxwell, 23 Mill St., Vicksburg, Miss.
Dr. James Minton, 29 Central Ave., Baltimore, Md.
Madame Shirley, 63 Cherry Lane, Birmingham, Ala.
Sir John Scott, 22 Thompson Park, Fond du Lac, Wis.
Sister Marie Winifred, St. Patrick's High School, Champaign, Ill.
Wilbur K. McLeese, LL.D., 240 Kent Lane, Canton, Ill.
Albert Saint Stephen, R. F. D. 6, Big Horn, Wyoming
Claudius F. Simpson, M.D., 12 Prospect Ave., Cheyenne, Wyo.
Pres. Henry M. M'Donald, 60 Pratt Ave., Sioux Falls, S. Dak.

Rule 6

Lincoln Snell, Jr., 211 Cass Rd., Indianapolis, Ind.
Kenneth O. Schuster, 213 Cherry Rd., Champaign, Ill.
Madeline Schuster, 436 Hawthorne St., Champaign, Ill.
R. J. Schusterbauer, Jr., 20 Windsor Park, Champaign, Ill.
Raymond Sine, Sr., 663 Dunning Blvd., Cairo, Ill.
Darius P. Marks, III, 231 Pardee Blvd., Belleville, Ill.
Edmond Marks, Jr., 238 Norwood Ave., Belleville, Ill.
Edward McFadden, Sr., 927 Henry St., Green Bay, Wis.

Rule 7

Barbara Morman, 917 Prairie Hill, Phoenix, Ariz.
Mrs. Edwin McHenry (Margaret), 938 Pickering Ave., Charleston, S. C.
Mrs. Frederick Stewart (Grace), 75 Silver Lake Rd., Providence, R. I.
Mrs. Hannibal Stewart (Anna), 927 Ray Ridge, Raleigh, N. C.
Mrs. Norman MacBeth (Olive), 923 Highland Ave., Wilmington, Del.
Mrs. Edwin N. McFadden (Dorothy), 226 Rose Ave., Madison, Wis.
Frederick Stewart, 75 Silver Lake Rd., Providence, R. I.
Mrs. C. J. Morman (Anna), 19 Francis Terrace, Abington, Ill.
Mrs. Robert T. Soutar (Susan), 392 Eastman Park, Chicago, Ill.

Nina N. St. Andrew, 42 Vistula Ave., Chicago, Ill.
Mrs. P. W. St. Andrew (Miriam), 123 N. River Blvd., Chicago, Ill.
C. J. Morman, 19 Francis Terrace, Abington, Ill.

Rule 8

Richard Albert Matzke, Raleigh, North Carolina
Alice Ann Spegal, Bangor, Maine
Fred P. Moody, Brookings, South Dakota
Alice Ann Spegal, Buffalo, New York
Richard Albert Matzke, Savannah, Georgia
Alice Ann Spegel, Birmingham, Alabama
Fred P. Moody, Bristol, Connecticut

Rule 9

Milwaukee Trucking Corporation, 283 Gates Ave., Milwaukee, Wis.
Sevenup Athletic Club, 35 Grove Ave., Charleston, Ill.
State Realty Company, 222 Elgin Rd., Clinton, Ill.
Standard Printing Company, Wakefield Rd., Carpenter, Ill.
S A S Delivery Service, 506 Garfield Ave., Canton, Ill.
Society Dress Shop, 39 Washington Ave., Barnett, Ill.
Sampson Incinerators, 25 Highland Rd., Alton, Ill.
Seaman Electric Company, 25 Duck Pond Rd., Alton, Ill.
S S Bottling Co., 1728 Avenue B, Chicago, Ill.

Rule 10

O. Sear Sons, 63 Hill St., Bloomington, Ill.
Robert Sear, 431 Canton Rd., Bloomington, Ill.
Francis L. SeMay, 380 Western Ave., Chicago, Ill.
Edward Maxwell Society, 160 St. Andrew's Lane, Butte, Mont.
William Macadam Company, 430 Crescent Dr., Boise, Idaho
James Madison High School, New York, N. Y.
Mathewstein Institute, 29 River Rd., Tucson, Ariz.
Benjamin McGowan, Haynes Company, 49 Collins Avenue., Colorado
    Springs, Colo.
M. R. Michael Company, 932 Watson Rd., Bridgeport, Conn.
Gifford L. Seland Company, 125 Quincy St., Champaign, Ill.
Matthew Smith College, Arcola, Ill.

Rule 11

Sudan Tea Importers, Cedar Point Rd., Cairo, Ill.
Strupes & Kelly, 21 Carter Ave., Camp Point, Ill.
Moot, Reiff & Son, 221 Ontario St., Chicago, Ill.

Beulah J. Mye, 35 Elm Ave., St. Louis, Mo.
Sud-Z-Soap Company, Allentown, Ill.
Moot-Reid Co., 183 N. Lake Ave., Chicago, Ill.
Scott-Boothe Co., 243 Marcus Ave., Winnebago, Wis.
Mye-Barkee Supply Co., 582 Osborn Rd., Wichita, Kans.
Seven-Up Fruit Distributors, 432 Craig Hill, Charleston, Ill.
Strupes-Keen, Inc., 44 Chestnut Hill, Calvin, Ill.
My-C-Cheese Products, 234 Eighth Ave., Bloomington, Ill.

Rule 12

Mary N. Sewaldjames, 59 Powell Ave., Ashland, Ky.
Arthur C. Sewald-James Circus, Inc., 41 Polk Ave., Allentown, Pa.
David B. Shillingshire, 932 North Lane, Arcola, Ill.
Shilling-Sten Paper Co., 490 Forest Ave., Arcola, Ill.
The Esther Shilling-Shire Shoe Store, 25 Persall Ave., Arcola, Ill.
Arthur C. Sewald-James, 54 Dosoris Way, Alton, Ill.

Rule 13

South Eastern Lumber Co., 771 Dale Ave., Clinton, Ill.
Mid West Paper Mill, 49 Westfield Rd., Akron, Ohio
South East Development Corp., 44 E. Witby Rd., Clinton, Ill.
Midwest Grain Corp. 232 Lakewood Rd., Kalamazoo, Mich.
Southeast Delicatessen, 25 Cypress Pl., Clinton, Ill.
Southeastern Book Company, 338 De Soto Dr., Clinton, Ill.

Rule 14

New Mexico Packaging Corp., 54 Argyle Rd., Memphis, Tenn.
New, Robert J., 825 Main St., Indianapolis, Ind.
New Rochelle Printing Co., 18 Monterey St., New Rochelle, N. Y.
Newmarket Textile Co., 58 Franklin St., Newmarket, Pa.
Newport News Dress Mfg. Co., 103 Clayton Ave., Newport News, Va.
Newport Optical Mfg. Co., 65 Shore Dr., Newport, R. I.

Rule 15

C. D. M'Connell, 726 Phelps Rd., Miami, Fla.
George E. Senning, 470 Trentwood Rd., Montgomery, Ala.
Arthur C. Sewell-Jones, 671 Samos Rd., Lincoln, Nebr.
Marden's Garage, 805 Westbrook Ave., Des Moines, Iowa
Senns' Beauty Parlor, 110 Livingston St., Denver, Colo.
Sewells' Appliance Co., 745 Wand St., Tacoma, Wash.
Sacketts' Delicatessen, 474 Kenwood St., Cairo, Ill.
Sackett's Delivery Service, 207 Wimple Rd., Carter, Ill.

Romeo Mason, 2496 Oxford Row, Chicago, Ill.
P. Mason's Sons, 692 Michigan Ave., Chicago, Ill.

Rule 16

Sixhey Co., 14 Michigan Ave., Chicago, Ill.
Six Hundred Seventeenth Street Café, Chicago, Ill.
794 Broadway Building, 794 Broadway, Charleston, Ill.
700 Club, 700 Bethany Rd., Charleston, Ill.
Seven Hundred Garage, 110 Brownson Ave., Charleston, Ill.
619 Grill, 619 Myrtle Ave., Chicago, Ill.
600 Fifth Ave. Bldg., Fifth Ave., Chicago, Ill.

Rule 17

Straft Sons, 55 Franklin Ave., Albany, Ill.
Alfred Geo. St. Louis, 43 Amsterdam Ave., Chicago, Ill.
Shermance Co., 14 Fulton Ave., Chicago, Ill.
Wm. J. McAllister, 49 Wilder Ave., Abington, Ill.
Sherman Coal Co., 4143 Clinton Ave., Chicago, Ill.
S. P. C. A., 42 Warren Ave., Bath, Ill.
Margaret Savit, 741 Lakeview Ave., Cairo, Ill.
Sayles Mfg. Co., 249 Norfolk Lane, Milwaukee, Wis.
Savit Mfg. Company, 253 Elsdon Ave., Cairo, Ill.
Sayles Manufacturing Corp., 88 Tappan Rd., Marinette, Wis.
Mfrs. Trade Assoc., 411 Benton Rd., Hartford, Conn.
A. Hallock Stile, 79 Sawyer Rd., Bedford, Ill.
Wm. A. Macadam, 397 Glen St., Little Rock, Ark.
Stillwater Ice Co., 632 Lincoln Rd., Bishop, Ill.
Mary Jane Saxby, 523 Seaton Dr., Boston, Mass.
Sampson, Inc., 932 Walnut Rd., Alton, Ill.
Mentor Optical Co., 12 S. Lake Ave., Chicago, Ill.
Meredith, Inclema Company, 58 Oak Lane, Abington, Ill.
Mt. Washington Observatory, 348 Tiffin Rd., Rainier, Wash.
Meredith, Inc., 43 Glen St., Abington, Ill.

Rule 18

Stevens Clothing Store, 394 Westmont Dr., Chicago, Ill.
Beatrice Mathews, 617 College Rd., Richmond, Va.
The McHenry Florist Shop, 458 Schoop Ave., New York, N. Y.
Servis & Aaron, 64 Allan St., New Orleans, La.
Mathews & Boucher, 11 Roy Rd., Norfolk, Va.
Springate, The Hatter, 627 Red Spring Lane, Seattle, Wash.
Society of Motion Picture Engineers, Inc., 43 Spencer Ave., Berwick, Ill.

Smith, Wilson & Adams, Ltd., 15 Westport Rd., Arcola, Ill.
Stevens and Wilson, Inc., 200 Michigan Ave., Chicago, Ill.
David C. Shelter, 45 Mads St., Chicago, Ill.
Shelter for Children, 192 Jackson Blvd., Chicago, Ill.
Mansion for the Maimed, 635 Parke Ave., Salt Lake City, Utah
Soutar & Soutar, 1439 Wipton Ave., Chicago, Ill.

Rule 19

Strickman, Williams & Co., 42 Winfield Ave., Portland, Ore.
Moux, Chappman, Snel & Co., 49 Sproot St., New York, N. Y.
Strickman, Williams & Co., 1733 Wingate Rd., Portland, Maine
Moux, Chappman, Snel & Co., St. Paul, Minn.
Moux, Chappman, Snel & Co., 422 Dodd Ave., New Orleans, La.
Moux, Chappman, Snel & Co., 619 Taylor Dr., Pittsfield, N. Y.
Strickman, Williams & Co., 333 Nichols Rd., Wheeling, W. Va.
Moux, Chappman, Snel & Co., 832 Sloan Dr., Pittsfield, Mass.

Rule 20

Soil Conservation Service of the U. S. Department of Agriculture, Omaha, Nebraska
Civil Service Commission of the United States, Cincinnati, Ohio
Federal Bureau of Investigation, U. S. Department of Justice, Chicago, Illinois
Bureau of Internal Revenue, Department of Treasury of the U. S., Los Angeles, California

Rule 21

Sacramento Clearing House, 219 Riverdale Rd., Sacramento, Calif.
Salem Coal & Fuel Co., 119 Covington Pl., Chicago, Ill.
Fire Department, City of Salem, 1 Sprague Pl., Salem, Ore.
Health Department of the City of Sacramento, Sacramento, Calif.
Department of Education, City of St. Louis, 43 Market St., St. Louis, Mo.
Department of Police, City of St. Louis, 218 Bridge St., St. Louis, Mo.
Mississippi Printing Company, 921 Haden Ave., Jackson, Miss.
Department of Labor, State of Mississippi, Jackson, Miss.
Commission for the Blind, State of Montana, 425 Erie Blvd., Butte, Mont.

Rule 22

Guaranty Bank of Salem, 289 Baden Place, Salem, Mass.
Masters Bank & Trust Co. of Macon, 432 Peach St., Macon, Ga.
First National Bank of St. Louis, 491 Club Rd., St. Louis, Mo.

Security Bank and Trust Company of St. Louis, 330 Town Path, St. Louis, Mo.

Rule 23

Middletown Hospital, Middletown, N. Y.
Hotel Statler, 14 Main St., Adair, Ill.
Secretarial School, 123 Erie Blvd., Syracuse, N. Y.
Public Library, Scranton, Pa.
Memphis Public Library, 938 Reading Blvd., Memphis, Tenn.
Secretarial School, Shrevesport, Pa.
University of Maine, Orono, Maine

3. Alphabetic tabs, which correspond to the guides for the letters *S*, *M*, and *U* in this alphabetic card index file, will be found on Sheet 67 of your Workbook. Paste them on cards and use them as guides in filing all the cards you have made out in these assignments. Paste just the lower portion of the tab on the card, so that the caption will be visible. The number in the lower right corner of the tab indicates the position on the card in which the tab should be pasted. The tabs are ⅓ cut and allow for three positions. The number in the lower left corner indicates the sequence in which guide cards are to be arranged before you file.

If a regular 5-by-3 filing drawer is not available, try to find a cardboard box of the approximate size and place your guides and cards in it.

Retain these cards for use in the next unit.

Optional

4. Often you will have to take hurried, fragmentary notes when your superior is rushed. Some of the things he tells you to do will have to be put off; others must be done at once. Your teacher will dictate to you instructions about things to be done after your superior leaves on a trip.

5. You need a personal "jogger," or "tickler," on your desk to be consulted by nobody except yourself. You will save time and writing space if you keep this record in shorthand. In an office, you may have a calendar pad to use for this purpose; but for this assignment you are to make your own reminder, as follows:

Divide a sheet of typing paper into halves by drawing one line down the middle. Then divide these halves into quarters by drawing three lines across. In the first section, top left, in the extreme left-hand upper corner, write today's date, thus:

THURSDAY
May
1

In the first section, top right, same position, write:

FRIDAY
May
2

Continue writing dates, including Sundays and holidays.

Certain notations that affect only you will appear. An occasional personal notation is quite ethical, but the young employee should be careful that his reminder does not become crowded with notations regarding parties and other social matters that might give the impression to an official who chanced to see it that the employee's mind was on social affairs more than on business.

The instructions dictated to you by your superior are to be transferred to their proper places in the reminder you have made.

In addition, jot down the following data of your own.

Get two boxes of carbon paper from the storeroom when returning from luncheon tomorrow. Stop after work tonight and get a new hat. Insurance premium due in the mail tomorrow—stop at the bank and the post office tomorrow noon. Don't forget to make a deposit in the Employees' Credit Union next Monday. Remember to ask Jim not to call at the office after this—will see him Sunday. Petty cash box owes me 40 cents—see Miss Freeman about this next Thursday.

Spelling Demons

pamphlet	pasteurize	physician
parachute	peculiar	possession
parliamentary	permanent	precede

Job Tips

1. Never "file" letters in your desk. You will probably forget them.

2. Never, for any reason, go away from the files and leave a drawer open—particularly a lower drawer. Another person, or you, could trip over the open lower drawer and be seriously injured.

3. Don't open more than one file drawer at a time in the same stack. A stack of file drawers can easily be tipped over in this way.

4. Onionskin is not the best type of paper for making file copies of correspondence. This thin paper has a tendency to crumple or slip down into the file folder.

5. Never leave a paper clip on material that is placed in the file. Important papers have been "lost" because they have been caught by such a clip.

6. Never place a paper smaller than half of a regular correspondence sheet in the file without first pasting or stapling it onto a full-size sheet of paper.

Personality Pointer

DO YOU FOLLOW THROUGH?

Have you ever faced a day's work feeling it would be impossible to accomplish even a portion of it, let alone *all* of it? That will be your problem on more than one occasion when you are employed in an office. You may have enough work to keep you extremely busy, yet someone will come to you with more work, and you will be expected to complete it *all* in the one day.

One secretary, George Scott, had to learn to adjust himself to such a situation. His work consisted of details too numerous to mention—and each detail seemed to be governed by a time limit. For example, the money received through the mail had to be in the hands of the accounting clerk before 11 a.m.; the outgoing mail had to be ready for the Mailing Department exactly at 4:15 p.m.; one type of incoming mail, which was voluminous and which was George's complete responsibility, could never be held over for more than two days. Just when he thought he had everything running smoothly, his superior would give him a rush job that would put him behind in his schedule.

George tried conscientiously to work under these conditions but found that he could not be so efficient as he wanted to be. He asked his superior's advice. Together they systematized the work of the department. George was given a part-time assistant, who relieved him of some of his duties.

June Humphrey's problem of adjustment was quite different from George's. June had the kind of secretarial position in which the work occasionally was very light. On these days, June had time to do all the

387

tasks that secretaries leave until the more urgent work is finished. The problem of adjustment came to June when, without much warning, her desk was piled high with work to be done in a hurry. June "rose to the occasion." Her superior admired her ability to meet the emergency without undue excitement.

Think ahead to the time when you will be holding a secretarial position. When your employer introduces you and says, "Mr. Customer, this is my secretary, Miss X," might he also have said:

"Mr. Customer, I *want* you to meet my secretary. She is my pride and joy. I know I can depend on her to carry out instructions fully and correctly. She knows my business likes and dislikes so well that I do not hesitate to give her tasks to do that involve a great deal of responsibility. She is conscientious and attends to her business, and you know, from experience, she is courteous when she meets our customers."

If you follow certain rules, you can be reasonably sure of being dependable on the job.

1. Have a correct understanding of the instructions regarding the work, whether you are to carry them out yourself or pass them on to others.
2. Note instructions in shorthand, if possible. This provides a written record. It also has a good effect on your employer, who under these circumstances is more likely to frame his instructions logically and state them carefully. However, it may not always be convenient to make a shorthand note of instructions. Often decisions must be made quickly. Concentrate closely on what your employer says and try to visualize the situation in such instances.
3. Organize the instructions, placing the most important item first. This practice will save time and avoid confusion. Review verbal instructions while the matter is fresh in mind, or write them out in shorthand as soon as you can.
4. Start carrying out the instructions promptly. Note deferred matters on your desk calendar, to be taken care of at the proper time.
5. Don't stop till the job is done.

UNIT 14

Filing Systems, Equipment, and Supplies

There are a number of manufacturers of filing equipment, and each one has developed his own variation of the four basic filing methods discussed in the preceding unit. The difference is usually in the type of guides and folders used and their arrangement within the filing drawers; basically each method is the same.

In addition to selling equipment or supplies, these manufacturers are eager to help any company to analyze its needs and develop a filing plan adequate for current needs, capable of expansion to take care of future requirements. Some firms specialize in giving professional filing service only. For example, professional filing experts from these firms are available to analyze needs, develop the basic plan, write a file manual, and train the office personnel in the efficiency of the system developed.

The first section in this unit discusses the distinctive features of alphabetic filing and describes briefly several such systems that have been developed by different manufacturers. In the second section, consideration is given to numeric, subject, and geographic filing systems. A number of other important kinds of filing equipment and supplies used in many business offices to meet particular filing needs are studied in the third section. You will remember, of course, that filing is the kind of office problem that should be studied constantly to improve it so that it will be accomplished in the easiest, quickest, and surest way.

Section 1. ALPHABETIC SYSTEMS

Distinctive Features of Alphabetic Filing. If you understand the distinctive features of alphabetic filing, you will quickly learn the par-

ticular variations of the system that is used in the office in which you work. The drawer of an alphabetic file is equipped with: (1) alphabetic guides, (2) alphabetic folders having name plates identical with the alphabetic guides, (3) special individual folders for active correspondents, and (4) special individual guides for active correspondents having a number of individual folders.

Alphabetic Guides. The alphabetic guides are arranged for twenty, forty, sixty, and on up to hundreds of divisions of the alphabet, the number of divisions depending on the volume of correspondence.

ILLUSTRATION OF ALPHABETIC DIVISIONS USED ON FILING GUIDES

25 Divisions	40 Divisions	60 Divisions	150 Divisions
A	A	A	A
B	B	An	Al
	Bi	B	American
	Bro	Bar	An-Ar
		Be	As-Az
		Bi	Bam
		Br	Bas
		Bu	Bea
			Bem
			Bi
			Bl
			etc.

The guides are made with name-plate projections, or "tabs," of different widths. If the size of the tab is one-third the width of the guide, the guide is referred to as a "⅓-cut guide." A ⅓-cut guide with a tab at the extreme left is known as a "⅓-cut guide in the first position." A ⅓-cut guide in the center or second position indicates that the tab is in the center of the guide. A ⅓-cut guide in the third position indicates that the tab is at the extreme right of the guide. (See page 370.)

Alphabetic Folders. Alphabetic folders (also known as miscellaneous folders) are intended to hold all correspondence, except very active correspondence, until such time as an individual folder is necessary. Correspondence within the alphabetic folder is arranged in exact alphabetic order. If there are two or more papers from one source, the paper with the latest date is on top. Folders, like guides, are made in different-sized cuts, with tabs in all positions. (See page 370.)

Special Individual Folders. As soon as six letters accumulate from one correspondent, the letters are taken from the miscellaneous alphabetic folder and placed in a special individual folder. This is done to make future reference more convenient and to relieve congestion in

Courtesy Remington Rand Inc.

Variadex alphabetic file.

the alphabetic folder. The name of the correspondent is typed on the gummed label which is pasted on the individual folder. Letters are filed with the latest correspondence at the front of the folder.

Special Individual Guides. When the volume of papers for one person or firm is such that a number of individual folders are required, it is customary to have an individual guide placed in front of the group of individual folders.

The Variadex Alphabetic Filing System. Study the Variadex filing system illustrated on this page and see how it follows the pattern of the typical alphabetic file, employing at the same time its own special features, such as the use of color to speed up filing and finding.

Alphabetic Guides. Alphabetic guides appear in the first and second positions. The first position is used for the letters of the alphabet and

the second position for the more common names. "Brown," for example, is given a guide in the second position, and all correspondence with names beginning with "Brown"—as "Browne" and "Brownlie" —is filed back of this guide.

Alphabetic Folders. In the third row, or third position, are the alphabetic folders having the same notations as the alphabetic guides. Papers are filed in these alphabetic folders until they become numerous enough or important enough to justify the making out of an individual folder for them.

Special Individual Folders. In the fourth position are the tabs of individual folders.

Special Individual Guides. Very active correspondents, to whom are assigned a number of special individual folders, are given a guide in the fifth position to head the individual folders.

Special Feature. One of the outstanding features of the Variadex file is the use of color for greater efficiency in filing and finding. The color plan for identifying guides and folders speeds up the filing and finding of papers, because the color steers the eye quickly to the desired folder. It also acts as a check to prevent misfiling. You stop at once if you try to file a folder with a green label with folders with blue labels.

The alphabet is divided into groups by the vowels, *a, e, i, o,* and the consonant *r.* Five colors, arranged in the sequence of the rainbow, omitting red—that is, orange, yellow, green, blue, and violet— are used on guides and folders to indicate *the second letter of the first unit* of a name.

The "Tailor-Made" Alphabetic Filing System. The "Tailor-Made" filing system, illustrated on page 393, also follows the pattern of the typical alphabetic file, at the same time incorporating certain individual features. In the following description, the numbers enclosed in parentheses refer to the numbers on the illustration of this system.

Alphabetic Guides (1). Alphabetic guides in the "Tailor-Made" filing system appear alternately in the first two positions.

Alphabetic Folders (2). In the first position are the alphabetic folders that correspond to the alphabetic guides in the first and second positions. These folders are used to hold the papers of persons or firms with whom correspondence is limited to less than five pieces.

Special Individual Folders (3). These wide-tabbed folders, alternating in two positions at the right, are used for firms or persons with whom there are more than five papers a year.

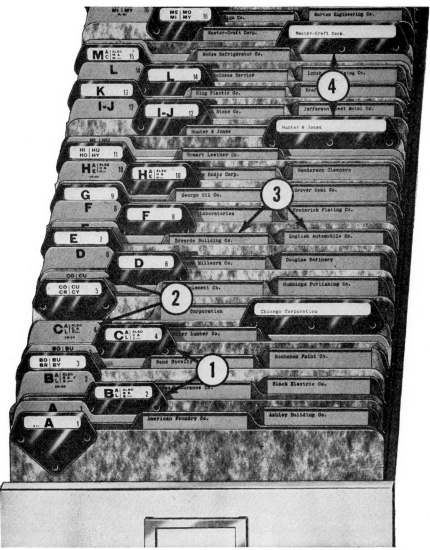

Courtesy Shaw-Walker Company

"Tailor-Made" alphabetic filing system.

Special Individual Guides (4). A wide-tabbed guide at the extreme right gives required prominence to the special correspondents—those having more than forty papers a year.

Other Features. Period folders and period guides head a series

of six or more period folders, where a chronological breakdown is desirable.

A follow-up folder automatically brings papers to the file operator's attention at a desired time.

Out guides replace any papers taken from the file. A requisition card bearing the name of the person to whom the papers are given is placed in the metal tab of the out guide. The guide is placed directly behind the folder from which material is removed.

A special alphabetic breakdown is used when a large number of individual organizations bear the same initial name.

A Special Feature. Tabs on all folders used in this system are five-eighths of an inch below the height of the guide tabs to permit complete visibility of guide captions.

Safeguard Filing Plan. The basic unit equipment of this plan is a four-drawer filing cabinet. In this alphabetic system, the files have individual folders marked with the name of the correspondent. The folders are placed in alphabetic order and separated by *primary guides.* These guides have a tab on which is printed one or more letters of the alphabet, or a combination of letters and numbers; this directs you to the folder you want quickly. For example, a one-drawer file might be marked "A-1," "B-2," "C-3," "D-4," etc. A two-drawer, or larger file, might have the alphabet subdivided into much smaller portions, such as "A-1," "ABR-2," "AD-3," "AN-4," and so on.

In this plan, the letters and numbers are printed on green tabs and placed toward the left on the primary guides. A miscellaneous folder for every alphabetic subdivision has a red tab, placed in the same left-hand position and printed the same as its corresponding green primary guide; this is the last folder in each subdivision of the alphabet.

Individual folders have, at the right, a tab to which is attached a gummed label. Each label is marked with the number of the primary guide behind which the folder belongs, in addition to the name. "Free Space" is available a little to the right of center between the primary guides on the left and the folder labels on the right to make it easier to use the files.

Auxiliary name guides are used when common surnames recur often in the file. These guides are either yellow or orange. Out guides and folders have tabs of blue. They also occupy the "Free Space" and are inserted in the file whenever a folder is taken out. Guides have insert

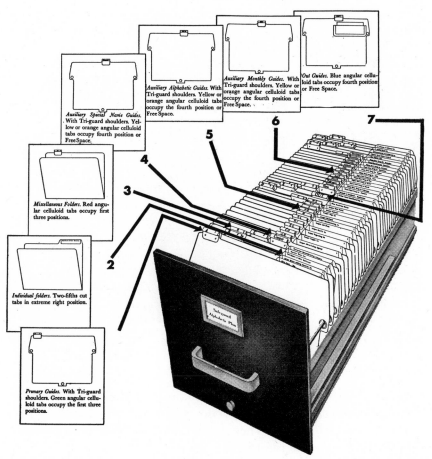

Auxiliary Special Name Guides. With Tri-guard shoulders. Yellow or orange angular celluloid tabs occupy fourth position or Free Space.

Auxiliary Alphabetic Guides. With Tri-guard shoulders. Yellow or orange angular celluloid tabs occupy the fourth position or Free Space.

Auxiliary Monthly Guides. With Tri-guard shoulders. Yellow or orange angular celluloid tabs occupy the fourth position or Free Space.

Out Guides. Blue angular celluloid tabs occupy fourth position or Free Space.

Miscellaneous Folders. Red angular celluloid tabs occupy first three positions.

Individual folders. Two-fifths cut tabs in extreme right position.

Primary Guides. With Tri-guard shoulders. Green angular celluloid tabs occupy the first three positions.

Courtesy Globe-Wernicke Company

Safeguard alphabetic file.

cards, and the folders have ruled spaces in which to enter the name of the correspondent, the date taken, by whom, and when returned. Many people prefer the folder to the guide because it can be used for filing new material that comes in while the regular folder is out.

"Y" and "E" Direct-Name System. The "Y" and "E" Direct-Name filing system, shown on page 396, also follows the organization of the typical alphabetic file, incorporating certain individual features.

Alphabetic Guides. The alphabetic guides in the Direct-Name system appear alternately in the second and third positions, the theory being that the eye first seeks the center of the drawer as it is opened.

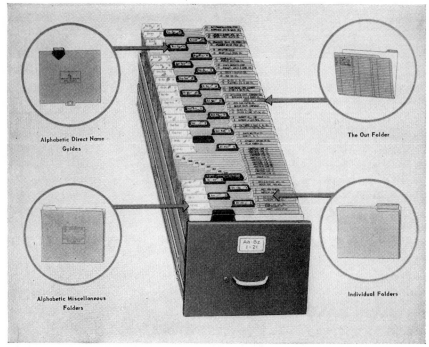

Courtesy Yawman and Erbe Mfg. Co.

Direct-Name alphabetic file.

Alphabetic Folders. In the first position, at the left of the drawer, are the alphabetic folders for correspondents that are not especially active.

Special Individual Folders. These folders, having a wider tab ($\frac{2}{5}$-cut), appear at the extreme right in one position.

Special Individual Guides. When correspondence with one firm or person is especially heavy and a number of individual folders are assigned, a special individual guide, with a large tab covering both second and third positions, is provided to facilitate finding.

Special Features. Because guide and folder tabs are in separate positions, an uninterrupted view of either is possible. Tabs of guides can be had tilted back at a slight angle, making for easy visibility without the necessity of stooping. Guides are numbered; all individual folders and all alphabetic folders bear the same numbers as those of the guides behind which they are filed. Folders, therefore, may be returned to the file by number. The number serves as a check against misfiling if the practice of coding correspondence with numbers before filing is followed.

Soundex Filing System. Many surnames can be spelled in more than one way. The filing system, known as Soundex, handily brings together in one place in the file all these various spellings. The system was planned to reduce errors in filing by grouping names pronounced alike but spelled differently.

When records are compiled from the spoken word or from longhand writing, the possibility of errors is great. Even the best penmen may make an *a* that looks like an *o*, an *e* that might be mistaken for an *i*, or the combination of *ie* that looks like a *u*. When names are spoken, it often is difficult to tell just how they are spelled, especially if the person giving the name cannot spell it. Actual statistics show, for example, that there are thirty-six ways to spell Baer; twenty-nine ways to spell Snyder; twenty-two ways to spell both Bailey and Burke; eighteen ways to spell Lehman.

If you were a file operator and you were asked for all the information about John Baher and you were not told the correct spelling of "Baher," where would you look for the name in a file arranged alphabetically? Perhaps you would look for the information under "Beyer," or "Baer," or "Beahr." You wouldn't find it in any of those places, as the name is spelled "Baher." In a large alphabetic file, "Beyer" and "Baher" will be widely separated.

The Social Security Board uses this system of filing for its largest and most important name file. Even though this file is so large, it takes, at the most, only 60 seconds to find any name in it.

Many insurance companies employ the Soundex index for lists of policyholders. Public-utility companies; hospitals; and Federal, state, and city governments also use it.

How the System Works. Basic sounds are represented by six fundamental letters, *b*, *c*, *d*, *l*, *m*, and *r*. These letters comprise the entire Soundex alphabet. Other consonants having the same relative sounds are considered as equivalents. All vowels and *w*, *h*, and *y* are disregarded. First, names are sorted according to initial letters of their first units and then are coded, using the following chart:

Code	Key Letters and Equivalents	Code	Key Letters and Equivalents
1	b, f, p, v	4	l
2	c, g, j, k, q, s, x, z	5	m, n
3	d, t	6	r

The following rules govern Soundex filing:
1. File by initial letter, but do not code it.

2. Code remaining consonants to three figures only. (If there are not enough consonants to make three figures, add zeros.)

    a. Double consonants or equivalents are coded as one consonant. (The double or equivalent of an initial letter is disregarded. See Rule 1.)

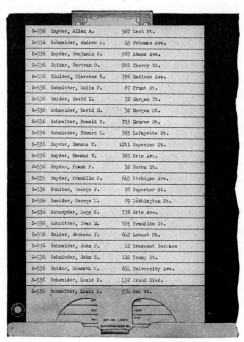

Courtesy Remington Rand Inc.

Index to a Soundex file.

    b. A, e, i, o, u, and *y* are not coded, but are considered as separators.

    c. W and *h* are disregarded entirely unless they are initial letters.

3. Arrangement of names coded alike in a visible file, or of all cards behind one guide in a vertical file, is alphabetic by *second* units. (The second units may be given names, or second words in firm names.)

Let us consider in detail the coding of the surname Snyder. The name is sorted and filed under the initial letter *S*, just as in alphabetic filing. The initial letter is not coded. The second letter, *n*, is coded 5; *y* is disregarded; *d* is coded 3; *e* is disregarded; and *r* is coded 6. The code number is 536.

Now let us code the surname Schneider. *S* is the initial letter and is not coded. The second letter, *c*, according to Rule 2*a* is disregarded, as it immediately follows the initial letter *S* and is an equivalent of *S*. The next letter, *h*, is disregarded; *n* is coded 5; *e* and *i* are disregarded; *d* is coded 3; *e* is disregarded; and *r* is coded 6. Again, the code number is 536.

No matter how this surname is spelled, it will be coded 536; so all cards or letters with this surname will be filed together, divided alphabetically by second units, according to Rule 3.

After names are coded, the cards are sorted numerically according to code numbers after each initial. The arrangement behind any one guide, or in each Soundex numeric group, is alphabetic by second units.

Section 2. GEOGRAPHIC, NUMERIC, AND SUBJECT FILING

GEOGRAPHIC FILING

In some businesses, geographic divisions are more desirable or more convenient than other divisions for the filing of correspondence. An organization or a department within an organization that finds it necessary to keep all orders and other correspondence together by localities should adopt the geographic method of filing. In filing geographically, it is usual to file first by state and then by town. Other adaptations, however, are also in use; for example, material can be filed by town, ignoring state lines entirely; by state and then by county; by state and then by name of person or firm. In all cases, the final arrangement within folders is alphabetically by name of person or organization.

Features of Geographic Filing. An illustration of a typical geographic file is given on page 400. You will see from a study of its organization that:

State guides for every state appear at the extreme left of the file drawer.

Alphabetic guides, to speed up finding of towns, appear in the first position.

Alphabetic folders, with the same name plate as the alphabetic guide, for inactive towns, appear in the last position.

Town guides for active towns appear in the second position. For very inportant cities (see "Boston" in the illustration), town guides are followed by an alphabetic breakdown.

Special individual folders for very active correspondents appear in the third position.

Operation of a Geographic File. To locate correspondence with the Interstate Leather Co., Boston, Massachusetts, for example, look, first, for the state guide, "Massachusetts"; then for the *B* guide in the first position; then for the town guide, "Boston," in the second position; and then for the individual folder, with the wide tab in the third position bearing the firm's name.

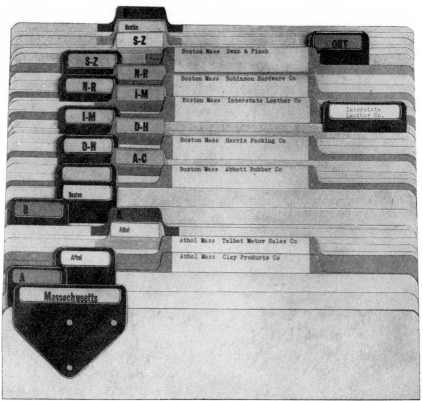

Courtesy Remington Rand Inc.

A geographic file.

Should the paper to be filed be the first or second letter received from a correspondent in Boston, it should be filed in the miscellaneous folder marked "Boston," the tab of which is at the extreme right of the drawer. The arrangement in this miscellaneous *town* folder should be strictly alphabetic according to names of correspondents. Two or more letters to, from, or about the same correspondent must be arranged by date, the latest to the front of the folder.

If the letter came from a correspondent located in a town for which a town guide and a town miscellaneous folder have not been provided, the letter should be filed in the miscellaneous alphabetic folder and arranged first alphabetically by town, then by name of correspondent. For example, a letter received from a correspondent in the town of Blackstone, Illinois, should be filed in the miscellaneous *B* folder at the end of the *B* group.

Expansion. When desired, additional town guides, with their corresponding miscellaneous and individual folders, are inserted for any towns not in the original list. The expansive features of the geographic system are identical with those of the alphabetic system.

The numeric method of filing, as it was defined in the preceding unit, is an indirect method necessitating the maintenance of a sepa-

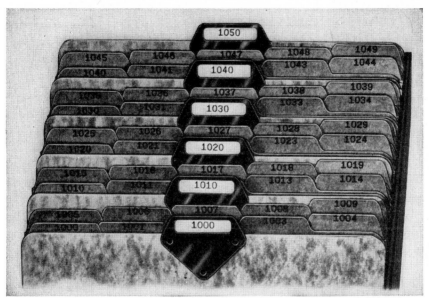

Courtesy Shaw-Walker Company

A numeric file.

rate card index for reference when filing or finding correspondence. For this reason, it is not used extensively in offices today. It is used mostly in professional offices where a permanent record or a great amount of cross-referencing is desirable. It is an accurate system that can be easily expanded by assigning new numbers to new materials to be filed. An illustration of a typical numeric file is shown above.

Features of Numeric Filing. The numeric method requires three units of equipment: (1) drawers containing numbered guides and folders for active correspondence; (2) drawers containing alphabetic guides and folders for inactive correspondence; and (3) a card index. Sup-

pose, for example, that several pieces of correspondence have been received from, or sent to, Howard Johnson. The next unused folder in the file, say 1033, is assigned to "Johnson," and a 5-by-3 card, similar to that illustrated on this page, is typed. The folder number is recorded on the card, and the card is filed in a card file alphabetically, geographically, or by subject, depending on the method used. All subsequent correspondence with Johnson is marked with the same number and placed in folder 1033.

Johnson, Howard	1033
74 Main Street	
Oswego, New York	

A card from the alphabetic card index showing the numeric file reference number in the upper right-hand corner.

Courtesy Shaw-Walker Company

In preparing correspondence for the files, the operator works with the card file before him and codes each piece of correspondence with the folder number. To look up correspondence, reference is first made to the card file to learn the number of the folder desired.

Subject Filing

Any system of filing may include certain folders of materials pertaining to a particular subject and filed in accordance with the system used. Moreover, the basic arrangement of the entire filing system may be according to subjects.

Subject filing is used more for storing material of a permanent nature than for filing everyday correspondence. Pamphlets, reports, clippings, booklets, and magazine articles that may be needed for future reference are kept in subject files. The use of subject filing for correspondence is usually limited to correspondence of interoffice and executive nature.

Features of Subject Filing. The illustration on page 403 shows a typical subject file. Though there are numerous adaptations of subject files, the one shown in this illustration follows the pattern of organization generally used in a business office.

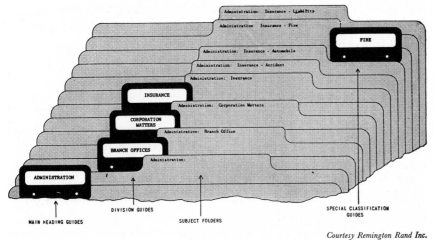

Courtesy Remington Rand Inc.

A subject file.

Principal Subject Guides. The principal subject headings appear on guides in the first position, in alphabetic order.

Division Guides. The divisions of the principal headings appear on guides in the second position, also in alphabetic order.

Subject Folders. Large-tabbed folders, on which are typed the main head, its division, and subdivision, follow in the third position.

Special Classification Guides. Where reference is frequent, a special classification guide may be inserted in the last position to spotlight the important subject.

The numeric system is sometimes used instead of the alphabetic system for subject filing. In such cases, a card index is necessary.

Some General Rules Regarding Guides and Folders

1. Always *file behind the guides.* Years of experience have proved that it works best, and therefore it has become standard practice.

2. There should be a guide for each inch of filing, or approximately every six to eight folders. This means that each file drawer will have about twenty guides.

3. The miscellaneous folder goes behind its matching primary guide and is the last folder before the next primary guide. There must be a miscellaneous folder for each alphabetic subdivision—not just one for the entire file.

4. No more than six letters with any one firm or individual should

be allowed to collect in the miscellaneous folder. Six letters (fewer, if they are bulky) are your signal to make out an individual folder.

5. Individual folders should have neatly typed labels, on each of which is marked the code number, if used, of the guide behind which it belongs, as well as the name of the firm or person.

6. Letters in *individual* folders should be arranged in order of date, the most recent at the front of the folder where, since it is the one most likely to be referred to, it can be quickly found. Keep material neat so that no paper extends beyond the edge of the folder. It not only looks better, but also prevents damage to the papers.

In alphabetic or miscellaneous folders the first order is alphabetic; then two or more papers about the same correspondent are in order of date.

7. A maximum of 75-80 letters in one folder usually gives greatest efficiency—though there may be as many as 100 pieces in a folder.

8. Allow four to five inches working space in letter or legal drawers to prevent jamming and tearing material.

9. When removing folders from the file, always grasp them by the side or center—NEVER by the tab. This saves wear and tear on the folders and keeps labels legible.

10. Transfer to inactive files at regular intervals and on schedule. This is usually done at the start of the calendar or fiscal year. Start getting ready for it a month or so in advance. Check your guides to see if the file has grown enough to need more (remembering the rule of one for each inch of filing) and if so, order them.

11. Most businesses use the two upper drawers for current filing and the two lower drawers for the most recent transfer.

12. When folders are transferred in the Safeguard file, red-tabbed miscellaneous folders go with them and are placed in front of the alphabetic subdivision they govern, to serve as primary guides. New miscellaneous folders are placed in the current file.

Section 3. OTHER FILING EQUIPMENT AND SUPPLIES

CARD FILING

Vertical card filing is simply an extension of the principles of vertical filing to record keeping by means of cards. It is principally used in recording names and addresses for a mailing list, in preparing a similar record in connection with numeric filing, or for cards to be used as a

"tickler," or follow-up, file. The cards are placed in a drawer that is provided with a set of index guides similar to those used in alphabetic correspondence filing. Cabinets for holding cards are obtainable in the same styles of units as those for the large-sized filing drawers. The tickler file is equipped with a set of month and day guides. Cards, as well as guides, may be procured in various colors.

Memo Tickler File. One of your most important duties will be the maintaining of an accurate tickler, or follow-up, file of matters to be brought to the attention of your employer, or matters that you yourself must attend to. The memorandums, written or typed on cards, should be sufficiently detailed to be clear and definite. Each matter should be entered on a separate card. As soon as matters have been disposed of, the cards should be removed from the follow-up file. If the cards are no longer useful, they should be destroyed. If there is a likelihood that the record will be of value later, the action taken should be recorded on the card, which then should be placed with related correspondence or records.

Courtesy Remington Rand Inc.

A memo tickler file.

Visible Records. One of the greatest advances in modern filing and record keeping has come about through the development of visible-record equipment. This equipment has made it possible to file records to which frequent reference is made in such a manner that the desired information can be found at a glance. With a visible record, one can *see* the information; with a blind record, one must *search* for the information.

In the most popular type of visible-record equipment, records are kept on cards 5 by 3 inches in size, or larger, which are slipped into the pockets of a steel tray (page 406). The pockets are arranged so that the bottom of each card shows through a "window" made of a transparent substance similar to celluloid. A line or so of essential information, such as the name and address of a person or firm, is typed on the visible margin of the card. On this margin may also be placed

Courtesy Globe-Wernicke Co.

Visible index tray with cards turned up to allow full visibility of one card.

Courtesy Revo-File Sales

Revolving visible file for cards and records with close-up view above.

Courtesy Remington Rand Inc.

Above: Kardex Linedex desk stand.

At left: Records made visible by resting back on steel Wobbleblock.

Courtesy Shaw-Walker Company

bright-colored celluloid signals to flash certain desired information.

The record cards are usually printed forms suited to the particular business using them. They may be specially ruled inventory records, with the visible part of the card given over to the names of the items inventoried. They may be specially prepared for customers accounts, with the visible part of the card given over to the name and address of the customer and his account number, followed by a series of numbered boxes in which can be placed a signal to show how many times the customer has placed an order in a given period of time.

Some Highlights of This Unit

1. Distinctive features of the alphabetic filing systems described are:

Name	*Variadex*	*Tailor-Made*	*Safe-guard*	*Y & E Direct-Name*
Numerals Used	No	Yes	Yes	Yes
Position of Alphabetic Guides	1st Alphabetic 2nd Common Name	1/5 cut 1st and 2nd alternately	1/7 cut Left 1st, 2nd, and 3rd alternately	1/5 cut 2nd and 3rd alternately
Position of Miscellaneous Alphabetic Folders	3rd	1/5 cut 1st	1/7 cut 1st, 2nd and 3rd, left alternately	1/5 cut 1st
Position of Individual Folders	4th	1/3 cut 2nd and 3rd right alternately	2/5 cut 4th and 5th right	2/5 cut 4th and 5th right
Position of Individual Guides	5th	1/3 cut 3rd	"Free Space" 2 inches	2/5 cut 2nd and 3rd
Special Features	Color Control; Uninterrupted View of Guides and of Folders	Tabs on Folders 5/8″ Below Height of Guide Tabs	"Free Space"	Uninterrupted View of Guides and of Folders
Directly Expandable	Yes	No	Yes, through "Free Space"	No

2. Soundex brings together in one place in the file all surnames that sound alike but are spelled differently.

3. Geographic filing is used when it is desirable to file correspondence by geographic location.

4. Subject filing involves the alphabetic or numeric arrangement of folders pertaining to particular subjects. These folders are filed according to a predetermined plan.

5. In vertical card filing, cards are placed in a drawer that is provided with a set of index guides similar to those used in alphabetic correspondence filing; the cards and guides may be procured in various colors.

Questions and Items for Discussion

1. What is the standard equipment for a drawer of an alphabetic correspondence file?

2. What is the purpose of the special individual folder? When should one be used? When is it desirable to use a special individual guide?

3. How is color employed in the Variadex file?

4. Describe the operation of a geographic file.

5. Name three types of businesses for which geographic filing is most suitable.

6. Discuss the four distinctive features of alphabetic correspondence filing.

7. Why is numeric filing referred to as an indirect method of filing?

8. What type of material is suitably filed in a subject file?

9. What is a tickler file? What is its purpose?

10. What type of information may be recorded in a visible-record file?

Personality Questions and Projects
(Based on Personality Pointer, page 387)

1. The scale in your Workbook, Sheet 43, offers you an opportunity to rate yourself on your dependability. Note first the words that explain dependability, then record your estimate of yourself on the scale. If you have acquired the habit of dependability in school, you will be dependable in business.

2. Apply the recommended rules for dependability to your daily school schedule:

   a. Make up work missed due to absence promptly and without prodding

   b. Follow specified routine in passing out papers or materials, or collecting them

   c. Give courteous, intelligent attention while instructions are being given

d. Take shorthand notes of instructions, assignments, and library reference material

e. Be prompt in completing and turning in assignments

f. Be sure you understand what is expected of you and do it, without further prompting or reminding

Secretarial Assignments

1. The head of the Advertising Department suggests that it would be more practical to file the names on the company's mailing list geographically than alphabetically. If your room is not equipped with a geographic file, change your alphabetic card index file to a geographic card index file. You will find on Sheet 67 in your Workbook geographic tabs to be pasted on cards, which may be used as guides. The guides given are not a complete set but merely a sampling of those found in a typical geographic file like the one pictured on page 400. The guides covering part of the state of Illinois are more complete, and include special guides for some towns in that state, as well as an alphabetic breakdown of the names for Chicago. Refile geographically the cards that you filed alphabetically in Unit 13.

2. On Sheets 68-78 of your Workbook you will find twelve pieces of correspondence. Following the model illustrated on page 358 of your text, mark each piece of correspondence properly for filing in an alphabetic file, indicating the name under which to file, the name under which to cross-reference, and the date under which to follow up, if a follow-up is required. It will not be necessary, however, to prepare actual cross-reference or follow-up sheets.

The twelve letters represent original correspondence coming to us and carbon copies of correspondence written by us. The latter are easily distinguished by the signature and by the fact that they do not have a letterhead.

3. Disregard the notations made in Assignment 2 on the twelve pieces of correspondence and prepare the correspondence for filing by subject, using the guides and folders listed below. These guides and folders represent a portion of the subject file illustrated on page 403 of your text. Write in the lower right-hand corner of each piece the subject of the main and secondary guides and of the folder covering the subject of the letter. For example, if a piece of correspondence is to be filed in the folder "Annual Statements," you will write on the letter in pencil:

Administration
  Corporation Matters
    Annual Statements

You may abbreviate if you wish.

Some correspondence may be filed in more than one folder, in which case make out a cross-reference sheet. Study the illustration of a cross-reference sheet on page 359.

Main Guides	*Secondary Guides*	*Folders*
Administration		
	Corporation Matters	
		Annual Statements
		Constitution and Bylaws
		Dividends
	Insurance	
		Automobile
		Fire
	Sales Department	
		Applications
Advertising and Publi-cations		
	Catalogues and Booklets	
		Card and Filing Supplies
		Vertical Filing
	Direct Mail	
		Form Letters
	Newspapers	
		New York
Factories		
	Equipment and Repairs	
		Boilers
	Reports	
		Labor Conditions
		Orders and Shipments
		Production

Optional

4. Examine the files in your principal's office and report on the filing system in use in that office.

5. If possible, inspect the files of some local office and write a detailed report. Include any recommendations you may have for the improvement of the system.

6. Make a report on the Dewey Decimal System of filing. You will find all the information you need in your school library or the local public library. State why this system is not suitable for the average business office.

Spelling Demons

precious	proceed	proprietor
preliminary	prominent	questionnaire
privilege	pronunciation	rarefy

Job Tips

1. Folder labels may be purchased in continuous rolls or strips.

2. Folder labels may be obtained in white and in solid color or with a color strip along the fold of the label only.

3. A small filing stool, on rollers, is a handy aid in placing material in the lower file drawers; but *never* stand on it to reach high shelves.

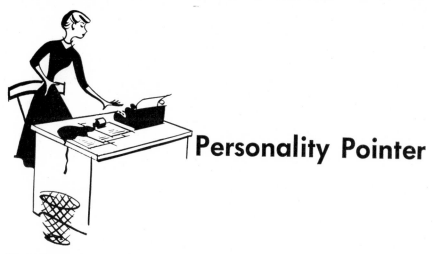

Personality Pointer

IS YOUR PERSONALITY PLUS?

Margaret Williams returned to school after spending most of the day making job-application calls. She went into the office of the school placement director to make her report. During the conversation Margaret said, "I overheard a remark made by one of the personnel men to his secretary. He said, 'You know, I liked that young lady I interviewed this morning. She had so much sparkle. I know she'd get along splendidly with everyone in the office.' What did he mean by 'sparkle,' Mrs. Evans?"

"Sparkle is rather difficult to define, Margaret. I was talking with a jeweler the other day. I asked him what to look for in a good diamond. He told me to look first at the cutting, because it is the cutting that determines the sparkle of the diamond. He told me that paste diamonds, or imitation diamonds, have little sparkle. Couldn't we say, then, that a sparkling personality is one that is genuine, radiating all the fine qualities we admire most in people?"

"I see what you mean, Mrs. Evans. It's just like the diamond on your finger. It is reflecting all the colors of the setting sun from the window there."

"Yes, that's another thing about sparkling personalities, Margaret. They don't hold the light within themselves but are constantly passing on to others their feeling of brightness and good will, just as this diamond is reflecting the beautiful colors of the sun."

"I wonder if it's possible to acquire a sparkling personality?"

"Oh, I think so, Margaret. But it's not something that can be put on and taken off at will. That kind of sparkle is too artificial; and it

413

won't stand the scrutiny of those who know the real thing, as a jeweler knows diamonds. Sparkle must come from within a person. One must be honest and sincere and have a genuine desire to please others, plus a zest for living."

"Don't you think that a sense of humor has something to do with sparkle, Mrs. Evans?"

"Yes, in a way, Margaret. A sense of humor is an accompanying factor—sparkling personalities usually belong to persons who also have a sense of humor. You know, of course, that a sense of humor doesn't mean the ability to tell a good story. It's the ability to take things good-naturedly."

"They say, Mrs. Evans, that you need a sense of humor in an office when you are working hard and your work seems to be more than you can handle. You need something to keep you from staggering under the load."

"Oh, yes, I know that's true. My psychology professor in college used to give terrifying examinations; but somehow we never seemed so nervous about them as you might expect, because he always was able to make us laugh and to put us in a good humor before we started to write.

"In other words, a sense of humor is a safety valve for your nerves. There's nothing so relaxing as a good laugh. Try chuckling to yourself the next time you get all 'tied up in knots.' "

UNIT 15

Travel and Transportation

The secretary sometimes performs duties that require a knowledge of transportation facilities and services. Almost every executive travels in order to keep in personal contact with important customers, to visit branch offices, and to attend conventions and conferences. In addition to business trips, he may travel occasionally for personal reasons.

You can be helpful to your employer when he is planning a trip by taking care of many of the details. The secretary usually (1) helps in the preliminary investigation necessary to decide the method of travel to be used, (2) prepares the itinerary to be followed, (3) makes transportation and hotel reservations, (4) obtains tickets, travel funds, and other items needed by the executive on the trip, and (5) makes any other arrangements that will enable him to get to his destination as conveniently and quickly as possible.

The traffic manager is the executive in the firm who is primarily responsible for decisions regarding the manner of shipment of the goods of his firm. The secretary, however, often must issue instructions for special shipments; she must correspond with customers relative to the transportation of goods; and she may prepare papers necessary for making a shipment. In order to fulfill these duties intelligently, you must be familiar with the services of the various transportation agencies and the printed forms used by them.

Your study of the travel and transportation information contained in this unit and the completion of the secretarial assignments at the end of the unit will prepare you to perform satisfactorily this phase of your future position.

Section 1. TRAVEL INFORMATION

To plan a trip it is necessary to have a good deal of travel information. You, the secretary, must be well informed about the methods of travel that may be used, the relative advantages of each method, the services available and their cost, and methods of arranging for all incidental details involved in making the trip. Of course the travel preferences of the employer will govern the kind of arrangements you make for his trips.

While you should be well informed generally about travel, it is obvious that the specific details of arranging a trip must be based on accurate, current information. It is the duty of the secretary to see that the latest timetables, *Official Railway Guide, Official Airline Guide*, and *Hotel Redbook* are available in the office. The secretary also knows that the local travel agencies are always anxious to be helpful in planning trips.

In this section you will be given the general information about travel that you should have to arrange trips and to prepare itineraries.

Timetables. The railroad timetable usually gives in each column the number of the train—or its name if it is a special train, like the "Twentieth Century Limited" for example—and the time of arrival at and departure from each station. The a.m. time is shown in light print and the p.m. time, in heavy print. A system of symbols in the time column,

Courtesy New York Central System

Traveling in an air-conditioned coach on a modern streamlined train is economical and pleasant.

and explained elsewhere in the table, indicates the type of equipment carried and the special accommodations offered on a particular train; for example, dining, sleeping, club, and parlor cars. (See below.)

It is important to remember that the United States is divided into four time zones—Eastern standard, Central standard, Mountain standard, and Pacific standard time—and that the time of any zone is one hour earlier than the time of the zone immediately east of it. There is a difference of three hours, therefore, between Eastern standard and Pacific standard time, as shown on the map on page 418. Bear in mind the observance of daylight-saving time when planning itineraries.

Timetables for planes or busses give essentially the same type of information as that given by railroad time-tables.

Courtesy Chicago, Milwaukee, St. Paul and Pacific R. R. Co.

A railroad timetable.

Some timetables include transportation fares between various points, maps of the territory served, and a great deal of other information.

Official Railway Guide. If extensive travel information is needed frequently, the office should be equipped with the *Official Railway Guide.* This publication includes detailed information for all railroads and air lines in the United States, Canada, Mexico, Central America, Cuba, and Puerto Rico. The latest schedules are given, as well as information regarding the stations served, connecting lines, services provided on various trains or flights, and other data. The *Official Railway Guide* is published monthly in order to keep the time schedules up to date.

Official Airline Guide. This guide is published monthly by the American Aviation Publications. It contains plane schedules, fares, and general air-travel information for all cities and points in the United States and for major foreign countries.

Travel by Railroad. Railroad rates are governed by the Interstate Commerce Commission and the public service commissions of each

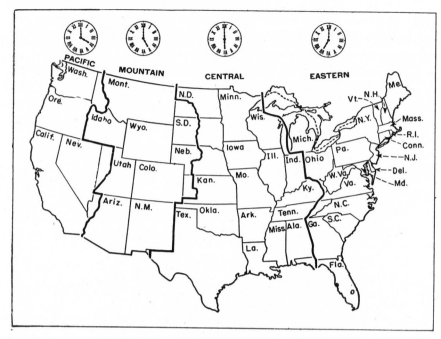

Standard time zones in the United States.

state. Two or more competing railroads running, for example, between New York and Chicago must charge the same rates. Where you have a choice in selecting the railroad over which you wish to travel, other things than the fare usually determine your selection: a saving in time, convenience of time of departure and arrival, scenery en route, and availability of special accommodations.

Coach travel is the most economical. Modern streamlined, Diesel-powered, all-coach trains are increasingly popular. Their equipment is comfortable and air-conditioned. The schedules of these trains are often geared to meet the needs of busy executives, with departure time near the close of the business day and arrival time in late evening or early morning before the opening of the next business day. Dining cars are carried on most through trains.

Certain railways operate extra-fare passenger trains between important points. These trains make faster time than the regular trains and offer some additional services. The "Twentieth Century Limited" operated by the New York Central System between New York and Chicago, the "Super Chief" operated by the Atchison, Topeka, and

Santa Fe System between Chicago and Los Angeles, are extra-fare, de luxe trains.

Pullman Service. For a charge, in addition to the regular first-class fare, one may travel in a Pullman car; these cars have equipment that gives additional riding comfort. Various types of sleeping accommodations are available at different costs, consisting of lower and upper berths, and the more commodious roomettes, bedrooms, compart-

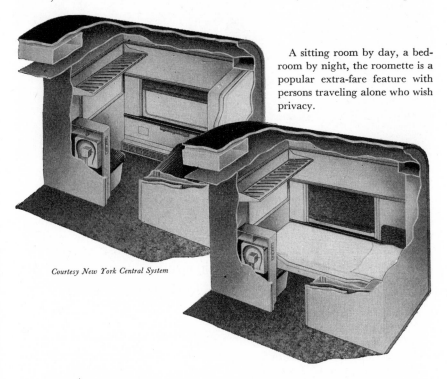

A sitting room by day, a bedroom by night, the roomette is a popular extra-fare feature with persons traveling alone who wish privacy.

Courtesy New York Central System

ments, and drawing rooms that insure greater privacy. Club, lounge, observation, and pleasure-dome cars are added services included on the de luxe and extra-fare trains.

Reservations for Pullman accommodations and for seats on some all-coach trains should be made in advance. They may be made by telephone. However, both the tickets and the reservations should be claimed and paid for without delay. A Pullman ticket cannot be purchased unless a railroad ticket has been purchased.

Additional Services. Some railroads offer additional services to their patrons, such as travel credit cards, rail auto service, rail traveloan,

Courtesy Chicago, Milwaukee, St. Paul and Pacific R. R. Co.

A diner and an observation car on a modern train.

and prepaid tickets. A person with proper credit rating may secure a rail credit card entitling him to charge rail, parlor-car, or sleeping-car tickets to any part of the country. The customer is then billed monthly. If desired, some railroads will furnish an automobile at your destination for a moderate cost. Also, tickets can be delivered to any point in the United States by making a deposit with the local ticket agent.

Baggage. Ordinarily, passengers carry with them their hand luggage containing their immediate needs and check their heavy luggage, such as a trunk, which is carried in baggage cars. Some railroads will check, free of charge, 150 pounds of baggage for an adult passenger and 75 pounds for a child; while other railroads levy a small charge for this service. Luggage should be securely locked and equipped with handles. The passenger must fill in a form declaring the value of each piece of luggage checked. The railroad company assumes responsibility for not more than $100 for each piece of baggage lost or damaged between two states; if the baggage is lost or damaged within a state, the railroad's liability does not exceed $150.

Travel by Air. Travel by air has become increasingly popular for two reasons: (1) it allows more time at your destination, and (2) it is

Courtesy American Airlines

You will get there fastest by plane.

comparable in cost to first-class rail travel. One can reach Boston or Washington, D. C., from New York in an hour; Chicago from New York in three hours; San Francisco from New York in ten hours; and San Francisco from Honolulu in about ten hours. Fares are the same for similar services on all scheduled air lines, which operate under strict government regulation.

Some transcontinental and overseas planes provide sleeping accommodations. As a rule, on flights during mealtime, passengers are served complimentary meals. In-between "snacks" are served on certain regular fare flights. Usually forty pounds of luggage are allowed each passenger without extra charge; sixty-six pounds are allowed on overseas flights.

Reservations can be confirmed quickly by telephoning the air-line office. To be sure of securing the desired flight, you should act early.

A schedule of flights and fares may be obtained from the air-line office or from an officially recognized travel agency that represents the scheduled air lines. This information is also available in the *Official Airline Guide*. Reservations may also be made through hotel travel booths and travel agencies. Travel agencies can also obtain hotel accommodations, and even arrange for the rental of a car if you wish. Generally there is no charge for these services, as the travel agent is compensated on a commission basis by the respective companies for serving you.

Transportation to and from the airport is ordinarily an additional charge. Stopover privileges within the time limit of the ticket are granted if requested at the time the reservation is made. Passenger cancellations are accepted if notice is given a short time before departure of the flight. The air line can cancel a flight entirely when such action is necessary to comply with governmental regulations or because of adverse weather conditions beyond the control of the carrier.

Travel by Bus. Thousands of commercial passenger busses are running daily on scheduled trips between points varying in distance from several miles to several thousand miles. For the long trips, busses provide sleeping arrangements.

Bus lines operate out of bus terminals in much the same way as do railroads out of stations. They maintain running schedules and issue timetables that are similar to railroad timetables.

Bus transportation is slower than train, but the cost of traveling by bus is less than the cost of traveling by rail.

Some bus lines are operated by railroads for the purpose of connecting two train lines or to continue service into territory not served by their trains.

Travel by Water. Business travel by water consists mainly of travel to and from foreign countries. It is suggested that for a trip by water all arrangements be made through a travel agency or a steamship line, especially if the trip is to include travel through foreign countries, in which case you will receive expert assistance in obtaining passports, visas, and so forth.

Section 2. PLANNING TRIPS

So that we may get a clearer picture of the preparations that have to be made, and of what your connection with these preparations will

Courtesy Greyhound Bus Lines

Modern busses are comfortable and usually more economical than other forms of transportation.

be, let us assume that your employer is planning to take a business trip.

Preliminary Preparations. As soon as your employer expresses his intention of making a business trip to a city or to several cities, it is wise to begin accumulating, in a trip folder labeled "Mr. . . . .'s Trip to . . . ., Date . . . .," all correspondence and memos relating to that trip. It is a good plan to include even such notes as "Remind Mr. . . . . to take a copy of the new catalogue with him."

The data in this folder will be used later in making up your employer's itinerary. Several days, perhaps a week, before your employer is to start on the trip, you should take all the material out of the trip folder and make a complete list of places to visit and of all appointments. When you have done this, consult railroad or other timetables, depending on how your employer wishes to travel. Use the *Official Railway Guide* if there is a copy in the office. Note which trains, busses, or planes he can take to make the best connections. Take special note

Courtesy Cunard Steam-Ship Company, Ltd.
Luxury liners serve both business and pleasure.

of the symbols in the timetables to see what type of special services are offered by the particular conveyance in mind.

If the schedule is an extended or complicated one, it is advisable to take advantage of the services offered by the transportation companies and travel bureaus in the preparation of itineraries. These organizations employ experts to assist in planning trips, and they do not charge for this service. You should not hesitate to call the offices of your local rail, air-line, or bus company for assistance in securing detailed information needed to plan the trip.

The Itinerary. Type the itinerary as soon as the route has been laid out and include all details of the journey. Incorporate in this itinerary the notes collected in the trip folder and refer to the correspondence in that folder if necessary. Arrange the facts in an easy, readable form, as in the illustration on page 425. Make several copies of the itinerary, so that, besides your employer, you and other members of the organization who may have to keep in touch with him will each have a copy.

Travel Accommodations. When you have submitted the finished itinerary to your employer, and he has approved it, telephone for train or plane accommodations. Call or send for the tickets at least the day before his departure. Because of the possibility of a change in the itinerary, many businessmen prefer to purchase tickets for the first part of the trip only and to make further reservations along the route.

Hotel Reservations. Write a short letter or send a reservation wire to the hotels where your employer intends to stop and specify the kind of room to reserve, the approximate price, the time of arrival, and the length of his stay. If you are not familiar with the hotels in certain cities, consult the *Hotel Red Book* or similar travel guides. Such books list the lead-

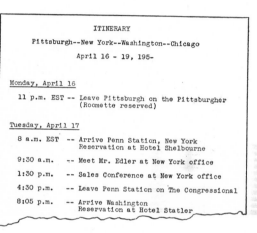

```
                        ITINERARY
        Pittsburgh--New York--Washington--Chicago
                   April 16 - 19, 195-

Monday, April 16

   11 p.m. EST -- Leave Pittsburgh on the Pittsburgher
                  (Roomette reserved)

Tuesday, April 17

   8 a.m. EST  -- Arrive Penn Station, New York
                  Reservation at Hotel Shelbourne
   9:30 a.m.   -- Meet Mr. Edler at New York office
   1:30 p.m.   -- Sales Conference at New York office
   4:30 p.m.   -- Leave Penn Station on The Congressional
   8:05 p.m.   -- Arrive Washington
                  Reservation at Hotel Statler
```

An itinerary for a busy executive.

ing hotels of the country, give rates, and describe the facilities offered by each hotel. The carbon copies of these letters should be included in your employer's trip folder of correspondence.

If time is limited, and there is the possibility of a shortage of rooms, perhaps because of a large convention, it is wise to telegraph or telephone for reservations.

Travel Funds. If your employer is going to travel in territory where he is not known and may not be able to cash personal or company checks, it is well to purchase traveler's checks or a letter of credit for the amount he needs (see description of both on pages 469-71) so that he will not have to carry a large amount of cash. Traveler's checks, which have been in use for over fifty years, are commonly called "blue money" because of their color. Many businessmen have credit cards issued them by the hotels that they patronize regularly. These cards permit the holders to cash checks and pay their hotel bills on a monthly basis.

OTHER RESPONSIBILITIES OF THE SECRETARY

Forwarding Mail. Your employer will give you instructions as to what type of mail he wishes you to forward to him while he is away. Place such mail in one large envelope and forward it daily or at whatever intervals he suggests. Copies should be made of important cor-

NAME William Wright

MONTH May	FROM	TO	TRANSPORTATION DATA AUTO MILES	@7¢ MILE	TOLLS & PARKING	PLANE	RAIL-ROAD	PULL-MAN	HOTEL	MEALS	STR. CAR & TAXI	TEL. & TEL. POST & SUPPLIES	APPROVED DUES (EXPLAIN)	ENTER-TAINING (EXPLAIN)	MISC. (EXPLAIN)	TOTAL	MONTH
DAY 26	New York	Albany					7 42		5 75	6 85	90					20 92	DAY 26
27	Albany	Buffalo					15 27		5 25	6 25	60	45			1 85	29 67	27
28	Buffalo	Cleveland					9 60		6 25	5 65	45	75				22 90	28
29	Cleveland								6 25	5 25	55	30				12 35	29
30	Cleveland	Chicago					17 69		6 60	7 20	70	2 65				34 84	30
31	Chicago								6 60	2 45	60	30		18 65		28 60	31
1	Chicago	New York				50 72					1 95	15				52 82	1

EXPLANATIONS: Entertainment, $18.65: Dinner with three clients at Edgewater Beach Hotel. Karl Hoerlein and Richard Dale, representatives of World Transport Association, and Elmer Sanders of Richards and Sanders, Inc.

Miscellaneous, $1.85: Laundry and cleaning service.

Form No. 5000

A travel expense report.

respondence, the copies being forwarded and the originals kept in the office to avoid loss in transit. It is advisable to keep a record of all correspondence forwarded.

Personal Expense Reports. The method of handling traveling expenses varies in different companies. One commonly used method is to advance the traveler a sum of money somewhat in excess of his actual needs if the trip is a short one. If he is to be away for several weeks, he is given enough money for a week or two, and arrangements are made to send additional remittances to him en route.

Most firms require that an expense report be sent in once a week. A typical expense report is shown in the above illustration. Executives often ask their secretaries to prepare these reports from notes that they give their secretaries upon their return. The reports are

usually made out in triplicate or quadruplicate, depending on the administrative routine of the company.

Appointments. You will recall the discussion in Unit 9 that the secretary anticipates the employer's schedule of appointments in advance. When your employer informs you that he will be away from the office on a trip, you will immediately "block out" that period of time on your record of appointments. If appointments have already been scheduled, it will be necessary to change them.

Section 3. SHIPPING SERVICES

As was indicated earlier in this unit, the secretary may be called upon to perform duties in connection with the shipment of goods. A knowledge of shipping services and procedures is necessary. This section will give you the general information you should have regarding the services of the various transportation agencies.

Choosing the Method of Transportation. There are various means for transporting goods—parcel post, express, and freight by railroad, airplane, motor truck, or steamer, or a combination of two or more of these means. So many factors must be taken into consideration when making a shipment that it is difficult to lay down general rules as to the method most suitable for a particular class of shipment. The nature of the goods in question, the size and weight of the shipment, its destination, the speed of service required, and the cost of shipping are factors that will have a bearing on the method of transportation used. If speed is important, a more expensive service may have to be chosen; if speed is not a factor, a slower and less expensive service may be used.

A number of shipping guides, among them *Leonard's Guide*, and *Bullinger's Postal and Shipper's Guide*, give detailed information on rates and regulations for air express, domestic and foreign air mail, domestic and foreign mail, domestic railway express, freight, freight routing, parcel post, motor freight companies, and other information pertaining to shipping.

The various shipping facilities available and the details of each service are explained in the following paragraphs.

Parcel Post. Parcel-post shipments, also known as fourth-class mail, are handled by the United States Post Office. Parcel post is one of the fastest means of sending packages that fall within the weight and size

limitations set by the Post Office. Packages must be over 8 ounces but less than 40 pounds in weight in the first and second zone; in the third through the eighth zone, the weight may not exceed 20 pounds. Packages must be within 72 inches total length and girth (at the widest point) combined.

No written message may be included in a parcel-post shipment unless the message is enclosed in an envelope, fastened to the outside of the package, and paid for at the rate for first-class mail. The cost of mailing by parcel post is determined by the weight and the destination of the package. The United States is divided into eight parcel-post zones. A rate per pound has been established for each zone.

If speed in delivery is important, air parcel post may be used. This service of the Post Office Department is expensive when compared to regular parcel-post rates.

For a nominal charge over the regular rates, special services are offered in connection with parcel-post shipments. A parcel-post package may be sent *special delivery*. This means that the shipment will be expedited from the point of origin to the post office of destination and then delivered to the recipient by special messenger.

A parcel-post package also may be sent *special handling*. This is similar to special delivery except that the package is expedited only from the point of origin to the post office of destination.

A parcel-post package may be sent *C.O.D.* The postman who delivers the package collects the price of the goods. He will also collect the cost of mailing and the collection charges if the shipper so requests. The sum collected is remitted by the post office to the shipper in the form of a money order, charge for which is included in the C.O.D. fee.

Parcel-post mail on which postage and extra fee have been paid by postage stamps may be *insured* against loss, rifling, or damage in an amount equivalent to its actual value or cost of repairs. Insurance fees vary with the amounts of indemnity and rise on a graduated scale. These fees are in addition to regular postage.

Rates and regulations for parcel post and its special services are changed from time to time. The secretary should, therefore, consult the *Postal Guide* or her local post office for current rates for the services that are required.

Express. Goods may also be shipped by express, a service provided by the Railway Express Agency, which utilizes the most rapid services of railroads and scheduled air lines. The shipper need give only the

destination of the package; the express company decides which means of transportation (except air express) is the fastest and most practical in each case. The shipper must give an exact address: the name of the consignee, his complete street address, the name of the town, the

Three steps in express service: pickup at home, delivery to railroad terminal, trucks loading at terminal for delivery at destination.

Courtesy Railway Express Agency

name of the state. The latter must be spelled out in full to avoid any confusion.

In addition to speed in service, an outstanding feature of express transportation is its free store-door delivery. The goods are picked up at the door of the shipper or "consignor," usually by express truck, delivered to the railroad, or other carrier, and then transported by truck from the railroad to the door of the recipient or "consignee."

At the time of the pickup, the express employee fills out a receipt in duplicate, leaving the original copy with the shipper. A receipt is

also obtained from the consignee upon delivery, so that there is a complete record of every transaction.

Express Rates. Rates for express transportation vary according to the type of goods shipped, their weight, and the distance shipped. They fall into two classes: *first class* for general merchandise, such as dresses, flowers, trunks; *second class* for articles of food and drink, such as fruit, vegetables. The second-class rate is three-fourths of the first-class rate.

Courtesy Railway Express Agency

A Railway Express receipt.

In addition there is a special commodity rate for large-volume shipments of special commodities.

A book listing the classification of goods and the rates charged may be obtained from the nearest express agency. *Leonard's Guide* also gives comparative rates and routings for freight, express, and parcel-post shipments.

The charges for sending goods by express may be prepaid by the shipper or collected from the consignee. Many business houses carry an account with the express company against which all prepaid shipments are charged.

Express charges include protection for valuation up to $50 for shipments of 100 pounds or less, or 50 cents a pound for shipments over 100 pounds. When the declared value is greater than the above, a slight additional charge is made for the extra insurance.

The express company, like the post office, offers a collection service. Packages may be sent C.O.D. at a slight extra charge. The selling

price of the item delivered, and sometimes the transportation fee and other fees, are collected from the purchaser; and the express company, after deducting whatever is due it, sends to the shipper the amount collected.

Air-Express Service. If speed is essential in the delivery of certain shipments, air-express service may be used. Rates are higher but delivery is fast, overnight from coast to coast. The express company will co-ordinate rail and air-express service if the shipping or destination point is not located at an airport city.

As planes grow larger, the size of shipments is limited only by the size of the aircraft. Such items as race horses and machine parts, weighing a ton or more, have been transported by air express. When shipments of unusual size or of a special nature,

Goods being chuted from plane to express truck in air-express service.

Courtesy Railway Express Agency

which may require the capacity of a full plane, are planned, special arrangements can be made with the local Railway Express agent. Air express is used for a wide variety of products, such as machine parts, style merchandise, flowers, newsreels, and medical supplies to mention but a few.

You may obtain detailed information about the rates and services of air express from any express office. A phone call is all that is necessary.

Express Personal Services. The Railway Express Agency makes available many services of a personal nature, such as collecting notes; obtaining signatures to notes, mortgages, deeds, or other legal docu-

Courtesy Railway Express Agency

Yes, it's possible to ship live birds by air express!

ments; paying taxes; depositing funds in a bank; transmitting and delivering papers to be filed or recorded by Federal, state, county, city, or town officials; purchasing or obtaining goods at another address; and picking up baggage or clothing that guests may have left in hotel rooms.

Freight. Heavy, bulky shipments are commonly sent by freight by rail, steamer, truck, or a combination of these. Freight is not so fast as parcel post or express, but it is a less expensive form of transportation. Such commodities as coal, iron ore, and large shipments of food and merchandise are sent by freight.

Transportation charges are figured on a minimum of 100 pounds, the rates being determined not only by the weight of the goods but also by the type of goods. A carload of gravel, for example, requires less handling and less insurance (the freight transportation rates include insurance) than a carload of textiles. Gravel, therefore, can be shipped at a much lower rate than textiles. The freight rates are set by the Interstate Commerce Commission according to classes of merchandise, and also according to various geographic areas.

Freight shipments gen-

Courtesy Railway Express Agency

A prize champion flies in by air express.

erally must be delivered by the shipper to the train or wharf and picked up at the other end by the purchaser—unless motor-truck freight is being used, in which case the trip is made from door to door. More and more transporation companies, however, are adopting store-door delivery, including the extra charge for this service in their total freight-transportation cost. They send their own trucks to pick up a shipment and deliver it to the train or wharf and at the other end again use trucks to deliver the shipment to the consignee.

When a shipper can use an entire railroad car for a shipment, he gets a special reduced carload rate; otherwise, shipments are charged at the regular l.c.l. (less than carload) rate.

Bills of Lading. The contract between the shipper and the freight company for transporting goods is known as a bill of lading. There are two types of bills of lading—the *straight* bill of lading and the *order* bill of lading—both of which are shown on pages 434 and 435.

The Straight Bill of Lading. The straight bill of lading is more commonly used. It is made in triplicate and signed by the agent of the transportation company when the goods are accepted for shipment by him. The three copies are used as follows:

1. The *original* copy is forwarded to the consignee (the person receiving the goods) and surrendered by him to the carrier's agent at destination. He can thus identify himself as the consignee and claim the shipment.

2. The second copy is the *shipping order*. It is retained by the carrier's agent (railroad company).

3. The third copy is the *memorandum copy*. This is kept in the file of the shipper for record purposes. Both the shipper and the railroad company agent sign all three copies.

There is also a short form of the straight bill of lading that does not have the contract terms and conditions printed on the back. This form has a brief statement on the front to the effect that the shipper certifies that he is familiar with the conditions included on the back of the uniform straight bill of lading.

Order Bill of Lading. An order bill of lading is commonly used with C.O.D. shipments, where a bank or other agency is to collect for the shipment before it is released. Three copies of the order bill of lading are made out. The shipper takes the first copy (the original) to his bank. This bank, in turn, sends this copy, with sight draft attached, to a bank in the city or town in which the consignee is located. In

Courtesy New York Central System

Uniform straight bill of lading.

Courtesy New York Central System

Uniform order bill of lading.

435

the meantime, the shipper has notified the consignee what bank is handling the collection, so that the consignee will know where to go to pay the draft and receive the bill of lading. He does this when the freight company has notified him that the goods have arrived.

The second and third copies of the order bill of lading are handled in the same manner as the second and third copies of the straight bill of lading.

Goods shipped on an order bill of lading cannot be surrendered until the bill of lading has been properly indorsed and given to the carrier's agent.

An order bill of lading is negotiable, and the goods may be transferred by indorsing the form. A straight bill of lading is made out to a specified consignee, who is the only one who may claim the shipment.

Freight-Forwarding Companies. By turning l.c.l. freight shipments over to private companies, known as freight-forwarding companies, a shipper will get faster service. The freight-forwarding company, by combining shipments from different sources, is able to fill a car with shipments to one city, thus saving the time ordinarily wasted in unloading and rerouting shipments at railroad junctions. Freight-forwarding companies are given the benefit of the reduced full carload rate offered by the freight company. A fee is charged for this forwarding service.

Water Shipments. In making shipments by water, the United States Government requires that a manifest be filled out. This is a form identifying the goods shipped and showing how much they are worth.

Motor-Truck Freight. This system of transportation has become popular for short hauls of several hundred miles. It is increasingly being used for longer hauls; coast-to-coast service is now offered by many motor-truck companies. It is a direct means of shipment, as the truck comes to the shipper's door and delivers to the door of the consignee. Thus, a shipment is handled only once. A bill of lading similar to that used for railroad and steamship freight is used for truck shipments.

Waybill. When a combination of rail, water, and, sometimes, truck facilities are utilized for transporting a shipment, a contract, called a *waybill*, is made with the freight company that first handles the shipment. The waybill contains complete instructions for routing the shipment from one carrier to another and accompanies the shipment until its arrival.

Courtesy United Fruit Company

A combination of water and rail shipping. The inset shows the bananas that came by boat and are being transferred on a conveyor belt to the freight cars.

Foreign Shipping. Shipping to foreign countries is a specialized field governed by many ever-changing regulations. If you should be employed as a secretary for an importing or exporting company, you will want to make a thorough study of this phase of shipping.

Frequently Used Shipping Terms. The following terms should be understood by the secretary who performs duties connected with the shipment of goods.

B/L. Bill of lading.

C.i.f. Cost, insurance, and freight. The shipper sometimes pays the cost of these items, depending on the conditions of an agreement.

C.O.D. Collect on delivery. The cost of goods plus transportation and collection charges are to be paid on delivery.

Carrier. A transportation company.

Common carrier. Railroad, truck, steamship line, or air line.
Consignee. The one to whom goods are shipped.
Consignment. The goods shipped.
Sold on consignment. Arrangement whereby unsold goods can be returned.
Consignor. The shipper.
Depot. A storage place for freight shipments.
F.o.b. Free on board. Free delivery from plant to train or other carrier.
Invoice. A bill for merchandise. See page 472.
Manifest. List of goods shipped by steamer.
Pier. A steamship terminal.
Route. The course a shipment takes from one point to another.
R.R. Railroad.
Ry. Railway.

Some Highlights of This Unit

1. The traffic manager is primarily responsible for methods used to ship the firm's goods; the secretary sometimes must (*a*) issue instructions for special shipments, (*b*) correspond with customers, and (*c*) prepare necessary papers for making a shipment.

2. A timetable gives information about (*a*) time of arrival and departure from each station or airport, (*b*) accommodations, (*c*) miscellaneous information.

3. Pullman cars provide additional travel comfort during the day and night for an extra charge.

4. Extra-fare passenger trains make faster time than regular trains and offer some additional services.

5. Coach fare entitles a passenger to space in a baggage car for luggage not exceeding 150 pounds. A nominal excess charge based on weight is made for transporting additional luggage.

6. Air travel allows more time at your destination.

7. Bus transportation is slower than train, but the cost is less; for long trips, busses provide sleeping arrangements.

8. In planning trips (*a*) accumulate all correspondence and memos relating to the trip in a file folder, (*b*) make a complete list of places to visit and of all appointments, (*c*) make an itinerary, (*d*) telephone for travel accommodations, (*e*) make hotel reservations, and (*f*) purchase traveler's checks or a letter of credit.

9. Other responsibilities of the secretary while her employer is out of town are (*a*) forwarding mail, (*b*) preparing the employer's personal expense reports, (*c*) canceling all appointments for the time the employer will be away.

10. There are various means for transporting goods—parcel post, express,

and freight by railroad, airplane, motor truck, or steamer, or a combination of these carriers.

Questions and Items for Discussion

1. Name some ways in which you can help your employer in planning the details of a contemplated trip.

2. What type of travel information can you obtain from the *Official Railway Guide?*

3. Name the four time zones into which the United States is divided. What additional time factors must be considered periodically?

4. If you were not familiar with the hotels in some of the cities that your employer will visit on an extended business trip, and he has not indicated his preference, what books would you consult for the information you need?

5. What procedure would you follow in forwarding mail to your employer during his absence?

6. Name some of the duties that the secretary may perform with regard to the shipping of goods.

7. What are some of the factors that enter into the choice of the method of shipment?

8. Name one or two sources for such shipping information as rates, time in transit, and the types of pickup and delivery service.

9. Name the two types of bills of lading and explain the difference between them.

10. What is meant by the following commercial abbreviations: *B/L, c.i.f., f.o.b., l.c.l.?*

Personality Questions and Projects
(Based on Personality Pointer, page 413)

1. The personnel manager of a large industrial concern has a motto hanging on the wall immediately behind his desk. The motto reads: "Don't get tragic about it."

Can you see what purpose this motto serves—what effect it has on applicants as they talk with the personnel manager? Would you say that a person who is continually getting "tragic" about things needs a sense of humor?

2. Does one necessarily have to be witty in order to show that one has a sense of humor?

3. Do you think there is some connection between the quality called "sparkle" and the quality of mental alertness? Is it possible to have a sparkling personality and not be wide-awake?

4. What is the difference between a sparkling personality and one that merely glitters?

5. Rate yourself on the mental-alertness scale in your Workbook, Sheet 43.

If you are not satisfied with your present rating, find out what makes your rating so low. Is it laziness? boredom? ill health? undernourishment? poor working habits?

6. Say aloud your answers to the interviewer's questions listed below. Show animation and sparkle in your voice and manner of speaking. The applicant's answer is given as a suggestion. Supply an answer as you would if you were the applicant being interviewed.

a. *Interviewer.* Where did you get your business training?
Applicant. I had my first training when I was a senior in high school. Then I went for six months to the Acme Business College.

What would your answer be?

b. *Interviewer.* Do you have any hobbies?
Applicant. Yes, I have two hobbies. One is playing table tennis, and the other is photography.

What would your answer be?

c. *Interviewer.* What did you do in school besides study?
Applicant. During my first two years in high school, I went out for all kinds of athletics. But during my junior and senior years I found dramatics and debating attracted me more. I did some reporting for the school paper, too.

What would your answer be?

TO THE STUDENT

Starting with Unit 15, whenever an assignment requires a letterhead or interoffice memorandum, use plain paper, as no further letterheads or memorandums are provided in your Workbook.

Secretarial Assignments

1. You have been transferred to the general manager's office to substitute for his secretary during a vacation period. Mr. Wright is leaving on Monday of next week to visit the branch offices of the United Products Corporation. His secretary has left notes regarding his itinerary. You are to type the information in the form shown on page 425. Make four carbons. Any personal items should be included only in the copy for Mr. Wright's own use.

Monday. Leave LaGuardia at 9:15 a.m., American Airlines. Arrive Boston,

10:18 a.m. Hotel reservations at Statler. Meet Mr. Richard March at Hotel Bancroft, 11:30. Conference, Boston office, 2:30 p.m. Dinner with sales representatives, 7 p.m., Hotel Bancroft.

Tuesday. Second session, sales conference, 9:30 a.m. Luncheon with Mr. March and new district manager, Mr. Lloyd T. Phillips, 12:30 p.m. Take 4:25 plane for New York, American Airlines. Arrive LaGuardia, 5:35.

Wednesday. Board of Directors meeting, 10 a.m., home office. Stockholders meeting, 1:30 p.m. Leave LaGuardia, 5 p.m., American Airlines. Arrive Chicago, 7:25 p.m., CST. Reservations, Hotel Stevens.

Thursday, District meeting, Chicago office, 9:30 a.m. Sales conference, 1:30 p.m.

Friday. Second session, sales conference, 9:30 a.m. Take 1:20 plane, American Airlines. Arrive San Francisco, 7:15 p.m. Pacific time. Meet brother, Mr. Elliott Wright.

Saturday and Sunday. Week-end guest of brother. Be sure to call Carl Pierce at his home, 1618 Jefferson Boulevard. TRiangle 6-2453.

Monday, 9:30 a.m., district meeting, San Francisco office. Sales conference at 1:30. 9:45 p.m., plane leaves San Francisco, United Airlines.

Tuesday. Arrive LaGuardia, 10:50 a.m. (half-hour stop in Chicago.)

2. After you have typed the itinerary, Mr. Wright dictates an office memo to the managers of the branch offices. Type the labels for the sample packages mentioned in the letter. Use Sheet 79 of your Workbook.

3. Write to a hotel in each city on Mr. Wright's itinerary (except New York) and reserve a single room and bath for the duration of Mr. Wright's stay.

4. While in Chicago, Mr. Wright wires you asking you to ship immediately 500 copies of the new United catalogue to the Chicago office and to the San Francisco office. As these new catalogues have not yet been received from the printer, you decide to send a night letter to the printing plant, Tennessee Press, Knoxville, Tennessee, asking them to ship the catalogues direct to the two offices. You also send a full-rate telegram to Mr. Wright telling him what you have done. Send a confirmation copy by mail and include a carbon of your night letter to the printer. Use Sheet 80 in your Workbook.

5. Prepare a handy reference list of *local* train, bus, and other passenger facilities. Type the information on a letter-size sheet of paper in a form that would be suitable for placing in a loose-leaf binder for the use of your employer. Include such items as:

Address and telephone numbers of various passenger stations
Skeleton timetable covering important towns within a radius of 200 miles
from your town

Time required to get to the station
Taxi fares, etc.

* * * *

Mr. Wright's secretary has returned from vacation, and you are now asked to help in the Order Department.

6. The head of the Order Department will dictate a series of letters having to do with shipments of goods and transportation problems. Transcribe the letters.

7. Our dealer in St. Louis, Mr. William French, sends an order to be shipped by freight. This will involve the following steps:

Typing an invoice for the goods in quintuplicate. (Allow 15 per cent trade discount.) Use Sheet 81 in your Workbook for the original.

Typing straight bill of lading in triplicate. Use Sheets 82–84 in your Workbook; also study the illustration on page 434.

Transcribing a letter of transmittal, which will be dictated to you by Mr. Martin.

The goods ordered are: 6 United electric ranges at $289.95. Freight charges of $22.08 are to be prepaid and the amount added to the invoice. The total weight of the shipment is 1,200 pounds.

The invoice number is 5063. Use plain paper for the duplicate copies of the invoice.

Note: Sight drafts are necessary for the solution of Assignments 8 and 16; a certified check for Assignment 15; and promissory notes for Assignment 18. For a discussion and illustrations of these forms, see pages 462, 464, 466, and 467.

8. An order for goods comes to you from a new dealer in Bangor, Pennsylvania—Mr. James Todd, whose address is 22 Elm Street. As we have not had credit dealings with him before, he instructs us to draw on him for the amount of the invoice. This transaction will involve typing the following: an invoice (allow 15 per cent trade discount), a sight draft for the total amount of the invoice, an order bill of lading, and two letters of transmittal, one to Mr. Todd and one to the bank. Use Sheets 85, 86, 87–89 in your Workbook.

The goods ordered are: 2 Torrid hot-air furnaces at $387.50; 250 square yards inlaid linoleum, No. 421, at $1.50 a square yard; 5 kitchen utility cabinets, No. 20, at $37.95; 200 gallons of Everlast paint at $4.60. Invoice No. 5064. Freight charges are to be paid by the customer. Use a calculating machine, if available, for figuring extensions and totals. The total weight of the shipment is 4,800 pounds.

9. You are asked to type express forms for three shipments to be sent by express today. The forms will be found in your Workbook, Sheet 90.

Here is a description of the three shipments:

a. Shipment to Keenly Building Company, Scranton, Pennsylvania. Four cartons of light fixtures, total weight 85 pounds; prepay express charges of $1.65; declared value of shipment, $100.

b. Shipment to Martine Brothers at 6220 Calumet Avenue, Plainfield, New Jersey. Two cartons Sun Ray bulbs, total weight 14 pounds; express charges to be paid by customer; declared value of shipment, $50.

c. Shipment to Leslie & Company, 107 Beacon Street, Buffalo, New York. Two cartons fireplace andirons, total weight 48 pounds; express charges to be paid by customer; declared value of shipment, $50.

Optional

10. Your instructor will dictate to you a "Rush" interoffice memo from the president to the general manager. Transcribe it quickly.

11. You have rough notes containing the following information. Put them into logical order and give the information in typed form to Mr. Wright.

Leave New York Tuesday on Congressional, Penn Station, 4:30 p.m. $23.12 round trip, plus parlor car reservations, $2.40 each way. Total, $27.92. Reservation at Mayflower, Tuesday night. Conference Wednesday, 9:30 a.m., with Mr. Jackson, Washington staff manager. Appointment at 11 a.m. with Mr. L. W. Montgomery, State Department representative. Conference with Mr. Montgomery and final briefing at 2:30 p.m. Take 5:15 from Washington, arrive Penn Station, 8:50 p.m.

New York to Rio, direct flight, takes about twenty-four hours, with one-hour stop in Port of Spain, Trinidad. Pan-American stratocruiser, El Presidente, leaves LaGuardia at 11 a.m. Arrives in Rio, 9:45 next morning. Daily flights. $460 one way, $828 round trip, no tax. Returning, leave Rio at 1 p.m., arrive New York, 5 p.m., next day. All meals are included. Baggage up to 66 pounds carried free. (Only 40 pounds on domestic flights.) Brief case not included when figuring this weight. Good hotels in Rio: Excelsior Copacabana, Gloria, and Copacabana Palace. Travel agency will make reservations.

Argentine lines have return sailings, but trip takes twelve days. (Conference is scheduled in Pittsburgh March 20.) The Argentina sails from Rio March 16, arrives in New York March 28. Fares begin at $500.

12. How would you send a message the quickest way to Mr. Wright in Port of Spain? to Mr. Wright in Rio de Janeiro? What is the literal translation of Rio de Janeiro? What language is spoken in Brazil? How do residents of Brazil spell the name of their country? What language is spoken in most other South and Central American countries? What is the capital of Brazil? What are its chief exports? What is the approximate area of Brazil in square

miles? Where did you find this information? What is the population of Brazil?

13. Write to the Hotel Mayflower in Washington and make a reservation for the Tuesday night that Mr. Wright will arrive there.

14. Your instructor or someone assigned by him will dictate some letters.

15. An order for office equipment comes to you from a newly organized firm—Warden, Hawkins & Wright, 14 Astor Avenue, Joliet, Illinois. (This firm is in the Chicago territory, but office equipment is shipped only from your New York warehouse.) The new firm is not able to give credit references but sends a certified check for $200 as evidence of good faith. The following equipment is ordered.

1	Wide counter cupboard	No. CS 1410	Olive green	$123.25
4	Legal-size 4-drawer files without casters	No. 4071	Olive green @	28.50
3	Card-size 2-drawer files	No. 1635	Olive green @	2.10
1	Combination wardrobe and supply cabinet	No. 2108	Olive green	39.25
1	Executive posture chair	No. 6718½	Olive green	39.50
2	Side chairs	No. 6715	Olive green @	30.00
	Extra for machine-buffed leather on one only			6.00
3	Typist posture chairs	No. 6413	Olive green @	27.25
1	Table	No. 296634T	Olive green	53.00
1	Double-pedestal typewriter desk	No. 7060DH	Olive green	90.25
2	Single-pedestal typewriter desks	No. 7045DH	Olive green @	74.75
1	Island-base desk	No. 7066	Olive green	75.50
1	Broadloom rug 12 x 15 ft.	No. HP17	Graystone	6.90
				sq. yd.

Make an invoice in triplicate, including the extensions. Allow a discount of 15 per cent except on the rug, which is net. Use Sheets 91, 92 in your Workbook.

16. Make a sight draft on Warden, Hawkins & Wright for the total, less the amount they have already paid. Use Sheet 86 in your Workbook.

17. Your teacher will dictate to you a letter concerning the order described in assignment 15.

18. Mr. Richard Robinson purchased today merchandise amounting to $1,000. The terms of the sale provided that Mr. Robinson shall pay $500 of the purchase price in cash or its equivalent. The balance thereof was to be represented by two promissory notes of a series, payable to the company in

equal monthly installments thirty and sixty days from date, at the Standard Trust Company, 27 East 45th Street, New York City. Prepare the promissory notes to be signed by the customer. Use the forms on Sheet 86 of your Workbook.

Spelling Demons

receipt	referred	rescind
recommendation	relief	responsible
reference	repellent	restaurant

Job Tips

1. An itinerary should be typed on the best quality paper the office has on hand—an itinerary is subject to frequent handling.

2. If the itinerary crosses time zones, be sure to indicate such information clearly.

3. Be sure the office carbon of an itinerary is readable!

4. In some instances, it is desirable to keep a file of itineraries for reference, particularly if the itineraries include reminders and marginal notes.

Personality Pointer

DO YOU HAVE A HOBBY?

A hobby is anything you enjoy doing that brings relaxation from a day's routine, that gives you a feeling of competence and inner satisfaction. You have a hobby because you *want* to have it—not because you *must* have it.

Hobbies may be classified into three groups: (1) mental: working crossword puzzles, collecting stamps, reading, etc., (2) physical: tennis, skating, golf, swimming, walking, (3) a combination of mental and physical: the manual arts, model making, photography, music.

A hobby that is fun to a high school pupil may not, necessarily, continue to be a source of pleasure after he leaves high school. A change of environment may demand a change of hobby.

You should seek in a hobby an interest that is unrelated to the day's routine. A lifeguard is more likely to choose a hobby *outside* the "physical" classification; a key-punch operator, on the other hand, will probably prefer a hobby *within* the "physical" classification; an executive whose responsibilities are heavy is likely to turn to music or some phase of art for relaxation from the day's tension; a certain surgeon has been known to play the piano nightly, not only because he seeks relaxation through music, but also because the practice keeps his fingers strong and supple.

You may expect an employer to ask you about your hobby when you are an applicant for a position. An employer asks the question for two reasons. First, he wishes to get you to talk about something

447

in which you are especially interested, so that you will be more at ease. The employer thus has a better opportunity to make a correct estimate of your personality. Second, your hobby indicates to some extent your outside interests, your manner of thinking, your social attitude, and your use of leisure time.

A hobby can be expensive. It's a good idea to invest *some* money in a hobby, but it's wise to try your hobby for a while before you invest much in it—you may tire of it soon. You should not feel under any compulsion to stick to a hobby when you are tired of it or have lost interest in it.

Life is never dull to the person who has an absorbing interest in a hobby of some kind. There is pure joy in knowing a great deal about one thing; it is fun to know even a very little about a great many things.

Handling Money and Keeping Records

One of the most exacting and important duties performed by the secretary is the handling of money and the keeping of financial or other records. This is true even though the secretary may devote but a relatively small amount of time to the actual execution of these particular responsibilities.

In the larger offices, the secretary handles a great deal of the employer's own personal business records; for example, his banking, investment, and insurance records. In the smaller offices, the secretary will probably do this and, in addition, handle money and keep some of the records of the firm. By their very nature, these duties require sterling qualities of integrity, confidence, loyalty, accuracy, and dependability.

Different types of business require different forms of records, but the underlying principles of all bookkeeping are the same—to make available information necessary to show the exact financial condition of the business or the person. Secretaries therefore need an adequate knowledge of the fundamentals of bookkeeping, and an understanding of such business areas as banking, investments, credit, and insurance. You have acquired considerable background knowledge in these business areas in other classes.

You will now have an opportunity to use that knowledge in performing the duties connected with the handling of money and the keeping of records for both your firm and your employer. You should be thoroughly acquainted with the common banking practices and procedures to be found in every business organization. You must know the common types of financial forms and their uses. Also, you

Courtesy First National Bank of Chicago

As a secretary, you may be asked to make deposits and cash checks.

must understand the kinds of transactions involving the payment of bills. In addition, you should be familiar with and be able to keep the more common kinds of records used in business.

If you know how to handle the money and records of the firm, you will have no difficulty applying this knowledge to the personal business affairs of your employer.

Section 1. RECEIVING AND HANDLING CASH

The type of transactions that a business has determines the records that are required and the procedures to be used. The more common transactions are those for cash, those for which a bill is rendered, and

those for which an invoice is received. Depending on the size of the firm, the secretary may be asked to keep the records for these and other transactions. It is quite likely that the secretary will be responsible for transactions involving the receiving and handling of cash, particularly the payment of small charges. Time will permit a discussion of only one or two types of transactions. They are, however, illustrative of what you may expect to do as a secretary.

PETTY CASH FUND

To take care of the small expenses that are paid in cash, a petty cash fund is generally set up. Such items as postage, carfare, telegrams, donations, express charges, and incidental office supplies are paid from this fund. The policy of the firm determines how the petty cash fund is to be operated. Responsibility for the fund is placed in one person, usually the secretary.

Establishing the Fund. The amount of the petty cash fund is determined initially by the probable need for small cash payments over a relatively short period of time. Two weeks to a month is the usual period. Later it may be desirable to increase or to decrease the amount of the fund. A check payable to "Petty Cash Fund" is drawn for the amount to be put into the fund. The check is then cashed by the secretary and the money put into the petty cash box.

Making Payments. If you are the person responsible for the petty cash fund, you must keep an accurate record of all payments made from it. The policy of the firm is followed as to how you operate the fund. For example, it may be that all amounts of less than $1 are to be paid from petty cash. Or it may be that all expenditures of a certain type, such as postage, are to be paid from petty cash.

The secretary will see to it that only authorized expenditures are paid from the fund and that a receipt for each payment is obtained. The bill that is being paid may be marked "Paid" and serve as the receipt when signed by the person receiving the money, or a petty cash voucher (illustrated on page 452) may serve as the receipt. In any case, the petty cash box must contain all receipts for the payments that have been made.

The amount of cash on hand, plus the total of the receipts and vouchers in the cash box, must always equal the original amount of the petty cash fund.

```
┌─────────────────────────────────────────────────────────────────┐
│ PETTY CASH VOUCHER                                    NO. 375     │
│                                                                   │
│ $   3.40                    Date     August 28, 19--              │
│                                                                   │
│ PAID TO:              Midwest Stationery Company                  │
│                                                                   │
│         Three and 40/100                            DOLLARS       │
│                                                                   │
│ FOR:                  Accounting Forms                            │
│                                                                   │
│ Paid out by   J.B.M.      Received Payment   Roscoe Smith         │
│                                                                   │
│ Account to Be Charged          Office Expense                     │
└─────────────────────────────────────────────────────────────────┘
```

A petty cash voucher.

Replenishing the Fund. While the exact procedure to reimburse the petty cash fund may differ in various offices, the following procedure is recommended:

1. Total all receipts and vouchers in the fund.
2. Prove the fund (as described above).
3. Have a check drawn payable to "Petty Cash Fund" for the total amount of all payments that have been made.
4. Attach receipts and submit check to employer for signature.
5. Cash the check and place the money in the petty cash box, thus replenishing fund to the original amount.

Analyzing the Fund. When it becomes necessary to replenish the fund, an analysis should be made to determine the amounts spent on various items. You may find it convenient to keep a petty cashbook to facilitate the classification of expenditures under certain headings. A petty cashbook record enables you to verify quickly the amount on hand, as well as to analyze the total expenditures under such headings as postage, carfare, telegrams, donations, etc.

Cashbook. While small payments may be made from the petty cash fund, records must be kept of all other transactions in which cash is received or paid out. Cash includes more than coins and currency; personal checks, bank drafts, money orders, certified checks, and cashier's checks are also called cash. Every office keeps a complete record in a cashbook of all cash received or paid out.

The simplest device for recording cash receipts and cash payments

is the two-column cashbook. It is frequently used by small business firms, professional organizations, and clubs, as well as by individuals, for their personal cash records. Special columns may be added in the cashbook for those items that occur repeatedly. Any number of special columns may be added. The total of each special column, at the end of a month, is the total amount spent on that item. The total of all special columns must equal the total of the payments column. If the firm has many cash transactions, it will probably use a cashbook with a separate page for cash receipts, on the left-hand side, and a separate page for cash payments, on the right-hand side.

CASHBOOK

Date	Description	Receipts	Pay- ments	Sal- aries	Sup- plies	Dona- tions	Gen- eral
195–							
March 1	Cash balance 297.50						
1	Sales	25 00					
1	Window Ventilator		7 50		7 50		
1	Rent		60 00				60 00
1	Sales	16 00					
2	Red Cross		10 00			10 00	
2	Invoice F607	30 00					
2	Sales	12 00					
2	Stationery		17 50		17 50		
4	Typist's salary		35 00	35 00			
4	Insurance		18 00				18 00
30	Sales	20 00					
30	Stationery		25 00		25 00		
30	Salvation Army		5 00			5 00	
31	Sales	30 00					
31	Typist's salary		35 00	35 00			
31	Garage—office car— gas and sup.		22 50				22 50
		718 25	543 30	140 00	62 50	25 00	315 80
		718 25	543 30	140 00	62 50	25 00	315 80
	Cash Receipts	718 25					
	Plus cash bal. March 1	297 50					
	Total cash payments		543 30				
	Cash bal. March 31		472 45				
		1,015 75	1,015 75				

Section 2. SECRETARIAL BANKING ACTIVITIES

The Bank Account. As commerce and travel have increased, the actual exchange of money has become inconvenient. Both individuals and firms today use substitutes for money known as "commercial paper."

Most persons receive their incomes in the form of checks, the most common form of commercial paper. If a person has a checking account, he deposits in the bank the checks he receives and pays his obligations with his checks. It is entirely possible to earn and spend a year's income without ever seeing or handling a tenth of the income in actual money.

Business firms now use commercial paper almost exclusively to carry on their financial transactions. The secretary's work will usually include some banking and financial duties. You should be thoroughly acquainted, therefore, with all common types of financial forms and their uses.

Making Deposits. When a person opens an account with a bank, he receives a passbook (see illustration), which he is expected to present each time he makes a deposit. Before making a deposit, a deposit slip supplied by the bank must be filled out. On this slip must be listed the various items included in the deposit, such as coins, bills, checks, drafts, and other instruments of exchange. The accompanying illustration shows the correct method of recording the items on a deposit slip. Be sure to write the figures in the correct columns—dollars under dollars and cents under cents.

When you have counted the money, listed the checks and other items, and totaled them, take the deposit, with the deposit slip and your passbook, to the receiving teller at the bank. He will check over the items and enter the total in your

Deposited with
MERCHANTS NATIONAL BANK
Natrona, New York

By *Reed Cleaning & Pressing Co.*

Sept. 3 19_–_

List checks separately	Dollars	Cents
Currency	*18*	*00*
Silver	*3*	*40*
Checks		
3-62	*3*	*50*
99-19	*5*	*00*
Total	*29*	*90*

A deposit slip.

passbook. As mistakes do occur, you should see that the correct amount is entered in your passbook before leaving the receiving teller's window.

In a business where the daily deposits consist of numerous checks, the amounts are first recorded on an adding machine (see illustrations on pages 494 and 495), each item being listed separately. Sometimes the adding-machine tape is wrapped around the checks and sent to the bank, the total amount only being written on the deposit slip. The receiving teller then verifies the items by comparing the tape list with the checks themselves. Many banks, however, require that the name of the maker, the name of the bank, and the amount be given for each check.

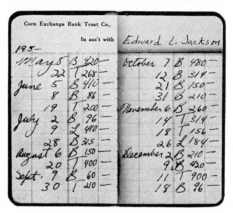

A depositor's passbook.

Occasionally, it may be necessary for you to make a deposit when you do not have your passbook with you. In such a case, make out a duplicate deposit slip, marking it "duplicate," and hand the duplicate to the receiving teller with the original deposit slip and the checks and money you are depositing. The teller will sign or initial the duplicate slip and return it to you. Retain the duplicate and have the amount entered in your passbook when you make your next deposit. Some firms require duplicate deposit slips made out for every deposit even though the passbook is used.

Overdrafts. Banks may not legally pay checks for amounts exceeding the balance of the depositor. Checks drawn for amounts exceeding the depositor's balance will be dishonored and a protest charge made against the drawer. Checks so issued will be returned to the payee marked "insufficient funds."

Overdrafts may result from any of the following causes:

·1. Failure to keep on the check stubs an accurate record of checks drawn.

2. Errors in arithmetic—such as adding in one deposit twice.

3. Taking for granted that the balance shown on the monthly bank statement is the same as that shown in the checkbook. If stubs are checked against the bank statement, it will be easy to tell whether

there are outstanding checks—that is, checks drawn that have not yet been presented to the bank for payment. This is explained in the paragraphs on "Monthly Bank Statement."

Special care must be taken to avoid issuing a check for a larger amount than is in your checking account at the bank. In some states the payee can bring criminal suit against the drawer of such a check.

It must be kept in mind that the mere act of depositing a check does not make the amount of the check available for withdrawal. The check first must be "cleared"—that is, collected by the bank. If, for example, a depositor in New York deposits a customer's check drawn on a bank in a western town, the proceeds from that check might not be available for a week or ten days—the time needed for the check to clear.

Postdated Checks. Some businessmen give their creditors postdated checks; that is, they date their checks ahead to a date when they believe they will have sufficient money on deposit so that the checks will be honored upon presentation. This is an undesirable practice and usually is considered an indication of a weakened financial condition. Postdating a check may add to the drawer's business difficulties in other ways. If he is unable to obtain and deposit sufficient money for the payment of the check upon presentation at his bank, the bank will refuse to honor it, thus necessitating its return to the person who presented it for payment. Banks frown upon the practice of postdating checks. It involves additional bookkeeping and other services, and some banks charge a service fee for the return of each item.

Stopping Payment. If a check should be lost or if one has been drawn in error, the bank should be notified at once so that it may issue a stop-payment notice to its paying tellers. This notice instructs the tellers not to honor the check described if it is ever presented for payment.

Average Daily Balance. To cover the handling cost for small accounts subject to numerous transactions, depositors are required to keep in their checking accounts a minimum daily balance, ranging generally from $100 to $500. Banks make their profits from the interest they earn by lending money that is deposited with them. If a depositor checks out his money as soon as it is deposited, the bank loses money on his account and must, therefore, charge a monthly handling fee.

Monthly Bank Statement. Nearly all banks send each depositor a bank statement at a certain date during each month. This statement shows

	In Account With		Name	Reed Cleaning and Pressing Co.
	MERCHANTS NATIONAL BANK			Louis Reed, Proprietor
	Natrona, New York		Address	125 Main Street

Checks		Deposits	Date: July 1, 19–	Bal. 000
		500.00	July 1	500.00
		26.50	July 2	526.50
		33.00	July 3	559.50
		30.00	July 5	589.50
4.00	105.00	40.40	July 6	520.90
60.00		54.25	July 7	515.15
		34.50	July 9	549.65
120.00		42.20	July 10	471.85
105.00		52.25	July 22	624.30
		28.00	July 24	652.30
		35.00	July 25	687.30
2.20		44.00	July 26	729.10
		39.60	July 27	768.70
2.60		46.00	July 28	812.10
105.00		36.30	July 29	743.40
		34.00	July 31	777.40

A bank statement.

the old balance, the deposits and withdrawals made during the month, and the new balance (see above). This statement is accompanied by the canceled checks that have been paid during the period covered by the statement.

As soon as the monthly bank statement is received, you should go over the figures and check them against your own checkbook records. This operation is called "reconciliation of bank balance." The bank's

Balance shown in checkbook, September 30 . . . . $389.98
Outstanding checks (not listed on bank statement) . . . . No. 435 $ 36.19
                         437   235.04
                         440   1.99
Total outstanding checks 273.22
Balance on bank statement $663.20

balance and yours will rarely agree because you will carry on your stubs the amounts of *all* checks issued, but all these checks may not have been presented at your bank at the time the bank's statement was prepared. The illustration presented here shows one method of bank reconciliation, based on the following steps:

1. Compare your canceled checks with the checkbook stubs.

2. List the outstanding checks and add the total to your checkbook balance.

3. If, after doing the above, your statement balance does not prove with your checkbook balance, compare the items on the statement with the deposits in your checkbook and with the canceled checks.

4. If the two balances still do not agree, consult the bank officers, first going over your figures carefully to see whether or not you have made an error in your calculations.

Safe-Deposit Box. An employer may find it convenient to give the secretary access to his safe-deposit box for the purpose of depositing or withdrawing important papers or securities. In carrying out these duties, be absolutely accurate and hold all these transactions in the strictest confidence. It would be wise to keep a perpetual inventory of the contents of the employer's box in the safe-deposit vault. If you keep the inventory, ask your employer to notify you of any deposits or withdrawals he makes so that you may keep the record clear.

Most banks have safe-deposit boxes for rental. The amount of rental depends upon the size of the box. These boxes are constantly guarded and only the box renter or his authorized agents are permitted to open the box. Each time a visit is paid to the vault, the renter must sign a slip of paper on which is stamped the exact time of his arrival.

Writing Checks

Convenience and Safety. A huge amount of business is done at a distance; buyers and sellers are often not even on the same continent. To put actual money into envelopes and send it through the mails would be impracticable, because it might be lost, stolen, or destroyed. A lost check, however, is not easily cashed by someone who has no right to it; furthermore, it can easily be replaced by another check and payment can be stopped on the original. The actual money, if lost, could be spent by anyone who found it; and if completely destroyed, it could not be replaced.

Instead of carrying a great deal of money around with him and paying it out as required, a person may leave it safely in a bank and issue checks that authorize the bank to transfer specified amounts to his creditors.

Let us say that we have issued such a check, for $100, to Albert Jones. He may deposit it in his own account, which may be in another

bank, and draw upon it by writing checks of his own; or he may obtain actual currency in exchange for the check. The bank will see that the money is transferred from the account on which we wrote the $100 check for Mr. Jones.

The original check is returned to our bank, where it is canceled, and is later returned to us, with our bank statement, to be checked against the statement and retained as a receipt.

We have made payment in a convenient and safe manner, Mr. Jones has his money, and we have the original check bearing his indorsement as evidence that we paid him $100.

Precautions in Writing Checks. In writing checks, the following precautions should be observed:

1. Never make a check out to "Bearer" or "Cash" unless you are cashing the check at once and are actually in the place where you plan to cash it. If such a check is lost, anyone may obtain the money for it.

2. Never sign blank checks. Anyone who has access to the check may fill in his own name and whatever sum he sees fit and may obtain the money. In this case, as in case 1, the person who signed the check —not the bank—will have to stand the loss, if any.

3. Write all checks in ink.

4. Write legibly.

5. Begin writing at the extreme left of each line; draw a line through unused space.

6. Make no erasures or alterations.

7. Void all checks that require alterations because of mistakes in the first writing.

To guard against the raising of amounts in checks, many organizations use what is known as a check writer or check protector—a machine that perforates the amount through the check. The cashier's check on page 461 was written on a check writer. A check writer is illustrated on page 460.

Most checks are printed on what is known as "safety paper," a guard against erasures. As soon as an attempt is made to erase on safety paper, the word "Void" appears.

With each check in a personal checkbook there is a stub that remains in the checkbook. The stub should always be filled out before the check is written, and care should be taken to carry over the correct balance from the preceding stub. The information that is to go on the stub is shown in the first check shown on page 461.

Company Checks. Some business firms use checkbooks and keep records on stubs, just as individual depositors do, although business checkbooks are usually larger, with two or more checks to a page, separable by tearing along perforations.

Courtesy Todd Company, Inc.

A check-writing machine.

Most large business houses do not use checkbooks with stubs in them. Instead of filling out stubs, they enter the data about their checks in a book called a "check register."

Voucher Check. The voucher type of check is widely used by business organizations. On a voucher check a space (or sometimes a detachable stub) is provided for making a notation of the item or items for which the check is drawn. When the space for this notation is on the face of the check itself, there is usually room only for a brief notation, such as "January rent on Watertown warehouse." When the voucher is a stub, either detachable or nondetachable, there is usually space for more detailed information; for example, an invoice number, order number, date of order, etc.

In some offices, a carbon copy of each voucher check is made and kept on file.

An ordinary personal check may be converted into a voucher check by writing across the face a brief statement of the purpose for which the check is drawn; as, "January garage rent."

A voucher check is illustrated on page 462.

Indorsements. A check is negotiable (that is, may be assigned or transferred to another person), and the extent of its negotiability is determined by the type of indorsement it bears.

To indorse a check, the payee (the person to whose order the check is made) writes his name *across* the back of the left end of the check, as shown on page 463. This indorsement should be placed close to

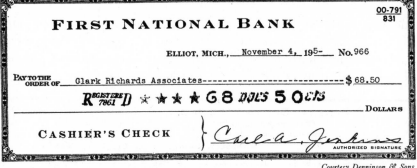

No. 62 ~ $7.65
July 18, 195-
To Logan's Store
For Blouse

	DOLLARS	CENTS
BAL. BROT. FOR'D	407	23
AM'T DEPOSITED	40	00
" " "		
" " "		
TOTAL	447	23
AM'T THIS CHECK	7	65
BAL. CAR'D FOR'D	439	58

July 18, 195- No. 62

PAY TO THE
ORDER OF *Logan's Department Store* $7.65

Seven and 65/100 ———————— DOLLARS

THE STATE BANK
SINCLAIR, VA.

Janet Marshall

Courtesy Dennison & Sons

A personal check with stub.

BY ENDORSEMENT THIS CHECK IS ACCEPTED IN FULL PAYMENT OF THE FOLLOWING ACCOUNT		
DATE	AMOUNT	
7-11-5-	210	143	16
7-16-5-	281	212	42
7-31-5-	327	87	42

TOTAL OF INVOICES	443	00
LESS 7% DISCOUNT	31	01
LESS Prev. Cr.	173	19
TOTAL DEDUCTIONS	204	20
AMOUNT OF CHECK	138	80

IF INCORRECT PLEASE RETURN
NO RECEIPT NECESSARY

NELSON REFRIGERATING, INC.
ELECTRIC REFRIGERATORS
85 EAST ELM BLVD.

TERHUNE, GA. August 3, 195- No. 852

PAY
TO THE
ORDER OF Roberts Chromium Company ----------$138.80

R **REGISTERED 7861** D ☆ ★ ★ ★ 1 3 8 DOLS 6 OCTS DOLLARS

TO NELSON REFRIGERATING, INC.
THE TERHUNE NATIONAL BANK
TERHUNE, GA.

Floyd L. Morey TREASURER

Courtesy Dennison & Sons

A canceled company check used as a voucher check.

FIRST NATIONAL BANK

00-791
831

ELLIOT, MICH., November 4, 195- No. 966

PAY TO THE
ORDER OF Clark Richards Associates----------------- $68.50

R **REGISTERED 7861** D ☆ ★ ★ ★ 6 8 DOLS 5 OCTS DOLLARS

CASHIER'S CHECK *Carl A. Jenkins*
AUTHORIZED SIGNATURE

Courtesy Dennison & Sons

A cashier's check written on checkwriter.

the top edge of the paper, so that nothing may be written above it.

The payee may indorse a check *in blank* by signing his name on the back. The check is then payable at the bank, upon identification, to anyone who presents it and adds his own indorsement below the first

GENERAL DECORATORS, INC.
"PAINTERS OF QUALITY"
1290 SOUTH DECATUR STREET
WOODSLEY, CONN ___April 23, 195-___ No. 421

Pay __Four hundred forty-one and no/100 ----------------__ DOLLARS $ __441.00__

TO THE ORDER OF
⌐ J. T. Ewing & Sons
1718 Twentieth Street
Hartford, Connecticut

GENERAL DECORATORS, INC.

TO THE
CENTRAL NATIONAL BANK
WOODSLEY, CONN.

Samuel J. Roth
AUTHORIZED SIGNATURE

DETACH AND RETAIN THIS STATEMENT
THE ATTACHED CHECK IS IN PAYMENT OF ITEMS DESCRIBED BELOW
IF NOT CORRECT PLEASE NOTIFY US PROMPTLY. NO RECEIPT DESIRED.

| DATE | INVOICE NUMBER | DESCRIPTION | AMOUNT | DEDUCTIONS | | NET AMOUNT |
				PARTICULARS	AMOUNT	
2-14-5-	216	Paint	$120	Trade Disct	10%	$108
3-30-5-	292	Wallpaper	250	" "	10%	225
4-10-5-	316	Paint	120	" "	10%	108
						$441

GENERAL DECORATORS, INC.

Courtesy Dennison & Sons

A voucher check.

one. Checks should not be indorsed in this manner except at the time the payee expects to have the check cashed or presents it for deposit.

If you wish to make it possible for the payee to cash a check without identification, draw it payable to his order, have him indorse it, then

GENERAL DECORATORS, INC.
"PAINTERS OF QUALITY"
1290 SOUTH DECATUR STREET
WOODSLEY, CONN.___June 24, 195-___ No. 894

00-791
831

PAY
TO THE
ORDER OF John E. McMichaels------------------------------ $62.17

REGISTERED ★ ★ ★ ★ G 2 DOLS 1 7CTS
7861

DOLLARS

GENERAL DECORATORS, INC.

TO THE
CENTRAL NATIONAL BANK
WOODSLEY, CONN.

Philip R. Potter
AUTHORIZED SIGNATURE

Courtesy Dennison & Sons

A certified company check.

CHECK INDORSEMENTS

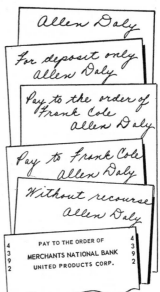

1. A blank indorsement—makes check payable to any holder.

2. A restrictive indorsement—check must be deposited, not cashed.

3. A special indorsement—check cannot be cashed or transferred until indorsed by Frank Cole.

4. A restrictive indorsement—check may be paid only to Frank Cole.

5. A qualified indorsement—identifies the holder without guaranteeing payment.

6. A special indorsement—made by a rubber stamp.

write under the indorsement, "Signature O.K.," and sign your name. When he presents the check for payment, he must indorse it again.

A depositor who wishes to draw money from the bank should draw the check payable to his own order, indorsing it when he is ready to present it for payment. If he is in the bank and does not have his checkbook, he may use a counter check supplied by the bank.

The form of the name in the indorsement should be identical with that on the face of the check. For example, if the name appears on the face as "Jno. C. Gray," the indorsement should be "Jno. C. Gray," not "John C. Gray." If the name on the face of a check is incorrectly spelled, indorse first as the name appears and again below that with the correct spelling. If a check is intended for deposit in a bank, write "For deposit only in (name of your bank)," above the indorsement. Should the check be lost, the finder would be unable to cash it, as he might do if the check were merely indorsed in blank. Business houses use a rubber stamp for indorsing checks for deposit.

Other Types of Checks. The checks thus far described—personal, company, and voucher—are the most common ones in business and are ordinarily accepted without question. In some situations, however, more definite guarantee of payment is required; for example, where the purchaser's credit standing is unknown to the creditor. In such

instances, certified checks, drafts, and cashier's checks may be required. These instruments are also commercial paper. Unlike the three kinds of checks just discussed, these papers have back of them the bank's guarantee that they will be paid. Each of these papers meets a definite need, as described below.

Certified Check. A *certified check* (see page 462) is a personal or company check that is guaranteed by the bank upon which it is drawn.

Bank Draft. A *bank draft* (see page 465) is an order of one bank to another with which it carries an account to pay a specified amount to a designated payee. A bank draft is purchased by the remitter from his bank, generally to pay an obligation in a distant city. It usually will be accepted by the payee without question, whereas a personal check might not be accepted. Banks usually, though not always, make a small charge for such drafts.

Cashier's Check. Your bank will give you, in exchange for cash or your personal check, a check drawn on itself, signed by the cashier of the bank and payable to you or a third person. The check is called a *cashier's check* (see page 461).

A cashier's check is the same as a bank draft except that the cashier's check is drawn on the bank in which the cashier is an officer, while the bank draft is drawn on another bank.

Section 3. OTHER FINANCIAL FORMS

Thus far in this unit we have discussed the handling of cash and the banking activities that are a part of the secretary's work. The discussion has included checks that are instruments of payment initiated by the debtor. The kinds of commercial paper described in this section—commercial drafts, promissory notes, and trade acceptances —are instruments usually initiated by the creditor for collection purposes. Stocks and bonds are financial papers with which the secretary should be familiar, although she will not be asked to write the fill-ins for these unless she is employed in the treasurer's department of a corporation.

Commercial Draft. Commercial drafts are often used in collecting debts. They are initiated by creditors to collect old debts or to convert the creditor's accounts receivable into cash when he needs money. Although a draft is a demand for payment, the debtor (drawee) is not

THE METROPOLITAN TRUST COMPANY

00-791
831

SHIRLEY, VA., <u>September 16,</u> 195-___ No. **00000**

PAY TO THE ORDER OF ___Elliott S. Smithfield--------------------------------$ 100.00___

R̲E̲G̲I̲S̲T̲E̲R̲E̲D̲ 7861 ☆ ⋆ ★ I O O D̲O̲L̲S̲ O O C̲T̲S̲ _____ **DOLLARS**

TO THE STATE BANK
SINCLAIR, VA.

William R. Burke
AUTHORIZED SIGNATURE

Courtesy Dennison & Sons

A bank draft.

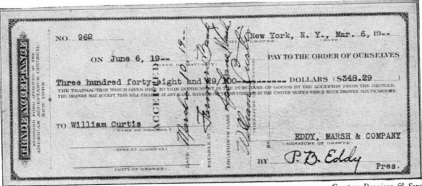

NO. 962 ....   New York, N. Y., Mar. 6, 19--

ON June 6, 19--   PAY TO THE ORDER OF OURSELVES

Three hundred forty-eight and 29/100----------- DOLLARS (S348.29)

THE TRANSACTION WHICH GIVES RISE TO THIS INSTRUMENT IS THE PURCHASE OF GOODS BY THE ACCEPTOR FROM THE DRAWER.
THE DRAWEE MAY ACCEPT THIS BILL PAYABLE AT ANY BANK, BANKING OR TRUST COMPANY IN THE UNITED STATES WHICH SUCH DRAWEE MAY DESIGNATE.

TO William Curtis

EDDY, MARSH & COMPANY

BY *P. B. Eddy* Pres.

TRADE ACCEPTANCE

Courtesy Dennison & Sons

A trade acceptance.

$75.00 _____ New York, New York _____ January 18, 19 5-

Sixty days after date --------------------------------- *Pay to*

the order of Merchants National Bank ---------------------

EXACTLY $ 7 5 AND 0 0 CTS *Dollars*

Value received and charge the same to account of

To Michael Prentice, Inc.

No 345   320 West 42 St., New York | United Products Corporation
James L. Stuart   Treasurer

Courtesy Dennison & Sons

A time draft.

obliged to accept it. If he fails to do so, however, he runs the risk of impairing his credit standing with his own bank.

The drawee signifies acceptance of a draft by writing the word "Accepted," the date, and his signature across its face. Thus he converts his verbal or implied promise to pay into a written promise. An accepted draft has the force of a promissory note. Banks will discount (that is, buy) accepted drafts under the same conditions as promissory notes, but they use extreme care in doing so, because the existence of a draft often indicates that the drawee pays his debts slowly.

A draft bearing the words "at sight" is a *sight draft;* it is payable as soon as the drawee receives it. Sight drafts are also used in foreign trade and in connection with order bills of lading (see page 433). A *time draft* is one that is payable at a specified time "after date" or "after sight."

When drafts are used for collection purposes, the drawer usually names his own bank as the payee. In this transaction, the bank acts as agent. Banks make a charge for collecting drafts.

Promissory Note. A *promissory note* (see page 467) is a written promise, in an accepted form, to pay to the order of a person or firm a stated sum of money, at a specified time. Blank forms of notes may be procured at a stationer's. The one who signs or promises to pay the note is called the *maker*, and the one to whose order the note is payable is called the *payee*. A note is a written evidence of a debt.

A *time note* is one in which the time of payment is specified. If no time is specified, the note is payable on demand and is called a *demand note*. A note made payable to the bearer or to the order of the payee is a *negotiable note*. A note that reads "Pay to the order of" must be indorsed by the payee before it is payable. Notes made payable to "Bearer" are payable to bearer without indorsement.

The words "with interest" written or printed in a note make interest payable from the date of issue; but if these words are omitted, interest at the legal rate can be collected only for the time the note runs after maturity. A note is said to *mature* on the date it becomes due.

The Collateral Note. The collateral note is similar to the promissory note except that a statement is made in it to the effect that the maker has deposited with the payee certain collateral (any kind of recognized negotiable instrument, such as bonds, stocks, mortgages, etc.) and has given to the payee certain rights in regard to these securities. The

GENERAL DECORATORS, INC.

No. C 16   *New York*   October 30, 19 5-

at sight ----------------------------------- *Pay to the order of*

Ourselves

One hundred and 00/100 ----------------------------- *Dollars* $100.00

Bill of Lading Attached ---

Value received and charge same to account of

To Jones & Son

     50 Wall Street, New York 5, New York   *Walter Marshall*

A sight draft.

Courtesy Dennison & Sons

No. 24   September 1, 19--

Sixty days after date we promise to pay to the order of

    The First National Bank of Denver $5,000.00

       ------Five Thousand and no/100-------------------------DOLLARS

Payable at: MAJESTIC OFFICE FURNITURE COMPANY
First National Bank   By:
of Denver   *Lee Wilson*
                        Treasurer

Maturity Date: *Wilbur Smythe*
October 31, 19--   Vice-President

A promissory note.

RECEIVED OF *October 1, 195-*

Martin L. Swift

Eighty-five and no/100 —Dollars for

Rent of *Apartment No. 413*

for one —————————————————Month

Ending *Oct. 31, 195-*

$85. no/100   *George F. Price*

RENT RECEIPT

MADE IN U.S.A.

A receipt for money.

collateral note is a negotiable instrument. If no time is stated in the note, it becomes payable on demand.

Trade Acceptance. A *trade acceptance* is an accepted draft, drawn by a merchant on a customer who has purchased goods from him. A trade acceptance differs from other drafts in three respects:

1. A trade acceptance is always accompanied by a bill for the goods sold.

2. It always grows out of the purchase of merchandise from the drawer.

3. It is never given in payment of old accounts or in return for loans.

A trade acceptance is given in the expectation that the sale of the merchandise will provide the means of paying the accepted draft when it falls due. Banks generally regard trade acceptances as better than ordinary accepted drafts or promissory notes. A trade acceptance cannot be renewed and the drawee cannot be given more time to pay.

After the acceptor has signed, the acceptance is complete. (See the illustration on page 465.) It is ready to be returned to the drawer, who holds it until maturity or converts it into cash by "discounting" it. When the acceptance is due, it must be presented for payment either directly to the acceptor or to his bank, if arrangements have been made for its payment there. When a firm gives an acceptance, it should notify its bank so that the sum called for in the acceptance can be charged to the firm's account at the bank without other formality than the presentation of the acceptance at the bank.

Stocks and Bonds. Shares of stock represent ownership in a corporation. Capital stock of a corporation may be divided into various classes, the principal ones being common stock and preferred stock. *Common stock* is the ordinary stock of a corporation and does not entitle the holders thereof to any preference over the other stockholders. *Preferred stock*, on the other hand, entitles the holders to certain preferences as to the payment of dividends and other privileges, all of which are set forth on the face of the preferred stock certificate.

Ordinarily, the holders of the common stock have the sole voting rights in a corporation, and the preferred stockholders have no voting rights except in certain instances where defaults may occur in the payment of dividends over a period of time.

Stocks are also classified as par-value stock and no-par-value stock. *Par-value stock* is that class of stock that sets forth the value of each

share on the face of the stock certificate. The par value of a share of stock, however, does not necessarily represent its actual value. *No-par-value stock* does not have any value on the face of the certificate.

Par-value stock, at the time of issue, should not be sold for any amount less than the amount of its par value. If it is, then the stockholder holding it is usually liable to any creditor, in case of dissolution, for the difference between the price he paid for the stock and the amount of the par value. After the stock has been issued, however, and the full par value has been paid, the stock may be resold or transferred for any amount whatsoever. No-par-value shares may be sold for any amount specified by the board of directors of the corporation.

Private corporations and governments issue certificates as evidences of indebtedness resulting from the borrowing of money. These certificates, usually interest-bearing, and promising to pay a principal sum at a stated time, are called *bonds*. Bonds, issued by private corporations, are secured by mortgages on real property or on personal property belonging to the corporations.

A bond differs from a certificate of stock in that it represents a *loan* to a corporation, secured by the property of the corporation, while a certificate of stock *represents ownership* in a corporation usually unsecured.

Receipt for Money. A receipt is a written acknowledgment of money received, or of goods, documents, or any business paper for which it is desirable to have a complete record of handling. A receipt should always be specific. Although printed receipt forms are in common use, a receipt does not have to be in any special form and may be a letter or memorandum. (See printed receipt form, page 467.)

Before signing a receipt for goods, packages, business instruments, etc., be sure that the delivery agrees with the statement on the receipt and is in satisfactory condition.

Letters of Credit. You will recall the discussion in Unit 15 that your employer may use a letter of credit when he travels. A person who travels extensively may obtain from his bank a letter of credit, which makes it unnecessary for him to carry large sums of money. The letter states that the person named therein, who may be identified by his signature, is entitled to draw on the bank issuing the letter of credit up to the amount stated. The holder, by presenting the letter of credit, can then draw money at any of the banks named by the

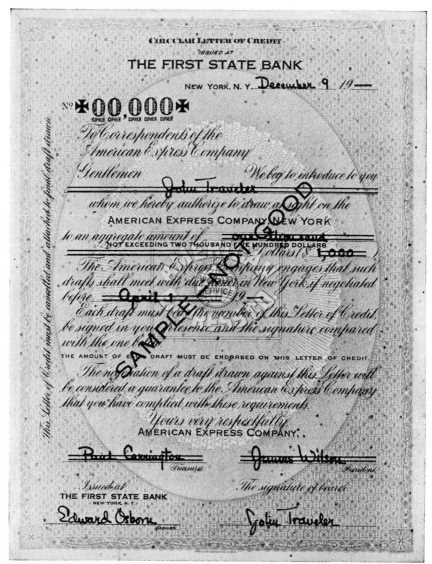

Courtesy American Express Company

A letter of credit.

issuing bank. The amounts drawn are recorded on the letter of credit so that the balance that can still be drawn is always known. (See the above illustration.)

Letters of credit can be bought by depositing cash or by having the amount charged to one's account in the bank.

Traveler's Check. Traveler's checks also make it possible for persons to procure cash when traveling. They come in varying standard denominations, from $10 up, and may be bought from banks, the American Express Company, and large travel agencies. Each check must be signed by the holder at the place of purchase and countersigned in the presence of the person cashing it. (See the following illustration.)

Courtesy American Express Company

A traveler's check.

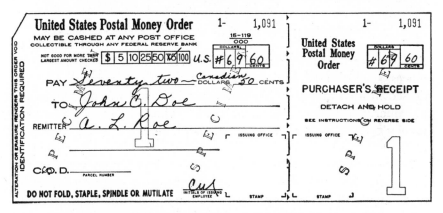

A United States postal money order for Canadian $72.50 or U. S. $69.60.

Postal Money Order. A means of transmitting money is provided by the United States Post Office through the medium of postal money orders. This form is an order from one post office to another, requesting that the amount named be paid to the person to whom the money order is made payable. It is transferable by indorsement, but only one indorsement can be made. It can be deposited like a check. (See illustration above.)

The largest amount that can be sent in one money order is $100. The fee is small, ranging from a few cents up, depending on the amount of the money order. The coupon should be detached and retained as a receipt.

Applications for postal money orders must be made on forms supplied by the post office.

The post office also sells international money orders. Applications for these must be made on a special international money order application form.

American Express Money Order. Express money orders are similar to postal money orders, except that, when buying them, no applica-

Courtesy American Express Company

American Express money order with stub and remitter's receipt.

tion form need be filled out. They can be bought at American Express offices, banks, and other agencies. Express money orders may be indorsed in the same way that checks are indorsed and may be cashed at American Express offices or banks. The coupon on an express money order should be kept as a receipt. (See the illustration given above.)

Telegraphic Money Order. When speed is a factor, money can be sent by telegraph. Cash for the money order plus the cost of transmitting a message and the money is paid at the office where application is made. A completed application form is shown on page 253.

Section 4. PAYING BILLS

Ninety per cent of today's business is conducted on a credit basis. Millions of bills are made out annually for these credit transactions.

The word "bill" is a general term used to refer to bills, invoices, or statements. A bill sent by a manufacturer or wholesaler to a retailer is generally referred to as an "invoice."

Billing. As billing is one of the important activities of many business firms, every secretary should be familiar with billing routine and with the usual business forms and machines used by billing departments. Also, the ability to type bills and to operate billing and calculating machines is a valuable addition to stenographic skill, for beginners often are able to find a combination stenographic-billing position when no other opening is available.

A. B. SLADE Wholesale Appliances				
No. 5430221				
Sold To Clark Electrical Appliances		Date February 1, 19 —		
Address 420 Main Street		Shipped Via Express Collect		
Local City, Missouri		Terms 2/20, n/60		
		FOB		
Quantity	Description		Unit Price	Extension
2	Radio, Carlton, Floor Model -- X-13		200 00	400 00

A merchant's bill of goods or invoice.

A typical bill, which is made out on a form called a "billhead," usually contains the following items: a date; an order number (taken from the order form sent by the customer); an invoice number; the name and address of the customer; a notation as to the method of shipment; the terms; and an itemized list of the purchases made, together with their cost.

The terms of payment of a bill are often printed on the billhead. For example, "2/10, n/30" means that the customer is expected to pay the bill in full in thirty days from the date of the bill; but if he will pay it in full within ten days, he may take a discount of 2 per cent of the net amount of the bill. In stating these terms to a customer, you would tell him the terms are "net thirty days and two per cent for

cash in ten days." Do not confuse these terms of payment with another type of discount known as "trade discount" or a dealer's discount. Most manufacturers advertise a certain price for each item they manufacture. This price, however, is often subject to a discount to jobbers, wholesalers, and retailers. The amount of the discount in some cases may vary with each firm or it may be the same for all. Before doing any figuring or typing of bills, be sure you understand thoroughly the terms of payment and the amount of the discount allowed on each bill.

Preparing Bills. The medium for preparing bills of course varies with the nature of the business and the number of invoices that have to be issued. In the office of the dentist, for example, bills may be handwritten; whereas in a large corporation, the thousands of invoices turned out each day are prepared on special billing machines.

In most medium-sized organizations, bills are typed on ordinary typewriters. Bills prepared by typewriter and by billing machine are illustrated on pages 473 and 476.

There are various steps leading to the typing of a bill. First of all, the sale is made. The order may be brought in by a salesman, or it may be received by mail. Mail orders are sometimes received in letter form and sometimes on order blanks. All orders are billed in the same way, however.

Before the order reaches the billing clerk, it usually goes to a pricing clerk, who checks the unit price for each item. The extensions and totals are figured with the aid of a calculating machine. (See illustrations of calculating machines on page 494.) Lastly, the order goes to the billing clerk, who types the finished bill.

At least one carbon copy is made—in most cases more. In many concerns the procedure is as follows: the original copy is mailed to the customer; one copy goes to the shipping department, which packs the order, cuts the bill in two, using the upper half as a shipping label and enclosing the lower half in the package for the customer to use as a check list; one carbon copy goes to the accounting department; one copy to the inventory clerk; and one to the representative covering the territory in which the customer is located.

When bills are made in multiple form, usually each copy is of a different color. Sometimes these copies come in sets "stuffed" (interleaved) with carbon paper, but this is an expensive billing process as the carbon is used only once.

MAJESTIC OFFICE FURNITURE COMPANY

1606 Clark Street
Denver, Colorado

August 12, 19--

X-L Furniture Company
280 North Wabash
Chicago 4, Illinois

Gentlemen:

Please ship us immediately the following
item listed in your latest general catalogue:

50 #347 Steel Office Desks, Green

This is our order number 659. Please be sure
that this number is placed on the invoice and
on other papers referring to this order.

Yours truly,

MAJESTIC OFFICE FURNITURE COMPANY

Judson H. Heywood
Assistant Manager

JHH:mb

MAJESTIC OFFICE FURNITURE COMPANY
1606 Clark Street — Denver, Colorado

PURCHASE ORDER NO. 659

Date	August 12, 19—
Terms	2/10, n/30
Ship via	Freight
FOB	Chicago

TO: X-L Furniture Co.
280 No. Wabash
Chicago 4, Illinois

Please ship us on or before August 16:

Quantity	Description	Price Each		Total	
50	#347 Steel Office Desks, Green per quotation of August 10	38	50	1,925	00

PLEASE SUBMIT INVOICES IN DUPLICATE

A purchase order may be either in the form of a letter or on a purchase-order form as shown here.

Various contrivances have been devised to cut down the cost of billing. One commonly used device is the "truck" attachment for typewriters. The several copies of the bills, printed in long strips for

SALESMAN'S COPY

SHIPPING ORDER

OFFICE SALES ORDER

ACCOUNTING DEPARTMENT COPY

UNITED PRODUCTS CORPORATION
500 Madison Ave. New York 22, New York

Refer to Invoice Number 749

			FOR CUSTOMER'S USE ONLY
Customers Order No. & Date	3-19	Invoice Date MAR 20	Register No.	Voucher No.
Requisition No.		Vendor's No.	F. O. B. Checked
Contract No.			Terms Approved	Price Approved
			Calculations Checked

. ACME SWEET SHOP

: BURROUGHSVILLE, OHIO

Transportation	
Material Received	
Freight Bill In.	Amount
19	Signature	Title
Date Satisfactory and Approved	

Shipped to & Destination		From		Adjustments
Date Shipped	3-20	F. O. B.		
Car Initials & No.		Prepaid or Collect COLLECT	Accounting Distribution
How Shipped and Route	HASTINGS EXP	Salesman PARKER	Audited	Final Approval
Terms	2%-10 DAYS			

QUANTITY	DESCRIPTION	UNIT PRICE	GROSS	NET
40 LBS	TRIPLE X CHOCOLATES	37	14 80	
75 LBS	ASSORTED GUM DROPS	22½	16 88	
25 LBS	PRINCESS MARSHMALLOWS	39	9 75	
20 BXS	CHOCO BARS	65	13 00	
15 BXS	BUSTER POPS	80	12 00	
80 LBS	PEANUT BRITTLE	16	12 80	79 23

Courtesy Burroughs Adding Machine Company

An invoice in multiple form, each carbon copy labeled for a specific use.

continuous fanfold billing, feed through the truck attachment, permitting the same carbon sheets to be used over and over again. The illustrations on pages 500–501 show various types of billing machines, including those with "truck" attachment for fanfold bills.

Credit Memorandums. If an error is made in billing or if goods purchased are returned for credit,

---

X-L FURNITURE COMPANY
280 No. Wabash
Chicago 4, Illinois

To   Majestic Office Furniture Company
      1606 Clark Street
      Denver, Colorado

CREDIT MEMORANDUM NO. CM 872

OUR INVOICE NO. D 56-23

Date   August 22, 19 —

We have credited your account as follows:

Reason for Return   Defective

Quantity	Description	Unit Price	Amount
1	#347 Steel Office Desk, green	38 50	38 50
	Return desk at our expense		

A credit memorandum.

STATEMENT

UNITED PRODUCTS CORPORATION
500 Madison Avenue
New York 27, New York

Alfred Allen
120 Cort Street
New York 27, New York

Amount enclosed $ _____

Please return this stub with your check.

Date	Reference	Charges	Credits	Balance
			BALANCE FORWARD	39.50 BAL
				47.00 BAL
				7.50 BAL
OCT 3	43356	7.50	39.50 −	.00 CR
OCT 8CS	615		7.50 −	3.00 CR
OCT 11RT	1857		3.00 −	
OCT 16AL	1984			244.00 BAL
OCT 20	44938	9.00		
OCT 20	44939	238.00		

CLARK ELECTRICAL APPLIANCES

Radios   Records   Appliances

Local City, Missouri

Sold to: Jane Lawson
           72 Dogwood Road
           Local City

The following goods have been charged for your convenience. They are sold on a cash basis and payment is due when bill is rendered. Return this coupon with your payment. Canceled check is your receipt.

Date	Item	Charges		Credits		Balance	
	Balance per last month's statement					40	00
3/24	Album—MM-413	4	00			47	75
3/24	Album—MM-612	3	75			43	75
3/26	Credit—Album MM-413 Returned			4	00		
	Pay last amount in Balance column						

Two types of customer's statements of account.

a credit memorandum is issued, usually in duplicate. The original copy goes to the customer and the carbon copy to the accounting department, so that the customer's account may be credited.

A credit memorandum is prepared in the same manner as a bill. It lists the items returned, their cost, additional charges for transportation paid by the customer, and other charges. The total is credited instead of charged to the customer's account. In order to distinguish

credit memorandums from bills, credit memorandums are sometimes printed in red, and, at the top of the form appears the head, "Credit Memorandum."

Statements. Statements are mailed every month or at any other time desired to those customers whose accounts show unpaid balances. In accounting parlance, this balance is called a "debit balance" and the customers accounts are known as "accounts receivable."

Two types of commonly used statements are shown on page 477. The statement at the top of page 477 merely gives the balance at the beginning of the month, the charges and the credits entered during the month, and the new balance due. The one at the bottom of page 477 is known as a "statement of account." This type of statement itemizes in detail all transactions since the issuance of the previous statement.

Section 5. MISCELLANEOUS RECORDS

Payrolls. In average-sized businesses, the handling of the payroll may be assigned to the accounting department, or it may be one of the secretary's many duties. Preparing a payroll for an office staff is a simple task, as office workers are usually paid a straight weekly or monthly salary. Factory workers, on the other hand, are usually paid on an hourly basis; and their weekly pay must be calculated from time cards that show the time they "punch in" and "punch out" each day. When the time-card system of record keeping is used, time cards for all employees are placed in a special rack next to the recording clock. Upon arrival and before leaving, employees insert the cards in the recording timer, which prints the hour and the minute of their arrival or departure. One of these recording timers and a typical time card are illustrated. Some recording machines can be set to print in red after a certain time in order to show tardiness.

Compensation for overtime is usually at the rate of one and one-half times the regular wage, commonly known as "time and a half." If the regular hourly wage is $1.00, for example, overtime is paid at the rate of $1.50 an hour.

The Federal Government and most states have laws setting minimum-wage and maximum-hour standards. These laws must be strictly adhered to.

Payroll Deductions. Two deductions are made from all salary checks: a tax for Federal Old-Age Benefits, commonly known as Social Security, and a Federal income tax.

Federal Income Tax. A Federal income tax is paid by all persons earning in excess of a stipulated amount a year. The installment payments on this tax are withheld by the employer from the employees' paychecks each payday. Payments to be withheld from earnings vary with the amount of the earnings and the number of exemptions claimed by an employee. It is advisable to obtain the latest information on the Federal income tax rate from the Collector of Internal Revenue in your city, so that you will know at the end of the year whether the payments made by means of payroll deductions have been sufficient to pay the entire tax, whether you must make an additional payment, or whether you have overpaid your tax and the Government will give you a refund.

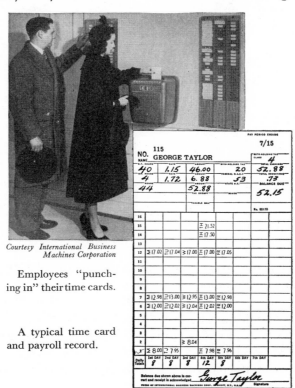

Courtesy International Business Machines Corporation

Employees "punching in" their time cards.

A typical time card and payroll record.

Social Security. Most payroll forms provide for a Social Security deduction. This deduction is in accordance with a Federal law for compulsory insurance to provide protection for a worker and his family in the event of death or at retirement at sixty-five.

The Social Security law specifies that a certain percentage be deducted by every employer from his employees' salaries. The employer is required to contribute an amount equal to that deducted from his employee.

Each worker should obtain from his local Social Security office a Social Security card with his account number printed on it. His earnings and Social Security payments will be credited to that account. (See illustration on page 523.)

UNITED PRODUCTS CORPORATION

CURRENCY MEMORANDUM

Department Mailing   Date May 5, 19--

EMPLOYEE	Salary	Bills			Coin				
		10	5	1	50	25	10	5	1
Ames, John	37.86	2	3	2	1	1	1		1
Miller, Marilyn	19.52	1	1	4	1				2
Parker, James	57.95	5	1	2	1	1	2		
Williams, Margaret	43.27	3	2	3			2	1	2

A departmental currency memorandum.

At the present time, wages subject to the Social Security tax include the entire amount up to and including $3,600 paid by an employer during a calendar year. The tax rate up to 1954 is $1\frac{1}{2}$ per cent.

In addition to these Federal taxes, there may be a deduction for a state unemployment tax, for hospitalization, for life insurance, and for the purchase of United States Government savings bonds. In preparing the payroll, it is necessary to take into account all these deductions and to rule up a form with columns for each deduction.

Preparing the Payroll. In the preparation of payrolls, certain forms are used for listing employees that are paid on a straight weekly basis; others for those paid on an hourly basis.

The hourly pay for employees working on a straight weekly salary is ordinarily determined by dividing the regular number of working hours in a week into the weekly salary. If payment is to be made in currency, a currency-memorandum form (see the illustration given above) is filled out after the salary forms have been completed. On this form are listed the bills and coins that will be inserted into each pay envelope, the object being to make each payment with the smallest number of pieces. To make up a salary of $19.52, for example, you would list a 1 in the column for $10, a 1 in the $5 column, a 4 in the

$1 column, a 1 in the 50-cent column, and a 2 in the 1-cent column. When this form is completed, the columns are totaled; and a bank currency-memorandum form, as shown, is filled out so that the proper number of each denomination may be withdrawn from the bank.

Insurance Register. The keeping of insurance records may be a responsibility of the secretary. It is important that a complete record of all insurance carried be kept. Policies may be carried on property, equipment, merchandise and stock, automobiles, etc. The following illustration shows the different kinds of information included on an insurance register.

UNITED PRODUCTS CORPORATION			
Currency Memorandum			
May 5, 19--			
TRADERS BANK TRUST COMPANY			
	NUMBER REQUIRED	DOLLARS	CENTS
Bills: $1	11	11	--
" 5	7	35.	--
" 10	11	110	--
" 20			
Coin: Pennies	5		05
" Nickels	1		05
" Dimes	5		50
" Quarters	2		50
" Halves	3	1	50
TOTAL		158	60

A bank currency memorandum.

INSURANCE POLICY RECORD

Date of Policy	Number	Name of Company	Property Insured	Amount	Time	Premium	Expiration Date
195–							
Mar. 4	187250	American	Auto—liab.	$10-20,000	3 yr.	$25.40	Mar. 3, 195–
June 5	T889321	Royal	Life—on pres.	15,000	1 yr.	75.00	June 4, 195–
July 3	65490	Mutual	Fire—off. equip.	5,000	3 yr.	12.25	July 2, 195–
Nov. 2	L 99855	National	Auto—collision	$50 deduct.	1 yr.	18.75	Nov. 1, 195–

Your Employer's Personal Accounts. It has been emphasized in this unit that the secretary will handle many personal records for her employer. They are confidential and must not be discussed with other employees or any persons outside the firm. Your boss has a right to expect genuine loyalty from you in this regard. Your efficient handling of his personal affairs, in accordance with his wishes, means that you will have the complete confidence of your employer.

Some Highlights of This Unit

1. The more common business transactions are those for which cash is paid, those for which a bill is rendered, and those for which an invoice is received.

2. Such authorized items as postage, carfare, telegrams, donations, express charges, and incidental office supplies are paid from the petty cash fund. A receipt must be obtained for each expenditure.

3. The amount of cash on hand plus the total of the receipts and vouchers in the cash box must always equal the original amount of the petty cash fund.

4. To place funds with a bank, a person makes out a deposit slip listing various items included in the deposit.

5. Checks drawn for amounts exceeding the depositor's balance will be dishonored and a protest charge made against the drawer.

6. A monthly bank statement shows the old balance in the account, the deposits and the withdrawals made during the month, and the new balance. The statement is accompanied by the canceled checks.

7. A check authorizes a bank to transfer specified amounts to a designated creditor and acts as a receipt for payment.

8. Many organizations use a check writer or check protector to write the amounts on checks; also, "safety paper" is usually used.

9. A record of checks issued may be kept on a check stub or in a "check register."

10. A voucher check carries a notation of the item or items for which a check is drawn.

11. A check is negotiable, and the extent of its negotiability is determined by the type of indorsement it bears.

12. In some situations where a more definite guarantee of payment is demanded, certified checks, drafts, and cashier's checks may be required.

13. A letter of credit states that the person named therein, who may be identified by his signature, is entitled to draw on the bank issuing the letter of credit up to the amount stated.

14. Traveler's checks may be bought from banks, the American Express Company, and large travel agencies, each check being signed by the holder at the place of purchase and countersigned in the presence of the person cashing it.

15. The U. S. Post Office sells domestic and international postal money orders.

16. Express money orders may be purchased from the American Express Company offices, banks, and other agencies, and are indorsed in the same manner as checks.

17. Money may be transmitted speedily through the medium of the telegraph.

Questions and Items for Discussion

1. Describe the procedure for establishing and for replenishing a petty cash fund.

2. What is the purpose of a cashbook?

3. What is the general term used by business for the substitute for money? Mention by name the financial form most extensively used; mention at least two other forms.

4. What is the object of indorsing a check? What is meant by "indorsement in blank"? By a "restrictive indorsement"?

5. Define the following: voucher check, certified check, cashier's check, bank draft. What is the chief difference between the two last named?

6. What is meant by the term "average daily balance," and why must banks insist that their customers maintain a certain balance in their checking accounts?

7. Define the following: commercial draft, promissory note, collateral note, acceptance.

8. In what major respect does the commercial paper named in Question 5 differ from that named in Question 7?

9. How may a traveler be assured of having sufficient funds with him without the necessity of actually carrying large sums of money?

10. What precaution would you observe if your employer gave you access to his safe-deposit box?

11. If you had a business in which clerks had to bill about an hour a day, would you purchase a special billing machine? Give reasons for your answer.

12. Discuss the two types of monthly statement sent to customers. Which do you think is the more practical?

13. If the volume of business warranted your employing two persons for billing, would you keep one person at the calculating and one at the billing machine, or would you ask each of them to calculate his own bills and then type them?

14. What is meant by fanfold billing?

15. Describe the circumstances that lead up to the typing of a bill, the steps through which the bill goes until completed, and the disposition of the various copies.

16. Describe an insurance register and the information which it may record.

Personality Questions and Projects

(Based on Personality Pointer, page 447)

1. Should a person choose a hobby that is related to his work?

2. Do you think reading or sewing are good hobbies for office workers?

3. Are hobbies that call for physical activity better for office workers than hobbies that call for little physical exertion?

4. How do hobbies contribute to the attractiveness of a person's personality?

5. Is it possible for a person to have more than one hobby at one time? Is it advisable to change hobbies occasionally?

6. What are your hobbies?

Secretarial Assignments

Because of an emergency, you have been temporarily assigned to the Accounting Department. The work will involve some calculating. Use adding machines and key-driven calculating machines, if available. (See illustrations of these on pages 494-95, 499-502.)

1. Sheet 93 of your Workbook represents the year's sales, by months, of all the offices of the United Products Company. Total the columns and fill in the figures on your typewriter.

2. The cashier has asked you to add the columns on the daily cash receipts record and enter the totals on the sheet. (This sheet is No. 94 in your Workbook.)

3. Six invoices will be found in your Workbook (Sheets 95–97). The treasurer has approved them for payment, and the number of the account to which they are to be charged has been indicated.

These bills must be paid today in order to take advantage of the cash discount. Check the extensions and totals, and figure the cash discounts. Then write checks in payment of the bills. Use the check forms on Sheets 98 and 99 in your Workbook. Fill in the stub for each check. Assume that the "Balance brought forward" on the first stub is $9,621.48, and that the number of the last check written prior to this assignment is 672.

4. Cash receipts for the day were as follows:

Checks

$195.95	$249.50	$106.47
22.98	79.45	1.98

Specie

16 1-cent pieces	17 dimes	32 half dollars
53 nickels	45 quarters	

Bills

26 $1 bills	31 $5 bills	6 $10 bills

Total the receipts on an adding machine. Then make out a deposit slip (Sheet 100), preferably on the typewriter.

Banks will not accept specie in large quantities unless wrapped in rolls as follows:

50 1-cent pieces	$ .50
40 nickels	2.00
50 dimes	5.00
40 quarters	10.00
20 half dollars	10.00

Banks will supply their depositors with special coin wrappers for this purpose. The firm name should be stamped or written on each roll before depositing.

5. A remittance of $4 is to be sent to the Register of Copyrights, Library of Congress, Washington, D. C., to cover the copyright on the company's new office manual. This remittance should be made in the form of a money order. (The Government will accept checks only when certified.) Make out the application form for a money order (Sheet 100). If you were actually getting the order, you would take the application with the cash to the nearest post office or send it by messenger. There is a fee for issuing a money order for this amount.

6. Mr. Wright wishes to send for a large sales map of the United States that he saw advertised in a magazine. It sells for 85 cents. In sending remittances for less than a dollar, it is customary to send a money order or stamps, if acceptable. In this case stamps are acceptable. Write a letter ordering the map. Mention the name of the magazine in which it was advertised, giving the date of issue and the number of the page on which the advertisement appeared. Select a current issue of a well-known business weekly. State that you are enclosing stamps in payment. Address the letter to the Graphic Record Company, 106 Lyons Avenue, Indianapolis, Indiana.

7. The chief accountant asks you to make a reconciliation of the company's bank statement for the month just ended. You will find the bank statements and the check stubs on Sheets 101 and 102 in your Workbook. Check each stub against the statement, placing a large check mark, preferably in red or blue, on the stub and cross off the corresponding item on the statement after you have satisfied yourself that the amounts are the same. If the canceled checks that the bank returned with the statement were available, you would compare them also with the stubs. After you have completed this checking process, type on plain paper a statement like that shown on page 457. The last figure on that form should be the same as your bank balance. Use an adding machine, if available, for listing the outstanding checks.

Optional

From the Accounting Department, you will go to the Billing Department to assist for a few days.

8. Type invoices for the following orders. Assume that the date is January 12. Make one original and one carbon copy of each invoice. Use the blanks in your Workbook for the originals only, Sheets 103 and 104.

Use a nonlisting calculator, if practicable, to figure all extensions and totals. Do not forget to allow the trade discount of 15 per cent from the total amount of each invoice.

a. Mr. O. L. Woolard, 206 Dumont Avenue, Hackensack, New Jersey. Invoice No. 731.

10 No. 330 Wastepaper baskets at $1.50
12 No. 18 Desk pads at $2.85
6 No. 68 Chair cushions at $2.50
4 No. 201 Desk trays (mahogany) at $1.75
3 boxes No. 100-5 file folders at $1.95 a box

b. Roper Department Store, 200 Fairview Boulevard, Rochester, New York. Invoice No. 732.

1 doz. Broadcloth shirts, white, size 16, at $30
35 doz. Men's handkerchiefs, white, at $2 a dozen
½ doz. Wool plaid lumberman shirts, size 15, at $45 a dozen
15 pairs Knitted gloves, size 9, at 85 cents a pair

c. Mr. Clyde E. Murray, 26 Chase Street, Philadelphia, Pennsylvania. Invoice No. 733.

12 No. DP-01 Desk pen sets at $4.25
50 sets Rubber casters at 50 cents a set
100 boxes HB Medium pencil refills at 10 cents
10 No. 3 Stapling machines at $2.50
75 pair Library book ends at 35 cents

d. Martine Brothers, 6220 Calumet Avenue, Plainfield, New Jersey. Invoice No. 734.

30 Sun-ray bulbs, No. 207, at 50 cents
30 Sun-ray bulbs, No. 209, at 40 cents
50 Sun-ray bulbs, No. 307, at 60 cents

e. Mr. Clyde E. Murray, 26 Chase Street, Philadelphia, Pennsylvania, had notified us that he is returning merchandise billed him on January 5 (invoice No. 459). The Shipping Department informs us that the shipment, consisting of one dozen de luxe fountain pens (unit price $15 a dozen) and a half-dozen standard fountain pens (unit price $7 a dozen) has been received in good condition. We had, of course, allowed Mr. Murray the regular 15 per cent dealer's discount on the order.

Issue a credit memorandum in triplicate in favor of Mr. Murray. Use Sheet 105 in your Workbook for the original.

9. Henry Duryea, of the Home Machines Company, 804-6 Main Street, Syracuse, New York, received six Model M sewing machines instead of the five he ordered and has returned one for credit. The Shipping Department reports the return of the machine in good condition.

Make out a credit memorandum in triplicate in favor of Mr. Duryea. The unit price of the sewing machine is $100, on which he will receive a discount of $15. Give him credit also for the prepaid express charges, which amounted to $1.35. Use Sheet 105 in your Workbook for the original.

10. The head of the Billing Department will dictate the letters to be sent to Mr. Murray and Mr. Duryea to accompany the credit memorandums. Transcribe the letters and attach the original copies of credit memorandums.

11. This is the time of month when statements of accounts are sent to your customers. You are to assist in the typing of these statements. Here are four accounts taken from the ledger. Use Sheets 106 and 107 in your Workbook, type statements for these four accounts. Make one carbon copy of each statement. Itemize the debits and credits, and show the balance still due. Use a calculating machine, if practicable, to find the balance due. A copy of a statement appears on page 477 of this text.

> O. L. Woolard, 206 Dumont Avenue, Hackensack, New Jersey.
> *Charges:* Jan. 2, $23.50; Jan. 12, $35.10; Jan. 22, $66.55.
> *Credits:* Jan. 15, $50.

> Roper Department Store, 200 Fairview Boulevard, Rochester, New York.
> *Charges:* Jan. 12, $47.17; Jan. 17, $47.51; Jan. 19, $30.22; Jan. 23, $24.48.
> *Credits:* Jan. 16, $25; Jan. 20, $65.

> Clyde E. Murray, 26 Chase Street, Philadelphia, Pennsylvania.
> *Charges:* Jan. 5, $15.72; Jan. 12, $66.94; Jan. 19, $9.62; Jan. 26, $65.78.
> *Credits:* Jan. 9, $10.26; Jan. 12, $15.72; Jan. 29, $100.

> Martine Brothers, 6220 Calumet Avenue, Plainfield, New Jersey.
> *Charges:* Jan. 6, $25.30; Jan. 12, $48.45; Jan. 27, $75.39.
> *Credits:* Jan. 9, $32.50; Jan. 23, $16.95.

12. Price sheets are typed in the Billing Department, on the basis of figures on incoming invoices. In typing these price sheets (which go in the price books kept in various departments of the organization), you must refer to the code shown below. Cost figures are usually shown in code, so that a customer who happens to see a price book will not be able to ascertain the price the store paid for the merchandise. On these price sheets, although cost figures are shown in code, selling prices are shown in plain figures.

The code used by your firm to show the cost price of any article is as follows:

LOW FIGURES

· 1 2 3 4 5 6 7 8 9 0

A cost of $1.59 would, therefore, be shown as L.IE.

The letter A is used as a "first repeater" and the letter B as a "second repeater"; that is, if a figure occurs twice in succession, the letter A is used to indicate the repetition—$1.19 would be L.AE. If a figure appears three times, the letter A indicates the first repetition and the letter B indicates the second; $29.99 would be OE.AB.

Price Sheet K-149 is shown here. You are to retype it on 8½-by-11 paper, making two carbon copies. Show code prices in the Cost column instead of the figures appearing there. (These figures would, in actuality, probably be penciled in by someone who had checked them against incoming invoices.) Your finished price sheet will show no figures at all for the Cost column— only code. Assume that the paper is to be punched for a ring binder, and leave room for the necessary holes at the left.

Price Sheet K-149

Stationery and Office Supplies

100% Rag Content Cards—White Only

Size	Weight	Blank or Ruled	Cost per 1000	Sell
3 x 5	Light	B	2.75	3.85
	Medium	R	3.57	5.00
	Heavy	R	4.29	6.00
4 x 5	Light	B	4.86	6.80
	Medium	R	6.39	8.95
	Heavy	R	7.29	10.20
5 x 8	Light	B	7.87	11.00
	Medium	R	10.78	15.10
	Heavy	B	11.82	16.55

13. You will be given dictation to be transcribed as quickly as possible.

14. Make a promissory note, payable sixty days after today's date, to Thredwell-Wilkison, Inc., for $1,575.32, at 6 per cent interest. The maker is the United Products Corporation. For the moment, imagine that you are the secretary-treasurer, and sign his name. Use Sheet 108 in your Workbook.

15. Mr. Martin gives his personal demand note for $200 to the First National Bank, Dumont, New Jersey, with interest at 6 per cent. Prepare the note for his signature. Use Sheet 108 in your Workbook.

16. United Products Corporation has notified Westphal & Rogan, wholesale grocers doing business in Helena, Montana, that it will draw on them for the amount of their past-due account, $137.52, today. Prepare a thirty-day sight draft. Use Sheet 109 in your Workbook.

17. Mary Ann Westbrook, treasurer of the senior class in the local high school, came in today and paid cash for some decorations for a class party. She forgot to bring the bill, and she had to have a receipt for the $3.72 she spent. Make out the receipt. Use Sheet 109 in your Workbook.

18. In your Workbook, Sheet 110, you will find the data for reconciling your company's bank statement. Follow the instructions dictated to you.

19. Your next assignment is to assist one of the clerks in the Billing Department whose duty it is to check all bill extensions. You are expected to find any errors in arithmetic that may appear on the bills. One of the invoices you are asked to check is given below. Check the extensions.

20. The Purchasing Agent has given you the following instructions: "Send this invoice back to the main office. Tell them they've made a mistake—tell them what the trouble is—and ask them to send us a corrected bill. Oh, and tell them what the difference is in the total, if there is a difference. Sign my name."

Write the letter and make one carbon copy. Assume that you return the original invoice by attaching it to the original of your letter. Indicate the number of enclosures below the identification initials on the "Enclosures" line.

UNITED PRODUCTS CORPORATION
500 Madison Avenue
New York, N. Y.

Date May 1, 19—

United Products Retail Store
  987 Jefferson Avenue
    Lynchburg, Virginia

Terms: 2/10, n/30

		Items	Unit * Price		Amount		Total	
4	doz.	Superstyle neckwear	6	00	24	00		
3	doz.	Sunstrype neckwear	9	00	27	00		
6	doz.	Wearwell neckwear	11	16	66	96		
6	doz.	Hi-Value hose	7	20	43	20		
3	doz.	A-1 hose	5	25	15	75		
3	doz.	S.T.B. hose	3	84	10	42		
2	doz.	Boy blue blouses	11	76	22	12		
5	doz.	Kalburn shirts	21	00	105	00		
3	doz.	Langley shirts	18	00	54	00		
7	doz.	Fancy hdchfs.	1	20	8	40		
							352	85

* The unit in this instance is 1 dozen.

Spelling Demons

rhythm	scholastic	similar
rotary	secretary	simultaneous
sacrilegious	separate	subsidy

Job Tips

1. If you make mistakes, admit them. Make every effort to avoid making the same mistake twice; never, a third time.

2. As an employee, never sign a check on which the name of the payee or the amount of the check has been left blank, unless specifically directed otherwise by your employer.

3. If your employer should find it necessary to leave a few signed, blank checks, guard them carefully.

4. In the day's routine, never mix even the smallest personal errand with the delivery or mailing of valuable papers or the handling of office money outside the office.

Personality Pointer

Before you can be a leader, you must learn to follow. Yes, it is quite true that many people are not even good followers—they are Caspar Milquetoasts. These individuals fear to step forward, to step backward, even to stand still! To become a good follower, you must at least make the decision to go along with a plan of action, an idea, or a group; you must participate; you must be acceptable as a person.

To be a leader, in the democratic sense, you must distinguish yourself in such a way that the group recognizes you not only as a person but also as an individual, in the complimentary sense of the word.

That it is possible for a person to have distinguishing characteristics is evidenced by the descriptive phrases "a sunny smile," "a kind word for everyone," "noisy," "evasive," "gullible," "timid." Nicknames, too, sometimes describe the most noticeable characteristic of a person, such as, "Tubby," "Giggles," "Mousey," "Freckles."

Of course, such descriptive terms do not necessarily mean that the individual is a leader in any sense of the word; but, if personal and physical characteristics can highlight a personality, how much more important it is that you develop leadership qualities to such a degree that they become a part of you in the same way. Needless to say, you must have knowledge in the field in which you choose to be a leader.

What are some of the desirable characteristics of a leader—the goal toward which every secretary must strive? Here are some desirable characteristics: responsibility, initiative, self-confidence, originality, enterprise, good judgment, resourcefulness.

491

Office Machines

Business offices are constantly increasing their use of business machines to expedite the work that has to be done. In many firms highly specialized office operations demand specialized skills. As business becomes more specialized, so do the machines it uses. This is especially true in those operations that can be done more efficiently by using calculating, accounting, billing, dictating and transcribing, duplicating, and other similar machines.

As a prospective secretary, you should know about the proper use of office machines in general, plus the basic features and devices of the more common machines. You should have at least a working knowledge of the operation and uses of many different machines and vocational competency on certain machines.

The amount of record keeping and statistical work that you will do as a secretary will depend mainly on the size and type of organization that employs you. You should understand the various types of office machines—adding, calculating, accounting, billing—that have been perfected to enable business to do the enormous volume of work of this nature.

You realize full well the fact that dictating, transcribing, and duplicating machines are necessary to handle the tremendous volume of "paper work" in the office. It is therefore obvious that the secretary must have an understanding of dictating machines and a marketable skill in the use of transcribing units. You recall also that Unit 12 pointed out your need for vocational competency in the operation and use of duplicating equipment.

The aim of this unit is to give you general information about office
492

Courtesy The First National Bank of Chicago

In a large office, an entire floor is often given over to the various types of record-keeping machines.

machines and to help you integrate the basic operating knowledge and skill you may have acquired. You will then be better prepared to develop on your job the ability to operate those office machines required by your employer.

Study the many illustrations of the makes and models of office machines contained in this unit. Your school will probably have demonstration machines typical of those used generally in your community. It may be possible for your secretarial practice class to visit certain business offices in your community and to study the machines in use. Perhaps you may find it possible to visit an exhibitor's booth at a business convention or equipment show and to see the latest machines and the proper operating techniques demonstrated. In some instances manufacturers send demonstrators to the schools to show students how to use and operate the equipment most advantageously.

A Friden calculator.

An electrically operated Felt and Tarrant comptometer.

The Marchant calculator with "push-button" multiplication.

Illustrations by courtesy of manufacturers of above machines

Section 1. ADDING AND CALCULATING MACHINES

Employers often prefer to use adding and calculating machines on even the simplest work to speed it up and to avoid costly errors. Surveys made in business offices indicate general figure work consists of about 53 per cent addition, 41 per cent multiplication, 4 per cent division, and 2 per cent subtraction. As a secretary you are almost certain to have occasions to use adding and calculating machines. It

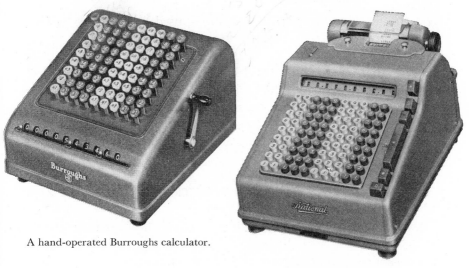

A hand-operated Burroughs calculator.

A National adding machine.

Burroughs hand-operated adding machine with subtraction.

Illustrations by courtesy of manufacturers of above machines

may be necessary for you to check figures that are included in the dictation. Or, you may be asked to assist other employees whose work involves the use of these machines.

Study the accompanying illustrations which show the more com-

mon adding and calculating machines used in modern business offices.

The most common type of calculating machine is the adding-listing machine that records on a tape. It may be a full keyboard machine or a ten-key machine. Calculating machines are also non-listing and use no tape, recording only totals shown on the dials. Two types of non-listing machines are the key-driven and the rotary type. Electrically operated models are generally preferred.

Section 2. DICTATING AND TRANSCRIBING MACHINES

In addition to taking dictation in shorthand, there are machines for taking dictation (see the illustration given below). The keyboard of these machines consists of letters. The different keys are operated with

Courtesy Stenotype

A machine for taking dictation.

the fingers of both hands, and the different combinations of letters are recorded on a tape that spaces automatically after each operation. The problems of transcribing, however, are essentially the same as those of the secretary who writes shorthand notes.

Several different types of dictating, or voice-writing, machines are used for recording dictation. The dictation may be recorded on a wax cylinder, on a plastic disk or belt, on a tape recorder, or on a wire recorder. The voice is played back on a transcribing unit in the first two types. In the case of the tape and wire recorders, it is played back on the recording machine for transcription.

Improvements are constantly being developed on all office machines, and dictating and transcribing equipment is no exception. The needs of the particular office determine the dictation method that should be used. For example, dictating machines are frequently used in recording conferences, speeches, interviews, telephone conversations, in inventory taking, or in "off hours" dictation. Points to com-

Courtesy Thomas A. Edison, Incorporated

This girl is transcribing the dictation recorded on a cylinder.

In these dictating and transcribing units, the dictation is recorded on plastic disks.

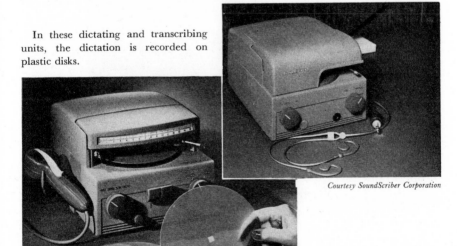

Courtesy SoundScriber Corporation

The executive's dictation is recorded by wire, and the secretary transcribes what she hears over the transcription wire.

Courtesy Webster-Chicago Dictating Machines

pare in selecting dictating and transcribing equipment are: clarity, simplicity, efficiency, economy, compactness, convenience, and ease of operation.

Again, it is emphasized that transcription problems are essentially the same for the secretary. In other words, the abilities you have in transcribing accurately and speedily on the typewriter may be adapted without difficulty to whatever dictation method is used.

The accompanying illustrations will give you a good picture of the variety of equipment that is available.

Section 3. ACCOUNTING, BILLING, AND OTHER OFFICE MACHINES

Bookkeeping and billing machines have been widely adopted in business and government offices. Today, practically all bank checks are posted on these machines. Many thousands of smaller offices also use this equipment to handle their figure work.

Some of these computing-billing machines perform all the opera-

Courtesy Monroe Calculating Machine Company, Inc.

This girl is operating a duplex register, all-purpose posting machine.

tions of invoicing, including typing, multiplying, discounting, subtracting, and accumulating. With special features, they are used for writing and figuring payrolls, stores, records, general accounting records, and so forth.

Accounts and Accounting Machines. Today, far more accounting is done by machine than by the traditional pen-and-ink method. Regardless of the method used, however, there are two definite steps in keeping accounts: the writing of amounts in proper columns, and the

Courtesy International Business Machines Corporation

This electric formswriter is designed to handle continuous fanfold and other web forms easily and quickly.

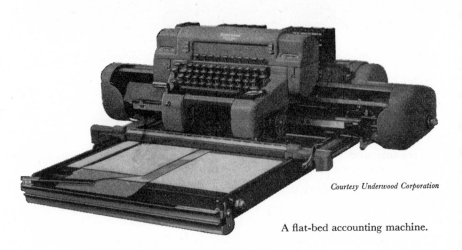

Courtesy Underwood Corporation

A flat-bed accounting machine.

balancing of these amounts by means of addition and subtraction. An accounting machine is equipped with an adding-subtracting device, a wide carriage, a dating attachment, and a mechanism that moves the carriage automatically into the positions for printing. As a rule, by operating certain keys, the machine carriage may be put in the debit position, credit position, and so on. (See pages 494-495, 500-501 for illustrations of accounting machines and calculators.)

Accounting machines may be either hand or electrically operated, may have either a ten-key or a selective adding-subtracting keyboard, and may be equipped with typewriters.

Statistics and Statistical Machines. Tabulating machines have been designed

Courtesy Burroughs Adding Machine Company

A desk model bookkeeping machine.

Courtesy National Cash Register Company

A bookkeeping machine with selective keyboard and typewriter.

This visible automatic punch machine perforates information in tabulating cards, such as the one shown below.

Courtesy Remington Rand Inc

This machine automatically sorts the punched cards.

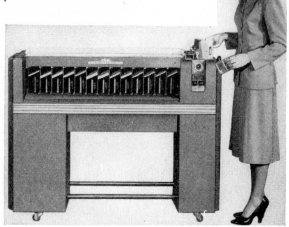

*Courtesy International Business
Machines Corporation*

to record and classify statistical information by means of a code system. The machines shown on page 502-503 are used for this purpose by large corporations; by colleges, where students are classified according to subjects, courses, etc.; and by other organizations where statistical information is necessary for the proper dispatch of business.

Before the tabulating machine can be used, the material to be tabulated must be specially prepared. A hole-punching machine is used to record the desired information on cards. Each perforation on the card represents a unit of information. When a total of all cards having certain units of information in common is desired, the cards are placed in a sorting machine that is adjusted to pick out automatically the cards according to the groups desired. Then

Courtesy Remington Rand Inc.

This tabulator automatically prints and adds information punched on cards after they have been machine sorted into proper sequence.

the picked group of cards is run through a tabulating machine, which tabulates as many as five columns at once and prints the result.

Some Highlights of This Unit

1. The amount of record keeping and statistical work done by the secretary will depend mainly on the size and the type of organization that employs her.

2. Employers often prefer to use adding and calculating machines on even the simplest work to speed up the work and to avoid costly errors.

3. The keyboard of machines for taking dictation consists of letters—the different keys are operated with the fingers of both hands and the different combinations of letters are recorded on a tape which spaces automatically after each operation.

4. Whether accounting is done by machine or by the pen-and-ink method, there are two definite steps in keeping the accounts: the writing of amounts in proper columns, and the balancing of these amounts by means of addition and subtraction.

5. Accounting machines may be either hand or electrically operated, may

have either a ten-key or a selective adding-subtracting keyboard, and may be equipped with typewriters.

Questions and Items for Discussion

1. Why should a secretary have at least a working knowledge of the operation and uses of many different office machines?

2. Name various types of office machines with which the secretary may come in contact.

3. Describe the different types of calculating machines.

4. How may dictation be recorded when voice-writing machines are used?

5. What operations do some of the computing-billing machines perform?

6. With what special devices is an accounting machine equipped?

7. How are statistical machines used?

Personality Questions and Projects

(Based on Personality Pointer, page 491)

1. Study the rating scale on leadership in your Workbook, Sheet 43. How would you rate yourself on this scale now? After you have thought about it, rate yourself on the scale.

2. Good judgment is one of the most desirable characteristics that an office worker can have. What would you say to the girl in the following story about the importance of good judgment in the performance of office duties?

Mae Reid's first job was in an investment broker's office where she assisted the secretary and acted as errand girl.

One of her duties was to take a deposit to the bank each morning. On the way out of the office one day she dropped the bankbook and one of the checks became separated from the rest of the papers. As Mae picked up the papers and saw the check, she gasped at the enormous sum for which the check was made out—and noticed that it was from a New York firm that was receiving much unfavorable comment in the papers at the time.

Upon entering the bank, Mae saw one of her friends, a clerk in a rival concern. Before she thought about what she was doing, she said excitedly: "Oh, Jack! Guess what! Right here in my hand I have the biggest check I've ever seen—thousands of dollars from that firm the papers are talking about." Jack raised his eyebrows and replied, "You don't say! That's a nice bit of news for me to tell my boss. Thanks a lot!"

Can you see where Mae failed to use good judgment?

3. In your notebook, make a list of your leadership characteristics or traits that seem to be outstanding now. Don't neglect to list the undesirable ones. Continue your list with the various nicknames by which you are known. Do you like the picture?

Secretarial Assignments

1. The Accounting Department has prepared for the Sales Department a rough draft of the figures showing the company's sales in leading cities in the United States during the first quarter of the year.

A copy of the rough draft appears on Sheet 111 in your Workbook. Calculate the totals for each city and type the table attractively on plain paper, making one original and four carbons. Use an adding machine to find the totals.

2. Mr. Wright will dictate a memorandum to accompany the report on sales in leading cities. Make a copy for each of the branch managers—New York, Chicago, San Francisco, and Boston. (This will require four carbon copies. Use plain paper.)

Optional

3. There are many, many types of office machines. Select a company that manufactures a machine different from that which you have available for practice in your classroom. As an individual, or as a member of a committee, visit this company and make a report to the class.

4. If there are no offices of company representatives in your locality, arrange to visit a local business office and make a report to the class on the business machines used in that office.

Spelling Demons

successor	superintendent	tailor
sufficient	surgeon	tariff
summoning	suspicious	temporary

Job Tips

1. Be willing to help check the accuracy of the work of others; also, be tactful in pointing out errors.

2. Keep your fingernails at an attractive, efficient length.

3. Your nails should not be filed in public. In an emergency, repair the damage as quickly as possible. Remove chipped or damaged polish the same night—at home.

4. Clean, well-taken-care-of machines do more attractive, efficient work.

Personality Pointer

ARE YOU PLANNING FOR THE FUTURE?

As you grow older, your ideas of what you want to be change. You become wiser in your choice of a life vocation. You begin to discover your talents and to realize that your greatest happiness will result if they are put to some constructive use. You begin to understand the value of money. Money is going to play an important part in the realization of your ambitions, and you hesitate to plan on something that is beyond your budget.

You consider the matter of education, too. For some of you, a college education will be necessary before you attain your goal. For others, one or two years of advanced education will be sufficient, while some of you will be able to step right into your chosen field immediately after high school.

How convenient it would be if we could look into a crystal ball and see exactly what the future holds for us!

However, of this much we can be certain: if our ambition is worthy, if it implies good citizenship, if it includes consideration of the rights and happiness of others—then we are justified in bending every effort we can to attain that ambition. We will obtain the necessary money—we will get the required education.

Don't let temporary problems obscure your view of the possibilities of the future. Planning for the future means more than planning ahead a year at a time.

Suppose your plans include a college education, and the money involved presents a serious problem. You can do as many have done be-

fore you—put your stenographic training to work on a job and take one or two university courses each semester at night school or by correspondence. Then at the end of two years, you will have saved enough money to go to the university full time and can use your accumulated night-school or correspondence credits to obtain advanced standing. Many young people, as you know, earn their way through college doing secretarial work in the offices of the university, typing student reports and theses, or doing stenographic work for members of the faculty. Your stenographic ability can always be a money-maker for you.

Our lives were meant to be full and abundant. Such lives call for courage and daring. Dare to be alive every minute of the day. Dare to follow your worthy impulses. Dare to tackle each new task with energy and will.

The great law of culture is: Let each become all that he was created capable of being; expand, if possible, to his full growth; resisting all impediments, . . . and show himself at length in his own shape and stature, be these what they may.—*Thomas Carlyle*

UNIT 18

Job Finding and Job Success

You are looking forward to the day, in the relatively near future, when you enter the business world as a full-time worker. This is the final unit in your present study of the many aspects of secretarial work. In the completion of the various secretarial assignments in this course, you have been given practice in qualifying yourself to succeed as a worker in this field. This final unit is devoted to those important factors that are so necessary to find a job and to succeed in it. Your success depends, as you know, on your all-round qualifications—technical stenographic skills, knowledge of business organization and practices, personal appearance, personality, attitudes, work habits, confidence, and the like.

The first section in this unit points out the importance of making adequate preparation for finding a job. Basic in this preparation is an analysis of your personal qualifications, the preparation of a data sheet, and the ability to understand and to complete an application blank. In section two, the need to plan a campaign to find the kind of job you want is stressed. Of primary concern in such a campaign are: job information sources, your letter of application, the letter campaign, and the personal interview. Section three emphasizes those desirable factors that make for success in your first job and prepare you to take advantage of the promotional opportunities that may come your way.

Section 1. PREPARATION FOR JOB FINDING

Set Yourself a Goal. Determine in your own mind the kind of position you want; then bend every effort to prepare yourself adequately for that position.

Courtesy Peggy West

The confident, well-groomed applicant has the best chance to get that coveted job.

When the time arrives for you to look for a job, you will be glad that, long before you were ready to sell your services, you started to think about the problems you would have to face.

It is not enough for you merely to say, "I want to get a stenographic or secretarial position." Your chances for getting a position will be much better if you can decide what is your special aptitude, in what kind of business you would like to work, and what department of that business would attract you most. Find the answers to these three questions:

1. What skill will be my major skill: typing, transcription, shorthand, bookkeeping, machine operation?

Let us say that you find that typing comes most easily to you; your speed and accuracy are excellent; you enjoy setting up good-looking tabulations; you know what it means to make each typewritten page a piece of artistic workmanship. You will develop this skill to as near perfection as you can.

Of course, in so doing you will not neglect your shorthand and transcription skills, and you will become as proficient in bookkeeping and other business subjects as time and opportunity will permit.

2. What organizations require employees with my particular major skill?

The answer to this question will necessitate a study of your local community and consultation with teachers and others who are familiar with employment opportunities.

With a particular aptitude for typing tabulations and planning attractive setups of statistical matter, you will probably find a market for your talents among the banks, insurance companies, credit associations, and accounting and statistical organizations.

3. In which department of a large organization would my talents be most usable?

If you are living in a large city, you will have an opportunity to make application for employment with firms made up of many departments—production, sales, credit, and transportation, for example. It may be that the business of a smaller town revolves around one industry, such as shoe manufacturing, oil production, or airplane manufacturing. In that event, your procedure will be adjusted to meet the local conditions.

When you make application for a position with a large firm, you will find your sales talk much more effective if you can indicate your familiarity with the departmental organization of the company and express the desire to work in a particular department, because in that department you can employ your talents most effectively.

You can say to the personnel manager to whom you make application: "I should like to work for your company as a stenographer. I am particularly interested in report writing and typing tabulated statements. My typing rate is rapid, and I am accurate in typing figures. Perhaps you could use my services in your accounting or statistical division."

No position may be open in either of these divisions at the time you apply, but the personnel manager may reply: "There is no opening in those departments just now, but we can use you in the Credit Department, and we will keep you in mind when an opening occurs in the Accounting Department."

Before you can talk intelligently about any particular department, however, you must be familiar with the rudiments of office organization and management. There are several books on this subject that you may read. Here are some suggested titles.

Cornell, W. B. *Organization and Management in Industry and Business,* third edition. New York, Ronald Press Company.

Robinson, Edwin M. *Business Organization and Practice.* New York, Gregg Publishing Division, McGraw-Hill Book Co., Inc.

Robinson, Edwin M. and William R. Blackler. *Today's Business: Its Organization and Practice.* New York, Gregg Publishing Division, McGraw-Hill Book Co., Inc.

Terry, George R. *Office Management and Control.* Chicago, Richard D. Irwin, Inc.

SELF-ANALYSIS

Don't wait until the last minute to plan your job-hunting campaign. There is a great deal of groundwork to be done if your campaign is to be successful.

First, you must take an inventory of your assets and liabilities, as of today, and make plans and organize your efforts so that you can turn your liabilities into assets in as short a time as possible.

The discussion in these pages will be very frank. If you do your part, this will be the most stimulating division of your secretarial-training course.

A graduate who is well trained for a secretarial position has the knowledges and skills listed below. Of course, many secretarial graduates have skills far above those listed. If you do not measure up to the secretarial graduate as described in the outline, set your goals accordingly—and do not let yourself be satisfied until you attain them.

MINIMUM SKILLS AND TECHNICAL KNOWLEDGES OF A
SECRETARIAL GRADUATE

Dictation speed, 100 words a minute for 5 minutes
Typing speed, 50 words a minute for 15 minutes

Transcribing speed, 25 words a minute for 1 hour
Thorough knowledge of mechanics of English
Ability to write a clear and complete letter
Knowledge of mechanics of bookkeeping
Working knowledge of common office machines, such as the adding
machine and a duplicating machine

On the outline on Sheet 112 in your Workbook, fill in the blanks
describing your own knowledges and skills.

What Are Your Outstanding Skills and Related Abilities? Each secretarial student should have some outstanding skill and related ability.
You will find it to your advantage to discover what yours is so that
you can capitalize on it when applying for a job. It may be that your
outstanding skill is a superior speed and accuracy in typing, for example, or an ability to take dictation at 140 or 150 words a minute.
Additional skills are listed in the following outline.

If you do not have any at this time, set your goals to develop one or
more within as short a time as possible.

OUTSTANDING SKILLS AND RELATED ABILITIES

Typing 60 or more words a minute
Taking dictation at 120 or more words a minute
Setting up difficult tabulations rapidly and accurately
Cutting stencils without error and with perfect touch
Operating accounting and statistical machines
Drafting
Writing original business letters
Excellent command of English
Speaking or writing a foreign language
Speaking in public
Dramatic ability

In the outline in your Workbook, list carefully your outstanding
skills and related abilities.

What Are Your Personal Characteristics? You must be very honest in
analyzing your personal characteristics. Do not overrate or under-
rate yourself. No matter how excellent your skills may be or how
strong your "pull" is in obtaining a job, you will not be able to hold
that job if you cannot get along well with the others in the office.
Your ability to get along with others depends on your personal characteristics and your skill in adjusting your personality to the personalities of others with whom you are associated.

Scientific investigations show that certain characteristics are primary requisites to secretarial success. Among these characteristics are the following:

PRIMARY REQUISITES TO SECRETARIAL SUCCESS

1. Intelligence—a keen, orderly mind
2. Health—vitality, energy
3. Social characteristics:
    a. Courtesy—creating good will
    b. Tact—in dealing with people under trying circumstances
    c. Tolerance—an understanding of human nature
    d. Poise—self-control
    e. Loyalty—to employer and his business
    f. Adaptability—ability to adjust oneself to personalities of other people
    g. Personal appearance—neatness
4. Work characteristics:
    a. Accuracy in everything done
    b. Ability to follow instructions
    c. Alertness
    d. Thoroughness—ability to see a job through to completion
    e. Resourcefulness—ability to meet emergencies
    f. Judgment in handling people and situations; ability to decide how and when to do things
    g. Executive ability—including initiative

Evaluate your personal characteristics in the Personal Characteristics section of the analysis chart in your Workbook, Sheets 112 and 113.

Detailed Analysis of Certain Characteristics. Good health is one of the basic elements of a pleasing personality. It is essential to success on your job. The intelligent control of diet, sufficient sleep and rest, and an abundance of physical exercise are necessary health habits.

Your personal appearance includes cleanliness and care of the body, dress that is appropriate and becoming, and facial make-up that does not call attention to itself.

Your manner of speech is a matter of habit. Find out, if you can, what speech faults and mannerisms you have. Have a recording made of your voice or ask the assistance of the speech instructor of your school in making an analysis of your voice.

It is well to examine your habits of conversation, too. Your voice, manner of speech, and conversation are indicative of your culture and refinement.

Study the following outline and decide which term best describes

your status in regard to each item on the chart; then rate yourself on the analysis chart in the Workbook, Sheets 112–114.

DETAILED ANALYSIS OF FOUR PERSONAL CHARACTERISTICS

Health

Diet	Intelligently controlled	. . . .	Given no consideration

Cleanliness of
body	Exceptionally neat	Neat and clean	Careless
Weight	Reasonable weight	Overweight	Underweight
Nervous tension . . .	Poised, without tension	High-strung	Lazy
Sleep	Sufficient, restful	Adequate	Insufficient and restless
Physical exercise . .	Adequate	Inadequate	. . . .
Posture	Excellent	Fair	Poor
Vitality	Abundant	Adequate	Lacking

Personal Appearance

Cleanliness of
body	Exceptionally neat	Neat and clean	Careless
Odors	Free from offensive odors	Careful to avoid offensive odors	Careless

Clothes—neat-
ness	Exceptionally neat	Neat and clean	Careless

Clothes—appro-
priateness	Always appropriate	Sometimes appropriate	Seldom appropriate

Clothes—becom-
ingness	Always becoming	Carefully selected	Seldom becoming
Posture	Exaggerated	Normal	Careless
Walk	Sprightly	Without energy	Lazy
Make-up	Artistic	Too much	Too little
Hair styling	Attractive	Extreme	Careless

Speech

Vocal quality	Pleasing	Acceptable	Unpleasing
Spontaneity	Spontaneous	Hesitant	Faltering
Enunciation	Exact	Careful	Careless
Grammar	Excellent	Acceptable	Careless
Laughter	Pleasing	Genuine	Uncontrolled

Conversation

Subjects chosen . . .	Interesting to others	Chosen to suit occasion	Thoughtlessly chosen
Skill as a listener . .	Good listener	Inattentive	Rude

What Are Your Other Qualifications? In filling in the Other Qualifications section of the chart, you have an opportunity to analyze the qualifications that make you different from others who have had

similar training and are of about the same age as you. What is there about you that distinguishes you from your fellow students? The following is a list of possible enumerations that you may make, but you should be able to add others. You realize, of course, that you become a more interesting personality when you add more and more items to this list.

SUGGESTED ACTIVITIES THAT REVEAL DISTINGUISHING CHARACTERISTICS

Leadership in school activities:

a. President of student body
b. Secretary of girls' league
c. Officer of Spanish club
d. Treasurer of class organization

Membership in honor societies:

a. Honorary society (high school)
b. Honorary campus fraternity (college)

Participation in athletics:

a. Captain of baseball team
b. Member of tennis team
c. Swimming champion

Membership in social societies:

a. Job's Daughters
b. Y. M. C. A.
c. Newman Club

Participation in school management:

a. Manager of student store
b. Ticket manager for athletic events

General:

Extensive travel in the United States
Foreign travel
Own a car
Hold a driver's license

Participation in speech-department activities:

a. Lead in senior play
b. Member of debate squad

Make your list on the form in your Workbook, Sheets 113 and 114, as lengthy as you can. If there is still time in your school career to take part in more activities than you have thus far, by all means begin now to do so. This experience in group situations is invaluable to you when you wish to develop a normal and interesting personality.

PREPARATION OF A DATA SHEET

When you have completed your self-analysis, you are ready to make up a data sheet. A data sheet is a presentation of facts about yourself that you want a prospective employer to know when considering you for employment. Like your application letter, your data sheet is your picture as you want the employer to see you.

It will help you in organizing your sales talk when looking for a

position and contains the information you will need when writing your application letters.

The information on data sheets is usually presented according to a simple outline, such as:

> Personal Data: Name, address, telephone, age, height, weight, marital status, type of employment desired
> Experience: What kind, for whom, where, when, salary
> Education: High school, college, other
> References: Name, position, address, telephone
> Other Qualifications

Be original in the setup of your data sheet, but be sure that it includes all the essential details. For example, set it up so that it itself represents your ability to type tabulations neatly; insert a paragraph that demonstrates your ability to use the English language correctly; arrange the data in the order that puts emphasis on your chief assets. As in the application letter, you can adapt certain sections of your data sheet to the occasion of its use. The sheet shown on page 518 is one that has been used successfully by students in obtaining positions.

Personal Data. Be sure that you have a telephone number available when you start looking for a position. If the telephone is not in your own home, then you should note, in parentheses beside the number, the location of the number; as, "Father's office," "Neighbor." Many times an employer would prefer to telephone an applicant rather than wait for the mail.

You can change the kind of employment desired according to the situation. For example, if a friend of your father's has referred you to a bank to apply for a typist opening, then you will put as the kind of employment desired: typist, stenographer, clerk. This calls to the reader's attention that you are qualified for the particular opening. Otherwise, you will list your best skill first, adding others to which you wish to call attention.

Education. In the Education section of your data sheet you can list subjects and grades that may enhance your desirability. Your excellent achievement in such subjects as English, economics, mathematics, and languages is always worth mentioning. Be sure to call attention to any special scholastic honor.

Experience. If you have worked at anything and have received pay for it, that experience is worth mentioning in the Experience section of

Applicant: PAULINE W. LAMBERT

Address: 1041 Joyce Place
                  Park Ridge, Illinois

Telephone: PArk 1-4385

Position Applied for: Secretary

Date: May 7, 19--

A. PERSONAL DATA
  1. Age: 18. I was born on March 9, 19--.
  2. Height: 5 feet 6 inches. Weight: about 110 pounds.
  3. Appearance: fair complexion.
  4. Marital status: single.
  5. Residence: living with parents.

B. EXPERIENCE RECORD
  1. Cashier at Forbes Department Store, Chicago, during summer
     months and at Christmas during the last two years.
  2. Part-time secretary in the office of the Dean of Instruction at
     Central City College, March and April of this year.
  3. Summer-camp counselor for two summers while in high school.

C. EDUCATIONAL RECORD
  1. Graduated from Park Ridge High School, May 29, 19--, after com-
     pleting the college-preparatory course.
  2. Will graduate from Central City College on June 3, 19--, after
     completing the two-year (executive secretarial) course.
  3. Academic and skill achievements--
     a. Shorthand: 120 words a minute (5-minute test).
     b. Typewriting: 75 words a minute (10-minute test).
     c. Accounting: secretarial record keeping.
     d. Business machines: duplicators, calculators, voice writers,
        addressing, billing, bookkeeping.
     e. Filing: comprehensive course.
  4. Have ranked on Dean's list throughout college program.
  5. Extracurricular activities--
     a. Secretary of student fraternity, Gamma Gamma Upsilon.
     b. Program chairman of the college's "Secretarial Clinics."
     c. Associate editor of the Central City College Courier.

D. REFERENCES
  1. Dr. John K. Youngman, Dean of Instruction, Central City College,
     6 North Michigan Boulevard, Chicago 6, Illinois.
  2. Mr. Richard L. Forbes, Forbes Department Store, 300 State Street,
     Chicago 2, Illinois.
  3. Mr. Adam Gerhold, director for the Community Youth Guild, Snyder
     Place, Park Ridge, Illinois.

A well-organized data sheet.

the data sheet. The work may be unrelated to stenography; but if it called for intelligent thinking, dependability, resourcefulness, and loyalty on your part, then you should include it. Sometimes you have done work for teachers or relatives for experience only. In that case

put the words "Experience only" in mentioning salary. If your school has a part-time training program, describe the work you did under this plan and put the words "Experience-in-training" in mentioning salary. Be sure to give the full name, title, and address of the person or persons for whom you worked. Many times these names and addresses are used as references, and the information must be complete.

If the work was temporary, at Christmas or on Saturdays only, for example, then in giving the date write "Christmas vacation," "Saturdays only," "After school," "On call during rush season," or whatever applies.

References. Obtain the permission of as many persons as you can to use their names on your reference list. You will probably not use more than three or four at a time, but you will find it helpful to have more than just that number available to you. There are several sources of references. Four are named here.

1. *School.* When you give a teacher reference, be sure that you know the full name—if a woman, whether she is "Miss" or "Mrs."—and what address is best to use. Be sure to indicate the subject the teacher teaches and his title if he has one.

2. *Experience.* Experience references are the names of your superiors in the firms listed on your data sheet under "Experience."

3. *Character.* Character references are the names of persons who can vouch for your honesty, sincerity, and loyalty. They will include friends of your family, your family doctor, your clergyman. Indicate the full name, the business position, the address, and the telephone number of each of these persons.

Reference letters from these persons will be more effective if they contain specific statements regarding you rather than merely general comments regarding your character. It might be well for you to help these persons write their letters, suggesting what statement from them will benefit you in your application. For example, if you have taught a Sunday-school class in your church and your minister is asked to write a letter for you, you should request that he mention your class teaching and any other of your activities in the church.

Character references from women in business are more effective than references from housewives.

4. *Political.* On occasions, a political reference strengthens your application. Politicians, however, receive so many reference inquiries that many of them have reduced their letters to a form that reads

something like this: "Miss Williams is a voter in my district. Any courtesy you can show her will be appreciated." You can see that such a recommendation would have little or no effect. If your political acquaintance can give you a genuine recommendation, then by all means put his name on your list.

You should have at least three or four references under each of the first three classifications so that you can choose the ones that will do you the most good on different applications. For example, the stenographer who applies for an office position with an investment firm or bank would put a bank executive and a well-known business owner on her list if possible.

Do not fail to obtain permission from each person on your reference list to use his name in your application. If you have not used a name for some time and feel that a reference inquiry might be sent to that person, get in touch with him and remind him of your qualifications and tell him to expect the reference inquiry. When you know that a person has written a reference letter to some company for you, the courteous thing to do is to write a thank-you note.

Other Qualifications. Refer to your self-analysis blank and choose from your list of other qualifications those that will add to the effectiveness of your data sheet. You might make this section of your data sheet in paragraph form, to indicate to the reader your command of English and your ability to express yourself on paper.

Ability to Fill Out the Application Blank

Many firms consider the filling out of an application blank a test of the applicant's intelligence. They take into consideration the applicant's ability to follow instructions, the time it takes to fill out the blank, and the completeness of the answers recorded on the blank. With a little thoughtful preparation you can make a good score on this test.

Application Blanks. Several application blanks are illustrated on page 521, and a composite blank, made up from many blanks, is reproduced on Sheets 115-116 in your Workbook. Practice in filling out this composite form will give you sufficient training for filling out almost any kind of application blank found in a business office.

Probably the first application blank you will be asked to fill out will be the one used in the office of the placement service of your school. The space on which the information is to be written is often extremely

Third form, courtesy Mrs. E. E. Brooke Personnel Agency

Applications for employment—Federal Government, private firm, employment agency.

small. When filling out blanks of this size, you will have to accommodate your penmanship to the space allowed. Sometimes this is rather difficult. Therefore, practice reducing your handwriting, at the same time retaining its legibility. When the space for the information is limited, it may be advisable for you to print your answers.

Follow Instructions. When the instructions on the application blank say to write in ink, then you must write in ink. If you receive the blank through the mail or the employer says that you may take the blank home with you to fill out, you will be tempted to take this opportunity to type the answers neatly on your typewriter. You must, however, follow instructions. A typewritten application will not make the desired impression if a pen-written one is specified.

The instructions usually say to answer every question. If you can find no logical answer to a question on the blank, indicate that you have read the question by placing a dash or some other symbol in the place provided for the answer.

Avoid Asking Foolish Questions. Avoid asking foolish questions of the person who gave you the blank. Here are a few typical ones that stamp you as a person who is not alert, would need supervision on the job, and would probably be a general nuisance if employed.

1. What is today's date?
2. Does "surname" mean the first or last name?
3. Shall I put my middle initial, or do you want the name spelled out?
4. Shall I put my father's full name? And what shall I put down for occupation if he is unemployed? Why do you want to know my mother's maiden name?
5. I stayed home from school one day because of a cold last year. Shall I put that down?
6. I'm interested in all sorts of outdoor sports. Do you want me to list them all?
7. I have never had any employment experience. What shall I put in that section?
8. What do you mean by "Have you ever been bonded?"
9. May I borrow your telephone directory? I don't know the addresses of some of my references.
10. I made a mess of my application blank. Will you give me another?

Tell the Truth. Do not try to evade the truth in answering the questions in your application blank. Many firms print a statement some-

thing like this on the blank to discourage applicants from making false statements:

If a false statement is discovered in this application, the blank will be destroyed immediately. If the erroneous statement is discovered after the applicant has been employed, then he shall be subject to immediate dismissal.

Social Security Number. Since every worker must have a Social Security number, you should get a card as soon as you are ready to apply for a position. To get your number, go or write to the nearest Social Security Board field office. If you do not know the address of the one nearest you, look in your local telephone book or inquire at your post office.

You should always have your card with you when you start a new job. Show your employer your card.

Before applying for a job, be sure to obtain your Social Security card.

See that your employer takes down your number and your name exactly as they are written on the card. (See the illustration given above.)

Date of Application. When giving the date, spell the name of the month in full; know the correct day; and write in the year date.

Name. If no specific instructions are given, write your name as you wish to have it recorded on the office records. If you prefer to use an initial instead of your second name, for example, and the blank does not specifically require your name in full, then write your initial. Write your name plainly so that there will be no chance of your application being misfiled.

Age and Date of Birth. Your age and date of birth should agree. The age desired is usually that on your last anniversary.

Kind of Work Desired. Many offices cross-index applications or file them according to the skills listed. When you make your application, you will want to have your name on as many prospect lists as possible. If you have prepared yourself to be a stenographer, then you can apply for three possible positions—stenographer, typist, clerk. If you have prepared yourself for a bookkeeping position also, then your list can read, "Stenographer, typist, assistant bookkeeper, clerk." Do not list any skill in this section, however, in which you have no confidence. Do not list, for example, "Comptometer operator" if you have had

only one week's training on the machine. There is another place on the application blank for you to list the various machines on which you are not expert but with which you are familiar.

Personal History. The next few questions seem to be very personal ones. Possibly you wonder why an employer wishes to know so many personal details about you. Perhaps your first impulse is to resent being asked for such information, but look at the matter from the standpoint of the employer. When you are hired, you become one of the members of a large family; and, to insure that this family is a happy one, the employer tries to employ only those persons who will prove congenial in the group.

These questions reflect something of your character and your social background; they suggest to the employer what you might be called upon to do with the money he pays you, what responsibilities are going to be on your mind when you are in the office. The employer is entitled to know about the person whom he is going to protect with insurance coverage and to whom he is going to entrust the tools of, and the private information about, his business.

If there is something in your background of which you are not proud, you can show by your own actions and abilities that you have risen above those circumstances.

Health. Answer the health questions honestly. If you were absent from school or work for any length of time because of your health condition, put in parentheses the reason for your absence. For example, "Three weeks (appendix operation)," "One week (wisdom-tooth extraction)." The purpose of these questions is to determine whether you will be absent from your work often because of common colds or some chronic ailment. The explanation of your illness will indicate to the employer whether he may expect you to be absent for the same reason again or not.

Membership in Associations. Do you know why the employer wants to know to what associations you belong? His main reason is to discover whether you like to be with people and to participate in group activities. You will be wise if you arrange your activities so as to include at least one association. Some that are acceptable in any situation are the Y.W.C.A., the Y.M.C.A., the K. of C., church clubs for young people, and social clubs. If your social club has a name, the significance of which is not immediately obvious—for example, if its name consists of one or more letters of the Greek alphabet—then you

should explain what type of club it is—whether a social club, a charity organization, or whatever it is.

Recreation. Your choice of recreation is indicative of your personality. Reading, outdoor sports (name some particular ones if you can), sewing, movies, and music are all acceptable activities.

Best Studies. You have a chance to sell yourself in answering the question, "In what studies did you do your best work in school?" You must tell the truth, of course; but if you are placing your application with a clothing firm and you can truthfully say that you were trained in home economics and textiles, you make your application more interesting to the employer. If you are applying for a position where you will be required to do some bookkeeping or number work, then you will mention mathematics if you can.

School Activities. List as many items as possible in answer to the question, "In what school activities have you participated?" Pick out those things that show your leadership ability, your diversity of interests, your social aptitudes. Do not forget committee memberships, debates, and dramatics.

Office Machines. Somewhere on the application blank you will be asked to list the different kinds of machines with which you are familiar. Know how to spell the names of the machines correctly—and do not omit any of those about which you have some knowledge, because a knowledge of office machines is becoming more and more important.

Employment History. Your employment history has already been discussed on page 517. One or two statements, however, will bear repeating. You should know the complete name and title of your immediate superior so that, if your prospective employer wishes to send a reference letter to him, he will have available all the necessary information.

You can make your experience sound more impressive by going into some detail under the Kind of Work section. Suppose you did some clerical work in your uncle's office on Saturdays. Clerical work can mean many things; so, list your duties, such as answering the telephone, running errands, typewriting, etc.

Even if you have had no employment whatever, you must not leave this section vacant—say, "In school."

If you have mentioned any actual jobs in the employment record, and the next question is, "Why did you leave your last job?" you must

give a reason. Your answer will probably be "Temporary job only," "Job terminated," "Employer moved away," or whatever statement is applicable.

Have You Been Bonded? Employees who handle valuable documents or large sums of money are usually placed under bond. The character and reputation of the employee are investigated thoroughly before he is placed under bond.

Fidelity bonds guarantee the employer against loss sustained by reason of an act or acts of larceny, theft, embezzlement, forgery, misappropriation, wrongful abstraction, willful misapplication, or other

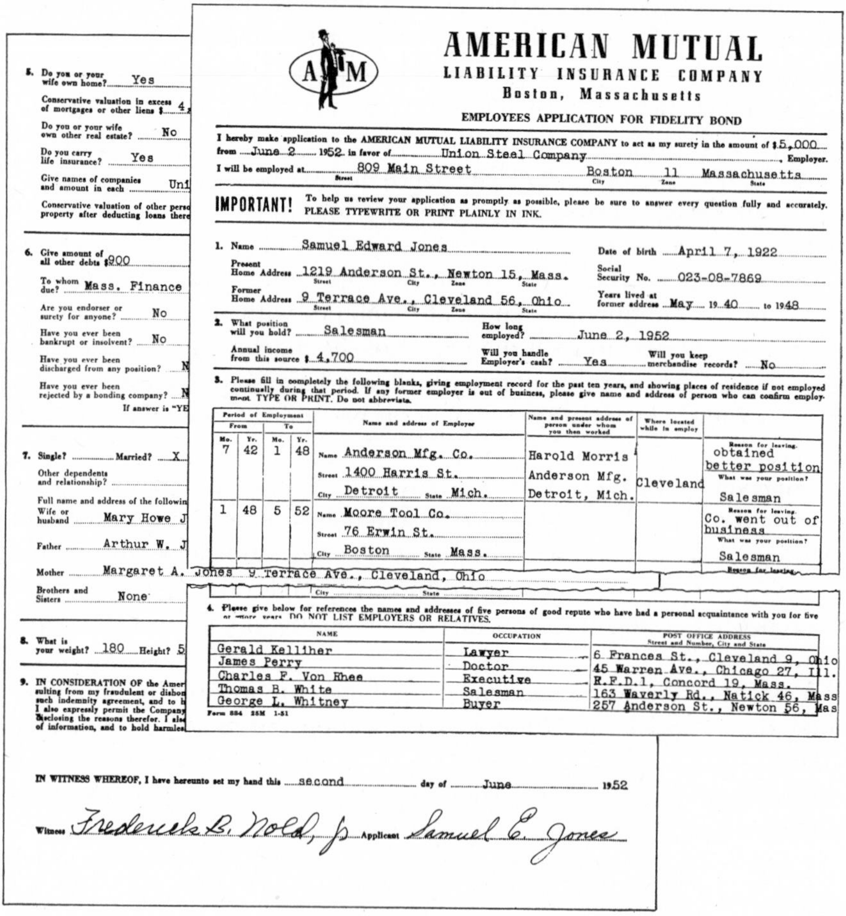

AMERICAN MUTUAL
LIABILITY INSURANCE COMPANY
Boston, Massachusetts

EMPLOYEES APPLICATION FOR FIDELITY BOND

I hereby make application to the AMERICAN MUTUAL LIABILITY INSURANCE COMPANY to act as my surety in the amount of $5,000 from June 2 1952 in favor of Union Steel Company, Employer.
I will be employed at 809 Main Street (Street) Boston (City) 11 (Zone) Massachusetts (State)

IMPORTANT! To help us review your application as promptly as possible, please be sure to answer every question fully and accurately. PLEASE TYPEWRITE OR PRINT PLAINLY IN INK.

1. Name Samuel Edward Jones — Date of birth April 7, 1922
Present Home Address 1219 Anderson St., Newton 15, Mass. — Social Security No. 023-08-7869
Former Home Address 9 Terrace Ave., Cleveland 56, Ohio — Years lived at former address May 19 40 to 1948

2. What position will you hold? Salesman — How long employed? June 2, 1952
Annual income from this source $4,700 — Will you handle Employer's cash? Yes — Will you keep merchandise records? No

3. Please fill in completely the following blanks, giving employment record for the past ten years, and showing places of residence if not employed continually during that period. If any former employer is out of business, please give name and address of person who can confirm employment. TYPE OR PRINT. Do not abbreviate.

From Mo.	From Yr.	To Mo.	To Yr.	Name and address of Employer	Name and present address of person under whom you then worked	Where located while in employ	
7	42	1	48	Name Anderson Mfg. Co. Street 1400 Harris St. City Detroit State Mich.	Harold Morris Anderson Mfg. Detroit, Mich.	Cleveland	Reason for leaving: obtained better position What was your position? Salesman
1	48	5	52	Name Moore Tool Co. Street 76 Erwin St. City Boston State Mass.			Reason for leaving: Co. went out of business What was your position? Salesman

4. Please give below for references the names and addresses of five persons of good repute who have had a personal acquaintance with you for five or more years. DO NOT LIST EMPLOYERS OR RELATIVES.

NAME	OCCUPATION	POST OFFICE ADDRESS Street and Number, City and State
Gerald Kelliher	Lawyer	6 Frances St., Cleveland 9, Ohio
James Perry	Doctor	45 Warren Ave., Chicago 27, Ill.
Charles F. Von Rhee	Executive	R.F.D.1, Concord 19, Mass.
Thomas B. White	Salesman	163 Waverly Rd., Natick 46, Mass
George L. Whitney	Buyer	257 Anderson St., Newton 56, Mas

Form 884 25M 1-51

5. Do you or your wife own home? Yes
Conservative valuation in excess of mortgages or other liens $4,
Do you or your wife own other real estate? No
Do you carry life insurance? Yes
Give names of companies and amount in each Uni
Conservative valuation of other perso property after deducting loans there

6. Give amount of all other debts $900
To whom due? Mass. Finance
Are you endorser or surety for anyone? No
Have you ever been bankrupt or insolvent? No
Have you ever been discharged from any position? N
Have you ever been rejected by a bonding company? N
If answer is "YE

7. Single? Married? X
Other dependents and relationship?
Full name and address of the followin
Wife or husband Mary Howe J
Father Arthur W. J
Mother Margaret A. Jones 9 Terrace Ave., Cleveland, Ohio
Brothers and Sisters None

8. What is your weight? 180 Height? 5

9. IN CONSIDERATION OF the Amer sulting from my fraudulent or dishon such indemnity agreement, and to h I also expressly permit the Company disclosing the reasons therefor. I als of information, and to hold harmles

IN WITNESS WHEREOF, I have hereunto set my hand this second day of June 1952

Witness Frederick B. Nold, Jr. Applicant Samuel E. Jones

Courtesy American Mutual Liability Insurance Company

An application for bond.

fraudulent or dishonest acts of employees acting alone or in collusion with others. The furnishing of a fidelity bond strengthens the moral fiber of employees and is considered a certificate of character. Employees with good records welcome the investigation of a surety company. A copy of an application for bond appears on page 526. Read the form over carefully so that you will be able to fill one out intelligently when called upon to do so.

References. The Reference section on your application blank is very important. You have already prepared a list of prospective references in making out your data sheet.

Some applications will contain a statement that relatives may not be used as references; others, that no school or experience references may be given. The employer can get school references from the detailed information in the Education section of your application, and he can get the experience references from the information in the Experience section. That leaves only character references.

Choose these references wisely, changing your list to suit the job desired, if that is possible.

Give the telephone numbers of your references. It may be that the prospective employer will wish to telephone your references and get an immediate report on you.

Be sure that each of your references knows you and your abilities and is conscious of the fact that you have given his name on your reference list. The propriety of having asked for and received permission to use the name of a reference was discussed on page 519.

Distinguishing Qualifications. So far on your application blank you are very much like all the other applicants of your age and experience. In order to distinguish yourself from the others, you should find some place on the application to stress those points that make you different from the other applicants. Some applications will give you several lines on which to write this information. Some will ask that you attach a letter describing yourself and your abilities. Some will seemingly be void of an opportunity for you to sell yourself because of any exceptional characteristics.

If no place is allowed on the blank for you to give this special information, then attach a copy of your data sheet or ask for permission to send the application in by mail, and then send with it an attractive application letter in which you sell yourself. If, as in the applications illustrated in this book, there is a place for you to describe your special

abilities or other qualifications, then choose, from the list you have already made up when you were studying the data sheet, those attributes that will get you the particular job for which you are applying. Word your statements in your best English and write them in your best penmanship. Make your list as long as you can without apparently "padding" it.

When you have reviewed your application and seen that it is in good order, every question answered, all details included, then you are ready to affix your signature.

The Applicant's Equipment. As speed is one of the elements judged in this so-called "intelligence test," always have available for quick reference:

1. A completed data sheet.
2. A full list of all available references with correct addresses and telephone numbers.
3. A record of the dates relating to your school experience.
4. A record of the dates and other pertinent information regarding your employment experience.
5. A list of all the machines with which you are familiar.
6. A list of all the "other qualifications" from which you can choose the ones that will be most effective.
7. Your Social Security card.
8. Several photographs of yourself so as to be prepared to submit one when it is required. The photographs, preferably, should be small; but be sure that they are attractive and that they do you justice.

Section 2. APPLYING AND INTERVIEWING FOR THE JOB

In planning your job-finding campaign, you must first know the sources of information regarding jobs. Your next step is to plan your application letters that will pave the way for interviews. Then, of course, your behavior during the interview needs to be carefully anticipated so that a call for employment will be the final result.

JOB INFORMATION SOURCES

You should familiarize yourself with the sources of information regarding jobs and the various placement agencies. Among these sources are the following.

School Placement Service. Almost every school offering training in business subjects maintains an employment service. Make this your first employment-agency contact, because here you are well known, the school is sympathetic with your particular problems, and the persons in authority are familiar with your special talents and abilities.

Friends. Someone has said that a job-seeker's friends are his best employment agency. Some people call this "friendly" agency by another name, "pull." This kind of pull is entirely legitimate. When you are ready for employment, let everyone you know "in" on the secret. Your social clubs and church affiliations are splendid mediums for spreading the news regarding your abilities. When one of your friends hears of an opening, he will say to himself, "Just last night Alice was telling us that she was ready for such a job—I'll call her and tell her to go down and apply"; or "John is just the boy for that job—I'll give him a ring right away."

Cultivate the interest of the friends of your parents. It is from persons older in years or in experience that you can expect employment; so seek the company and gain the confidence of such persons.

There may be an opening in the office where one of your own friends is working. If he is familiar with your abilities, he can suggest to his employer that he interview you for the job. This is the best kind of "pull" you can have, because many employers would rather employ someone recommended by one of their present employees than to take into the organization a stranger about whom they know nothing. It will be well for you, therefore, to have among your friends as many employed office workers as possible.

Be sure to make a courteous report to the person who referred you to a position no matter what the outcome of the interview may be. Should you fail to obtain the position, perhaps the person can refer you to another. If you obtain the position, then your friend should know the outcome so that he will not send another applicant.

Employment Agencies. There are many kinds of employment agencies. There are those that are supported by the city and the state or by the Community Chest and like organizations. These agencies are usually free; that is, you do not have to pay them a fee if you obtain a position through them.

Typewriter and office-machine companies also maintain employment services for those capable of operating their machines.

There are also many private placement agencies. These agencies

charge applicants a fee for their services. Sometimes the agency charges the employer instead of the applicant. Private agencies have more calls for experienced workers than for inexperienced workers. The latter calls usually go to schools. Be sure to read the agency contract before you sign it. A typical agency application blank is shown on page 521.

Personnel Offices. Many corporations that employ large numbers of office workers maintain a personnel department to take care of all applications for employment. Many personnel offices require all applicants to take a skill test. You can get in practice for these employment tests by considering each test that you take in school from now on as an employment test. Harden yourself against any possibility of becoming nervous during an employment test. Your effectiveness in making application in these offices will depend on your ability to sell yourself and make them believe that there should be a place for you in their organization.

Civil Service. The state and Federal governments often hold examinations for clerical and stenographic openings. Information regarding the Federal examinations can be obtained through the post office, and you can ask to be put on the mailing list for notification of state examinations. The offices of large city governments operate under civil service also. You can call at the city hall for information about these examinations.

Announcements regarding the various Federal examinations, together with descriptions of the tests and some sample questions, are mailed to persons who have requested that their names be placed on the mailing list to receive announcements of the tests in which they are interested.

For a very nominal fee, you may procure from the United States Civil Service Commission, Washington 25, D. C., a booklet, *Federal Employment under the Merit System*, which gives full details regarding the civil service.

Appointment to civil-service positions is determined by placement on the official civil-service list of those who have passed examinations. Taking these examinations is an excellent test of your ability, and you can regard a high number on the list as distinctly to your credit. If you can say to a prospective employer, "I placed among the first ten in the state examination for junior stenographer," the employer knows pretty well that your abilities are above average.

Classified Ads. An important source of jobs—namely, classified ads —is discussed in detail in the following section. Many replies to classified advertisements are made by letter.

ELEMENTS OF AN EFFECTIVE LETTER OF APPLICATION

Do you know why you are beginning now to think about the construction and wording of an effective job-getting letter? Because a good application letter cannot be written in a few minutes. Careful thought and planning are necessary.

It is almost impossible to state any set rules by which you can construct an application letter. Writing your application letter is something like taking your photograph—you try to eliminate all the blemishes (poor grammar, incorrect spelling, careless construction) and bring out your best qualities—your sincerity, your character, and your abilities. A retoucher can work on your photograph and make it arresting and intriguing. That's what you want to do with your application letter—make it reflect your personality, ring true to your character, and hold the attention of the employer.

Your letter may be alive and interesting and still fail in its objective. To be successful, it must lead to a personal interview. Three essential items must, therefore, be included in your letter: the opening, which draws attention and states your purpose in writing; a few statements regarding your training and experience that will be of interest to the employer; and a closing paragraph that makes him want to pick up his telephone and call you in for an interview immediately.

Mechanical Setup. As you are applying for a stenographic position, your letter should be representative of your very best typing and letter setup. Avoid any erasing and keep the paper free of thumbprints. The best paper to use is white bond paper 8½ by 11 inches in size, inserted in a plain white envelope. Sometimes a letter can be made outstandingly attractive on white paper of a slightly smaller size, with a matching envelope. Never use social stationery.

Conservative stationery and letter style give an impression of dignity and refinement. If your name is Brown, and you use brown ink on brown stationery, some reader may be impressed; but most readers would consider your letter freakish.

Address your letter to some one person if possible. Use your initiative to find out the name of the person to whom the letter should be addressed. A letter addressed to the personnel manager would be much

more effective if addressed to "Mr. John Anderson, Personnel Manager" than merely to "Personnel Manager." Then you could use the salutation, "Dear Mr. Anderson," and make your letter sound personal.

Your letter should always contain your full name, address, and telephone number. And don't forget to sign your letter.

A handwritten letter is acceptable if your handwriting is especially neat and legible. A typewritten letter, however, can be made more attractive and is more easily read.

Letter Content. Your application letter is essentially a sales letter. It should, therefore, be brief—every word and every sentence adding to its selling power. Avoid negative statements.

Even though you may use the same basic letter in applying to several organizations, each letter must appear and read as if it were addressed to one concern alone. Make each letter an original copy, changing the wording and points of emphasis to suit the recipient, if necessary.

A good piece of advice to novices in application letter writing is to write down first everything that you could possibly put into the letter. Then check those items that qualify you especially for the position for which you wish to apply. Pick out from these checked items the one that will probably be the deciding factor in your obtaining the position. This item should be named first.

Then start writing your letter. Write a good introductory paragraph. Write a good second paragraph. Then cross out the introductory paragraph and start your letter with the second. Do you know why you do that? Because you will have worked so hard to make the first paragraph unusual that it will not sound like you at all. It will sound unnatural and forced.

On the following page is a successful application letter. As you read it, you may say to yourself, "If this has been successful, why don't I copy it and sign my name?" The answer, of course, is that your letter will not be sincere and will not be a reflection of your own personality.

Read this letter, however, and let it suggest to you the essentials of a job-getting letter.

Dear Sir:

Out here we don't believe in Santa Claus any more, and if there are any soft jobs left in the world I wouldn't know what to do with one.

Getting through four years at the University of Montana in these times fits a man for work. (My B.A. in Business Administration was granted in June, 1951. My senior thesis did not attempt to solve world problems.) We're used to working, by the time we finish school. Summer of 1948 I worked in the harvest fields; summer of 1949 I sold washing machines (second paragraph from the last tells more about that); and in 1950 a crew of us picked spotted-fever ticks for the Government and good wages. Spotted-fever ticks are nobody's pets.

Here is a transcript of my completed courses and grades received. A high school honor scholarship paid my fees all four years; you lose them if your grades get down to C average.

"Active in a leadership way," your advertisement reads. So: Bearpaw (honorary Sophomore men's organization), M Club (varsity basketball two years), Duniway prize books in 1950.

I couldn't afford a fraternity, but two years spent managing the "barb" house helped out the social graces. My freshman year was spent in the men's dormitory; they're used to rubbing the rough edges off aspiring business men in South Hall. I can still get by with the boys in the Butte mines, too.

Salesmanship?—I sold twelve washing machines in two weeks in a railroad town of 4,000 one summer when half the men in town were cut off the board.

I would like to sell you the services of one James Birch, who could do more good in your organization than he could as a deputy sheriff. But he has to earn a living; and while he is ambitious, he isn't fussy. Would you like to ask questions about this merchandise, and look it over?

Sincerely yours,
James Birch

Your Planned Letter Campaign

As pointed out on page 529, your best sources of information regarding openings are your school placement office and your friends. But you will not wish to stand idly by waiting for someone to find you a job. A letter campaign, well planned, will bring you the returns you wish.

Study Classified Ads. From the classified section of your newspaper become acquainted with the style of ads as they occur from day to day. Typical ads are shown on page 536. After reading a few pages of ads, you will soon discover that only one or two each day will have any application to your problem. When you have decided to answer an ad,

be sure that your letter is placed in the mail the same day on which the ad appears.

This letter must have all the characteristics of a good application letter. You will want to be careful, however, to answer only those ads for which you qualify.

Your letter must be outstanding among the scores of answers received by the advertiser. An advertiser usually sorts application letters into three piles—the no-good, the possible, the outstanding letters.

What makes an application letter no good? When letters are received in quantity, notice is first taken of the envelope—its neatness and the correctness of address. The envelope may be of an unusual color, and therefore be outstanding; but the employer may suspect that the letter inside is freakish and will eliminate it before it is read.

The letter itself may be eliminated because of poor setup, faulty grammar, incorrect spelling. Applications written on torn sheets or half sheets or on the backs of old envelopes are immediately thrown out. Letters from persons who are not qualified for the position open are not considered.

The letters in the "possible" pile are all right but not quite good enough to be put in the "outstanding" pile. Why not be first choice instead of second choice?

The persons whose letters get into the "outstanding" pile are called for an interview.

Read the following good letters, which were written in response to a want ad.

Gentlemen:

In applying for the position of "rapid and accurate stenographer," the best evidence I can offer you to show that I am qualified for this position is a brief outline of my preparation for this work.

I have just completed a four years' high school course, during which I devoted two years to stenographic work. I have had thorough training in bookkeeping, shorthand, office training, business English, commercial law, and typewriting.

During my school years, accuracy was always stressed as vital. Speed, we were taught, followed upon accuracy. In this respect I feel I can be of service to you. I can write at an average of 50 words a minute without error on the typewriter and can take dictation at the rate of 100 words a minute, transcribing accurately. I am free to take the position immediately and shall appreciate it if you will name the day and hour

when you can see me. At an interview you can judge better of my personal qualities.   Very truly yours,

Gentlemen:

Speed.   Accuracy.   Intelligence.   Reliability.   Honesty.   Ambition.
You are looking for a stenographer with these qualities.

Speed. I can write 60 words a minute on the typewriter and take dictation at the rate of 125 words a minute. I can transcribe quickly, and you will find that my transcriptions are marked by their

Accuracy. Not only is the mechanical side of my typewriting correct and accurate, but the matter itself is thoughtfully written, with the meaning kept intact. The grammar and punctuation are also correct, as I make use of my

Intelligence. I earned membership in the Minnesota Scholarship Federation while at high school and had Phi Beta Kappa standing during the one year I attended Middle West Teachers College. I finished the course at Secretarial School in half the time usually required. I am twenty-one years of age—old enough to have

Reliability. I believe in doing every bit of work with the highest possible efficiency. Though loyalty alone would command strict reliability on my part, I realize that it is to my own interest to do your work well; and as to getting it done promptly, I consider that a matter of

Honesty. You will pay me for my time, and none of it will be wasted. If there is any spare time, I can use it to further my

Ambition. I want to learn the business thoroughly, not only because I am deeply interested in it, but because I hope some day to be fitted for a position of responsibility where thoroughness and initiative are required.

May I have a personal interview?   Respectfully yours,

Examine Situation-Wanted Ads. When you are reading the classified section of the newspaper, examining the help-wanted advertisements, study, too, the situation-wanted advertisements. Typical ads are shown on page 537. Ask yourself as you read them which ones you as an employer would answer and why. You will find that they are miniature application letters, written in telegraphic style. They state the kind of position wanted, the education, and the experience of the applicant.

If you are able to couch this information in arresting language, then your ad will be a good one. Don't expect too much of your situation-wanted ad, however. A good application letter written direct to some company or corporation is more apt to get results than a situation-wanted ad.

HELP-WANTED ADS

FEMALE

1 ACCOUNTING clerk, pleasant downtown insurance office: 5-day, 35-hour week; salary $170 mo. Write P1034 Times

2 ADVERTISING agency, opportunity for clever young woman who knows switchboard, can type. Excellent advancement. $45 to start. Write fully, giving background and experience. Y6250 Times.

3 AIR LINE clerk, required for Revenue Accounting Department of permanent scheduled air line; midtown area; air line experience not essential; salary $184 month. State age, education, and experience. S246 Times.

4 ASSISTANT BOOKKEEPER, Lumber office, knowledge of bookkeeping machines helpful, 5 days. State references, school background, salary desired. P.O. Box 583.

5 CLERICAL, $42-$48 START

Large nationally known company has several select positions available in financial, accounting, purchasing, statistical, and clerical divisions of its organization. Intelligent young woman with good general clerical aptitude, incl. ability to compile and handle figures, may apply. Salary based on qualifications. 5-day week. Y6519 Times.

6 COMPTOMETER-CLERICAL

Require services of bright beginner; good at adding and subtracting; good handwriting essential. 5-day week. S283 Times.

7 DENTAL ASSISTANT. Experience preferred, but not necessary. Call Monday, between 9-10 A.M. Mu 6130.

8 FILE CLERKS

Beginners and Experienced
NATIONAL ORGANIZATION
5-DAY WEEK
Reply stating age, schooling, experience, and salary expected.
S320 TIMES.

9 STENO monitor-board operator. Light shorthand, typing, congenial downtown office, bright beginner considered, 5 days. $45. Start Dec. 10. Submit resume. P1000 Times Downtown.

10 STENOGRAPHER $50

Experienced or willingness to learn Ediphone required as well as stenographic experience. Permanent position in midtown office of nationally known fashion-accessories manufacturer. 5-day week, attractive surroundings, lunchroom and liberal benefits. Give age, education and experience. S367 Times.

11 SWITCHBOARD operator, monitor. Knowledge of general office work. S85 Times.

12 TYPIST-EXPERIENCED

To learn letter writing from Sound-Scriber: large national organization: 5 days, 35 hrs.: $180 mo.: state age, education, experience. S67 Times.

13 TYPIST-RECEPTIONIST

Exceptional environment, varied duties, art educational firm. Permanent. State age, education, salary. S282 Times.

14 YOUNG girl, just out of high school preferred: typing, filing; pleasant working conditions. $150 month. Small publishing firm. Y6542 Times.

MALE

15 BOY (OFFICE)—$39

Excellent career position on office staff, noted corporation; intelligent, H. S. grad. (age 17-19) may apply: training program: early salary advancement. S263 Times.

16 OFFICE BOYS
Junior Clerks

Major oil company needs ambitious, energetic young men 17-18 years of age for immediate and future openings.
Write giving full particulars regarding personal history and education. Please include telephone number.
Y6846 TIMES.

17 SHIPPING clerk, to handle receiving, shipping and stock: old-established firm; downtown area; 49-hour week. Time and a half for overtime; state age, experience, salary expected. P1026 Times.

18 YOUNG MAN

Age 21-25, H. S. grad. Exceptional opportunity as production assistant in large, well-known printing company. No previous printing experience required. P1065 Times.

19 YOUNG MAN

Single; general office work in sales organization; opportunity for advancement; state age, experience, references, salary desired. S149 Times.

20 YOUNG MAN

Must be high school graduate. General clerical work, Must make neat figures. Salary to start $45. S65 Times.

Study these ads before you construct one of your own. Read all of them and then ask yourself these questions:

Why would a telephone number be better to put in your ad than a box number at the newspaper office?

SITUATION-WANTED ADS

1 ASSISTANT BOOKKEEPER, light steno., own correspondence, efficient, adaptable. GL. 6500

2 BOOKKEEPER, typing, one-girl office, $60. JE 4318, 1-7 p.m.

3   EXECUTIVE SECRETARY

Confidential; diversified experience, excellent skills, personable; $75. TE 3200

4 MEDICAL secretary-assistant, personable, thoroughly experienced; references; permanent. Y6541 Times.

5 SECRETARY, purchasing assistant advert., publ., experienced; $60. Call YO 7000.

6 SECRETARY-steno., experienced, efficient; prefer 1-girl office. Y6883 Times.

7 SECRETARY, executive ability, diverse experience; midtown; $65-60. TR 5417.

8 SPANISH-ENGLISH stenographer, experienced; competent; reads French, Portuguese. O442 Times.

9 STENO-type, general office work, experienced, neat appearance; H. S. grad., moderate salary OL 6489.

10 TYPIST-CLERK, knowledge billing, statistical, steno; Govt.-private experience; neat appearance; $50-45. PR 6262.

Do you think that the words "moderate salary" add to the pulling power of the advertisement?

What kind of personality would you guess the young woman in No. 4 possesses? Is it necessary for her to mention the word "personable"? Would you say she was conceited?

Would a beginner strengthen his application by mentioning shorthand and typing speeds, transcription speed, number of bills typed in a minute, number of envelopes typed in an hour, or other definite measures of his skills?

Send "Shotgun" Letters. Shotgun application letters are so called because the letter writer, like the shotgun hunter, fires at an object with many pellets, hoping that one pellet may hit the mark.

With your goal in view—a stenographer in some advertising agency, for example—select a group of firms for which you would like to work and address the same letter to each of these firms. Each letter, of course, will be typed as an original and will be so worded that it does not sound like a "form" letter. These letters are really the easiest to write because you are talking about something most important to you and expressing your sincere ambitions.

The names of advertising concerns may be obtained from trade magazines or the classified telephone directory. You will discover that the classified telephone directory is one of your best friends when you are job hunting.

You have already learned that it is better to address an application letter to a particular person. The best way to find out the name of the proper person to address is to telephone the office of the company and ask for the name and the mailing address of the person in charge of employment of office help. This information will never be refused;

but if you are asked why you wish the name, say, "I am planning to write him a letter."

Or, suppose your business experience has consisted of clerking in a grocery store after school and on Saturdays. You know the names and the quality of most of the products sold in the store. Why not capitalize on this knowledge and send your shotgun letters to wholesale grocers or food brokers? In this letter you would emphasize the knowledge you had gained from your part-time employment.

Sometimes a letter to a department head gets better results than one sent to the personnel director. To illustrate, suppose your special aptitude is handling legal matter, and you are familiar with legal terminology—then you can address your shotgun letters to the heads of legal departments in the larger firms of your city. The department head does not receive many letters of this kind; and if yours is a particularly good one, he will probably say to his secretary: "This chap sounds all right. Send this letter to the personnel office and ask them to call the young man in and see what he looks like. If he's all right, tell them to send him up to me."

One caution: when you stress a special ability, such as your interest in advertising, your knowledge of grocery information, or your familiarity with legal work, you must be able to follow through on your statements and "produce the goods."

Read the following letters and determine why they would obtain an interview for the writers.

Dear Sir:

Isn't there a place in your organization for a young man to whom responsible work can be assigned, with the knowledge that it will be done satisfactorily, and on time?

I am employed at present but can leave on short notice.

I shall be glad to have the opportunity to be acquainted personally with you, whether or not we come to an agreement. I should very much appreciate it if you will use the enclosed envelope to let me know when it will be convenient for me to call on you.

A "specification sheet" is enclosed. I shall be glad to send you a photo upon request.

Respectfully yours,

Dear Sir:

You are a busy man—but perhaps you have a moment to consider the many uses to which you could put the services of a young lady who

writes well, has had a year's experience in a publishing company, and a course in the fundamentals of advertising.

During the period of my employment in the publishing house, I had the opportunity to learn something of all sides of the business, from writing editorials, feature stories, and reviews, to proofreading.

After high school graduation, I attended a junior college, where I studied psychology, economics, government, sociology, finance, American literature, and business administration. In both high school and college I edited the school publications.

For the past year I have been a teacher-secretary-solicitor in a business school, which has given me a well-rounded background in the operation of such an institution. I am taking, also, extension courses in literature and poetry in a local college, and I write occasional articles and features for my former connection.

I am twenty-two years of age, American, of pleasing personality, and contact people readily and easily. I have traveled somewhat and lived during the past summer in Puerto Rico. Though interested principally in the editorial department, any of the routine of publishing your magazine would be a pleasure to me.

If you find that you can use my services, I will furnish references to confirm my qualifications.

Very truly yours,

Preparation for the Personal Interview

Let us suppose that you are planning for an interview with a prospective employer. How will you appear? What will you do? What will you say? How will you convince him that you are the one for the position that is open?

How Will You Appear? You are not ready for a personal interview until you have done certain "homework."

Give yourself a mirror test. Stand in front of a full-length mirror to see whether you have that "employable" look. Could you pass under the close scrutiny of the interviewer; or do you have a split seam somewhere, an uneven hem line, careless make-up, run-over heels, or unpolished shoes?

Are the colors you are wearing in harmony? Do your clothes look as if they belonged to you, or do they look "borrowed"? Are they appropriate for the occasion?

Your appearance should be such that the employer could say, "Take off your hat. Sit down at this desk. We shall be proud to introduce you as our new employee."

Courtesy Shaw-Walker Company

Look relaxed, yet eager, in your job interview. Never place any of your belongings on the interviewer's desk.

When you are satisfied that your appearance will be an asset to you, then put all concern for your appearance from your mind, at least until after your interview. Much of self-consciousness, which is definitely not desirable, comes from being overconscious of your appearance. You must be able to take your mind off yourself and think about the person with whom you are talking and about the subjects under discussion.

What Will You Take with You? When you go for an interview, be sure to take with you the things mentioned in the following paragraphs.

1. Your own pen (filled with ink), one or two sharpened pencils, typewriter eraser, and shield.
2. A small memorandum book or notebook in which you have your job-hunting calls listed and in which you keep your interview records.

3. All the data you will need to assist you in filling out an application blank. These data are listed on page 528.
4. A good pocket dictionary.

What Will Be Your Attitude? If you have planned your campaign carefully and thoughtfully, then you will enter every office in which you wish to leave an application for employment with this idea in mind: "This is the one place in which I want to work." Then what you say will radiate such enthusiasm that the employer will realize that you really want to work for him.

What Will You Say to the Receptionist? The receptionist can open the door to the employer's office for you or she can keep it closed. You should, therefore, make a friend of the receptionist by respecting her authority and not letting yourself become a nuisance. Sell yourself to the receptionist to the extent that she will say to her employer, "Mr. Employer, there's an applicant outside whom I think you will want to see. I told her there was no job open at this time, but she looks very capable."

Your approach to the receptionist may vary according to circumstances. For example, there are several ways of approaching the receptionist at an agency. She must, of necessity, follow a definite routine in receiving applicants and, at times, may seem impersonal. Nevertheless, a pleasant attitude on your part and a carefully planned sales talk will make an impression.

What Will You Say to the Employer? Treat the employer with respect but not with fear. He is going to be as interested in you as you care to make him. Be yourself. Your natural enthusiasm touched with a bit of the excitement of the occasion will make a better impression than a forced personality that probably wouldn't fool the employer anyway. Be your best self, in full control of the situation.

When you enter the employer's office, wait for him to invite you to sit down. After seating yourself, keep your belongings (gloves and purse) in your lap; don't put anything on the employer's desk.

If you have asked for the interview, then you must take the initiative and conduct the interview as a salesman would conduct a sale. When you have introduced yourself and told of your qualifications and why you wish to place your application, the employer will follow with questions on points that he thinks are important.

If you have been called for an interview on the basis of a former ap-

plication or letter, the employer will very likely wish to direct the discussion.

The employer may have your application, letter, or data sheet before him. Supposedly, everything about you that is necessary for him to know is in these documents; but, in order to carry on a conversation, the employer asks you identical questions that you have answered on the written papers. Don't look at the employer as if you thought he couldn't read or was asking foolish questions. He is trying to open the conversation so that you can start talking and show him what kind of person you are and what kind of personality you have.

You will, therefore, not only have to be able to write your qualifications well, but you will also have to have verbal answers ready on any topic mentioned in the application blank. The employer will glance over the blank or data sheet; and when some item attracts him, he will ask you to state the facts orally. Some of the questions to be expected are:

> What skills do you have? or What can you do?
> What did you do in school other than study?
> What are your hobbies?
> Why do you wish to work for this company?
> What salary do you expect?

Whatever you answer, say more than "Yes" or "No." Answer in complete sentences and even in paragraphs, if the subject warrants it. For example, when the employer asks, "Can you operate a bookkeeping machine?" you might answer, "No, but I have been trained in hand bookkeeping and can operate the adding machine and calculator." In this way you follow your negative answer with a positive statement and thus try to convert a liability into an asset.

A good practice exercise in preparation for your oral interview is to take each item mentioned in the application blank and prepare a sales talk of one minute or less. Don't memorize these explanations—that would take away from their spontaneity. Just try to prepare yourself for any emergency.

How Should You Terminate the Interview? An application interview should rarely last over fifteen minutes. Be sensitive to the reactions of your interviewer so that you will not prolong the interview unnecessarily. Smile as you say "Thank you" for the interview. Take all your

belongings with you as you leave so as to avoid the embarrassment of having to return for your gloves, handkerchief, or fountain pen. Be sure to thank the receptionist, also, as you leave.

Understand Use of Rating Sheets by Employer. During the interview the employer is making a mental picture of you, or he is noting certain factors about you that he can record on a rating sheet when you have left his office.

In his mental estimate of you, the employer is classifying you according to a scale somewhat like the following:

Characteristic	Poor	Average	Good	Excellent
Appearance			√	
Personality				√
Initiative		√		
Mentality		√		
Speech	√			

Very often, however, the employer uses a printed check sheet on which to record his opinion of the various characteristics that you reveal in your personal interview. A typical interview rating sheet is shown on page 544. The knowledge that you are being rated on such a scale will make you self-conscious unless you ascertain your weaknesses early in your training period and prepare yourself to make a good impression and to have a high rating on the scale.

Follow Up Your Interview. On the evening of the same day in which you have your application interviews, write thank-you notes to the persons who expressed an interest in your abilities, even though they gave you no encouragement for employment. If you did receive some encouragement in your interview, then follow your thank-you note with a telephone call within a few days or ask one of your sponsors to write direct to the employer and recommend you for consideration for any openings that might occur.

Your follow-up technique is an important part of your campaign. Don't overlook it.

TYPICAL RATING SHEET FOR INTERVIEW

(Position of check mark on the line indicates rating. Note that checks at either end of scale in some instances may indicate undesirable characteristics. A check in the fourth position on each section is desirable.)

Name of Person Rated...................................Date...............

1. APPEARANCE

Untidily and inappropriately dressed	Carelessly dressed	Acceptably dressed	Well dressed	Exceptionally well dressed

2. PHYSICAL ENERGY

Listless	Below par	Average amount of activity	Active	Full of pep and energy

3. SELF-ASSURANCE

Marked feeling of inferiority	Timid and ill at ease	Normal self-confidence	Well poised	Aggressive

4. SOCIABILITY

Constrained	Reserved	Meets one half way	Cordial and congenial	Very informal

5. ORAL EXPRESSION

Inarticulate	Expresses self with difficulty	Adequate expression	Good choice of words	Speaks distinctly and convincingly

6. MENTAL ALERTNESS

Dull and stupid	Somewhat slow	Normally alert	Grasps ideas quickly	Keen, alert mind

Here are some thank-you notes from applicants. Notice how the personality of the applicant is evident in the manner of expression. Never lose sight of the fact that your personality must ring true in every contact with the employer.

Dear Mr. Brandon:

When I first set out to write you a letter of thanks, I only had to say "Thank you" in acknowledgment of your valuable time spent in speaking to me this past Friday afternoon.

But now—I have been told to report for duty Monday morning; and so I have a twofold reason for sending my sincere thanks to you.

Very respectfully yours,

Dear Mr. Edmonds:

Thank you for giving so generously of your time in our interview this afternoon regarding my application for employment as a stenographer with your company.

You expressed an interest in my ability to do original writing. I am sending a copy of our annual school publication of student compositions, *My Pen Speaks*. On pages 2 and 12 appear two essays of mine of which I am very proud, and on page 8 is a poem of which I am not so proud.

I should like to say again that I do enjoy writing letters and feel that I have a command of English fundamentals.

If, in the near future, you have need of a stenographer who is ambitious and willing to work hard to succeed, I hope you will refer to my application and call me for another interview. My telephone number is Main 5200.

Yours very truly,

To a follow-up letter sent several days after your interview, you could attach a data sheet, if you have not already given the employer one; or you could enclose specimens of your work or copies of recommendation letters. If you have done some investigating about the business, mention of this study will be effective. When you do this, however, you must be sure that your interest and investigation are honest and sincere. The employer can see through a bluff very quickly.

SCHEDULE OF CALLS FOR FEBRUARY 11, 195-

Firm	Time of Call	Results
Reynolds Rubber Co. 75 West 44th Street Miss Ellen Forbush	9:15	There may be opening. Return Wednesday, Feb. 4 for test and interview.
Richard and Adams, Inc. 514 Fifth Avenue Mr. J. Williams	10:15	Filled in application. No openings at present.
Mrs. Egan's Agency 41 East 43d Street	10:40	Filled in application, had interview. Two promising leads.

Plan your schedule of calls efficiently.

```
                RECORD OF CALLS MADE ON ONE FIRM

Firm:  Reynolds Rubber Company

Address:  75 West 44th Street

Interviewed by:  Miss Ellen Forbush, Mr. L. Sand

Positions available:  Stenographer, clerk-typist, bookkeeper

Record of Calls:

Date              What Occurred                   Follow-up

Feb. 2        Interview with Miss          Return for test Feb. 4.
              Forbush.  Filled out         There may be an opening.
              application blank.

Feb. 4        Took test.  Saw Miss         Return Feb. 6 to meet
              Forbush again.  Looks        Mr. Sand, learn results
              promising.                   of test.

Feb. 6        Interview with Mr. Sand.     Will let me know by
              Informed test scores         Feb. 9.
              satisfactory.

Feb. 9        Miss Forbush called to
              tell me to report to
              work next Monday!
```

How to follow through after the interview.

When making a follow-up telephone call, you can say you are still interested in your application; ask if your application is still in the active files, or if you can come in for a second interview. For example:

MISS ARMSTRONG (*Over the telephone.*) Hello, Miss Green. This is Jane Armstrong. I took your employment tests last Tuesday afternoon. I am calling to inquire whether my tests were satisfactory.

MISS GREEN. Yes, Miss Armstrong. You did very well on the tests. We were planning to call you tomorrow.

MISS ARMSTRONG. Oh, you were? Would you like to have me come in tomorrow morning?

MISS GREEN. Yes. Come in tomorrow at 8:45. Be sure to come direct to this office.

MISS ARMSTRONG. Thank you so much, Miss Green. I'll be there promptly at 8:45. Good-by.

Keep a record of all your calls. A card file is good, or a small loose-leaf notebook. The calls you plan for each day should be so arranged that you do not waste time and effort traveling from one section of town to another. Plan as many calls in the same neighborhood as you can. A suggested report record of calls made on one firm and a calling schedule for one day are illustrated on pages 545 and 546.

Section 3. YOUR JOB SUCCESS

Your first job may not be a very important one, but it will give you an opportunity to prove your worth and to gain experience. The thing to remember is that your ability to handle more important responsibilities will be gauged by the way you take care of the duties assigned you on your first job.

Follow Instructions to the Letter. For the first few weeks, you will spend most of your time becoming adjusted to the new routine with as little lost motion as possible. You will perform your duties without a full understanding of their significance in some cases, because you will know little about the business. Your ignorance of the whys and wherefores of your duties, however, will not excuse mistakes caused by not following instructions. After some experience on the job, you will learn the "why" of the procedures you may not fully understand at first. For example, you may be told to double space and block the addresses on outgoing envelopes. Don't modify this style just because you don't happen to like it or because you may have learned another style at school. *Follow instructions to the letter. Keep a special notebook of instructions* for constant reference—no matter how reliable you may consider your memory.

Do Your Level Best on Every Assignment. Whatever the duty assigned to you may be, do your best. An assignment may seem trivial to you at the time—perhaps only the pasting of clippings in a scrapbook. Nevertheless, do your best. Trim the clippings neatly. Be careful and exact in your pasting. The resulting favorable comment by the user of the scrapbook will be worth the care you have taken.

Welcome New Duties. Your work will become more interesting as it becomes more diversified. Each new assignment will give you an opportunity to learn more about the business, thus increasing your chances for promotion.

Do Some Constructive Thinking. You will learn about the business, also, by reading the publications of the company, trade journals, and books. If you work for a publishing company, then become familiar with the types of publications handled and read some of them if it is practicable to do so. If you work for a wholesale paint concern, find out all you can about paint. Learn the names of the products, the colors, the container sizes, and other technical details, so that each day your work will become more meaningful and interesting to you.

The following scale will give you an idea of what the employer looks for in a junior employee. He places check marks on the lines to indicate his rating.

RATING SCALE FOR NEW EMPLOYEES

APPEARANCE. Neat, appropriately dressed.	Neat and appropriate	Ordinary	Slovenly
ABILITY TO LEARN. Ease of learning and following instructions.	Very quick	Catches on slowly	Needs repeated instruction
ACCURACY. Freedom from errors.	No errors	Few errors	Many errors
DEPENDABILITY. Can be relied upon to work without supervision.	Very reliable	Sometimes reliable	Unreliable
SPEED. Amount of work accomplished.	Fast	Moderate	Slow
CO-OPERATIVENESS. Ability to work with others.	Co-operative	Endeavors to co-operate	Fails to co-operate
CONSTRUCTIVE THINKING. Ability to grasp a situation and draw correct conclusions.	Shows originality	Carries out suggestions	Needs detailed instruction

Notice that this scale includes a section on constructive thinking. As you become accustomed to your routine, an idea for the improvement of the routine will occur to you. If the change will not affect anyone else—for example, the rearrangement of papers and equipment in your desk—then you should make the change. Otherwise, present your suggestion to your immediate superior before you inaugurate any

change, provided your suggestion is good and you can justify your point.

Sometimes you can show your constructive thinking by giving your employer the benefit of your own experience. Suppose you are working for a shoe-manufacturing concern. The advertising manager is dictating an advertising letter and says to you, "What else should I say in this letter to make these people buy our evening slippers?"

You are justified in making a helpful suggestion, saying something like this: "I've found that a lower-heeled slipper for dancing is much more comfortable than an extremely high-heeled shoe. Maybe you could stress the attractive and flattering styles of our evening slippers and call attention to the fact that they are just as good-looking with low heels as with high heels. Low-heeled dancing slippers are better for tall girls, anyway."

Early in your career *form the habit of learning names and faces of everyone in your organization.* If your office is just a small part of a large organization, learn the names and titles of as many officers and executives as you can. By learning names and titles, you can also learn the location and functions of many different departments in the organization. All this stored-up information may become very helpful to you some day.

The illustration of how one accomplished young graduate, Dale Kane, used his memory of names and titles to good advantage in his first position proves the value of this habit. When someone would greet him in the elevator with a polite "Good morning," he would smile and say, "Good morning, Mr. Sullivan." Mr. Sullivan would be pleased to think that a new employee had learned his name so quickly—besides, there's nothing so flattering to a person as to be called by his name on any occasion. When an executive would enter Dale's office and ask to see his superior, saying, "I'm Mr. Adams. May I see Mr. Martin?" Dale would say, "I'll be glad to inquire, Mr. Adams. You're from the Accounting Department, aren't you?"

Consider Personal Relationship Factors. Doing assigned duties exceptionally well, as was said earlier in this chapter, is an important factor in success. Equally important, however, are personal relationships. These may be divided into three classifications: relationships between employer and employee, relationships between employees, and relationships with the public.

Relationships Between Employer and Employee. Who is your employer? Think of your school organization and you can better understand a business organization. Your class instructor is like your immediate superior. Your instructor works under a department head, and the department head works under the principal. If you are employed as a typist in the accounting department, for example, your immediate superior will be the person who assigns your work to you. This person may be a minor executive in the department who reports to the chief accountant. The chief accountant is responsible to the manager of the company or to the president of the board of directors, depending on the type of organization.

If you have occasion to come in contact with the manager, be prepared to call him by name and be sure to treat him with every respect. You may seldom have an opportunity to see the manager or to talk with him; but when you do have such an opportunity, be sure that you are looking your best and are behaving in a businesslike manner. Also, you will, perhaps, have few occasions for coming in contact with the department head; but when you do, you must take care that the impression you make is a good one.

Your greatest concern will be the contacts you make with your immediate superior. He is the one to impress with your ability, initiative, pleasing personality, and co-operativeness. He is the one who will be asked about you when you are being considered for a salary increase.

Treat all your superiors with respect but not with fear. If you are doing your best on your job, then you will have no need to fear any one of your superiors.

Office etiquette is not always the same as social etiquette. Remember, if you are a girl, that the business world is still a man's world. Don't expect to be waited upon because you are a girl. If you drop a filing tray, no man is going to jump up and rescue it for you. You cannot expect your employer to get up from his chair when you enter his office. Although some employers may make a practice of observing the social niceties in the office, you must not expect them as your rights.

At some time—we hope not often—you will be reprimanded for doing something in error. Say, "I'm sorry. What can I do to correct the error?" If you try to argue or attempt to justify your actions, you are likely to lose your temper or say things that you will later regret. Be calm and controlled in this sort of situation, and your employer will generally retain his composure also, and the matter will be soon for-

gotten. Under no circumstances, let your emotions get the best of you. The office is no place for tears. If you must cry—and sometimes crying relieves the tension—go off by yourself in some private corner until the storm blows over. Don't ask for sympathy from any of your fellow employees. Keep your troubles to yourself. Instead of holding a feeling of resentment towards your employer, take steps to insure that the error will never occur again.

The secret of pleasant relations with all your superiors is a cheerful disposition and a willingness to do your work to the best of your ability.

Relationships Between Employees. A slogan to have in mind when considering your relations with your fellow employees—especially when you are new in a situation—is to be friendly with everyone, intimate with no one. Being friendly with everyone includes fellow workers of all ages, regardless of their employment status. Don't restrict your smile and friendly conversation to those of your own age. Your best friend, professionally speaking, may be the gray-haired woman—or the elderly man—who holds a relatively minor position. There is no reason why you should snub the elevator operators, and the custodian will appreciate your attitude of good will and kindness.

"Breaking in" socially in an office sometimes takes a little time, so don't be discouraged if you do not seem to be popular instantly. Maintain an attitude that invites kindness and consideration and avoid an attitude of aloofness or fright. You will soon find your place in the group. Just remember that the office is not a social organization; there is no reception committee, no hostess whose business it is to make you feel welcome.

Some offices provide a lunchroom for employees where they may eat lunches that they bring from home, or the company may run an employees' cafeteria. In any case, if you are invited to join a group at luncheon, accept the invitation. Try to contribute to the conversation. As it is important for you to be friendly with everyone in the office, try to avoid identifying yourself with any one group before you have had an opportunity to meet other groups. If, on the other hand, no one asks you to join a group, keep that "I'm-scared-and-want-to-crawl-into-my-shell" look from your face and eat your lunch alone. A ready smile and friendly attitude will soon attract acquaintances to you.

Avoid Conversation about Yourself. What to say when in conversa-

tion with other employees presents many problems, especially to a beginner. Perhaps the best way to prevent your making mistakes and saying things for which you would be sorry is to enumerate some of the topics of conversation that should be avoided.

Topics of conversation that come most readily to your mind are related to those things most closely associated with you. Oddly enough, these are the topics that should be avoided. For example, your love of your family and your pride in its members will cause you to believe that others are also interested in the activities and accomplishments of your family. While this may be true of your intimate friends, casual acquaintances are interested only to the extent of curiosity.

Your personal health is another matter that becomes a boring topic when given too much emphasis. Reserve remarks regarding your health until you have been asked regarding it. Ideally, your answer to such questions should be, "I'm feeling fine. How are you?"

Religion and politics are such controversial subjects that you had better avoid these, too.

Avoid Conversation about Your Job. Avoid any discussion of salaries —either your own or that of a fellow worker. Doubtless, someday soon after your employment in a new office, someone will say to you, "I know I shouldn't say this to you, but—what salary are you getting?" You need not answer this question directly because it should never have been asked. You can say, "I'm just a beginner, you know," or make light of the question by answering, "Well, my income tax certainly won't be very large this year!"

You may be receiving more money than the person asking. Or you may be receiving, as a beginning salary, the same as another employee is receiving after some time of employment.

Some salary rating scales are published. Civil-service salary rating scales in printed form, for example, are available to anyone.

One enthusiastic young beginner said to his immediate superior, "I want to work up from where I am to the very top in the organization." His superior remarked, "That's a very good ambition, Charles. But let me give you one word of advice. Don't discuss your ambitions with anyone but your superiors. Do your work well, show initiative and interest, and you will realize your ambitions."

Other members of the organization may resent promotions that come your way; they will be jealous of your success. If you have boasted about your ambitions, then they will feel justified in saying,

"He pulls all the wires he can to get recognition." If you keep quiet, however, and get your promotions through merit, then your actions will belie any "catty" remarks others may make.

Until you are quite familiar with the details of your own job and with the policies of your company, you will be wise if you never "talk shop" with other employees or even with your family. You must avoid telling "office secrets," and you had better consider everything that goes on as an office secret. Should you remark to someone that your employer was "stewing over the books all morning, and is he worried about expenses," you are telling that person too much about your employer's business.

Avoid Conversation about Other Employees. Furthermore, you must avoid any semblance of gossip in your conversation. One office employee said to a friend, "I never say anything about another employee in our office unless I can say something nice." The friend replied, "That's a good idea. My rule is to say nothing about the others in the office; but if I must say something, I'll say only nice things."

Never say anything disparaging about your company or its policies. You really have no right to make such remarks so long as you are receiving your pay from the company. The company is paying you to do its work. It has a right to expect your co-operation and should, of course, deserve your good will. When you are dissatisfied with the treatment you are getting, then you had better find another employer.

The real secret to success in getting along with your fellow workers is to realize that every one is a human being and may be expected to display varying reactions to favorable and unfavorable situations. A person who shows too many ups and downs in his reactions is said to be temperamental. You may have one or more persons of this kind in your office. If you do not understand them, they will disturb you and perhaps cause you some uneasiness.

Very often one of the employees in the office is ill or recovering from an illness. Such persons are sometimes difficult to get along with unless you understand their condition and make allowances for their behavior. Sometimes you will have to work with a person who is and acts like a "spoiled baby." Don't try to reform this person, but adjust yourself so that your contacts with him will not result in unpleasantness.

A practical knowledge of the psychology of human behavior will help you work in harmony with others.

Relationships with the Public. Remember that—no matter how lowly a position you may hold—*you are the company* when you come in contact with the public. You know that people form opinions of department stores, for example, from the treatment given by the counter clerks, the telephone-order clerk, or the delivery boy. Haven't you heard someone say, "I'll never trade at that store again. Why, the telephone operator was actually rude to me!"

The public may be judging your employer by you when you are unconscious that you are being observed. Suppose you are going from your own office to another office of your company in the same building. In the elevator you meet one of your co-workers with whom you are quite friendly. You throw off your usual office dignity and "let yourself go," using careless speech and indulging in childish behavior. The distinguished gentleman in the elevator with you may be an important customer of the company or a very desirable prospective customer. How chagrined you would feel if you knew that your careless behavior had so disgusted the gentleman that he would not consider doing business with your company! An extreme case? Perhaps, but a very probable one.

It is no wonder that an employer is careful about whom he puts at the reception desk, in the outer office, at the switchboard, and on the sales force. Any employee who comes in contact with the public can bring customers to the business or turn them away from it.

The appearance of your office is almost as important as your own appearance so far as the favorable impression on the public is concerned. A customer or a client coming into an office where the desks are kept neat, where the furniture is tastefully arranged, where there is an atmosphere of order and organization—takes away with him the impression that the company's business must be reliable and conducted on an orderly and efficient basis.

In conversation with outsiders, guard carefully details about your company that should be discussed only within the organization.

How to Win a Promotion. There is a strong desire for recognition and promotion within the hearts of most beginners. Many employers recognize the value of this ambition and prefer to employ beginners because they usually possess this quality in a high degree. The enthusiasm of the new employee enlivens the general spirit of the office.

You can help yourself progress on the job. Margaret Staff was employed in the Policy Department of a large title insurance company.

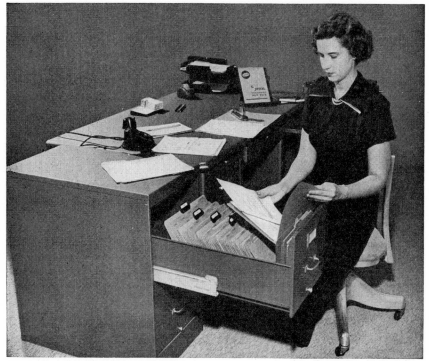

Courtesy Shaw-Walker Company

Always use your spare time profitably. Those slow periods are a good time to straighten out the files.

She was a very fast and accurate typist and had gained an enviable reputation with her immediate superiors. Her duties consisted of filling in data on the vacant lines of the title policies—a tedious and exacting task. Margaret was learning about the business and was making valuable contacts, but she felt that she would be much happier making use of her stenographic ability.

The supervisor of her department gave his dictation to his secretary, one of Margaret's good friends. One day, as Margaret was passing the secretary's desk, the supervisor asked the secretary to come in to take some dictation. The secretary, noticing Margaret, said, "I'd be glad to take the dictation, Mr. Supervisor; but these reports will be delayed if I do. May I suggest that you give the letters to Margaret Staff? I know she'd do the work very well." The supervisor accepted the secretary's suggestion, and Margaret had a chance to show her stenographic ability.

You can guess the rest of the story. In a very few days, Margaret's desk was moved so that she could be near the secretary; and she was made the secretary's assistant. Margaret had won her first promotion.

Another young beginner, Ruth Travis, had to make several changes in the same organization before she finally arrived at her stenographic position. She was employed first in the Claim Department of an automobile insurance company. She filled in policy numbers and dates on 5-by-3 cards—hundreds of cards, all day long. Ruth wasn't suited to this routine and wished to be transferred. She planned her campaign carefully.

One day she finished her day's basket of cards in one hour's less time than usual. It was a struggle to do this, but Ruth needed this extra hour to work on her campaign. At four o'clock, she went to her supervisor, said that she had finished her assigned work, and asked whether she might help someone else for the rest of the day. The supervisor told Ruth to ask the chief file clerk to give her some work to do.

Ruth was then given a stack of 5-by-3 cards to put in a visible-file index. She worked so rapidly that the chief file clerk asked that she return the next day at the same time—and after several days asked Ruth whether she would like to work in the Filing Department permanently. Ruth replied, "Thank you so much. I like the work, but my heart is set on doing stenographic work. Perhaps you can suggest a way for me to get a transfer to a stenographic position." The chief file clerk suggested that Ruth speak to the head of the central typing division because, in that company, all the stenographers were given a trial period in that division. Ruth obtained her transfer to the central typing division and learned the correspondence policies of the company quickly.

One day a call came to the head of the central typing division from the Legal Department, where they needed a good stenographer in a hurry. Ruth was chosen for the assignment, and so she had her first chance to take dictation. Ruth had been wise enough to keep in constant practice with her shorthand—and did a good job on this assignment.

A week went by. The Legal Department called again, this time asking that Ruth be sent. It wasn't long before Ruth received a transfer to a stenographic position in the Legal Department—she had attained her goal in just six months.

Another young beginner, Maurice Zale, obtained his first position as a stenographer in the Accounting Department of a large publishing concern. Maurice was a college graduate and was as proficient at bookkeeping and accounting as he was at shorthand and typing. When one of the bookkeepers was on his vacation, Maurice was given some of the bookkeeping work to do. He found himself fascinated by this new work; and when the bookkeeper returned from his vacation, Maurice asked his department head to consider him for a bookkeeping position when one was open. Maurice is now in charge of the payroll books of this large company.

Suggestions to Ambitious Beginners

1. Cultivate the friendship and admiration of those about you.
2. Do excellent work on every job assigned to you.
3. Keep in practice on any skill that you anticipate using in the future.
4. Welcome new assignments as opportunities to prove your abilities.
5. Don't be afraid to let your employer know your ambitions—but never discuss your ambitions with persons other than your superiors.

Enjoy the Thrill of Self-Improvement. No chapter addressed to young people about to enter the business world would be complete without this friendly advice: Any kind of work may become so routine that the mind of the worker is dormant most of the time. You can avoid this deadening effect of a routine job by consciously trying to improve yourself either in professional skills, in physical ability, or in leisure-time activities.

Keeping up your professional skills through night school or home practice will quicken your ambition and maintain your readiness for promotion on the job.

Office work often is so confining that you tend to neglect your physical health. Taking part in active sports after work, or participating in a night-school gymnasium class, will keep your body fit and will renew your physical energy. Get out into the open air as much as you possibly can.

There are a great many things that you can do in your leisure time after a hard day's work at the office that are interesting and that will contribute to your self-improvement.

If your work calls for much standing on your feet, then get the habit of reading good books as you sit at home resting; or take up some handicraft—leatherwork, needlework, or art.

Conversational groups or study groups in your own home lead to new and interesting experiences. Go to night school and explore study fields that have been attractive to you but for which you have never found time. Or continue your study toward a college degree. Employers always have great respect for employees who keep their minds active.

Success in Your Job Becomes Your Best Recommendation. In the files of the personnel office of a large engineering concern, detailed records are kept on each employee. These records include his application for employment, his physical-examination card, a record of his absences, his salary and promotional history, and other pertinent information.

When the employee leaves the company, his immediate superior sends to the personnel office a rating sheet so that an estimate of the employee's work is in the files, should he wish to be reinstated in the company. This final statement from the employee's superior is also used when a recommendation letter has been requested on this former employee by another firm.

Study carefully the copy of the following rating sheet. Notice the different qualities on which the employer is asked to judge the employee. How would someone rate you on these qualities as you are now? Do you think it would be well for you to develop some of these good qualities before you are employed so that, when you leave any position you may hold, your employer will have nothing but complimentary things to say about you?

Perhaps at the end of this secretarial course you would like to ask your teacher to rate you on this chart and give you some suggestions to help you make plans for self-improvement.

CONFIDENTIAL INFORMATION

TO   Personnel Manager   Date . . . .

FROM

SUBJECT   Termination of . . . .   Position . . . .

The employee named above has been terminated for reasons as given in detail on the reverse of this sheet.

(One line to be checked under each numbered qualification)

1. *Ability and Industry*—With reference to performance of work in an energetic manner:
. . .A. Exceptionally reliable and thorough.
. . .B. Reliable and thorough.
. . .C. Well-meaning but not always reliable.
. . .D. Work incomplete and unreliable.

2. *Judgment*—With reference to ability to differentiate between the important and the unimportant:

...A. Reaches sound decisions promptly; not easily disconcerted; discreet

...B. Exercises common sense; careful; clearheaded.

...C. Fair judgment in normal and routine things.

...D. Draws illogical conclusions; careless.

3. *Co-operation*—With reference to the faculty for working harmoniously with others:

...A. Exceptionally effective in working with others to a common end.

...B. Works in harmony with others but not particularly considerate.

...C. Indifferent to leadership.

...D. Obstructive, selfish, or inconsiderate.

4. *Loyalty*—With reference to constancy:

...A. Considers his and the company's success as synonymous; builds up morale.

...B. Loyal to the company but somewhat selfish regarding associates.

...C. Selfish and mercenary.

...D. Hypercritical; faultfinding.

5. *Fortitude*—With reference to the ability to act effectively and with firmness under difficulties, disappointments, or pressure of duties:

...A. Difficulties stimulate.

...B. Difficulties do not inhibit effective performance of duties.

...C. Needs considerable support and encouragement.

...D. Difficulties seriously depress and obstruct efficiency.

Moral character and personal reputation:.....................................

do not

I do   recommend this employee for reinstatement with the company.

(*Signed*) ....

Some Highlights of This Unit

1. Analyze yourself and your preparation with regard to (*a*) your skills, (*b*) your technical knowledge, (*c*) your personal characteristics, (*d*) other desirable distinguishing qualifications.

2. Know how to prepare a data sheet.

3. Be prepared to fill out an application blank intelligently and completely.

4. An effective letter of application needs careful thought and planning and attention to letter content and mechanical setup.

5. Plan and execute your letter campaign by studying classified ads, examples of good letters of application, and situation-wanted ads; also by sending "shotgun" letters.

6. When you prepare for the personal interview, check your appearance, the items you will take with you, your attitude toward the interview as a

whole and toward the receptionist, your approach to, and conversation with, the employer, and the termination of the interview.

7. Follow up the interview properly by writing a thank-you note and, depending on the situation, making a telephone call later.

8. It may be desirable to keep a card-file record of all your calls.

Questions and Items for Discussion

1. Why should a student who has chosen secretarial work as his vocation study other business subjects than shorthand and typing?

2. A friend remarks to you, "An exceptionally smart student never has trouble getting a job. I am just average in ability. How can I sell myself to an employer?" What suggestion would you make to help your friend recognize his personal assets?

3. How might a person who is in apparent good health and neat in appearance betray his lack of refinement and cultural training?

4. When you are working in close contact with others, is there any one personal habit more desirable than the others, if you classify personal habits into health, personal appearance, and speech habits? Give the reason for your answer.

5. How does participation in extracurricular activities affect one's personality? Why is it desirable to take part in as many activities as possible while in school? How can these activities help you to get a job?

6. What justification is there for an employer's considering the application blank as an intelligence test? What can you do to bring up your score on this so-called "intelligence test"?

7. What sources of information are available to you in your job-finding campaign?

8. Where would you find examples of good letters of application?

9. What is meant by the term "shotgun" letters?

10. What items will you take with you on a personal interview?

11. What is meant by the term "constructive thinking"?

12. What may become some of the "personal relationship" problems?

Personality Questions and Projects
(Based on Personality Pointer, page 507)

1. Check the catalogues of the prominent universities in your state and list the courses which you feel would help you toward your goal. Separate the courses into campus courses, correspondence courses, and adult-education evening classes. Of particular importance to you are those universities having evening divisions in your city.

2. Investigate scholarships that are available in your locality.

Secretarial Assignments

1. Ask at least three successful, employed stenographers or secretaries—and as many more as you can conveniently approach—the following questions regarding their jobs:

   a. How long have you been employed?

   b. Do your present duties differ from your duties during your first days of employment?

   c. What are some of your specific duties?

   d. What further training do you wish you had had before you were employed in the position you now hold?

   e. What part of your school training have you found to be most valuable to you on your job?

Tabulate the results of your investigation and compare your tabulation with the recommendations given in your text. If there are differences in the two tabulations, determine, if you can, the reasons for the differences. By which tabulation would you prefer to set your goals? Why?

2. Construct a data sheet describing yourself and your abilities at the time you will be ready to look for a position. You may have to anticipate some details, such as your skills, extracurricular activities, and experience. You can make this data sheet approximately true, however; then, when the time comes to use it, all you will have to do is to adjust a few details.

3. Fill in the application blank in your Workbook, Sheet 115, as carefully as if you were going to present it to a prospective employer. How would you modify your blank if you were applying for the position of typist-clerk; ledger clerk; receptionist; stenographer in an insurance company; typist-receptionist in a doctor's office; bookkeeper's assistant?

4. With the help of your telephone directory, classified section, make a list of employment agencies with which you could place your application. Employment agencies for domestic help will not interest you, of course. Check your list against the want-ad section of your newspaper to see which of these agencies advertise that they have calls for applicants. The Sunday edition of your paper (if there is one; if not, the Saturday edition) usually has the best want-ad section. Consult with your teacher and your friends who would be acquainted with employment agencies and make notes regarding their comments on particular agencies—whether they are likely to take applications from beginners, whether their services are free to the applicant, whether they are of good reputation.

When you have finished your investigation, revise your original list of employment agencies so that it will include only those agencies that offer a prospect of being of assistance to you.

5. With the aid of the classified telephone directory, make a list of preferred firms with which you would like to place your application for employ-

ment. Classify these firms as to the kind of business and in the order of their attractiveness to you.

If you feel that you would like to be connected with a lumber company, look in the classified section under "Lumber." If you are interested in dress designing, you can probably find interesting prospects under "Dresses—Manufacturers" or "Designers—Clothing." Look under "Automobile—Agencies and Dealers" if that business attracts you.

When you make up this list, include the full name, address, and telephone number of each prospect.

6. Choose one of the following newspaper ads and write an answering application letter. Be sure your letter gets into the outstanding group of answers by using a good grade of paper, typing without error, and presenting yourself in a sincere and effective manner.

GIRL, for general office work; must be rapid, accurate typist; knowledge French preferred but not essential; state age, salary wanted. G 182 Times.

GIRL, young, knowledge of bookkeeping and typing; write stating age, salary and qualifications. P. B. Hoyt Engraving Company, 100 West 24th St.

HIGH SCHOOL GRADUATE

If you are one of the ten top boys who graduated last June or are about to graduate, this may be of interest to you. Wanted—a boy for office work, to start from the bottom with plenty of opportunity for advancement to one of ability and desire to progress. C 589 Times.

OFFICE ASSISTANT, college, 23; care for correspondence, clerical details; accuracy essential; large professional office; $45. S 285 Times.

SERVICE and Complaint Department— Young woman, college, good telephone voice, ability to handle complaints over phone; outline background in full. P. H., 250 Times.

STENOGRAPHER, bright beginner; state age, experience, salary. W 679 Times Downtown.

STENOGRAPHER, mechanically inclined; state education, experience, age, salary desired. S 127 Times.

STENOGRAPHER, typist, high school graduate; publicity; $40-$45. Reply Y 2537 Times Annex.

STENOGRAPHER, typist, young man, for small, growing advertising agency; some knowledge of production; $45 start; this position presents an unusual opportunity for advancement to the right person; state age, etc. R. T., 499 Times.

Spelling Demons

tenant	truancy	unusually
tranquility	unanimous	vehicle
transparent	unconscious	warrant

Job Tips

1. Be sure the contents of your purse are in neat order at all times, but especially when you apply for a job.

2. Enumerate work experience, paid or voluntary, in detail—school, office, church, club, neighborhood.

3. For references, select persons who can write businesslike letters.

4. Don't fidget while you are waiting for an interview.

5. Just because you are nervous or are trying to make an impression, don't try to entertain the receptionist while you wait. She usually has work to do.

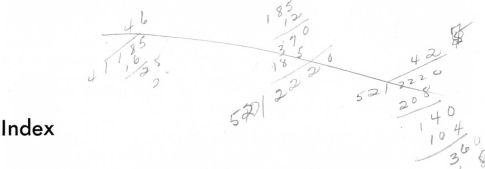

Index

Crutcher, Roberta Pers. & Reason. London, the
  David press.; 1931

Desmond, Shaw Pers and Power, London, Rad & Liff, 1950.

Garnett, Arthur Campbell. Instinct & Person London,
  G. Allen & Unwin, 1928.

Honingman, John Joseph, culture & Pers. N.Y,
  Harper, 1954

Messick, John D. Pers. & character Development
  New York, Fleming H. Revell, 1939